Freedom and Democracy in an Imperial Context

Freedom and Democracy in an Imperial Context: Dialogues with James Tully gathers leading thinkers from across the humanities and social sciences in a celebration of, and critical engagement with, the recent work of Canadian political philosopher James Tully. Over the past thirty years, James Tully has made key contributions to some of the most pressing questions of our time, including: interventions in the history of moral and political thought, contemporary political philosophy, democracy, citizenship, imperialism, recognition and cultural diversity. In 2008, he published *Public Philosophy in a New Key*, a two-volume work that promises to be one of the most influential and important statements of legal and political thought in recent history. This work, along with numerous other books and articles, is foundational to a distinctive school of political thought, influencing thinkers in fields as diverse as Anthropology, History, Indigenous Studies, Law, Philosophy and Political Science. Critically engaging with James Tully's thought, the chapters in this volume take up what is his central, and ever more pressing, question: how to enact democratic practices of freedom within and against historically sedimented and actually existing relationships of imperialism?

Robert Nichols is Assistant Professor of Political Theory at the University of Alberta (Canada). His areas of research include nineteenth and twentieth-century continental philosophy and the study of imperialism and settler-colonialism in the history of political thought.

Jakeet Singh is Assistant Professor in the Department of Politics and Government at Illinois State University. His research interests include imperialism and postcolonialism, social justice and critiques of (neo)liberal-democracy.

Freedom and Democracy in an Imperial Context

Dialogues with James Tully

Edited by
Robert Nichols
and Jakeet Singh

LONDON AND NEW YORK

First published 2014
by Routledge
2 Park Square, Milton Park, Abingdon, Oxfordshire OX14 4RN

and by Routledge
711 Third Avenue, New York, NY 10017

First issued in paperback 2015

Routledge is an imprint of the Taylor & Francis Group, an informa business

© 2014 Robert Nichols and Jakeet Singh

The right of Robert Nichols and Jakeet Singh to be identified as editors of this work, and the individual chapter authors for their individual material has been asserted in accordance with sections 77 and 78 of the Copyright, Designs and Patents Act 1988.

All rights reserved. No part of this book may be reprinted or reproduced or utilised in any form or by any electronic, mechanical, or other means, now known or hereafter invented, including photocopying and recording, or in any information storage or retrieval system, without permission in writing from the publishers.

Trademark notice: Product or corporate names may be trademarks or registered trademarks, and are used only for identification and explanation without intent to infringe.

British Library Cataloguing in Publication Data
A catalogue record for this book is available from the British Library

Library of Congress Cataloging in Publication Data
Freedom and democracy in an imperial context: dialogues with James Tully / edited by Robert Nichols and Jakeet Singh.
pages ; cm
ISBN 978-0-415-81599-4 – ISBN 978-0-203-49146-1 (ebk.) 1. Tully, James, 1946–Political and social views. 2. Democracy–Philosophy.
3. Liberty–Philosophy. I. Nichols, Robert, 1979– , editor of compilation.
II. Singh, Jakeet, editor of compilation
JC423.F7517 2014
321.8–dc23
                                                                                       2013036832

ISBN 13: 978-1-138-95081-8 (pbk)
ISBN 13: 978-0-415-81599-4 (hbk)

Typeset in Baskerville by
Servis Filmsetting Ltd, Stockport, Cheshire

Contents

Contributors vii
Acknowledgements xi
Abbreviations xiii

1. **Editors' Introduction** 1
   ROBERT NICHOLS AND JAKEET SINGH

PART I
Recasting Public Philosophy

2. **Engagement, Proposals and the Key of Reasoning** 13
   ANTHONY SIMON LADEN

3. **Freedom as Practice and Civic Genius: On James Tully's Public Philosophy** 32
   EDUARDO MENDIETA

4. **At the Edges of Civic Freedom: Violence, Power, Enmity** 48
   ANTONIO Y. VÁZQUEZ-ARROYO

5. **'[Un]Dazzled by the Ideal?'—James Tully and New Realism** 71
   BONNIE HONIG

PART II
In Dialogue with the Past

6. **Vattel, Internal Colonialism, and the Rights of Indigenous Peoples** 81
   ANTONY ANGHIE

7. On the Moral Justification of Reparation for New World
   Slavery   100
   DAVID SCOTT

8. Postnational Constellations? Political Citizenship and the
   Modern State   121
   CHRISTIAN J. EMDEN

PART III
Re-Imagining Civic Freedom Today

9. Spaces of Freedom, Citizenship and State in the Context of
   Globalization: South Africa and Bolivia   147
   EUNICE N. SAHLE

10. 'Becoming Black': Acting Otherwise and Re-imagining
    Community   174
    ALETTA J. NORVAL

11. Accessing Tully: Political Philosophy for the Everyday and
    the Everyone   202
    VAL NAPOLEON AND HADLEY FRIEDLAND

PART IV
Conclusion

12. Responses   223
    JAMES TULLY

    Bibliography   273
    Index   293

Contributors

Antony Anghie is the Samuel D. Thurman Professor of Law at the S.J. Quinney School of Law at the University of Utah, where he teaches various subjects in the international law curriculum including public international law, international business transactions, and international law and the use of force. His research interests include the history and theory of public international law, international law and globalization, and international development institutions. He has published on each of these themes, and is the author of *Imperialism, Sovereignty and the Making of International Law* (Cambridge University Press, 2005). He has also taught at various other universities including the University of Tokyo, Cornell Law School, the London School of Economics, the University of Auckland and the University of Melbourne.

Christian J. Emden is Professor of German Intellectual History and Political Thought at Rice University. His current research focuses on questions of political citizenship and the public sphere, and political realism in German thought from Max Weber and Carl Schmitt through Hannah Arendt. Recently he co-edited *Beyond Habermas: Democracy, Knowledge, and the Public Sphere* (New York: Berghahn, 2012) and *Changing Perceptions of the Public Sphere* (New York: Berghahn, 2012). Among other books, he is the author of *Nietzsche's Naturalism: Philosophy and the Life Sciences in the Nineteenth Century* (Cambridge: Cambridge University Press, 2014) and *Friedrich Nietzsche and the Politics of History* (Cambridge: Cambridge University Press, 2008).

Hadley Friedland is a PhD candidate and Killam Scholar at the University of Alberta, Faculty of Law. Her research focuses on the articulation and revitalization of Indigenous, and particularly Cree, legal traditions and theories. She previously completed an LLM thesis entitled 'The *Wetiko* (Windigo) Legal Principles: Responding to Harmful People in Cree, Anishinabek and Saulteaux Societies – Past, Present and Future Uses', and has published in the areas of criminal justice and child protection law.

Bonnie Honig is Nancy Duke Lewis Professor of Political Science and Modern Culture and Media at Brown University. She is author of, most recently,

Antigone, Interrupted (Cambridge, 2013), as well as *Political Theory and the Displacement of Politics* (Cornell, 1993), *Democracy and the Foreigner* (Princeton, 2001), and *Emergency Politics: Paradox, Law, Democracy* (Princeton, 2009).

Anthony Simon Laden is Professor of Philosophy at the University of Illinois at Chicago. He is the author of *Reasonably Radical: Deliberative Liberalism and the Politics of Identity* (Cornell, 2001) and *Reasoning: A Social Picture* (Oxford, 2012), as well as numerous articles on democracy, democratic reasoning, civic education and the work of John Rawls.

Eduardo Mendieta is Professor of Philosophy at the State University of New York, Stony Brook, where he is also the director of the Center for Latin American and Caribbean Studies. He is the author of *The Adventures of Transcendental Philosophy* (Rowman & Littlefield, 2002) and *Global Fragments: Globalizations, Latinamericanisms, and Critical Theory* (SUNY Press, 2007). He is presently at work on another book entitled *Philosophy's War: Logos, Polemos, Topos*. His most recent book publications are a collection of interview with Angela Y. Davis, entitled *Abolition Democracy: Beyond Empire, Torture and War* (Seven Stories Press, 2006), and an edited volume of interviews with Richard Rorty, *Take Care of Freedom, and Truth Will take Care of itself* (Stanford University Press, 2006), and with Chad Kautzer, *Pragmatism, Racism, Empire: Community in the Age of Empire* (Indiana University Press, 2009).

Val Napoleon is of Cree heritage and is an adopted Gitksan member. She is Associate Professor with the University of Alberta, teaching in the Faculties of Native Studies and Law. Her research focused on a substantive articulation of Gitksan law and the development of a Gitksan legal theory. Val was awarded the University of Victoria's Governor General's Gold Medal for her doctoral dissertation in June 2010. She has published in areas of indigenous legal traditions, indigenous feminism, oral histories, restorative justice, and governance.

Robert Nichols is Assistant Professor of Political Theory at the University of Alberta. He has also been a Fulbright Faculty Fellow at Columbia University in New York and a Humboldt Research Fellow at the Humboldt Universität-Berlin. His areas of research include nineteenth and twentieth-century continental philosophy and political theory, as well as the study of imperialism and settler-colonialism in the history of political thought. Work of his on these topics has recently appeared in such journals as *Philosophy and Social Criticism*, *Foucault Studies, Contemporary Political Theory* and *Philosophy Today*.

Aletta J. Norval is Reader in Political Theory and Director of the Doctoral Programme in Ideology and Discourse Analysis in the Department of Government, University of Essex, UK. She is also Co-Director of the Centre for Theoretical Studies in the Humanities and Social Sciences. Her publications include *Aversive Democracy: Inheritance and Originality in the Democratic Tradition* (Cambridge University Press), and *Deconstructing Apartheid Discourse* (Verso). She is co-editor of *South Africa in Transition: New Theoretical Perspectives* (Macmillan) and *Discourse Theory and Political Analysis: Identities, Hegemonies and Social Change* (Manchester University Press). She has written widely on democratic theory; post-structuralism and contemporary political theory; South African politics; theories of ethnicity; feminist theory; the construction of political identities. She is currently working on a book on Rancière and Cavell.

Eunice N. Sahle is Associate Professor at the University of North Carolina at Chapel Hill with a joint appointment in Africa and African American Studies and Curriculum in Global Studies. Her current work focuses on the history and role of ideas in the making of the modern world order, imperialism and decoloniality, African diaspora formations, human rights, ethics and justice, constitutionalism and transitional justice in Africa and elsewhere, political violence and the political economy of land and displacement. Her publications include, *World Orders, Development and Transformation* (Palgrave Macmillan, 2010). She was educated at the University of Toronto and Queen's University in Canada.

David Scott teaches in the Department of Anthropology at Columbia University. He is the author of *Formations of Ritual: Colonial and Anthropological Discourses on the Sinhala Yaktovil* (University of Minnesota Press, 1994), *Refashioning Futures: Criticism After Postcoloniality* (Princeton University Press, 1999), *Conscripts of Modernity: The Tragedy of Colonial Enlightenment* (Duke University Press, 2004), and *Omens of Adversity: Tragedy, Time, Memory, Justice* (Duke University Press, 2014).

Jakeet Singh is Assistant Professor in the Department of Politics & Government at Illinois State University. His research is rooted in a decolonial approach to political theory, and explores the ways in which the progressive, critical, and emancipatory traditions of Western modernity marginalize subaltern practices and ways of life. He is currently completing a book manuscript entitled *Beyond Free and Equal: Decoloniality and the Limits of Liberal-Democracy*. He holds a PhD from the University of Toronto, and his work has appeared in *Third World Quarterly* and *Theory, Culture and Society*.

James Hamilton Tully is the Distinguished Professor of Political Science, Law, Indigenous Governance and Philosophy at the University of Victoria. After completing his BA at UBC and PhD at the University of Cambridge he taught in the departments of Philosophy and Political Science at McGill University 1977–96. He was Professor and Chair of the Department of Political Science at the University of Victoria 1996–2001. In 2001–03 he was the inaugural Henry N.R. Jackman Distinguished Professor in Philosophical Studies at the University of Toronto in the departments of Philosophy and Political Science and the Faculty of Law. In 2003 he returned to the University of Victoria. He is Fellow of the Royal Society of Canada and a Fellow of the Trudeau Foundation. He is the author or editor of eight books and many articles in the field of contemporary political and legal philosophy (or theory) and its history, and in Canadian political and legal philosophy.

Antonio Y. Vázquez-Arroyo is Assistant Professor in the Department of Political Science at Rutgers University. His areas of teaching and research interest are interdisciplinary and mostly engage with contemporary political questions, albeit always drawing from the history of political thought broadly understood. His recent work has been located at the intersections of the tradition of critical theory and the dialectical legacy of the twentieth century. Currently, he is finishing a book titled *Scenes of Responsibility: Power and Suffering in a Post-Political Age* and is currently working on a book-length manuscript tentatively titled *Shadows of Catastrophe*. Additionally, he continues to work on two long-term projects on the idea of universal history and the critical import of dialectical thinking.

Acknowledgements

This volume would not have been possible without the dedication, hard work and assistance of many people, to whom we owe an enormous debt of gratitude. In the summer of 2010, we held a workshop in Victoria, British Columbia, Canada, where the majority of the chapters in this volume were initially presented. Those two incredibly stimulating days of dialogue were supported by a workshop grant from the Social Sciences and Humanities Research Council of Canada. Generous support was also provided by the Dean of Social Science, the Faculty of Law, and the Department of Political Science at the University of Victoria, as well as the Department of Political Science, Faculty of Arts and Office of the Vice President (Research) at the University of Alberta. A number of individuals provided us with invaluable assistance and advice in the planning and organization of the workshop, including Jeremy Webber, David Owen, Andrée Boisselle and Alex Robb. We thank all of these various institutions and individuals, without whose generosity and commitment to the project it would never have come to fruition. We would also like to acknowledge the many colleagues – faculty and graduate students – who attended the workshop, and whose interventions undoubtedly enriched the final versions of all of the chapters.

Of course, our greatest debt is to the contributors of this volume, not only for their outstanding contributions, but also for their patience and unwavering support in seeing this project through to completion. The contributors were initially charged with the enormous task of not only critically engaging with the work of James Tully, and positioning their own work in relation to his, but also of addressing the broader themes of 'freedom and democracy in an imperial context'. What's more, we then asked them to critically engage with each other's chapters, both at the workshop itself and later in small editorial groups. We could not have imagined a richer, more diverse, and more stimulating result, and we thank them for all of the work they have invested in this volume.

We would also like to thank everyone at Routledge who guided this project through the publication process, including the anonymous reviewers of the volume. An earlier version of Bonnie Honig's essay, '[Un]Dazzled by the ideal?', was published in *Political Theory*, Vol. 39, Issue 1 (2011): 138–44. We gratefully acknowledge Sage Publications for their permission to reprint her essay here, as well as Cambridge University Press for the permission to cite extensively from James Tully's *Public Philosophy in a New Key, 2 volumes* (Cambridge: Cambridge University Press, 2008). Special thanks are owed to Janet Phillips at the University of Alberta for doing a great deal of editing and proofing on the final manuscript, and to Takao Tanabe for the use of his painting 'English Bay at Dawn' as the cover art for the book. A piece that so vividly captures the Pacific coast at dawn is the perfect complement to a volume celebrating James Tully's work, which has long been rooted in this part of the world.

Finally, we want to express our deepest gratitude to Jim Tully. For many years, he has been an invaluable interlocutor, friend, mentor, and now colleague to both of us, as well as to many of the contributors to this volume. His work has been a source of unending inspiration and insight. But beyond his writings, Jim manifests in his own comportment and relations with others the very courage and integrity that are so integral to the notion of 'civic freedom' he elaborates. His work and life are exemplary in the harmony they exhibit between word and deed. We could not be more grateful to him for writing such a rich, far-reaching, and thoughtful reply to the chapters in this volume, as well as for his ongoing example of scholarly and ethical life.

Abbreviations

All quotations from James Tully's *Public Philosophy in a New Key: Volume I, Democracy and Civic Freedom* and *Public Philosophy in a New Key: Volume II, Imperialism and Civic Freedom* (Cambridge: Cambridge University Press, 2008) are cited in the text using the abbreviations *PPNK I* and *PPNK II*.

Chapter 1

Editors' Introduction

Robert Nichols and Jakeet Singh

Part One: The polyvalence of freedom and democracy

> *[T]he dominant forms of representative democracy, self-determination and democratisation promoted through international law are not alternatives to imperialism, but, rather, the means through which informal imperialism operates against the wishes of the majority of the population of the post-colonial world.*
>
> PPNK II, 158

With these words, James Tully identifies one of the key tensions at the heart of global politics today. While freedom and democracy are often understood as emancipatory ideals, their prevailing instantiations provide the very language and institutions through which imperial power relations operate today. 'Imperialism' is understood here in a broad sense, as a web of global power relations, built over the course of the last 500 years, which establishes a number of deep disparities between Global North and Global South through a multiplicity of practices of dispossession, exploitation, environmental destruction, dependency and inequality. If freedom and democracy serve a double function of not only challenging and critiquing such practices, but also of facilitating and legitimating them, then what does it mean to struggle for freedom and democracy in our contemporary imperial context? Or, as Wendy Brown puts it, at a time when 'we are all democrats now'—when democracy stands both for and against imperialism—'what possibilities are there, in theory and practice, for resurrecting or rehabilitating the radical promise and potential of democracy? Alternatively, given the disrepair and misuse into which it has fallen, ought democracy to be abandoned for other visions and practices of popular justice and shared power?'[1]

In his recent two-volume collection, *Public Philosophy in a New Key*, James Tully offers a striking response to these questions. Far from abandoning the language of freedom and democracy, Tully aims to struggle over these terms, and to retrieve and reinvent alternative meanings of them. In his words,

> the economic, political and military elites and their ideologists have inherited not only much of the earth and its resources but also many of its languages,

including the manipulable language of citizenship, democracy, civic goods and freedom. Yet, it is precisely this ordinary language that the oppressed and exploited of the world have always used to express their outrage at the injustices of the present and their hopes and dreams of another world. Like Edward Said, I refuse to surrender it to our adversaries without a fight and abandon the repository of the history of struggles from which we derive. (*PPNK* I, 10)

Tully's aim, then, is to develop alternative notions of freedom and democracy that can be woven into a non-imperial, or in fact de-imperializing, way of life. In other words, this new language is to provide the basis not only for an immediate response to imperialism, but also for a more general alternative to imperialism. At the heart of Tully's approach is an innovative understanding of the 'practices of freedom and democracy' that are to play this role. As such, it is helpful to unpack the three parts of this phrase.

First, Tully places a priority on *practices* over institutions. Relations of oppression and injustice are understood here not primarily as impersonal, material structures or institutions to which human beings are subject, but rather as 'practical systems' in which humans participate, and which are made up of complex networks of organized and coordinated human activities that are simultaneously structured by, and structuring of, the actions of others. As a result of this first step, Tully's approach remains grounded first and foremost in thinking and acting differently as the basic unit in the transformation of any relationship of power, rather than the imposition of an ideal institution or structure as the precondition for such a transformation.

Secondly, Tully's approach emphasizes practices *of*, not simply *for*, freedom and democracy. Because of the priority of practices over institutions or structures in his framework, freedom and democracy are no longer primarily understood as institutional forms to be fought *for* and demanded *of others* by those seeking the transformation of an oppressive relation, but rather as practices that can always be enacted and exercised here and now—without the purportedly necessary institutional preconditions—by human agents who conduct themselves differently.

But what, more specifically, are these practices of *freedom* and *democracy*? This third step involves Tully's distinctive redescription of both terms. For Tully, *freedom* is no longer understood as it is in the modern, civil tradition, as a tiered set of institutionalized rights or liberties that are coercively bestowed and enforced by international law and the modern constitutional state. Rather, it is understood here as the type of situated, critical freedom that is practised whenever we call into question any norm by which we are governed. Again, 'relations of governance' for Tully are not limited to juridico-institutional relations, but include the vast multiplicity of formal and informal relations of power that guide the conduct of the actors involved in any number of ways. These actors are both subjects and agents of these relations, and are both enabled and constrained by them in a way that inevitably leaves room for the guiding norm(s) to be called into question, either in words or in deeds. The exercise of this type of creative, relational freedom, Tully insists, provides the ground or basis of any other form of freedom, including the modern rights that are usually understood as most basic or foundational.

Finally, Tully's recast understanding of *democracy* is also not primarily institutional, and therefore departs from the modern notion of democracy as embodied in the modular, low-intensity forms of representative democracy of the Western-style constitutional state. Democracy, for Tully, is a type of relationship in which all those who are subject to, or affected by, a relation of governance have an effective say over that relation. He characterizes this mode of shared authority as an essentially non-violent and dialogical practice of action-coordination, decision-making, and conflict resolution, in which the diverse co-authors struggle over the norms that govern their interactions in a way that is open-ended and never final.

For Tully, these lived and embodied practices of freedom and democracy—practices in which we are always engaged, if only we would take notice—offer the beginnings of a de-imperializing response, and a non-imperial alternative, to the grand theories and institutions of modern freedom and democracy which serve as the very basis and justification of contemporary imperialism. Once we become attuned to these practices, we will, according to Tully, be able to see 'that we are much freer and our problems more tractable than the grand theories ... make it seem. For while we are still *entangled* in conditions that constrain and enable, and are difficult to change, we are no longer *entrapped*' by them (*PPNK* I, 9).

Part Two: The function of political philosophy

Tully's primary contribution to a critical apprehension of contemporary politics does not lie exclusively, however, with the specific problematization of freedom and democracy in relation to imperialism. Rather, it also lies with the particular approach he brings to these questions, which he terms a 'public philosophy'.

To get clearer on the novelty and import of this approach, it is helpful to begin with a contrast regarding the task of political philosophy. There is an important tradition of thought that approaches the question of political philosophy by way of its subject matter. That is, for thinkers in this long and internally differentiated tradition (really a set of distinct traditions), the predication of philosophy with 'political' refers to its object of investigation. 'Political philosophy' is thus understood to be a species of philosophy pertaining to 'things political': the *res publica*. Those within this tradition do not agree on what properly belongs to this domain, but they will concur that the question is an important, even indispensible fulcrum around which the discipline orients itself. This will be as true of those working within a field of investigation fixated upon the ontologizing of 'the political' (often drawing upon a vocabulary indebted to Carl Schmitt amongst others) as it is for those concerned to distinguish a theoretical inquiry into the 'fundamental political structures of society' from competing branches of inquiry into moral or metaphysical problems. (It is, for instance, in this sense that Rawls sought to clarify in what way *The Theory of Justice* presented a vision of liberalism that was 'political, not metaphysical'.)

Over against this set of approaches, we find a second community of thinkers for whom the predication of philosophy by politics refers not to subject matter but to *function*. These thinkers are concerned not merely with philosophy *about* politics, but with philosophy that *is* political. They will ask the question of how it is that philosophy—or perhaps more generally, critical thought—can perform an act, exercise a function, or have an effect beyond itself. (Perhaps the most famous exhortation to political philosophy in this sense is Marx's eleventh thesis on Feuerbach.) Of course, it will follow that these two broad approaches overlap in important ways. In order to determine what could count as a political effect, one must have a provisional sense of the sphere of politics itself. And yet, these approaches are not reducible, for the latter will be concerned with relevance, impact, and the way that ideas and propositions are actualized in the world of action in a manner not necessarily entailed by the former approach.[2]

James Tully's work is exemplary of political philosophy in this second sense. While the interventions presented in his collected works range over a host of diverse topics including globalization, cultural diversity, ecological politics, and indigenous rights, they are unified in their disclosure of this model. Here, political philosophy is clearly understood in the functional sense—as concerned with relevance and grounding in everyday praxis. In his words, public philosophy 'starts from the present struggles and problems of politics and seeks to clarify and transform the normal understanding of them so as to open up the field of possible ways of thinking and acting freely in response' (*PPNK* I, 37). Tully invites us to see political philosophy as starting from, attending to, and interrogating the contestatory practices of citizens that make up our political worlds or systems of governance. Hence, his political philosophy is also a *public* one.

One important resource for the development of this distinctive style of public reasoning is the late, so-called 'ethical' writings of Michel Foucault. In Foucault's later lectures, essays and interviews, he worked to demonstrate how key thinkers in the Classical Greek, Hellenistic and Roman worlds were concerned with according philosophy a political efficacy.[3] Foucault's model for this was that of the *parrhesiastes*, one who does not rest content to search after truth in a life of contemplation and public withdrawal, but instead operationalizes truth through frank, free and fearless speech. *Parrhesia* stages a confrontation with power, putting the speaker at risk and modelling political philosophy in a new way.

A second relevant thread running throughout Foucault's reflections is that of integrity. Foucault suggests that the political function of philosophy hinges considerably upon the speaker's capacity to bind together *thought*, *word* and *deed* as closely as possible. Foucault returns to Socrates as a model for this, noting in a reading of Plato's *Laches* for instance, the 'harmonic relation between what Socrates says and what he does, between his words (*logoi*) and his deeds (*erga*). Thus not only is Socrates himself able to give an account of his own life, such an account is already visible in his behavior since there is not the slightest discrepancy between what he says and what he does ... [Socrates is] someone who exhibits a kind of ontological harmony where the *logos* and *bios* of such a person is in harmonic accord'.[4]

This *parrhesiastic* courage and integrity is a central element of James Tully's public philosophy. Interestingly, however, Tully also moves beyond the Foucauldian model, bringing in aspects of this practice not thematized by the French philosopher. Foucault's model of *parrhesia* finds its paradigmatic manifestation in relations of asymmetry: in the courageous act of standing up to a greater force.[5] Tully's model, by contrast, also finds room for *isonomia*: for relations of equality and reciprocity. In this way, it prefigures democracy; indeed, it helps us to think about how, and what it means, to transform relationships of inequality, injustice, and oppression into democratic relationships (*PPNK* I, 6). Tully operationalizes critical thought in a way that does not command, but invites, and in so doing reveals the philosophical import of everyday activities of questioning and problematization. This is the specific sense in which Tully's work is not merely a *political* philosophy, it is a *public* one. He makes this linkage explicit early on in his recent collection:

> What is distinctively 'democratic' about public philosophy in a new key is that it does not enter into dialogues with fellow citizens under the horizon of a political theory that frames the exchanges and places the theorist above the *demos*. It rejects this traditional approach. Rather, it enters into the relationships of normativity and power in which academic researchers and civic citizens find themselves, and it works historically and critically on bringing them into the light of public scrutiny with the particular academic skills available to the researchers. Every reflective and engaged citizen is a public philosopher in this sense, and every academic public philosopher is a fellow citizen working within the same broad dialogue with his or her specific skills. Studies in public philosophy are thus specific toolkits offered to civic activists and civic-minded academics working on the pressing political problems of our times. (*PPNK* I, 4)

It is perhaps for this reason that in the end it is Gandhi who holds an exemplary status in Tully's work. For Gandhi did not merely engage in spiritual practices of self-transformation so as to equip *himself* to be a *parrhesiastes*, he did so in a manner that spread outward from his own person into a world-wide movement of global citizenship that took direct aim at empire, war and violence (*PPNK* II, 308–9). For Tully, Gandhi reveals the public, cooperative and non-violent spirit of true *parrhesia*. To speak truth to power is to invite others into a relationship of collective empowerment in a way that realizes the critical capacities within others while, at the same time, opening oneself to transformation through relations with them. Through this process of mutual struggle and self-transformation, we become citizens in the oldest, classical sense of the term: active agents in relations of governance (*PPNK* I, 3). The goal of a public, political philosophy then is not to observe and codify this process, nor to serve as a replacement for it. Rather, it is to incite and participate within these activities:

Civic empowerment and enchantment do not come from grand narratives of universal progress but from *praxis*—actual participation in civic activities with others where we become the citizens we can be ... This is a meditative relationship of working truthfully on oneself and one's attitude to improve how one conducts oneself in the challenging yet rewarding civic relationships with others. These are daily practices of becoming an exemplary citizen. (*PPNK* II, 309)

Part Three: Volume overview

The chapters in this volume grapple with the many questions raised by Tully's work through three main lenses: philosophical, historical and legal–political. Rather than merely commenting upon Tully's work, the chapters here put his studies to work, explicating and testing them precisely by employing them as the 'toolkit' he suggests they are (*PPNK* I, 4). Contributors consider questions such as reasoning as an activity of critique, moral justification of reparations for historical injustices, the rights of indigenous peoples, global citizenship and the persistence of the nation-state, and the role of violence in political life. In so doing, they all model (in their own ways) public philosophy in a new key.

Part I of this volume is concerned with *recasting public philosophy*. It opens with a chapter by the noted philosopher, Anthony Laden. Here, in Chapter 2, Laden argues that one of the most important features of James Tully's approach to constitutional deliberation and political philosophy more generally is the claim that the value of deliberation does not lie in the agreements it produces, but in the very activity itself. In order to understand this point fully, he argues, we need to situate it in a somewhat unfamiliar picture of the activity of reasoning, one that views this activity as a sub-species of conversation in which we offer proposals rather than propositions and proofs. Laden outlines that picture and its important features, arguing that deliberation is best understood as a form of 'engagement': reasoning that requires a heightened level of responsiveness to our reasoning partners. Its value can then be seen to lie in that responsiveness and not in the agreements it produces.

In Chapter 3, Eduardo Mendieta critically commends Tully's philosophical–political work for attending to specific social and political struggles as it theorizes and synthesizes across different philosophical traditions. Here, Mendieta aims to clarify and explicate some of Tully's proposals by pushing some specific questions. First, there is the question of the relationship between citizenship and the public sphere, or rather on the relationship of becoming citizens—what Tully calls citizenisation—and the development of publics. By way of reference to Habermas, Mendieta pushes on the notion that publics have to be created and that part of the process of citizenisation is precisely the forming of counter-publics that may become (mainstream) publics. Secondly, he problematizes the project of public philosophy, not in terms of the ideal that this project entails, but rather in terms of a genealogy of philosophy in the modern world. In this regard, he engages

Rorty's call for a post-philosophical culture that returns us to the deliberations of citizens in an agonistic field of public practices, arguing that Tully sometimes neglects the adverse consequences that the professionalization and academization of philosophy has had on its 'public' function. Thirdly, Mendieta returns to the Foucault/Habermas confrontation that in very fundamental ways informs Tully's project. He argues that a thread running through the two volumes of *PPNK* is precisely the endorsement of a Foucauldian injunction to practice freedom over against the Habermasian preoccupation with questions of normativity and justice. Mendieta suggests that this juxtaposition is artificial and prevents us from actually seeing the degree to which the Foucauldian project of sketching an ontology of the present is not adversarial but instead complementary to a Habermasian project of elucidating the cultural accomplishments of competencies that allow us to cope with a complex world while domesticating the violence of capitalism and imperialism. Fourthly, and finally, following on the attempt to bring about a rapprochement between genealogical critique and reconstructive social sciences, Mendieta broaches the status of rights and law in Tully's work.

In Chapter 4, Antonio Vázquez-Arroyo situates and critically engages with Tully's original contribution to contemporary political theorizing by paying close attention to his account of democratic freedom as a critical vector to imperial forms of power. Vázquez-Arroyo begins by situating Tully's interventions in their political and theoretical contexts. The political context for Tully's public philosophy of democratic freedom includes the aftermath of the Cold War, the collapse of communism, and the demise of anti-colonial nationalisms, while the theoretical context involves the collapse of the liberal–communitarian debates of the 1980s, as well as subsequent debates surrounding minority and group rights, and an emergence of ethical tropes, such as ethos and sensibility, within contemporary democratic theory. He argues that Tully's formulations offer the most compelling formulation of the critical import of 'ethos', which for Tully signifies 'a mode of civic conduct' that is necessary for the sustenance of public freedom. Tully has not only offered a compelling theorization of ethos—out of original readings of Arendt, Foucault, and Wittgenstein—he has also re-set the terms of the discussion by providing an account of democratic freedom that goes beyond the liberal–communitarian divide, one firmly anchored in the critique of imperial forms of power and knowledge. And yet, Vásquez-Arroyo contends, for all its normative and explanatory power, Tully's account falters in its interrogation of capitalism, imperialism and, most specifically, the logics of violence that underwrite them. Accordingly, the chapter proceeds to interrogate these limitations and articulate some possible ways to overcome them.

In the final chapter of Part I, Bonnie Honig engages Tully's reading of *Antigone*. She notes that it is not Sophocles' lamenting title character that attracts Tully, nor is it the playwright's tragic message. Rather, it is Haemon, the 'exemplary citizen of the intercultural common ground', who sees the justice of Antigone's claim and pleads with his father, Creon, for restraint. Like Haemon, Tully here positions himself between the worlds of dissidence and governance, speaking to the powerful in soft reasonable tones on behalf of subaltern subjects, and arguing that we can break out of seemingly tragic impasses if we take instruction from the 'rough ground' of politics and the pacific ways of nature. The chapter then employs the reading of *Antigone* as a means of suggesting that Tully does not attend to this example's essential contestability. Thus, while the vision presented in *PPNK* re-orients us away from the tragic zero-sumness of politics and towards broader ways of conceiving public goods and shared fates, it does not do so without some measure of loss.

Part II of the volume offers a series of exemplary *dialogues with the past*. In Chapter 6, Antony Anghie offers a reading of Emer de Vattel and the rights of indigenous peoples. Here, Anghie connects two of the major themes of *PPNK*: Tully's enduring concern with the predicament of indigenous people, and his examination of the role of imperialism in the contemporary international system. The chapter explores Vattel's view of colonialism, and compares his work with that of other eminent jurists such as Grotius and Vitoria. More particularly, by focusing on his views of the role of political economy in international law, Anghie shows how Vattel's jurisprudence was crucial to the construction of an entity now known in contemporary international law as 'indigenous peoples'. He argues that Vattel formulated a series of ideas that have structured thinking about indigenous peoples since that time. Further, Anghie examines contemporary developments in international law relating to indigenous peoples, and shows how these can be viewed as attempts to redress the problems that arose from Vattel's jurisprudence.

In Chapter 7, David Scott places Tully's work in conversation with that of Janna Thompson to productively interrogate the question of reparations and historic injustice, with particular emphasis on the legacy of slavery in the United States. Scott argues that, between *Strange Multiplicity* and the volumes of *Public Philosophy in a New Key*, Tully has re-set the terms of moral–philosophical argument in such a way as to draw it more meaningfully and productively into an agonistic dialogue with the political demands of the present. One significant domain of demands in the present concerns the various claims for the repair of historical injustice. And one of the most intractable of these claims involves reparations for New World slavery. Through an examination of Thompson's book, *Taking Responsibility for the Past*, which seeks to offer an intergenerational and obligation-dependent account of the justification of reparation for slavery, this chapter tries to show how approaches to moral–philosophical inquiry into such historical injustices often do not historicize and thereby criticize some of the essential terms of their own intervention, as Tully's approach urges us to do. As such, they are apt to reproduce questionable conceptions of the harms of the past and the warrants for their repair.

In Chapter 8, Christian Emden argues that Tully's formulation of civic freedom and political citizenship do not stand in opposition to either the normative framework of constitutional law in the modern tradition or the regimes of power that characterize the modern constitutional state as a democratic polity. Bringing Tully's approach to political philosophy into a conversation with both cosmopolitan theory and Jürgen Habermas's model of a procedurally grounded deliberative democracy, the chapter suggests that an emerging European polity is a particularly interesting example in this respect, precisely because of the way in which it brings together both the traditional nation-state and post-national forms of governance and political action. In much the same way that nation-states, and political associations that have taken over central functions of the nation-state, can only be successful in the long term if they are able to integrate civic practices in a meaningful way, Emden argues that civic practices—as the most direct manifestations of political citizenship—ultimately depend on the constitutional and institutional structures of the nation-state to realize their goals in terms of real politics.

The central theme of Part III is *re-imagining civic freedom today*. Eunice Sahle begins in Chapter 9 with an examination of Tully's approach to neoliberal globalization, and the possibilities for practices of freedom within and against it. While neoliberal globalization does constitute a structure of domination, Sahle argues that one of the great contributions of Tully's approach is that it does not treat such structures as one-way impositions on passive victims; rather, it highlights a mediating process between structures of domination and practices of freedom that reveals not only the way 'global' processes are pluralized when they are instantiated in localized spaces, but also the room that is available for resisting, modifying, and transforming these processes within localized spaces. Sahle's rich and detailed case studies of South Africa and Bolivia illustrate the innovative ways in which state spaces can be and are being reconfigured within the context of neoliberal globalization, as well as the broader 'politics of realist hope' that Tully's work helps to underpin.

In Chapter 10, Aletta J. Norval presents a reading of the third volume of a trilogy by the South African poet, writer and activist Antjie Krog, titled *Begging to be Black*. Noval explores Krog's writings through an engagement with Tully's work on practices of citizenship in *PPNK*. Tully asks how it is possible for 'diverse citizens' to avoid being captivated by a picture of 'one familiar form of national citizenship as the only acceptable form, projecting its hierarchical classifications over others' (*PPNK* II, 268)? This raises the question of how we, as citizens, exercise our critical faculties so as to sustain a multiplicity of alternative forms of citizenship. Reading *Begging to be Black* as an engagement with this central question, Norval explores the role of imagination, the telling of stories, and of historical narratives in opening up possibilities of 'acting otherwise'.

Finally, in Chapter 11, Val Napoleon and Hadley Friedland explore ways to incorporate the expansive insights from Tully's public philosophy within particularly challenging local sites of everyday struggle, including street involved youth, inmates, battered women, and the growing number of murdered and missing indigenous women in Canada. The chapter seeks to connect these local struggles to global struggles, to struggles 'for and of freedom' and addresses how and why people at the local level could re-imagine their everyday practices as practices of citizenship. Napoleon and Friedland address two inter-related sites of struggle and citizenship using these local examples. First, they question how individuals who cannot imagine themselves as citizens in any sense—let alone the active citizen-agents that Tully describes—and whose perceptions of powerlessness are continually reinforced through their interactions, can connect their actions to the practices of citizenship. Secondly, they examine how diverse individuals, groups and agencies, working tirelessly at the local level, can connect their practices with those of others working in different localities, and how they can situate their work dealing with very immediate and urgent concerns within broader struggles and practices of freedom. They argue that finding concrete ways for citizens in these local sites to access Tully's insights would aid in disclosing the purpose and meaning of individual and group actions beyond unavoidable, exhausting everyday struggles. Reframing local struggles as 'glocal' practices of citizenship, connection and cooperation, as Tully suggests, would provide a much-needed source of strength, encouragement and hope at the local level.

The twelfth and concluding chapter provides James Tully an occasion to respond to the provocations and invitations of the previous pieces. He provides a lengthy, original essay that engages each chapter individually, as well as recasting the general terms of a long conversation over freedom and democracy in an imperial context. At the heart of Tully's response is a fascinating and passionate defence of the transformative potential of creative, non-violent practices of freedom and democracy, even in the face of entrenched structures of exploitation, oppression and imperialism.

Notes

1 Wendy Brown, 'Editor's Introduction: We are all democrats now ...', *Theory & Event*, 13(2) 2010.
2 Of course, thinkers in the second school will not agree on what a 'political function' will look like. Followers of Leo Strauss, for instance, might see philosophy as exercising only a very limited and highly mediated political function. From their standpoint, philosophy must hide and disguise its operations in untruth (noble lies) and operate politically only in a highly mediated manner, that is, through the ostensibly apolitical realm: the closed and private community of elites.
3 See especially, *The Hermeneutics of the Subject*; *The Government of Self and Others* and *The Courage to Truth*.
4 Michel Foucault, *Fearless Speech* (Los Angeles: Semiotext(e), 2001), 100.
5 Tully makes explicit reference to this tradition, via Euripides' *The Phoenician Women* and Foucault's reading of it, at *PPNK* II, 282.

Part I

Recasting Public Philosophy

Chapter 2

Engagement, Proposals and the Key of Reasoning

Anthony Simon Laden

James Tully has taught me more about political philosophy and being a philosopher than could be brought together in a single chapter. But of all the lessons I have learned with him, I think the two most significant for my work are these: first, that the value of the sort of political interaction that he calls negotiations and I call deliberations lies not only and perhaps not primarily in the agreements they may produce but in the sorts of activities they are.[1] And second, that this is also true of political philosophy, and so it is a mistake to think of political philosophy as a theoretical exercise divorced from actual politics.[2]

That these are lessons that Tully's work tries to teach us should be clear to anyone who reads it. And yet, many of his readers have been hampered in their full appreciation of the distinctiveness and importance of these points because political philosophy lacks an adequate framework within which to absorb them. In the absence of such a framework, one can talk all one wants about the value of deliberation beyond any agreements it produces, but there will be a moment when one slips back into thinking that the main value must still lie in the end of the deliberation itself: if not the actual agreement then the production of conditions conducive to further agreements or a sort of meta-agreement to keep working things out peacefully. And one can try to make political philosophy practical, but find oneself, despite one's best intentions, taking up a theoretical stance, laying down foundational truths and principles, perhaps thin and procedural and enlightened truths, but theoretically laid down and established ones nonetheless.[3]

This chapter offers the outlines of an alternative framework that develops in part out of an attempt to learn these lessons, and then suggests how some of the central activities of democratic politics look within it. The key idea will be that deliberation can be understood not as a morally constrained form of bargaining, but as a species of a wider genus of conversational interactions that call for responsiveness, a genus I call 'engagements'. Engagements, in turn, fit within a wider picture of reasons and reasoning in which reasons are conceived as proposals fit for rational creatures, and reasoning the activity of interacting with others without commanding or blindly deferring to them.[4]

The activity of reasoning: an alternative picture

According to our standard philosophical and social scientific pictures, reasoning is an activity of rational or logical calculation and determination, a norm-governed intellectual process guided by the forms, structures or principles of reason. Reasoning thus contrasts with thinking that is emotional or intuitive or arbitrary. But there is an alternative picture that can be found in certain philosophical corners, in which reasoning is pictured as a particular way of relating to and interacting with others. In this picture, the relevant contrasts are with commanding and ordering, ignoring and manipulating, blindly obeying and deferring. Reasoning, so pictured, is a value-rich activity: one whose value lies in its role in structuring and constituting our relationships to one another and to ourselves as relations of reciprocity and mutual respect and recognition. It is, first and foremost, an intersubjective practice, rather than a mode of thinking and directing action, and one whose central characteristic is responsiveness to one's fellow reasoners.

Picturing the activity of reasoning as contrasted with commanding and ignoring leads to a second feature: reasons are proposals, invitations, and so the activity of reasoning amounts to a kind of inviting. Offering someone a reason for action is neither ordering her to act nor merely making noise in her general vicinity. When I order someone to act, I leave no space for her reasons to affect what she does. When she hears my words as mere noise, she leaves no space for my reasons to affect what she does. Taking my words as potential reasons means she leaves some space for them to make a difference in what she does. And offering her a reason rather than issuing a command means that I leave space for her to rebut or criticize it. It is thus to offer her a genuine proposal rather than the justification for an already reached decision or conclusion. Reasoning with her requires not so much that my words show a proper responsiveness to a pre-determined set of relevant considerations in favor of what I propose, but that in making a proposal, I show proper responsiveness to her. I show that responsiveness by not determining ahead of time, in the absence of her response, what can count as reasons or relevant considerations for her. Reasoning, that is, is a matter of being responsive to each other, reasonable. Note that so understood, what will count as reasoning on this alternative picture will not be determinable by starting from more standard pictures of what reasons are, and then applying that to the intersubjective case. In this alternative picture, we learn what reasoning is and thus what reasons there are, by looking at actual cases of responsive interaction, what I will call below 'engagements', and seeing, in all their variety, how they proceed.[5]

Such responsiveness cannot be a one-off affair. And yet, according to most accounts of the activity of reasoning, reasoning is a kind of episodic activity, encapsulated in time and space, and directed at an end: reaching a conclusion or decision. This assumption provides one of the most stubborn blocks to fully appreciating the first of Tully's lessons: that the value of political interaction lies not only in what agreements it produces but in the interaction itself. If we are unable to imagine the activity of reasoning except as taking place in discrete packets directed at conclusions, then it is hard to see what is being claimed by those, like Tully, who want to direct our attention to the intrinsic values of the activity itself. As long as we continue to imagine reasoning as taking place in end-defined episodes, then the suggestion to stop focusing only or primarily on agreements and consensus will have to be understood as suggesting that we focus on a different set of ends, such as respectful or peaceful coexistence. But Tully's point goes beyond this, and its interest and importance is missed if it is so read. Imagining democratic politics in terms of practices of civic freedom requires that we see value in the activity itself and not only in what it produces or otherwise brings about.

According to the alternative picture, reasoning is part of the background activities of our shared lives. That is, reasoning is how we occupy a social space of reasons, just as swimming is how fish occupy water. So, the space of reasons is something we inhabit, not merely invoke and deploy, more like our home than our office, and reasoning is just the ongoing activity of inhabiting that space. As with inhabiting a home, inhabiting a space of reasons involves interacting with it, occasionally changing or re-modeling it and in turn being changed by it.[6]

If reasoning is not episodic, then we cannot exhibit neatly packaged episodes of reasoning as cases to study. Rather, we will have to look at the more general interactions that shape and constitute our lives, and describe features of those interactions that make them reasoning. So, we need to pay attention not to the solving of isolated problems, but all the interactions that Stanley Cavell describes as the "whirl of organism":

> our sharing routes of interest and feeling, modes of response, senses of humor and of significance and of fulfillment, of what is outrageous, of what is similar to what else, what a rebuke, what forgiveness, of when an utterance is an assertion, when an appeal, when an explanation—all the whirl of organism Wittgenstein calls "forms of life."[7]

To see what reasoning looks like in this second picture, we need to think, then, as Cavell and Wittgenstein do, of scenes of instruction, or attunement or the lack of it. These are moments when someone is brought to see the world as another sees it, or is confirmed in her own view by finding that another sees things similarly or is threatened or struck by the recognition that they do not, after all, inhabit the same space of reasons. They are often moments that pass in idle conversation, even if the conversation is emotionally charged.[8]

To shift our perspective away from episodes of reasoning toward reasoning as an ongoing background activity, I situate the activity of reasoning within the broader category of conversation. Whereas calculation and deduction and the other familiar activities associated with reasoning are naturally defined by their ends, and thus brought to an end when brought to their end, conversation has no natural termination point or goal, and thus succeeds precisely insofar as it is ongoing. If, then, we can re-orient our conceptual maps so that the activity of reasoning, and in particular the kinds of reasoning together that form the heart of democratic political interaction, can be seen as a specialized form of conversation rather than a joint exercise in decision-making, then we will be in a position to appreciate Tully's lessons in full.[9]

The basic idea is this: conversation, and the various specialized forms of it in which reasoning plays a central role, can be characterized as governed by a set of constitutive or characteristic norms. These norms not only serve to characterize the activities of conversation, but specify the conditions for its success and the values it realizes when successful. Thus, if we can describe political deliberation in terms of such norms, and these norms do not rest on the ends of that deliberation, then we will have a way of capturing Tully's point without slipping into our old ways of thinking. Note that this does not require also denying that deliberators' shared ends play a role in their activity. We can accept that one of the features that shape a particular deliberation is the set of ends, shared and not, of its participants, while defining and articulating the value of deliberation without reference to those ends.

Conversation and engagement

In order to see that casual conversation might have its own characteristic norms, note first that although casual conversations may be aimless and thus do not derive their structure from particular ends, they are not formless. Not all instances of human beings gathered together and speaking are forms of conversation. Sometimes we speak past one another and sometimes our words are heard as mere noise. Sometimes we lecture or hold forth or pronounce our sentiments. Sometimes we cry out. Part of what makes such instances of speaking not forms of conversation is what we try to do with our words, and part is how those words are received. We can distinguish conversation from these other forms of speaking in each other's proximity by saying that while these may involve speaking at or to someone, conversation involves speaking with them. In speaking with others, one of the many things we do is to construct, maintain and shape our relationships with others. From these humble observations, we can develop various norms of conversation, norms that require that we use words in ways that our conversation partners can understand, or that we are sincere in the positions we take in the course of our conversations.[10]

Narrowing our focus somewhat, we can notice that among the many things we say in the course of casual conversations, some of them amount to offering the kind of proposals that I suggested are characteristic of reasons. As we saw above, part of what is required in order for my speaking to count as offering you a reason, a proposal, is that I am open to your rejection of it, and this openness brings with it further norms, norms that govern the activity of reasoning generally. But although reasoning in conversation requires that I propose and not profess, invite and not command, there are still a large variety of ways to invite. Not all invitations are offered with the expectation or even the hope that they will be accepted, and not all rejections of our invitations lead us to revise them. I can invite you to my wedding out of mere politeness, not expecting you to make the cross-country trip to attend, especially given our not very close relationship. And even if we are closer friends, and so I am very hopeful that you will come, it is rather unlikely that I will offer to change the time or place or my partner if it turns out that you cannot accept the invitation as offered. Similarly, I can genuinely offer you reasons without being all that interested in whether or not you will take them up as yours as well. I might do so in the course of stating my position, and not thereby be committed to revising that position if it is not one you hold as well.

Thus, we need a further specification of the activity of reasoning to cover the activity of truly reasoning together, reasoning where I am not only concerned to issue invitations, but to have them accepted. In order to do so, we need to think about cases where we offer invitations that we expect or hope will be accepted and which we are willing to revise if they are not so accepted. Inviting you to marry me is, in some sense, inviting you to my wedding, but it is an invitation of a very different sort. My concern that my proposal be accepted requires further levels of responsiveness to you, both in the kinds of invitation I offer and how we go on if you decline it. Conversations characterized by this heightened level of responsiveness are the ones I call engagements, and this is the genus of which deliberation is a species.

There are a variety of circumstances that may lead us to engagements, and this will make the category initially appear somewhat heterogeneous. They include conversations that have no aim or goal, but where, as it were, the stakes are higher, because the people speaking with one another care more deeply about the topics under discussion or about each other, as well as conversations that aim at reaching agreement or making a joint decision, or coming to some sort of shared understanding. Nevertheless, the variety of forms of engagement turn out to share at least some of their governing characteristic norms, norms of what I will call reasonableness. Since these norms arise out of the general features of engagements, and not the specific ends or other features that lead some conversations to be engagements, they give us a way of characterizing the value of deliberation without reference to its ends and goals.

Varieties of engagement

Since the category of engagements is not a familiar one in philosophical work on reasoning, it will help to look at a variety of examples, and bring out their common features. First, think of otherwise idle conversations that take place between people who care for or admire one another. One consequence of my admiring you or caring about you is that it matters to me whether we can and do share a space of reasons, just as it matters to me that we spend time in the same physical spaces. It is not exactly that I want you to approve of me and my views, though I may also want that, but that your failure to share my views gives me a special kind of reason to re-consider them, and not only because I take your disapproval as evidence of them being wrong. The development of a friendship or romance, whether depicted in literature or found in our lives, is often marked by just such increasing sensitivity to the reactions of others to our invitations. In the face of someone about whom I care, it will no longer be enough that I clearly articulate my position on the matter under discussion, but also that she not reject it out of hand. And so I will be led to issue invitations with an eye to their acceptability and be differently responsive to their rejection. To fix terms, I will call engagements brought on by mutual concern or affection friendly engagements.

Next, consider a case where I converse with strangers or those toward whom I am more indifferent but the topics we are discussing are important to me. We are at a party and having an idle conversation that wanders over a variety of relatively unimportant topics and in which we each take up our turns and say things that are appropriately responsive and sincere to count as reasons. But the conversation remains on the surface, a way to pass the time, until a topic arises that one of us is passionate about. All of a sudden, the tone changes, the invitations are more insistent and the possibility of disagreement becomes more threatening. The conversation becomes less idle, more engaged, as we each find ourselves more concerned that what we say is not dismissed or rejected or rebutted. Faced with disagreement, perhaps we re-phrase our position, perhaps amend it. We don't let what we consider to be irresponsible counter-positions stand, but subject them to criticism.

What I have in mind here is not a case where a conversation touches on a point about which one of us has deep but dogmatically held convictions, but where, rather, our attachment to the issues under discussion is sufficiently deep that we become concerned both with how what we say is received and with having something to say that others can accept. It is, we might say, the subject matter more than our positions and opinions that concern us or to which we are attached. Just as when we care about one another, caring about the subject under discussion will alter the dynamics of our interaction, and give it the characteristic features of engagement: a greater concern that our invitations are acceptable and a greater responsiveness to their rejection. Call such engagements debates.

Third, consider the kind of case that is most important to the domain of political philosophy where Tully works: deliberations and negotiations, where people who disagree reason together in order to reach a joint decision. Parties who aim to reach an agreement by reasoning together have to be attentive to the invitations they offer and more concerned that they meet with acceptance. After all, they will only reach an agreement when their invitations meet with acceptance. And it is precisely a lack of this kind of responsiveness, whether in the offering of unacceptable proposals or in a failure to change course in the face of a proposal's rejection, that is generally taken to be a sign that one is deliberating in bad faith.

In such deliberative situations, one and perhaps the only reason each side needs to be responsive to the other is that they share a goal or need to find common ground or reach a decision. As I suggested above, this end-directed characteristic of such interaction makes it tempting to treat such cases by extending our standard pictures of reasoning to cover cases of reasoning together. For although such reasoning together is interactive, it appears to have the same structure as episodes of individual reasoning: a goal or end or problem sets the reasoning in motion and provides criteria for determining when the reasoning is finished and whether it has been successful. By situating such cases within the broader category of engagements, however, we have a framework for analysis that avoids this standard picture, and thus from which we can finally appreciate Tully's lessons.

Norms of reasonableness[11]

Although there is much that separates them, friendly engagements, debates and deliberations involve parties who are concerned to offer invitations that will be accepted, and thus to work out what reasons they share. They represent, so conceived, a category of interaction that is narrower than, but nevertheless a form of, reason-giving conversation. This means that they are guided by the characteristic norms of conversation and reason giving alluded to above, but also by a set of additional norms that are particular to engagement. In particular, engagement places two further requirements on its participants. First, they must offer one another reasons they in good faith take to be reasons for all of them. Second, as we have seen, participants must be properly responsive to the way their invitations are received. I will describe this condition as a requirement that the rejection of an offered reason must have an impact on the future course of the engagement. When both of these requirements are satisfied, then we can say that the participants in the interaction are engaged with one another in an activity of reasoning together. Moreover, it turns out that abiding by these two norms in the course of our engagement makes our interaction reasonable, in the sense this term has come to have in moral and political philosophy.[12]

Note that these norms do not prevent engagements from themselves transforming the reasons we face. We form and shape and maintain our relationships in part through reasonable engagement, and yet we engage with one another in the context of those very relationships. Even in the context of a given piece of deliberation or debate, we may begin the engagement with a particular understanding of a relationship and then over the course of and as a result of the interaction, come to find ourselves with a very different understanding of our relationship. It turns out, then, that a constitutive requirement on those who participate in engagements is an openness to be moved by the engagement itself and this is part of what the second norm tries to capture.

Moreover, we sometimes engage with someone in the hopes of forming a relationship that does not yet exist.[13] Offering reasons in reasonable engagement, no less than in casual conversation, ought not be seen on the model of premises in a practical deduction. Rather, even in the more restricted field of deliberation, the offering of reasons amounts to inviting (with a greater or lesser degree of confidence) one's deliberative partner to share a space of reasons. Such an invitation can be extended both to someone with whom I already share a well-defined and mutually understood relationship and to one with whom I do not yet share anything but the possibility of forming such a relationship.[14] The course of an engagement can alter the relationship or the circumstances that prompted the engagement, and it can alter the agreement, the shared will, or the shared understanding that the participants eventually construct or re-affirm. The first norm of engagement is meant to get a handle on this problem without thereby reducing engagement to a less open-ended process.

In order to engage with others, each of the participants must work to offer reasons to the others on the presumption that these are reasons they can share, what might be called "we"-reasons. Note already that thinking about deliberation from the perspective of this norm begins to give us a way of distinguishing productive vs. unproductive moves in any engagement, including a deliberation, without making reference to the end of agreement. Thus, someone who claims to be deliberating, but who merely articulates his own position without any regard for how that informs the relationships in which he might stand to his deliberative partners is not deliberating, but negotiating or stalling or trying to bulldoze opposition. Even someone who offers possible positions for agreement, but who makes no effort to show how they are supported by "we"-reasons, or how those reasons are in fact the "we'-reasons of the engaged groups, is failing to engage with his fellow participants.

Note that the requirement that people engaged with one another work toward a determination of the plural subject they form and the "we"-reasons it supports does not rule out all reference to specific differences among the engaged parties. One of the ways that they can mutually clarify their relationship to one another is by making clear to each other how their own positions are influenced or constrained or otherwise shaped by factors that apply to them but not to their partners. Sometimes, narratives of how I got to where I am, or genealogical accounts of the roots of some of my commitments, despite being idiosyncratic and not themselves the foundations of "we"-reasons, may play a role in the process of coming to understand together what sort of "we" we do or can form. In those cases, such moves, though not, strictly speaking, involving offering presumptive "we"-reasons, contribute to our engagement. But we can still say of such moves that they contribute to the deliberation only insofar as they are offered with the thought that they will help to shape or clarify the space of "we"-reasons we can come to share.[15] The importance of such interactions to deliberation is, of course, an ongoing theme of Tully's work.

The first norm of engagement serves to describe the form of its subject matter. The second norm covers what might be thought of as its mode of proceeding. That is, we can observe the first norm and thus offer each other "we"-reasons or considerations that help to map out our shared space of reasons while nevertheless failing to be responsive to how our invitations are taken up. In such a case, we are not centrally concerned with the acceptance of our invitations, and so not, in the sense I have defined the term, engaging with others. I can discuss with you where we each stand, and even explore the possibility that we share some standpoints without thereby engaging with you if I enter that discussion with the attitude that it is a matter of settled fact where we do and will stand, or am unwilling to alter my position in the face of what you say. In order to genuinely engage with you, I need a further commitment: to, at least in some cases, be willing to be moved by what you say so as to find common ground in a shared space of reasons that may not have previously existed. In order to be genuinely engaged with you, then, our conversation must leave appropriate space for the reasonable rejection of proffered reasons to affect the further course of the deliberation. And this is the second characteristic norm of engagement. Rejection of a given "we"-reason is reasonable if it rests on a warranted criticism of the presumption which sustains the original claim. I won't here have much to say about what might ground such a warrant, but it might rest on a rejection of the identity in virtue of which one is being presumed to be a member of the plural subject, or its particular contours or its presumed relationship to other aspects of one's position which themselves have a claim on others' recognition and respect.

Note that while we may be led to engagement by the need to reach a joint decision, and we might be more likely to successfully reach such a decision by following the norms of reasonableness, we are now in a position to begin to see the inherent value in such engagements without making reference to such agreements or ends. The very commitment to remain engaged involves a different kind of agreement: to privilege the reasonableness of our deliberation over the need to reach a (possibly imposed) consensus, to remain engaged with one another even when we can't find further common ground. Coming to the topic of deliberation and reasoning together to reach agreement from the side of engagement thus leads us to focus more on the interaction that precedes the decision rather than the nature of the decision reached, to concentrate on whether our interaction is reasonable rather than whether our choice is rational. And it is from this perspective, I want to suggest, that we can fully appreciate Tully's lessons about the value of democratic practices of civic freedom.

Deliberation vs. negotiation

To bring out these lessons, and place them within the framework I have been constructing, we can more fully contrast two descriptions of the reasoned interaction of people who disagree but are trying to come to an agreement. On the first description, we analyze this interaction from the point of view of the rationality of the final outcome and the means and likelihood of achieving it. Seen in this light, such interactions appear as negotiations. On the second description, we treat these interactions as engagements, and our questions concern whether the engagement is reasonable. When interactions are described in this light, they appear as deliberations.[16]

Seeing an interaction as a deliberation leads us to think about the interaction differently than if we see it as a negotiation. We will, for instance, evaluate its successes and failures differently. Moreover, to the extent that the parties involved in such an interaction see it one way rather than another, this may influence how they proceed, what they regard as helpful or appropriate moves and so forth. At the same time, however, though many interactions can be properly seen as both, this need not be true of all of them. Some interactions may properly be thought of as negotiations but not deliberations or *vice versa*. Even, and perhaps especially, when the categories diverge, coming to see that there is another category of interaction that counts as a form of reasoning together can be helpful as we figure out both how to relate to one another and how to satisfy our various aims and ends.

The logic of negotiation[17]

If, then, we look at an interaction as an interaction whereby rational creatures aim at an agreement as these terms are understood on a standard picture of reasoning, then that interaction will look like a negotiation. In negotiation, people who disagree or have divergent interests reason together in order to try to reach an agreement. Negotiated agreements are compromises amongst parties who have different pre-existing interests. Negotiation serves as the means by which they attempt to maximize the satisfaction of their particular ends or interests given the presence of others with different interests and the obstacle this places in their way. That is, parties involved in negotiation see each other as obstacles to the maximal satisfaction of their own interests. The point here is not that negotiating parties treat each other purely instrumentally, and negotiation as merely more cost-effective than outright domination. We can see someone as an obstacle to our plans without seeing them as an object.

Nevertheless, picturing our interaction as a negotiation involves seeing others as obstacles and thus the need to deal with them as an unfortunate fact. This, in turn, makes negotiation a kind of concession to the unfortunate plurality of our social world: if everyone just agreed with us, we wouldn't have to negotiate. And that attitude, in turn, may reinforce or generate an attitude toward those with whom we find ourselves negotiating as problems for us. If I have to accept an alternative that I find less attractive in order to reach an agreement with you, then I can come to see you with resentment, as it was your presence or position that required me to compromise.

Interpreting reasoning together on the model of negotiation has several further consequences. First, negotiated agreements always require further compliance mechanisms. To see why, it helps to distinguish between the ends I adopt and the interests they serve. Imagine that I have a set of interests that can be advanced or realized by my adopting and reaching a given end. And imagine further that I am unable to pursue this end unimpeded because you, pursuing the ends you have adopted to advance your interests, stand in my way. If we decide to negotiate our way past this situation, then we reason with one another in order to find an agreement. This agreement will involve our adopting new ends that are either joint ends or at least jointly satisfiable. The agreement counts as a compromise for each of us, however, insofar as the new ends we each adopt serve to advance each of our interests less well or less fully than the ends with which we began. In other words, the agreement that negotiation aims at is an agreement in ends, not interests, and most negotiation works not by transforming people's interests but by leading them to adopt new ends. But this means that negotiated compromises thus necessarily leave some pre-existing interests unsatisfied. As a result, each side in a negotiation has a motivation to break the agreement when doing so will serve their interests better than keeping the agreement will. And this is why negotiated agreements always come with problems of compliance. Since nothing internal to the process of negotiation fosters trust or a sense of a shared project, even if negotiations can end or forestall open conflict, they may not lead to a true cessation of hostility. Even successful negotiations—ones that reach agreement—are always in danger of breaking down.

Second, negotiation leads each side to exaggerate its claims and thus paradoxically drives parties apart as they try to reach agreement. The basic idea is that the less I am willing to give up, the better deal I can make, and so I have an incentive to exaggerate my interests and their importance to me. It is important to be clear about the force of this claim. I mean to say more than that sometimes people enter negotiation in bad faith and thus violate accepted practices to get a better deal. Clearly that happens. My point here is that the structure of negotiation itself can push even those who enter negotiation in good faith but who nevertheless view their interaction as a form of negotiation, to exaggerate their claims. Each side may respond to resistance to their claims from the other side by, as it were, pulling harder and digging in its heels. The rejection of a claim may serve to make its satisfaction seem more important, giving it new symbolic value as a question of respect or recognition. Insofar as negotiation involves not only interaction between the groups negotiating but also the at least symbolic separation of those groups into separate sides, it may have the effect over time of solidifying intra-group ties and emphasizing inter-group differences. All of these dynamics, then, have the effect of exaggerating the opposing claims of the negotiating groups even in the absence of bad faith and an initial intention to deceive.

Third, when negotiations fail to reach agreement, or that agreement breaks down, this can leave the conflict more intense than before, the failure of negotiations taken by both sides as a sign that their differences really are irreconcilable, and that the only full solution to the problem will come from one side overcoming the obstacles that the other side represents. The problem here stems in part from the way that the process of negotiation generates centrifugal pressures, but also from the underlying fact that negotiation is an end-defined activity: failure to achieve a negotiated agreement is seen by all sides as a sign that negotiation has failed.

One common way of describing the motivation for entering into negotiation is that it allows parties to realize something of value in their situation: that it is one that admits of the possibility of mutual advantage. That is, negotiation and bargaining are most likely to be successful means of reaching agreement when there is a kind of surplus to be had in the face of agreement, and so the question the negotiators face is how to divide up the surplus.[18] If the parties do not face a problem of this form (and so there is no mutual advantage to be had), negotiation may either seem like a pointless or hopeless task. It is pointless if there is no interaction with or without an agreement. Two groups inhabiting separate islands that have no contact or possibility of joint enterprise have no reason to negotiate with one another. It is hopeless if there is interaction but no possibility of one side benefiting from the agreement, perhaps because of their current relative inequality.

Despite these problems, viewing interaction among rational agents as negotiations has been the dominant means of interpreting them in philosophy and especially the social sciences and has tended to be the dominant interpretation given by participants to their interactions. Of course, there are clearly cases where the kind of interaction that we need to participate in is best thought of as obeying the logic of negotiation, even when our joint aim is not the dividing up of some good but making some joint decision about what to do or what to believe. One ground for engaging in negotiation or regarding our interaction as a negotiation is the importance of our reaching an agreement or shared decision. Another is that, as we will see, genuine deliberation requires forms of responsiveness that we might be unwilling or unwise to accept in certain circumstances. In those cases, understanding our interaction as a negotiation may, despite all of its shortcomings, be the best alternative. My aim in distinguishing negotiation from deliberation is merely to highlight certain characteristics of reasoning together that, though they may appear inevitable, are really tied to the special features of negotiation. Note, then, by way of wrapping up this discussion that many of the values—of reconciliation and recognition, of the realization of the values of practices of civic freedom—that Tully associates with the possibility of just constitutional and political dialogues will be hard to realize through negotiation as described here. Thus, if we look to such dialogues through a framework that treats them as negotiations, we will miss the very values Tully is calling to our attention.

The logic of deliberation

Whereas regarding our interaction as a negotiation involves seeing it as a means to search for a compromise that balances a set of our competing pre-existing interests, interpreting our interaction as deliberation involves picturing it as, first and foremost, a form of engagement with others. Despite deliberators' concern that their invitations are accepted, they often come to deliberation with different perspectives, and thus offer considerations, concerns, and proposals that may compete with one another and thus not meet with shared acceptance. What is distinctive about deliberation is that despite their differences, all parties attempt to work out a set of shared reasons. They do not merely hold out for the best deal they can get, but rather try to figure out what authority to give the various offers that others make, and how they can, together, respond appropriately to the complex terrain of reasons that their competing positions generate. Part of their task in deliberation, then, is to find a way to understand their divergent claims in terms of shared reasons, for it is in doing this that they can bring others to accept their invitations, and offer, in turn, invitations that others can accept. And part of that understanding may involve seeing that the reasons they do or can come to share do not support any further agreement.

Understanding our interaction as deliberation involves understanding what we and our partners do as offering proposals to one another, and being responsive to one another's rejection and acceptance of those proposals, possibly by allowing ourselves to be moved by what others say. Since the reasons we offer and those we accept depend upon the nature of our relationships to one another, deliberation may involve an investigation of our relationships to one another and the reasons they support. If we come to the deliberation with different understandings of just what relationship we bear to one another or what sorts of reasons that relationship authorizes, then the very process of deliberation may involve one or both of us changing our understanding of these matters and thus what reasons we have, both collectively and severally. If deliberating together moves us from an unarticulated disagreement about our relationship to a new understanding of that relationship, we may resolve our competing claims by understanding them in a new and common light. When we reach agreement in this fashion, our agreement will not have the features I highlighted in the compromise that results from negotiation. Because the agreement rests on a shared understanding of the merit of the various reasons that support it, the parties to the agreement need not regard it as merely the best they can do under the circumstances, a necessary but unfortunate concession to the obstacles the others represent. Through deliberation, each party genuinely refines her understanding of herself, her relationship to others, and the reasons they authorize. If a shared understanding is reached in this manner, the original claims that go unsatisfied do not continue to exert their pull because they are seen to have insufficient authority. The final agreement expresses where each side now stands. Interestingly enough, then, parties who approach their interaction as a deliberation and thus an engagement, and so do not treat their positions as constrained by the aim of reaching a joint decision, thus put themselves in a position to arrive at agreements that can be stronger, more stable and more lasting.

Note that this possibility in deliberation arises from its being a form of engagement, and thus governed by the norms of reasonableness. In particular, in order to be reasonable in my engagements with others, I have to be open to being changed by the engagement itself, to being moved by what my deliberative partners say. In the absence of such openness, I won't be able to alter the course of our engagement in light of my partner's rejection of my offered reasons, and so I won't be able to adhere to the second norm of reasonableness.

My being open to being moved by what you say amounts to my giving you some say over where, as it were, I stand, and thus, in a deep sense, who I am. Being open to being moved does not require always moving or having no principled stands. It is important to recognize the possibility of taking up another's reasons and responding reasonably to them without thereby accepting them. Thus, being reasonable need not forestall the possibility of having deeply held beliefs, positions and commitments. In such cases, though I am open to being moved by your reasons, the reasons you offer me do not in fact move me. Nevertheless, being open to being moved by another's reasons requires a certain kind of vulnerability to the influence of one's deliberative partners, and this vulnerability means that participants in deliberation must be able and willing to trust one another.

Note two consequences of this fact. First, whereas negotiation requires situations with the possibility of mutual advantage, deliberation requires situations of mutual intelligibility and the possibility of mutual trust. Since deliberation involves making proposals to others to share a space of reasons with us, it must, at a minimum, be already possible to speak with them. We can, that is, only deliberate with those with whom we are mutually intelligible. Situations of mutual intelligibility cut across those with the possibility of mutual advantage, and they are created where they didn't exist before via different pathways than those that create the possibility of mutual advantage. The possibility of mutual advantage can be constructed by tweaking incentive structures. The possibility of mutual intelligibility is realized, in large part, through conversation and the general work of living together. On this analysis, then, it should come as no surprise that so much of Tully's work is about bringing seemingly incompatible positions and traditions into conversation with one another, showing how each side's claims and moves and ways of speaking can be intelligible to the other, and on the other hand, how certain traditions of Western political thought can get in the way of such engagement.[19]

Second, there will be situations where straightforward engagement in deliberation is not a feasible alternative because one or both sides lack sufficient trust to accept the vulnerability that good faith deliberation entails. We cannot, it turns out, reasonably deliberate with just anyone on any topic of disagreement. There is a large difference, however, between an analysis that concludes that deliberation is not a live option in a particular situation and one which lacks the conceptual resources to see it as a distinct alternative to begin with. For one, if understanding our interactions as deliberations holds out attractive possibilities for reconciliation and yet circumstances (such as a lack of trust between the parties) make acting on that interpretation impossible or unwise, we have reasons to think about how to change those circumstances to make true deliberation possible, and a further reason to try to implement such policies beyond whatever direct good they do. We might, as successful mediators in peace talks often do, try to get the parties together to talk about anything as a way of building up some initial trust. This also leads us to see certain forms of conversation, including but not limited to other forms of engagement, that are neither deliberations nor agreement-producing negotiations as productive nevertheless, insofar as they lay the necessary groundwork for future reasonable deliberation.[20]

Even when there is sufficient trust to engage in good faith deliberation, it can fail to reach an accord. Nothing guarantees that parties to deliberation will find sufficient common ground on which to stand together. Nevertheless, the dynamics of deliberation can generate some level of solidarity even in the absence of a final agreement. Unlike negotiation, deliberation does not generate incentives for exaggeration. In deliberation, each party is motivated not solely or primarily by getting as many of its own claims as possible satisfied, but in coming to a set of shared understandings, in finding invitations that can be accepted. In order for such shared understandings to be reached, each side must come to understand the demands others make, and under which they find themselves. Seeing ourselves as deliberative partners can lead us to think more about our relationships to one another, and not to dwell solely on intra-group commonalities. Moves in a deliberation thus do not function as tugs on a rope, provoking stronger counter-tugs from the other side. Rather, even when rejected, good faith suggestions of what the sides share draw the other side into thinking together. Thus, rather than having the effect of hardening initial differences, deliberation can serve to bring different sides toward mutual acknowledgment and understanding even when it fails to bring them to embrace a fully shared decision.[21] The internal dynamic of good faith deliberation serves to increase rather than erode what trust exists. As a result, deliberation that does not arrive at a final agreement is less likely to generate an even more divisive conflict.

Here we come to one of the lessons of Tully's work with which I started: that the values of deliberation are realized through the activity itself and not only the agreements it produces. First, deliberation can be ongoing without this being a sign that it has failed.[22] As we have seen, the very participation in the activity of deliberation expresses a willingness and interest on the part of those participating to resolve their differences cooperatively and on mutually acceptable terms, to search for and perhaps develop shared spaces of reasons that can support mutually acceptable claims, to continue to live together and work as partners. Participation in deliberation thus involves each party showing respect toward and recognition of the status of the other parties as parties whose claims matter.[23] Such respect is not a product of deliberation, nor can it be one of deliberation's aims. Contrast this with what is required to engage in negotiation: recognizing the other party as an obstacle to the unimpeded pursuit of one's ends that must be dealt with, and cannot be merely ignored or overrun.[24]

In addition, since deliberation involves an attempt to determine jointly the authority of various competing reasons, it provides parties who disagree with one another a wider array of responses to the claims of others short of fully satisfying them. Thus, in the course of deliberation, it is possible for one side to acknowledge the legitimacy of the other side's offer without thereby fully accepting it, by acknowledging that it gives rise to a reason, but urging that it is a reason that is overridden in this context. Such recognition of legitimacy can, in certain cases, go a long way toward resolving disputes without agreements, in part because they serve to (re)-establish at least some shared ground.[25]

The continual recognition of one another as engaging together in a shared project then serves to maintain deliberators' relationships to one another as ones that can serve as the basis for further deliberation and reasoning and interaction even in the absence of a more complete lining up of interests or desires or positions.

The result can be what, in the political realm, Rawls calls "stability for the right reasons," and which he describes as resting on "the deepest and most reasonable basis of social unity available to us in a modern society."[26]

Note that stability so conceived is not an end that can be pursued through legitimate or illegitimate means, but is, rather, a by-product of pursuing other ends legitimately. As Rawls describes political stability for the right reasons, it is generated by citizens deliberating in good faith with one another, and recognizing this fact. What leads citizens to feel allegiance to their shared political society is precisely the recognition that society leaves room for them and their particular demands, and recognizes those demands even when it does not satisfy them. The allegiance that generates stability for the right reasons relies on the ongoing commitment to reasonable deliberation. Any attempt to achieve such stability through coercive or manipulative tactics, or by excluding certain voices in the name of unity and agreement is bound to fail, as precisely such tactics are what will undermine the very features of the deliberation that command the allegiance that generates stability for the right reasons in the first place. If, on the other hand, we engage with our fellow citizens by deliberating with them, then in the course of such deliberation, we demonstrate that we take the issues of our common life seriously, and them as civic friends.

Philosophy and the field of civic engagement

James Tully brings the first volume of *Public Philosophy in a New Key* (2008) to a close with his essay "Towards a New Field of Democracy and Civic Freedom," in which he traces what he takes to be the development, out of and beyond work in deliberative democracy, to a new field, that of civic freedom. I can sum up what I have been offering in these pages, then, as offering a conceptual terrain in which such a field might be planted: the terrain of civic engagement.

Now, civic engagement is generally used as a term to describe certain sorts of activist citizenship, and in particular, educational programs that stress involving students in political and social action rather than mere book-learning. And I certainly mean my suggestion here to pick up on those resonances, while nevertheless giving it the somewhat technical meaning this chapter has explored. The new field that Tully invites us to study and contribute to is one which not only imagines democracy as an intellectual exercise, a political debating society, but also as a practical matter, a set of practices and activities. And this brings me to the other lesson of Tully's that I highlighted at the beginning: the idea that political philosophy is not a purely theoretical endeavor, but a kind of critical activity. How are we supposed to understand this thought? Well, it will come as no surprise if I invite you to hear this lesson, hear this new key for public philosophy, as the suggestion that we treat political philosophy itself as a form of engagement. That is, political philosophy in Tully's new key does not aim to uncover transcendental or universal truths about social or political practices, or to derive abstract principles, but to propose to us reasons as ones we might accept, and to instantiate by its very methods and tones, an intellectual space where we can decide which of these proposals to take up, which to suggest need changes, and which to reject. So, Tully's public philosophy is engaged philosophy not only in the sense that it takes up political and social causes, but because it makes proposals to and enters into responsive reasoning relationships with citizens and activists, and offers us ways to see those relationships and the activities that make them up, as well as our own participation in those relationships through our philosophical interventions, as engagements.

When a proposal meets with acceptance, resulting in an engagement, that is often the end of the story. But what is true of romantic comedies and fairy tales is not true of democratic politics and philosophy. For, as with real life, an engagement is not an end, but a beginning. And no matter how polished and well-thought out our proposals are, they must, if they are to remain reasonable, always be open to retraction and revision as we embark on the always ongoing, always unfolding, hard work of living together.

Notes

1 James Tully, *Public Philosophy in a New Key: Volume I, Democracy and Civic Freedom* and *Public Philosophy in a New Key: Volume II, Imperialism and Civic Freedom*, Cambridge: Cambridge University Press, 2008, hereafter referred to as *PPNK*.
2 Tully, "Public Philosophy as a Critical Activity," *PPNK* I, 15–38.
3 This happens to many who work downstream of both Habermas and Rawls. One in the Habermasian tradition who may have escaped is Rainer Forst. See his *The Right to Justification*, New York: Columbia University Press, 2011. For a discussion of Rawls as also teaching us this lesson about the place of political philosophy, and Habermas as either rejecting this lesson or not seeing it as a clearly different option, see my "Justice of Justification," in *Habermas and Rawls: Disputing the Political*, ed. Fabian Frayenhagen and James Gordon Finlayson, New York: Routledge, 2011, pp. 135–52.
4 I develop this picture at much greater length in my *Reasoning: A Social Picture*, Oxford: Oxford University Press, 2012, from which much of the material is taken. That a reason is a proposal fit for a rational creature is meant to echo the scene in *Pride and Prejudice* where Elizabeth Bennet refuses Mr Collins's marriage proposal as not so fit because it has been offered as if to "an elegant female" whose refusal can only count as coquettish. See Jane Austen, *Pride and Prejudice*, Oxford World Classics, ed. James Kinsley, Oxford: Oxford University Press, 2008, volume 1, chapter XIX, pp. 80–4.
5 That this should be our method of understanding key philosophical concepts, whether reason, justice, recognition or democracy is, of course, a lesson that Tully often credits Wittgenstein with teaching him.
6 Thinking of reasoning in terms of a social space of reasons will perhaps be most familiar from the work of Wilfred Sellars and, following him, Robert Brandom, who takes himself to be engaged in a basically Hegelian project. As will become clear below, one can find variants of this picture in the work of Stanley Cavell, who takes himself to be articulating thoughts he finds in Wittgenstein and sometimes Emerson and sometimes Kant, and in Onora O'Neill's work on and deriving from Kant. The image of reason as a home, though most evocative of Hegel's project of reconciliation, finds expression as well in Kant's 1st Critique (A707/B735).
7 Stanley Cavell, "The Availability of Wittgenstein's Later Philosophy," in *Must We Mean What We Say?*, New York: Charles Scribner's Sons, 1969. Cavell is unpacking what he

takes to be Wittgenstein's understanding of what supports our confidence that others will go on as we do, will understand what we mean by our words.

8 They can also be the work of philosophical activity, and not surprisingly, Tully's work is full of them: moments where a familiar trope or idea is re-described under a new and often unflattering light, where verities of Enlightenment Western thought are shown to be tied up with an imperialist project and a failure to genuinely hear and respect other voices, moments where we are taught how to see things from a new perspective, and thus to see that such a perspective is one we have hitherto ignored or marginalized.

9 We might also thus be in a position to appreciate the lessons of others who have emphasized the importance of what Cavell calls the conversation of justice, and Oakeshott calls the conversation of mankind. In addition to Cavell and Oakeshott, prominent names here would have to include Hannah Arendt and Richard Rorty.

10 The ideas in this paragraph are developed and defended in chapters 5 and 6 of *Reasoning: A Social Picture,* op cit.

11 Much of this section is adapted from my "Outline of a Theory of Reasonable Deliberation," *Canadian Journal of Philosophy* 30, 2000, pp. 551–80, where the connection of these norms with the reasonable and the contrast between reasonable deliberation and rational choice is more fully developed.

12 My use of the term "reasonable" is meant to follow that of John Rawls, *Political Liberalism,* paperback edition, New York: Columbia Unversity Press, 1996, although not necessarily many of his commentators.

13 Again, peace negotiations are the most prominent example of such cases. It should, in light of the discussion so far, not be surprising that many successful peace negotiations begin by getting the parties to the same place for long enough that they have to talk to one another, about anything. Such dialogue helps create a relationship on which later deliberation can rest and build.

14 My thoughts on this point have benefited from several discussions with Avner Baz.

15 I mean this to be a weak, though not an empty requirement. It should allow forms of dissent, denial and distancing from an emerging consensus in the name of some particular aspect of a participant's positioning or history or worldview, when this rejection is meant to clarify a flaw in the emerging consensus's claim to be shared or universal or neutral, and it should allow such moves to be initially inarticulate or not expressible in a dominant mode of communication, but nevertheless rule out as unreasonable such rejections when they are merely meant to reject any possibility of looking together for common ground anywhere but where the deliberator currently stands.

16 Note that this terminology departs from Tully's. He calls "negotiations" what I call "deliberations" in part because he does not draw the distinction between his preferred form of interaction and the one he is rejecting that I do here.

17 The material in this section and the next is adapted from my "Negotiation, Deliberation and the Claims of Politics," in *Multiculturalism and Political Theory,* ed. Anthony Smon Laden and David Owen, Cambridge: Cambridge University Press, 2007, pp. 198–217.

18 Of course, the surplus can come in the form of avoiding a penalty. A negotiated settlement may keep us from conflict as well as provide the basis of our cooperative interaction.

19 Thinking about the conditions and actions that can make our deliberative partners trustworthy may also shed light on the reasonableness or not of a variety of more subtle forms of rhetorical persuasion, and whether they are properly thought of as rhetorical devices that bring our partners to see an aspect of a situation in a way that moves them to see reasons where they did not before, or forms of manipulation that unreasonably change our partners' viewpoint with seemingly the same effects. Working out the details here goes beyond the scope of this chapter. I am grateful to the ever trustworthy David Owen for bringing me to see the importance and difficulty of the question.

20 It also provides the beginning of an argument for the importance of public spaces where serious and engaged interaction among diverse members of a society take place, such as common schools, public forums of discussion and debate, and to a lesser degree public modes of transportation as all necessary for a deliberative democracy to thrive.

21 Of course, the mere fact that deliberation encourages good faith participation is no insurance against the possibility that some parties will enter deliberation in bad faith. My claim is merely that the logic of deliberation does nothing itself to pervert the incentives of those who enter such deliberations in good faith, whereas the logic of negotiation can itself have the effect of pushing those who enter negotiation in good faith further apart.

22 Tully stresses this aspect of deliberation (though he calls it negotiation) in *Strange Multiplicity*, Cambridge: Cambridge University Press, 1995, 135–6, and connects it to what he calls practices of freedom in "A New Field of Democracy and Freedom." See also my *Reasonably Radical*, Ithaca, NY: Cornell University Press, 2001, p. 127.

23 For a longer discussion of the relation between engaging in reasonable deliberation and forms of recognition, see my "Reasonable Deliberation, Constructive Power and the Struggle for Recognition," in *Recognition and Power*, ed. Bert van den Brink and David Owen, Cambridge: Cambridge University Press, 2007, pp. 270–89.

24 This recognition is neither trivial nor empty as it includes the rejection of domination as a means to satisfy one's claims, whether because it is not practically feasible or not morally acceptable. Nevertheless, it is minimal compared to the recognition afforded in deliberation, and, within negotiation, it is merely considered a necessary condition for something else rather than one of the points of the activity itself.

25 Something like this hope seems to me to animate Tully's responses to Canada's various constitutional crises and developments. See, for instance, "Multinational Democracies: An Introductory Sketch," "The Negotiation of Reconciliation" and "The Struggles of Indigenous Peoples for and of Freedom," *PPNK* I, chapters 6, 7, 8.

26 John Rawls, "Reply to Habermas," reprinted in John Rawls, *Political Liberalism*, paperback edition, p. 391. Rawls says that the basis of such unity is a reasonable overlapping consensus, but I think it is clear from the preceding passages and other parts of his work that this consensus is best thought of not on the model of a negotiated agreement, but as the sort of joint commitment to address differences through reasonable deliberation of the sort discussed above. Compare here Tully on "Reimagining Belonging in Diverse Societies," *PPNK* I, 160–84.

Chapter 3

Freedom as Practice and Civic Genius: On James Tully's Public Philosophy

Eduardo Mendieta

Introduction

Engaging the work of James Tully entails for me at the very least two formidable challenges. First, there is the insurmountable challenge of coming to terms with decades of pioneering work on modern political philosophy that is both prodigiously researched and ecumenical in scope. Reading through the two volumes of *Public Philosophy in a New Key* (2008) is a humbling experience.[1] The level of engagement with the most interesting work in political philosophy of the last couple of decades is simply staggering. One can only approach this synthesis of both historical and theoretical work with trepidation and extreme humility. Second, there is also the challenge of having to say something that is critical, or insightful, with and against so much that I agree with. There is the danger of taking specific arguments and saying something to the effect: "I agree with this, but I would have put it differently." The challenge, then, is to say something that is not simply a nuanced repetition of what Tully has already written and argued so eloquently and persuasively. Still, in the sea of agreement, I found a couple of archipelagos where I discerned some points of divergence, not full-fledged disagreements, but perhaps points on which I would want to engage Tully so as to elicit further clarification. Let me briefly mention what I think are these archipelagos of divergence: first, there is the question of the relationship between citizenship and the public sphere, or rather on the relationship of becoming citizens—what Tully calls wonderfully citizenization—and the development of publics; second, I want to briefly problematize the project of public philosophy, not in terms of the ideal that this project entails, but rather in terms of a genealogy of philosophy in the modern world. More specifically, I have in mind Rorty's call for a post-philosophical culture that returns us to the deliberations of citizens in an agonistic field of public practices. Third, I want to touch on the Foucault/Habermas confrontation that in very fundamental ways informs Tully's project. In fact, a running thread throughout the two volumes of *PPNK* is precisely the endorsement of a Foucauldian injunction to practice freedom over and against the Habermasian obsessions with questions of normativity and justice. I want to suggest that this juxtaposition is artificial and prevents us from actually seeing the degree to which the Foucauldian project of sketching an ontology of the present is not adversarial, but instead complementary to, a Habermasian project of elucidating the cultural accomplishments of competencies that allow us to cope with a complex world while domesticating the violence of capitalism and imperialism. Fourth, and finally, following on the attempt to bring about a rapprochement between genealogical critique and reconstructive social sciences, I would like to broach the status of rights and law in Tully's work.

Making publics, becoming citizens

Could we say that civil society is to Hegel's philosophy of law and the modern state, what "the public sphere" is to Habermas's philosophy of the rule of state law? The analogy gets us only half way. Civil society operates in Hegel's philosophy of the state as an intermediary social space between the family and the state, in which agents are acting in accordance with their private interests and where they tend to abide still in accordance with local and historically sedimented ethical practices (see paragraphs 183, 235, 236, and 241 of the *Philosophy of Right*). Civil society is still in the grip of what Hegel called "Sittlichkeit," or ethical substance. It is only when we ascend to the level of the state, of right, of law, that we have overcome our particular and selfish interests and assume the standpoint of generality by submitting to the abstract form of law. It is only in the form of the law that the ethical substance is translated into a universal principle. The state is the embodiment of reason. It is accomplished reason. Of course, for Hegel such an accomplishment is not possible without the struggle for recognition that takes place in "civil society." Yet, the struggles for recognition in civil society are mostly articulated as struggles over pecuniary and selfish interest. There is no deliberation, only conflict. One of the great virtues of Habermas's epochal 1962 book *The Structural Transformation of the Public Sphere*,[2] was to offer a historical reconstruction of a social space where we are not simply self-interested economic contenders, but above all, "deliberating" agents. The other virtue of Habermas's work was to, in a Hegelian vein, show how this new social structure contained normative principles that embodied and unleashed in modern society an emancipatory potential that remains both operative and inchoate. In contrast to Hegel, for whom the rational is embodied in the state or the form of law, for Habermas rationality is achieved through the deliberation of citizens in a space in which the force of the better argument prevails by persuading. In other words, for Habermas reason is embodied in practices of democratic deliberation. If reason becomes static in Hegel's state, reason becomes dynamic and yet to be accomplished in Habermas's public sphere. The public sphere is the place where reason is generated, regenerated and made substantive through the deliberation of social agents.

True, as soon as the book was published it generated heated debates not just in Germany, but also in Europe. When the book was finally published in English three decades later, it spawned a new series of debates. The debates circled around two main issues: the empirical deficits of Habermas's description, and whether there was "one" public sphere, and not many. The second type of criticism is the one I want to foreground for my purposes here. The work of Nancy Fraser,[3] as well as that of Oskar Negt and Alexander Kluge, tried to demonstrate that the public is never one, but plural.[4] There is always a dynamic, tense, dialectical relationship between "subaltern" or "counterpublic" and what we can call the "hegemonic" or "official" public, as Michael Warner has shown so eloquently and definitively.[5] In response, Habermas acknowledged that the public has never been one and that it is always under contestation.[6] It is part and parcel of the "public sphere" that questions of who and what form part of it are *sine qua non*. A public is formed through negotiation and deliberating about precisely who is part of the public. The public is not simply constitutive of a certain social group; it is a regulative idea that remains always shy, short, of any completeness. A public is a horizon that recedes as we engage it; meaning, a public can never be sure of its having achieved publicness. It is for this reason that integral to the conception of *Öffenlichkeit* is that publics are called into being so that something like the "public" can be constituted, even, as the univocity and stability of that "public" is undermined. There is only a public sphere that is ceaselessly being revitalized by the creation of counter-publics. It may be said that it is indispensable to the public sphere as a social space that is never identical with itself; its aim is to generate dissent. Yet, the public sphere is not the mere aggregation or summation of different publics. It is when these publics engage each other, by overlapping, by engaging in different practices of contestation, challenge, agonistics, that something like a public begins to materialize, even if ephemerally. There is only publicness—*Öffenlichkeit*—so long as publics are ever forming that challenge received notions of what counts as either public or private, a matter of private concern, or general social importance. Nothing is *prima facie* to be excluded from discussions in the public sphere. Everything can be a subject for deliberation. Publicness, in the sense of public sphere, means precisely that anything can potentially become the subject of democratic deliberation insofar as what is under discussion can be shown to have consequences for the bodypolitic. No one can be excluded, even if some are *de facto* left out by the material configuration of the way in which those publics interact. All are nominally included in the formation of the public *qua* synergy of publics.

Even if Habermas's work on the *Structural Transformation of the Public Sphere* can be faulted for certain empirical lacunae, there is an aspect that even today deserves praise and admiration, and that is what I would call the material–practical elucidation of what enables the public sphere. Part of Habermas's original insight was to locate, in the very material transformation of society, the resources for the emergence of new normative structures. He did this by paying close attention to the emergence of material institutions and spaces that provided the material framework for the deliberations of social agents: the mass newspaper, the emergence of a reading public that was fed by bourgeois literature, the evolution of public spaces for the gathering of masses where a *societas* independent from the state and the pursuit of private affairs could be pursued and enjoyed. Interestingly, it is in the public sphere that social agents can participate in the state, indirectly but just as efficaciously. Citizens recognize each other as such only within a vibrant public sphere, and not simply on the day of voting. We vote once a year, or once every two years, depending on what election is taking place. But we are ceaselessly engaging in an agonal exchange about what constitutes the public interest by reading, debating, demonstrating, and posturing, in the public sphere. Habermas accepted and built on Hannah Arendt's insight that totalitarian societies are those that obliterate the public sphere, precisely so as to squelch and neutralize the communicative power of deliberating citizens. It can be safely averred that Habermas's work since the early 1960s has been to carry to its further conceptual conclusions the insight that citizens generate normative claims by engaging each other in public deliberations—citizens generate not just insights about the good, but also the just, through their public use of reason. As the title of a volume produced for his 70th birthday puts it: "the publicness of reason and the reason of the public sphere [*Die Öffenlichkeit der Vernunft und die Vernunft der Öffenlichkeit*]", which can lend itself to the interpretative translation to the effect that the public sphere is the place, the *topos*, where reason is made reasonable to itself—accessible, not to say transparent—because the public sphere is itself a space for the giving and taking of reasons, reasons that remain always yet to be redeemed and cashed in.[7]

A public is surely more than a citizenry, but there is no citizenry that is not always at some point a public. To recognize itself as a citizenry that is exhausted neither by the Bill of Rights, nor by the number of senators and congresspersons in the Capitol, citizens must engage each other as what Dewey called the "public." To use Tully's language, we practice citizenship first and foremost by engaging each other as a public. The most fundamental form of practicing citizenship is precisely to participate in the formation of publics. Now, I want to go along with Tully and say that we become citizens, not by passively submitting to an extant script, but by forming publics. I would claim that we become citizens by forming publics, publics that may begin locally and with what at first sound like exorbitant and unrealistic claims, but that after long processes of deliberation, and persuasion, become acceptable and even common sense claims. This is how feminism began and transformed not just our conception of what it means to be citizens, but also what kinds of rights and duties needed to be codified in our citizenship rights to embody that new self-understanding. A "public" philosophy, therefore, must attend to the ways in which publics are formed, what kind of material means of possibility enable or disable the formation of such publics, and how it is that a "subaltern" public becomes eventually part of the pedestrian consensus of a civic public.

The ivory tower, birth of a post-philosophical culture, undisciplining political philosophy

Chapter four of volume one of *PPNK*, one of my favorite chapters, makes use of Rorty, in one of the most hermeneutically generous ways that I have seen Rorty being used. I am not sure whether Rorty ever read this text, but I am sure he would have approved of his work having been read in this vein. I think he may have said, "yes, practice has priority over norms," but he may have also added: "but why do you have to call this project 'public philosophy'?" There is an aspect of Rorty's work that has made him the *enfant terrible* of US philosophy. Rorty was the establishment philosopher that became an anti-establishment anti-philosopher. In fact, Rorty spent the last 20 years of his life trying to free philosophy from its disciplinary chains.[8] If Heidegger railed against Plato's betrayal of the pre-Socratics, Rorty railed against the shackling of philosophy by Kant. He called for the emergence of a post-philosophical culture, one in which our pursuit of ultimate truths would become a private matter, and issues of the common good would be deliberated by citizens without reference to ultimate truths, dispensing with the requirement that we discern an unassailable Archimedean levering pivot. Democracy does not require philosophical justifications, much less foundations. It was in this sense that Rorty read Rawls's project of political liberalism, namely as an attempt to clarify and make explicit the practices of the US polity, and not to derive the justification of those practices from some abstract, rational, universal principles. In the famous essay, "The Priority of Democracy to Philosophy,"[9] Rorty sought to argue that Rawls's political project was post-metaphysical and made do without philosophy. Philosophers are at best useless and at worst an actual obstacle to the practice of citizenship. Philosophers never convince citizens that they ought to respect the rights of excluded minorities. Novelists and artists, prophets, in fact do that better than philosophers. At best, in fact, all that philosophers can do is to serve as "underbrush" removers, clearing the ground for trailblazers. It is up to feminists, civil rights leaders, civic geniuses—to use the expression of William James—to lead, guide, and transform citizens by enlarging their imaginations. We become better citizens by expanding our loyalties, not because we have been persuaded but because our moral imaginations have been moved in the direction of recognizing the suffering of others. Just as Rorty spoke of the priority of democracy over philosophy, it can be said that he argued for the priority of literature over philosophical books. For him, the way to save philosophy was to dissolve it in the public deliberations of citizens. It is for this reason that he called for more political projects and less philosophical principles, more social movements and less philosophical argumentation.

Just as Rorty's work was one of de-institutionalizing philosophy, it was also one of provincializing US philosophy. Philosophy for Rorty, as he never tired of saying by way of quoting Hegel, "is its own time comprehended in thought," by which he meant that philosophy, when it does its best work, is local, national, very historicized, thinking. It was for this reason that he set out to rescue and revive the heroes of US thinking. In his own words, Rorty was a postmodern bourgeois ethnocentrist, by which he meant that he could not but think from the standpoint of the present situation of the US. He could only participate in the dialogue that is Western culture, from a particular locale, and time, in history. In what I take to be one of Rorty's most moving books, *Achieving our Country: Leftist Thought in Twentieth Century America*[10] (1998), Rorty engages in an impassioned critique of what he called the "spectatorial" left. He may as well have written, "the philosophical left." These spectatorial left battles are over department budgets and arcane philosophical debates that have rendered them irrelevant and embarrassing to the larger public. As against this overly philosophical left, Rorty extols the virtues of the socialist, democratic, romantic left of the early part of the twentieth century. This was a left that took seriously the promise of the US, and did not feel shame at being part of the transformation and achievement of that promise. Part of what had gone wrong, according to Rorty, is that the left became academicized. As philosophy became professionalized, the left also became academicized. If there was to be a future for the left, and any role for philosophy in that left, both had to abandon the academy. It is not mere serendipity that Rorty spent the last three decades of his life teaching outside a philosophy department.

I take it that Tully's civic freedom and agonistic citizenship are eloquent articulations of what Rorty meant when he said aphoristically "take care of freedom and truth will take care of itself."[11] What I wonder is whether Rorty would have been as willing to go along with Tully's project of public philosophy. I wonder if Rorty would have had the same reaction that he had to Cornel West's call for prophetic pragmatism, namely to say that prophets are as in need of pragmatism as fish are of bicycles. I underscore Rorty's deep suspicion of institutional, professionalized philosophy not because I want to cast doubts upon Tully's call for a public philosophy, but because I think such a project needs to think through the very complicated history of philosophy, in general, and political philosophy, in particular, over the last 50 years, at the very least. In fact, in the introduction to *PPNK*, as well as in chapter one of volume one, Tully discusses the ways in which political theory has been made foundational, abstract, procedural and thus disembodied, rationalistic, monological, and highly dehistoricized. What Rorty was trying to do for philosophy, by deprofessionalizing it, is what we can take Tully to be doing for political philosophy. Yet, I take it that if that project is to be successful we have to engage in a bit of meta-institutional self-reflection. I think that the call for a public philosophy implies that philosophy has ceased to be public. The call for a political philosophy of civic freedom is to loudly complain that political philosophy has become professionalized, academicized, bureaucratized and scienticized. If we are to make explicit this tacit critique, we must also engage in a bit of genealogical critique of the evolution and transformation of modern political philosophy. By this I mean that we have to unmask the ways in which the rise of European and North American imperialism has been masked and legitimated by the emergence and development of a certain type of political theory that condones and naturalizes the distribution of post-Westphalian state sovereignties—a project in fact that is not at all foreign to Tully, as is amply demonstrated by many of the chapters in volume two of *PPNK*, and *Strange Multiplicity*.[12]

What I mean may be illustrated with reference to the work of Immanuel Wallerstein, more specifically his work with the Gulbenkian Commission, which argues that the way in which we have divided the social sciences (including political science) reflects the fact of European Supremacy.[13] In this way, we produce knowledge that only confirms the ontology of Euro-American hegemony.[14] Thus, a cosmopolitan public philosophy would be one that would attend to the ways in which political philosophy itself bears the marks of an epistemic perspective that privileges the political experience of Euro-America. To become aware of this embedded skewing perspective, while also recognizing that it can't be jumped over as one can't jump over one's shadow, requires at the very least doing a counter-history of the emergence of modern "Euro-American" political philosophy. Here, I can only indicate two authors who have undertaken this type of "decolonizing" of political philosophy. First, there is Charles W. Mills, a Caribbean political philosopher who now teaches in the US, whose *The Racial Contract* (1997) remains one of the most devastating, and persuasive, critiques of the hegemony of "the social contract" in modern political philosophy (from Hobbes to Rawls).[15] Second, there is Enrique Dussel, an Argentinean-Mexican philosopher, who has produced one of the most comprehensive histories of global political philosophy, which demonstrates the ways in which non-European political experience has been appropriated and covered up by the political philosophy of modernity.[16]

I have made use of Rorty to argue a point about Tully's own commitments to the task of emancipating political philosophy from its disciplinary shackles: If there is to be public philosophy, it is a philosophy that is less academic, and thus also less disciplinary, and disciplining. Part of that task of un-disciplining political philosophy would be to walk it through its own history, attending to the matrix of knowledge that naturalizes and ontologizes the structures of Western societies to the detriment of other forms of social formation. I don't think, however, that this process of un-disciplining political philosophy is inimical to what Tully does. In fact, in volume two of *PPNK*, in the chapter on Kant and Europe, there are traces of how we may go about both un-disciplining political philosophy while also provincializing it.

With Foucault against Habermas, with Habermas beyond Foucault: Genealogies and reconstructions

Rorty had three philosophical heroes, who presided over the dining table at his Parthenon of philosophical pioneers: Wittgenstein, Heidegger and Dewey. Tully seems to have three as well: Foucault, Wittgenstein and Habermas. Most of volume one of *PPNK* in fact is built around a confrontation between Foucault and Habermas, one that is refereed by Wittgenstein. Still, volume two of *PPNK* builds creatively and approvingly upon Habermas's project of deliberative democracy and his elaboration of discourse ethics. There is indeed a tension, or let us say, asymmetry between the substantive criticism of Habermas in volume one, and the positive and constructive use Tully makes of his work in volume two. This asymmetry in fact appears as ambivalence. In volume one, the project of civic freedom calls for the construal of freedom as the practice of freedom (see chapter 4). In such a project, as Tully puts it: "… anyone with a general interest in freedom and autonomy will choose Foucault's approach over that of Habermas" (*PPNK* I, 119).

Of course, when Tully makes reference to Foucault's approach, what he makes reference to is Foucault's genealogical approach, and in particular, the use of genealogy in order to diagnose the ontology of our present, as well as the ontology of our ethical selves. One may say, thus, that genealogy is to freedom in Foucault, as critique is to un-circumventable limits in Habermas. The imputation is that if Foucault's method allows us to see how freedom is the practice of freedom, Habermas's prevents us from seeing how it is that freedom is always creative and not merely a process of submission to norms. I think that Tully's ambivalence about Habermas's project and method has to do with what one could call a deficit of the recognition of the agonistic character of freedom in Habermas's political philosophy.

In what follows, I want to argue that the root of Tully's ambivalence about Habermas's work can be productively resolved if we pay attention to two aspects of the latter's work that I think are neglected in Tully's own reconstruction of his work. I will focus on two specific aspects of Habermas's work that are directly relevant. First, I will briefly discuss Habermas's notion of communicative freedom. Second, I will try to show that Foucauldian genealogies are not inimical or orthogonal to Habermasian reconstructions. I would argue that genealogies at the service of critical ontologies of the present are complementary to fallible reconstructions of moral, political and discursive competencies.

It can be shown that Habermas has been developing what he later called "communicative freedom" since 1976, when he wrote his first essay on Hannah Arendt: "Hannah Arendt's Communications Concept of Power." The essay was later edited and included in the expanded edition of his *Philosophical-Political Profiles*.[17] The essays on "Individuation Through Socialization: On George Herbert Mead's Theory of Subjectivity,"[18] as well as his *Between Facts and Norms*,[19] however, go on to develop more explicitly what has been called by Quentin Skinner a "third concept of liberty."[20] This is a freedom that is neither negative nor positive, in Isaiah Berlin's sense.[21] It can also be argued that already in his essay on Hegel's *Jena Philosophy of Mind*, titled "Labor and Interaction," from 1967, Habermas had undertaken a critique of the monological, productivist, objectifying, instrumentalist, goal-oriented model of subjectivity that culminated in Marx's concept of the subject as self-objectifying subjectivity.[22] From his earliest to his most recent work, Habermas's critique of the Cartesian, Kantian, epistemological and productivist subject has been undertaken with a view to elucidate the ways in which freedom is truly recognized not when we see the subject as being liberated from reification and material need, but when we recognize that the subject becomes one only through interaction.[23] As he concludes in his 1967 essay on Hegel's *Jena Philosophy of Mind*: "*Liberation from hunger and misery* does not necessarily converge with *liberation from servitude and degradation*, for there is no automatic developmental relation between labor and interaction."[24] The socially constituted subject is one that becomes itself—it is individuated—only through being socialized. There is no "I" before socialization. By the same token, there is no freedom outside communicative interaction. To put it pithily, if subjectivity is always linguistically constituted and mediated, freedom is only freedom from and through others. There is no freedom that is not communicative freedom, freedom that I am socialized into, through being individuated by socialization in and through a certain culture. Communicative freedom is incomplete freedom; it is freedom always being negotiated. Thus, in as much as agency and subjectivity are always dialogically constituted and mediated, freedom is dialogically constituted and mediated.[25] In fact, Habermas's conception of communicative freedom is in perfect accordance with Tully's definition of what he calls "civic freedom": "Civic freedom is not an opportunity but a manifestation; neither freedom *from* nor freedom *to* (which are often absent or suppressed), but freedom *of* and *in* participation, and *with* fellow citizens" (*PPNK* II, 272).

The agonistic model of freedom that Hannah Arendt championed is preserved in Habermas's model of communicative freedom. It is this freedom that is practiced, enabled, and empowered within the public sphere. Indeed, it is precisely the deliberations of citizens and mutually free subjects that energize what Arendt called the communicative power of interaction, as opposed to the mere "management" of subjects that take each other as objects; not free co-subjects, but entities to be controlled. The public sphere is the proper social space for the practice, enablement and empowerment of communicative freedom. When that freedom is practiced, it generates a power that then gets institutionally cashed out in the legal power of the state. Contrary to the view that could be imputed to Foucault, that Habermas's work projects a utopia of interactions neutralized and denuded of power, Habermas argues for the power of communicatively empowered subjects that becomes authority through juridification. Communicative freedom projects communicative power that is *jurisgenerative*, to use an expression that Benhabib has used recently in the context of her Tanner Lectures.[26] Its efficacy and authority lies precisely in that it allows our collective power to be transformed into administrative power. One may say that freedom is the practice of freedom, indeed, but remains both blind and inefficacious unless it takes the form of institutionalized power. If communicative freedom is empty without civic acknowledgment, civic freedom remains blind without legal institutionalization.

Even if "freedom is the practice of freedom" (*PPNK* I, 136), one can and must still ask, "is the practice of freedom always the same, and is that freedom that is practiced the same freedom always?" Every practice has a history, and part of knowing how to go about, keep going with the practice, as Wittgenstein puts it, is knowing the history of the practice. There is no freedom without the history of freedom—at the very least, knowing that the freedom we can practice is the result of many, many struggles that have refashioned the ways in which we can all practice freedom. Foucault was very explicit in linking his genealogical deconstructions to unleashing the possibilities for new forms of freedom.[27] Tully is right to link Foucault's methodology to the liberation of freedom, to the freeing of freedom. If practices are contingent and not ineluctable, constructed and not necessitated, there is then the possibility that we can do things differently. If freedom is the product of contingent *dispositifs*, we can configure new *dispositifs* of freedom. Of course, as we configure new *dispositifs* of freedom, we also configure new *dispositifs*, or exactly the very same *dispositifs*, that command new regimes of docility and subjectification. In Foucault's genealogical reconstructions, we practice freedom, or rather, we enact freedom by contesting the powers that are transmitted through the *dispositifs* that enable our own modalities of subjectivity. These "apparatuses" of control, of both subjection and subjectification, operate at different levels, in interlocking ways: the prison, the school, the factory, the psychoanalyst's couch, the court's witness stand, the pulpit, and the bathhouse stall. It may be said that in contrast to Habermas, Foucault gives us thicker and more nuanced pictures of the diverse and rich ways in which we generate freedom. But just as Foucault is profligate, Habermas is more disciplined and focused. We get better, if not sexier, pictures of how it is that freedom is generated, and above all, preserved to be passed on to future generations. To the degree that Foucault teaches that freedom is ever new, Habermas teaches us that freedom is also something that we practice in certain ways because of what past generations and societies before us have been able to accomplish. Freedom as a practice is always an accomplished, learned, inherited practice.

It could be argued that over and against Foucault's view of history as the field of contestation in which we have become whom we have become, so that we may become different, Habermas has always thought history from the standpoint of historical materialism. One of Habermas's key texts, albeit little known in the English-speaking world, is his *Zur Rekonstruktion des historischen Materialismus*[28] from 1976. Unfamiliarity with this text hinders one from properly understanding the move that Habermas makes from the project of a philosophical anthropological grounding of knowledge interests towards a reconstruction of normative structures and the bifurcation of society into the systems level and the life-world that culminated in his *The Theory of Communicative Action*.[29] In any event, at the heart of "Towards a Reconstruction of Historical Materialism" (1975) is the idea of social evolution as a societal process of learning, of the acquisition of certain competencies, whether they be moral, political, legal, hermeneutical, and communicative, that are passed on and preserved at two levels: at the level of social systems and at the level of life-world interactions. As against the first generation of the Frankfurt School, with its view of every process of rationalization as a process of reification, *qua* mere alienation and objectification, Habermas argued for a different understanding of rationalization. Rationalization, as the institutionalization of instrumental rationality, may and does lead to alienation and reification. Yet rationalization qua reification is only one aspect of reason. Social progress can be measured in the ways in which we have succeeded in controlling and exploiting nature, both external and internal. But social progress is better measured in terms of the rationalization of communicative interactions. Just as important as how we control nature is how we have rationalized human interactions. This is not the place to map the ways in which Habermas's three knowledge interests from his *Knowledge and Human Interests*[30] book have turned into the three different competencies and corresponding validity claims of *The Theory of Communicative*

Action; but, suffice it to note that if knowledge is about coping with objective nature, cognitive, moral and expressive competencies are about coping with the complex disenchanted natural and social worlds. What Habermas called in the mid-1960s "the emancipatory knowledge interest" became the competency for mutual understanding through communicative freedom. The important shift, however, is from structures of knowledge, what he called knowledge interests, to contingently achieved competencies that are preserved in social systems. If there is progress, it is social progress, that is to say, in the ways in which ways of producing knowledge have been institutionalized and passed on as learnable competencies. If there is progress in knowledge, it is because we as a society have learned how to produce better systems of knowledge.

As against Hegel, and even his teachers, Habermas argued that we can grasp reason as the process of the rationalization of the life-world and the social system in terms of processes of rationalization that have to be reconstructed by the social sciences. Philosophy must paint its grey in grey precisely because it must rely on the hypothesis building, testing and disposing of the reconstructive social sciences that aim to trace the ways in which we evolve social, personality and psychic structures that both embody and pass on certain competencies. History is the field of contingent processes of learning—things could have been different, but we cannot think differently than we presently can precisely because of the competencies we have acquired.

If Foucault's genealogical deconstructions are linked to his views of productive freedom, Habermas's reconstructive genealogies are linked to his communicative freedom. Both highlight their contingency, their constructedness, their laborious production, their fragility, and their need to be protected and preserved. Against the plausible imputation that Habermas's project is utopian, I would claim that it is Foucault who is utopian when he argues for a freedom that does not translate into some sort of administrative or institutional wherewithal. The freedom of the courageous dissenter and transgressor remain at worst a luxury and at best a tolerant indulgence lest it can take on the form of communicative freedom that translates into legal power. Nonetheless, perhaps Foucault was not that far off when he called Habermas a utopian thinker. Very recently, Habermas has argued on behalf of utopia, a realist utopia. In two recent essays, one on "The Concept of Human Dignity and the Realistic Utopia of Human Rights" (2010),[31] and in a response essay to a collection of essays on his debate with Rawls,[32] Habermas has argued that "human rights" embody a utopia that is not some transcendental and metaphysical dream, but rather the embodiment of dreams and yearning that remained unrealized but that nonetheless have guided the development of the best institutions we have contingently constructed as humans. As he writes at the end of his essay in response to critics on his debate with Rawls:

> Human rights constitute a *realistic* utopia insofar as they no longer paint deceptive images of a social utopia that guarantees collective *happiness*, but anchor the *claim to a just society* in the institutions of constitutional states

themselves.[33] The translation of the first human right into positive law gave rise to a *legal duty* to realise exacting moral requirements that has become engraved into the collective memory of humanity.[34]

Indeed, the practice of freedom has become engraved in the collective memory of humans because our collective struggles have given birth to a civic freedom that has taken shape and flesh in fragile institutions of public deliberation.

Corporeal and subjective injurability and juridification: on the critique of rights

After studying Tully's work, from *Strange Multiplicity*, through *Democracy*, to *PPNK*, one cannot but be left with the very general impression that he is deeply suspicious and critical of any form of legalism, institutionalism, or what one can call in short hand, the rights discourse. This suspiciousness is exacerbated when it is coupled with a critique of Euro-American imperialism. It is a suspicion, furthermore, that is warranted by the long history of the uses of legalism, and rights discourse, to justify and legitimate many and much of the long history of Euro-American colonization and neo-imperialism. One of the virtues of *PPNK*, especially of volume two, is to have shown the extent to which a low-intensity, and ultimately self-eviscerating, democracy and ineffective cosmopolitan citizenship, have been propagated through the channels of international law—with its normative and teleological assumptions. In Tully's critique of the last 500 years of Euro-American imperial colonization, law has played the role of both vehicle and shield for a metaphysically sanctioned theodicy of world history that neutralizes every criticism of its violence and alleged ineluctability. This metaphysically sanctioned theodicy is succinctly embodied in the synecdoche Kant. As Tully writes: "… Kant combined two very powerful imperial stories: a presumptively universal and Eurocentric narrative of historical development or modernization and a presumptively universal and Eurocentric juridical theory of global justice" (*PPNK* I, 148). In Kant's name is congealed a whole tradition that brings into convergence a teleology of history and the supposed normative rationality of law.

This critique of juridification resembles Habermas's pre-*Between Facts and Norms* critique of the colonizing effects of law on the life-world. In fact, one could see Tully's work as championing what we could call a "culturalism" or "anti-institutionalism." Or, perhaps, more accurately, Tully's work champions what he calls "civicism" (*PPNK* I, 271). By "civicism" he means: "the activities and practical *arts* of becoming and being a citizen …" in which being a citizen is not "… seen as being the bearer of civil rights and duties but of the abilities, competences, character and conduct acquired in participation, referred to as 'civic virtues'" (*PPNK* I, 271). I think Tully's deep commitment to "civicism" as a metonym for anti-institutionalism and anti-legalism is summarized in this formulation:

> Civic citizenship does not take a "practice" of civic activity as a *form* of organization within which civic activity takes place, for this would be to treat civic activity as resting on some proto-institutional background (rules, conditions, processes). Rather, civic citizenship consists of *negotiated* practices all the way down. It comprises civic activities and the on-going contestation and negotiation of these practices by the participants and by those subject to and affected by yet excluded from them, and so on in turn. There is never the last voice or word (*PPNK* I, 269–70).

Tully recruits Wittgenstein and Gadamer to develop the argument that in fact there is never a self-implementing and self-evident rule, and thus, there are no norms, laws, or rules that do not require immersing oneself in the thick and thicket of "negotiated practices." If we use the Apelian-Habermasian language of justification (*Begründung*) and application (*Anwendung*), we could say that for Tully there is no justification outside a game of application.[35] Or to put it in the discourse of law: there is no legal norm that is univocally and unambiguously self-applying, i.e. every legal norm entails a juridical interpretation, but interpretation is a hermeneutically embedded practice that entails a life-world suffused by "strange multiplicity." Still, I would like to ask: "can one play a game without rules? Is not the definition of a game that there are rules, even very provisionary and arbitrary ones? Even if all rules are negotiated, isn't it the point that we do begin by negotiating some rules?" In other words: does not civic citizenship presuppose at least a bare minimum of some basic institutions of citizenship, such as: a bill of rights, laws and rules about participating in a civic community, laws and rules by which conflicts among citizens can be arbitrated, and rules and laws by means of which delegated members of the citizenry can relate to those they represent and rule for a time or turn? Tully may be right that all we have are "negotiated" practices all the way, but this does not mean that we don't have a set of institutions that frame and enable our practices. The rights and duties that constitute modern citizenship indeed have not come about because of some ineluctable unfolding of some *logos*. The rights of citizens were not discovered. They were invented. They were made. Citizenship is the built dwelling of the political animal that we are. I would go a bit further: the contemporary human rights discourse may be the stage for the rituals of geopolitics and the theology of a certain idolatry, but it is also the stage on which a global legal matrix for the protection of the most vulnerable is being slowly built. Universal human rights take the built dimension of citizen rights to a global level. What both citizen and human rights show is that all law is always produced, made, invented, and not discovered. But, all law is contingently made and negotiated against the background of extant law. Tully is right. All law is always a product of a hermeneutically embedded practice, but those practices let it be buried in the sands of forgetfulness, and leave always a trace. The recent work of scholars such as Micheline R. Ishay,[36] Lynn Hunt,[37] and Samuel Moyn[38] can be said to have established that human rights have been an accomplishment that came about because of political struggles that have followed changes in the moral imagination of citizens across the world. Their work can also be said to show that human rights, and the web of international law that supports them, have been accomplished partly in struggle with Euro-American legal hegemony. Their contructedness makes them no less monumental, no less worthy of both celebration and respect.

When we begin to recognize that citizenship is a legal canopy built over centuries of struggles, we also begin to recognize that the juxtaposition between civil and civic conceptions of citizenship, where civil stands for institutions and laws and civic stands for practices and interpretations, may be a misleading opposition. If we adopt Wittgenstein's terminology about language being a form of life, we could say that citizenship, civicness, belongs to forms of life. There is no citizenship without the ceaseless renovation and revitalization of the culture of citizenry that is maintained by engaged citizens. But that engagement always takes form against, through and beyond an extant institution of citizenship. I cannot engage in either the pedestrian use or poetic innovation of language without a background set of rules, norms, and accepted practices. I can break a grammar rule, but only if the rule is there. There can't be civic innovation without the edifice of civil rules and norms.

I will close with a brief, though risky, exegesis. There is an aphorism, attributed to Heraclitus of Ephesus, fragment 44 to be precise, which I think can be used to illustrate my point about the relationship between laws and the civic practices of citizens that enable political innovation. The fragment reads: "The people should fight for the Law (*Nomos*) as if for their city-wall."[39] One way in which we could read Heraclitus's aphorism is that the *nomoi* of a polis are as important as the protective city-walls of the polis. When the laws of a polis are not heeded, when they are eviscerated by either their abuse or non-compliance, it is as if a citizenry had been rendered defenseless, and the city-walls had been breached. Conversely, the laws of a polis, the laws of a nation, are as monumental and worthy of admiration as are that polis's or nation's defenses. In our time, a constitution is the embodiment of a people's achievement. A constitution is the temple of a people's civic genius.[40] At the same time, a constitution that remains both sacred, but revisable, is even more of a magnificent monument to a people's civic genius; for as both commanding though revisable, it reflects the maturity of a people who recognize that constitutions are human inventions, but for that reason no less worthy of respect and admiration. Tully's work, I argue, is not diminished, but on the contrary, amplified, when it is read as precisely the elaboration of the civic genius of nations, of citizens within nations, whose great works of art are constitutions with their Bill of Rights, and all the laws that are by them demanded, enabled and implied.

Notes

1 James Tully, *Public Philosophy in a New Key: Volume I, Democracy and Civic Freedom* and *Public Philosophy in a New Key: Volume II, Imperialism and Civic Freedom*, Cambridge: Cambridge University Press, 2008, hereafter referred to as *PPNK*.

2 Jürgen Habermas, *The Structural Transformation of the Public Sphere: An Inquiry into a Category of Bourgeois Society*, trans. Thomas Burger with the assistance of Frederick Lawrence, Cambridge, MA: The MIT Press, 1989.
3 Nancy Fraser, *Unruly Practices: Power, Discourse and Gender in Contemporary Social Theory*, Minneapolis: University of Minnesota Press, 1989.
4 Oskar Negt and Alexander Kluge, *Public Sphere and Experience: Toward an Analysis of the Bourgeois and Proletarian Public Sphere*, trans. Peter Labanyi, Jamie Owen Daniel, and Assenka Oksiloff, Minneapolis: University of Minnesota Press, 1993.
5 Michael Warner, *Publics and Counterpublics*, New York: Zone Books, 2005.
6 For Habermas's response to some early criticisms, see his "Further Reflections on the Public Sphere," in *Habermas and the Public Sphere*, ed., Craig Calhoun, Cambridge, MA: The MIT Press, 1992.
7 Lutz Wingert and Klaus Günther, eds, *Die Öffenlichkeit der Vernunft und die Vernunft der Öffenlichkeit*, Frankfurt am Main: Suhrkamp Verlag, 2001.
8 See in particular the last volume of his *Philosophical Papers*, Richard Rorty, *Philosophy as Cultural Politics, Philosophical Papers*, Vol. 4, Cambridge: Cambridge University Press, 2007.
9 See Richard Rorty, *Objectivity, Relativism, and Truth: Philosophical Papers, Vol. 1*, Cambridge: Cambridge University Press, 1991, pp. 175–96.
10 Richard Rorty, *Achieving our Country: Leftist Thought in the Twentieth Century*, Cambridge, MA: Harvard University Press, 1998.
11 See Richard Rorty, *Take Care of Freedom and Truth Will Take Care of Itself: Interview with Richard Rorty*, edited and introduced by Eduardo Mendieta, Stanford, CA: Stanford University Press, 2006.
12 James Tully, *Strange Multiplicity: Constitutionalism in an Age of Diversity*, Cambridge: Cambridge University Press, 1995.
13 Immanuel Maurice Wallerstein, *Open the Social Sciences: Report of the Gulbenkian Commission on the Restructuring of the Social Sciences*, Stanford: Stanford University Press, 1996.
14 See also Immanuel Maurice Wallerstein, *The End of the World as we Know it: Social Science for the Twenty-First Century*, Minneapolis: University of Minnesota Press, 2001.
15 Charles W. Mills, *The Racial Contract*, Ithaca, NY: Cornell University Press, 1997.
16 See Enrique Dussel, *Politics of Liberation: A Critical World History*, London: SCM Press, 2011, as well as *Ética de la liberación en la edad de la globalización y la exclusión*, Madrid: Editorial Trotta, 1998. See my discussion of Dussel in my *Global Fragments: Latinamericanisms, Globalizations, and Critical Theory*, Albany, NY: SUNY Press, 2007, chapters 6 and 7; see also my foreword to Dussel's *Twenty Theses on Politics*, Durham, NC: Duke University Press, 2008, pp. vii–xiii.
17 Jürgen Habermas, *Philosophical–Political Profiles*, trans. Frederick G. Lawrence, Cambridge, MA: The MIT Press, 1983, pp. 171–87. In this edition, the essay appeared under the title of "Hannah Arendt: On the Concept of Power" (1976).
18 Now in Jürgen Habermas, *Postmetaphysical Thinking: Philosophical Essays*, trans. William Mark Hohengarten, Cambridge, MA: The MIT Press, 1992, pp. 149–204.
19 Jürgen Habermas, *Between Facts and Norms: Contributions to a Discourse Theory of Law and Democracy*, trans. William Rehg, Cambridge, MA: The MIT Press, 1996.
20 Q. Skinner, "A Third Concept of Liberty," *London Review of Books* 24(7), 2002, pp. 16–18.
21 See also Albrecht Wellmer, *Endgames: The Irreconciliable Nature of Modernity: Essays and Lectures*, trans. David Midgley, Cambridge, MA: The MIT Press, 1998, especially the first part on Negative and Communicative Freedom.
22 In Jürgen Habermas, *Theory and Practice*, trans. John Viertel, Boston: Beacon Press, 1973, pp. 142–69.

23 The most succinct articulation of a communicative, dialogic, post-Cartesian conception of the subject is to be found in Jürgen Habermas, *The Philosophical Discourse of Modernity: Twelve Lectures*, trans. Frederick Lawrence, Cambridge, MA: The MIT Press, 1987, chapter XI: "An Alternative Way out of the Philosophy of the Subject: Communicative versus Subject-Centered Reason," pp. 294–326.
24 Ibid., p. 169, italics in original.
25 See my essay, "Communicative Freedom, Citizenship and Political Justice in the Age of Globalization. On Seyla Benhabib's *The Claims of Culture: Equality and Diversity in the Global Era*," *Philosophy and Social Criticism* 31(7), 2005, pp. 739–52.
26 Seyla Benhabib, *Another Cosmopolitanism, with Commentaries by Jeremy Waldron, Bonnie Honig, Will Kymlicka*, New York: Oxford University Press, 2006.
27 I have argued in "The Practice of Freedom" in *Michel Foucault: Key Concepts*, ed., Dianna Taylor, Durham: Acumen, 2011, pp. 111–24, that we should read Foucault's work from the mid-1970s until the end of his life as an attempt to offer a political philosophy as a genealogy of practices of the self that enable modalities of freedom.
28 Frankfurt am Main: Suhrkamp, 1976. Part of this volume was translated by Thomas McCarthy as *Communication and the Evolution of Society*, Boston: Beacon Press, 1979.
29 *The Theory of Communicative Action*, 2 Volumes, trans. Thomas McCarthy, Boston: Beacon Press, 1984–87.
30 Jürgen Habermas, *Knowledge and Human Interests*, trans. Jeremy J. Shapiro, Boston: Beacon Press, 1971.
31 Jürgen Habermas, "The Concept of Human Dignity and the Realistic Utopia of Human Rights," *Metaphilosophy* 41(4), 2010, pp. 464–80.
32 James Gordon Finlayson and Fabian Freyenhagen, eds, *Habermas and Rawls: Disputing the Political*, NY: Routledge, 2011.
33 Ernst Bloch, *Natural Law and Human Dignity*, trans. Dennis J. Schmidt, Cambridge, MA: MIT Press, 1987.
34 Jürgen Habermas, "Reply to my Critics," in Finlayson and Freyenhagen, eds., *Habermas and Rawls: Disputing the Political*, pp. 283–304, at 304.
35 See Klaus Günther, *The Sense of Appropriateness: Application Discourses in Morality and Law*, trans. John Farrell, Albany, NY: SUNY Press, 1993.
36 Micheline R. Ishay, *The History of Human Rights: From Ancient Times to the Globalization Era*, Berkeley, CA: University of California Press, 2004.
37 Lynn Hunt, *Inventing Human Rights: A History*, New York: W.W. Norton & Co, 2008.
38 Samuel Moyn, *The Last Utopia: Human Rights in History*, Cambridge, MA: Belknap Press of Harvard University Press, 2010.
39 In Kathleen Freeman, *Ancilla to the Pre-Socratic Philosophers: A Complete Translation of the Fragments of Diels*, Fragmente der Vorsokratiker, Cambridge, MA: Harvard University Press, 1983 [1943], p. 27.
40 See my "The Unfinished Constitution: The Education of the Supreme Court," *Newsletter on Hispanic/Latino issues in Philosophy* 9(1), 2009, pp. 2–4 for further elaboration of this argument, as well as my "The City to Come: Critical Urban Theory as Utopian Mapping," in *City* 14(4), 2010, pp. 442–7.

Chapter 4

At the Edges of Civic Freedom: Violence, Power, Enmity

Antonio Y. Vázquez-Arroyo

> To sleep: perchance to dream: ay, there's the rub:
> For in that sleep of death what dreams may come
> When we have shuffled off this mortal coil,
> Must give us pause. There's the respect
> That makes calamity of so long life;
> For who would bear the whips and scorns of time ...
>
> <div align="right">Shakespeare, <i>Hamlet</i>, III.1</div>

I.

The onset of a new world order ushered in new themes and significantly reset the terms of the discussion in North Atlantic political theory, thus unbinding the concepts of the overstated liberal–communitarian stalemate within the liberal family. Retrospectively, it could be argued that the emergence of a vibrant discussion of the politics of recognition in the context of North American multiculturalism represented a transition to a new set of questions—identity, difference, group rights, secularism—which were already embedded in theoretical terms that reached beyond the liberal–communitarian divide. In the 1990s questions of justice became increasingly conceptualized in cultural terms and "difference" and "identity" emerged as important markers of the age. The transformation of emphases in the two commanding formulations of John Rawls's liberal theory is revealing of this trend: however tamed, the predominance accorded to redistribution in the initial formulations of "justice as fairness," and the salience of civil disobedience in *A Theory of Justice* (1971), conceived within the context of the Great Society, yielded to the different tribulations of US *Kulturkampf* in *Political Liberalism* (1993). The latter text stages the encounter of a liberal culture with religion and other sources of diversity.[1] Meanwhile, Charles Taylor, another central figure associated with this debate, took an analogous path: drawing from a richer Canadian multicultural tradition, largely anchored in anti-Quebecois nationalism, not only inaugurated a new set of discussions on the question of recognition, but as the first decade of the twenty-first century unfolded, he produced *A Secular Age* (2007), a commanding if de-historicized theory of secularism and modernity. Ethics and a hyper-moral view of power and political life—surely a subterranean current already running through the humanities in the late-1970s and 1980s that was still mostly *terra incognita* for political theory—also developed into important themes that eventually displaced the thematic of justice during this decade. Equally important in this context was the status of rights, now cast in an international dimension as human rights at once victorious and complacent about its ethical valences, and in terms of cultural rights for historically marginalized minorities. Humanitarianism and human rights became the valences of the former, usually anchored in an "international individualism," to borrow Étienne Balibar's apt phrase.[2]

Unsurprisingly, the most distinguished work on multiculturalism came from thinkers reflecting on the Canadian experience. Indigenous groups and secessionist nationalism (Québec) provided the immediate occasions for not just Taylor, but also Will Kymlicka, Joseph Carens, and James Tully, among others. In the last two decades, culture and ethics, multiculturalism, recognition, and politicized (and anti-political) identity, humanitarian and human rights—as well as their corollary virtues: tolerance, cosmopolitanism, responsibility to the other—became preeminent themes in the world of North Atlantic political theory.

This is the relevant context to situate James Tully's original account of civic freedom. In *Public Philosophy in a New Key*, his impressive *summa*, Tully has productively worked through, sublated as it were, the different turns in contemporary political theory and the humanities—culture, ethics, postcolonial theory—and framed these in a coherent theorization of public freedom with a strong democratic, anti-imperial edge.[3] In doing so, he has impressively drawn from the strengths found in different theoretical and scholarly traditions, while avoiding the commonplaces and pitfalls usually associated with them, especially their indifference to history. Indeed, Tully has reflected on all of this with an acute sense of history, a sharp and non-pious assessment of contemporary empires, and a stout commitment to a form of public freedom as a *sine-qua-non* of democratic practice. He has thus coupled democracy and freedom in ways that go beyond not only the old liberal–communitarian stalemate, but he also cuts significantly deeper than the liberal–republican divide that quickly replaced it, and his recasting of freedom entails a strong sense of shared ruling that goes beyond the terms recently theorized by Philip Pettit and Quentin Skinner. *PPNK* also compellingly recasts the relationship between democracy and the rule of law without reverting to the apodictic conceits found in Jürgen Habermas's influential mythology of their co-originality. Equally decisive and insightful is the way in which these volumes offer the best account of Kant and imperialism to date, along with a powerful critique of neo-Kantian justifications of US imperial might (*PPNK* II, 15–42, 142–3).[4]

A thorough recasting of freedom, trenchant critiques of contemporary empires and their pieties, democratic constitutionalism, and civic citizenship: these are some of the most important concepts that accompany Tully's formidable theorization of an anti-imperial ethos of citizenship. And if these achievements were not enough, *PPNK* is written with clarity, political trenchancy and verve. This is a well-conceived project, a bravura performance, in which an astonishing historical erudition is matched by an original mind that also happens to be one of the most rigorous yet generous scholars of political thought writing today.

Understood on its own terms, there is very little to object to in Tully's formidable theoretical edifice and any critique of it runs the risk of either nit-picking, or self-referential narcissism. Even so, precisely because Tully's public philosophy deals with questions of crucial importance today, it is worth it to raise some critical inquiries and, at least, sketch out an interpretation that maps the edges of Tully's project and thus interrogates some of the tensions and silences that can be sporadically glimpsed in the otherwise chiseled architecture of his theory. How, and to what extent, Tully's new public philosophy effectively conceptualizes contemporary predicaments of power and the forms of structural violence that permeate and constitute these political spaces? Can Tully's civic freedom, however attractive its democratic and critical import is, dispense with a sustained analysis of capitalism, the forms of state and market power and their respective "cagings" of political life in the present, as well as the ineluctability of enmity lines?[5] Does a principled commitment to non-violence fully capture these complexities?

2.

One of the most remarkable features of Tully's public philosophy is the historical sense found galore in his reflections. In his hands, political philosophy does not take the ethereal character often associated with many of its most prominent North Atlantic practitioners, where political philosophy only meets history, if at all, as an afterthought, or as an extremely selective add-on, and it is treated as amorphous fodder for a preconceived scheme that is ultimately independent of it. Not so in Tully's account. For not only the political, social and cultural histories of planetary scope have nourished his reflections, but his accounts of imperialism, past and present, convey a degree of historical sense and detail that has no counterpart in the current scholarship on empire within North Atlantic political theory.[6] Moreover, in Tully's work historical sense is matched with conceptual rigor and precision. Indeed, no other contemporary political theorist in the world of North American political thought works as industriously and scrupulously with such a vast array of sources—historical, textual, political commentary—as Tully, which is one of the attributes that set his enterprise apart.

How does this vast reservoir of sources conform Tully's public philosophy? Broadly speaking, Tully characterizes political philosophy as an endless dialogue among practitioners across space and time: "Dialogue partners gain insight into what ruling, being ruled and contesting rule through the exchange of questions and answers over different ways of studying politics and over different criteria for their assessment relative to how they illuminate different aspects of the complex worlds of politics" (*PPNK* I, 16). In the version that Tully makes his own, political philosophy is a public philosophy—"a species of 'practical philosophy' (politics and ethics)" that is defined by three main attributes: it is practical, critical, and historical (*PPNK* I, 16). It is a philosophical ethos, a critical activity that initially consists of "questioning whether the inherited languages of description and reflections are adequate to the task" of critically and historically apprehending the practices of freedom necessary for the sustenance of democratic life (*PPNK* I, 19). Accordingly, in *PPNK* contemporary predicaments of power are historicized. In it, Tully offers an invitation for the reader and the citizen to conceptualize and reconfigure the meaning of practices of freedom and governance in the present.

Yet there is a slight structural inconsistency in the architecture of this public philosophy between Tully's political commitments and the main conceptual and historical signposts that guide his inquiry. Tully has brigaded a series of thinkers—Arendt, Foucault, Skinner, Wittgenstein—to forge an agonistic concept of freedom, which is the pivot for the critical ethos that is the signature of his public philosophy. But to formulate a thoroughly historical and materialist account of the forms of power, including the new imperial forms that constitute the present—as Tully does—one could not think of less congenial company than the historically and socially disembodied accounts of Wittgenstein, the proto-oracular de-historicized history of Arendt and Foucault, let alone Skinner's asocial intellectual history.[7] This is not to say that Tully simply bundles these thinkers together—there is certainly no room for eclecticism on the cheap in *PPNK*. Tully rather scrupulously works his way through his sources and mines them to good effect in order to buttress and formulate his own conception of civic freedom. Likewise, he effectively curbs some of the temptations that Wittgenstein's language of "family resemblances" notoriously invites. Even so, some traces of their original locus remain in Tully's theorizations. Blind spots, so to speak, that he inherits from these thinkers. These are, first and foremost, the question of power and determinations—conceptual, historical and institutional.

The question of historical determinations is best considered by exploring the understanding of the history of political thought that informs Tully's enterprise. Even if Skinner is a valuable point of departure, the forms of history that Tully avows are not always in sync with the usual protocols of the Cambridge School: his are culturally and socially thick in ways that the commanding historical narratives of, say, Dunn, Pocock, and Skinner, are not. Still, Tully sometimes seems to be overawed by Skinner's achievement—he credits Skinner with "a revolution in the history of political thought"—even if he is a more substantial and politically minded thinker than the Cambridge doyen (*PPNK* I, 141). Better still, the important and highly influential innovations associated with the Cambridge School are everything but revolutionary. If emphasizing the importance of historical context is the signature of this school's achievement, there is a downside in the ways in which "context" is conceived. Namely, "context" has been overwhelmingly thematized in terms of languages, words, and utterances. Influenced by Wittgenstein, Skinner casts the interventions of past political theorists in the context of their times primarily in linguistic and rhetorical terms that are conceptually indeterminate —not the meaning of words but "the different ways they are put to use" is what matters—and following J.L. Austin, words are understood as deeds, as "forms of social action."[8]

Yet the material and social context in which these words are signified and transmogrified is bracketed out and thus emptied of meaning. Not only that, but some words are debarred in the contexts that Skinner construes, say, those of the Levellers during the English Civil War.[9] Similarly, there is next to nothing about the socio-economic underpinnings of the transformations Skinner maps out in his formidable *Foundations of Modern Political Thought* (1978), his attempt at putting his "philosophical position" to work.[10] This is not to say that Skinner's body of work is entirely indifferent to these other historical contexts. *Foundations* is a formidable, erudite work in which the flight from the social—which is, at any rate, more prominent in Pocock's writings—is occasionally curbed by attention to political upheavals and institutional struggles. Still, the balance is considerably tilted in favor of considering the connections between utterances rather than the external conditions for their political valences.[11] The latter context, however, would force into historical narratives a sense of continuity and historical sedimentation, as well as an account of the binding economic and political continuities and discontinuities shaping the evolution of European political thought, that the self-enclosed analysis of words as deeds conceals.

Now, not only *PPNK* stakes out a concept of civic freedom that cuts much deeper than Skinner's rather labile third concept of freedom, but Tully's historical accounts also go beyond Skinner's in his attention to social and cultural history and the ways in which he avows the existence of structures, even if he significantly downplays their obduracy (*PPNK* II, 265–6, 296ff). Like Skinner's, though, Tully's excavations of the past not only serve an academic vocation, but have a civic one: to expand the horizons of citizens by providing accounts of "the background conventions of the contemporary problematisation and practices" (*PPNK* I, 16).[12] A laudable civic role is thus accorded to the study of the history of political thought, but one that is somewhat compromised by Skinner's narrow contextualism. Herein lays a conceit that Tully has unwittingly inherited from Skinner's so-called revolution: as will become clearer below, Tully ultimately misrecognizes the history and structures of contemporary forms of power and ends up reverting to a quest for silver linings in the present and an antinomian anti-politics of non-violence. Similarly, in addition to conceptualizing the practical, material and social conditions for the exercise of civic freedom—which throughout *PPNK* Tully acknowledges, even if these are never accorded the role they deserve to have in his public philosophy—it is necessary to critically apprehend the ways in which contemporary forms of power exceed the political mechanisms and constitutions that historically have been devised to tame them, or at least to hold these accountable. To accomplish these critical tasks, a more robust social (and political) sense of material history than the one avowed in these pages is paramount.[13]

3.

These tensions and limitations, however, are not the exclusive upshot of the playfulness that Tully ascribes to Skinner's excavations of the past and the sense of possibility that these certainly conjure, especially in Skinner's elegant *Liberty Before Liberalism* (1998) (*PPNK* I, 141). The lack of social and economic determinations that is appended to this view of civic freedom also stems from Arendt, Foucault and Wittgenstein, all of which Tully casts as complementary for an agonistic ethos of freedom. In *PPNK*, Wittgenstein offers an anchorage for a non-foundational concept of freedom that is grounded in practices and games situated in our everyday life interactions. These are central in Tully's account of civic freedom and the different ways in which what he calls "proto-civic" practices undergo processes of "citizenisation" and "civicisation" (*PPNK* I, 211–12, 311–13; *PPNK* II, 99–100, 119, 279–83). The appeal of Wittgenstein for this project is thus not hard to fathom: he understood language as an indefinite, undetermined multiplicity of incommensurable language games, a (non)-foundational account that sets the stage for a conception of meaning and signification whose basis resides in heterogeneous practices of linguistic usage, as part of language games that are governed by discrete rules. There is no meta-game to encompass all of the games, a tenet that disallows any idea of totality, or comprehensiveness. It is little wonder that such tacit avowal of common sense became so predominant in Oxford, where Englishry provided a fertile ground for it to harvest: a conception of philosophy and language whose radical openness to multiplicity of practices and rules nonetheless acquiesce to the *status quo* by disavowing any comprehensive account of it. For all its playful openness, which opens the door to endless associations, philosophy hardly interferes with the use of language. It could only describe it. It "leaves everything as it is."[14]

This philosophy of "language games" and "intermediate links,"—reproducible almost *ad infinitum*—at once conceptually and historically indeterminate in which the mastering of techniques for obeying rules is paramount, underpins Tully's idea of an apprenticeship in civic freedom. But language games and their links, in and of themselves, do not carry any critical or democratic import. Indeed, in Wittgenstein's own philosophy these are everything but, as well as socially adrift. But it is precisely these less appealing attributes that Tully's work has sought to reverse, albeit he is not always able to do so. On this notion of language and practice, he pivots a conception of variability with no fixed demarcations that he recasts as central to the democratic edge of his public philosophy. Analogously, Tully has revamped Wittgenstein's disavowal of any meta-context, or foundational principle, politically. "When we look at the uses of a general term," Tully writes, "what we see is not a determinate set of essential features that could be abstracted from practice and set out in theory along with rules for their application." He then goes on to approvingly cite Wittgenstein's anti-philosophy of language games: "We 'see complicated networks of similarities overlapping and criss-crossing: sometimes overall similarities, sometimes similarities of detail' and these 'family resemblances' among uses of a concept change over time in the course of human conversation" (*PPNK* I, 27). Tully rereads Wittgenstein as precisely offering a conception of practices *situated* in social life, language games of "critical reflection": "The contemporary *and* historical study of these practices of critical reflection in Western and non-Western societies might be called 'a genealogy of the critical attitude'" (*PPNK* I, 69).

In the last formulation the centrality of Foucault is already adduced. What Foucault offers is a coruscating account of what a philosophical ethos of critique entails, which Tully, following David Owen, identifies with a sort of prolegomenon to the practice of freedom, the agonistic ethos of Enlightenment that Foucault's oracular essay, "What is Enlightenment," conjures up (*PPNK* I, 19, 127–8). It is this understanding of freedom as a practice, with its ontological connotations, that allows Tully to productively juxtapose it to Arendt's reflections under the sign of an agonistic conception of freedom. Arendt famously theorized freedom in stark opposition to what she saw as the conceit of sovereignty and proceeded to conceive of it in relation to political activity and her miraculous conception of boundless action. Tully goes on to draw the importance of activity in Arendt's theory of freedom and agency and relates it to Wittgenstein—with whom she shares "an orientation to activity"—and then to Johan Huizinga's discussion of *Homo Ludens*, where emphasis is placed on "game playing" as constitutive of agonistic freedom (*PPNK* I, 137, 139).[15] Here, however, Tully seems to uncharacteristically yield to the looseness of family resemblances—Arendt, Foucault, Huizinga, Skinner, and Wittgenstein (and *Public Enemy*) all speak about games and practices, but overwhelming attention to the family resemblances between them could obfuscate more than enlighten. And yet they share something that has had an imprint in *PPNK*: Arendt, Foucault, Skinner, and Wittgenstein shared a disavowal of conceptual determinations, comprehensive knowledge, and the pervasiveness of binding historical continuities; and all of them had in common an indifference to capitalism as a political–theoretical problem and historical process (*PPNK* I, 142–3).

Yet what is even more vexatious in Tully's formulation of agonistic freedom is the way in which the "agonal" element of political life is completely sanitized from the violence that has historically been part and parcel of this form of contestation, as well as the exaggerated political import granted to it. Tully's theorization, to be sure, is not as prophylactic and self-satisfied as William E. Connolly's agonized liberalism.[16] Yet the idea of political agonism involving *fun* is tendentious. A careful look at the Greek understanding of this notion shows that agonism is awash with violence and agonistic contestation is often far from playful. Tully, however, cannot be accused of frivolity here—for very few thinkers have displayed the ethical and political sympathy to the plight of the have nots, the dispossessed, than Tully. How, then, could the centrality accorded to this rather aseptic conception of agonistic freedom be explained?

4.

Lineages for an answer can be found in the ways in which the theoretical underpinnings of Tully's project betray a lack of conceptual determinations—indeed, indeterminacy is sometimes elevated to a virtue—that equally dispenses with any dialectic of the universal and the particular, or of collective identity and its political forms, which parallels the difficulty in accounting for the historical and structural determinations of the political field.[17] Tully shows awareness of them, but the theoretical armature that he has forged is ill-equipped to conceptualize these determinations. For instance, he mentions the extent to which "scientism, administration, routine, mass warfare, and the professionalization of sports and politics" afflict and compromise "the play element in Western culture," and yet these are brushed off as upshots of cultural pessimism (*PPNK* I, 137–8). To get around the obduracy of these insights, which however compromised by some of their sources (Wittgenstein was notoriously spellbound by Spengler) present the argument of *PPNK* with important questions, he brigades Richard Rorty. And drawing from Rorty, Tully then suggests that the crucial activity is to focus the beam on "the language game as the primary thing" (*PPNK* I, 138). Unfortunately, the unintended effect of this nod to Rorty is to sidestep the question without actually addressing it.

The displacements of these formulations are clear enough. Its sources: the uncritical celebration of indeterminate fluidity that anchors this idea of civic freedom. It is at once attractive and problematic. Attractive insofar as it promises diversity, pluralism, and multiplicity, notions with an intuitive appeal that is hardly negligible; problematic in the ways in which these politically and ethically indifferent tropes—empty signifiers, if there ever were any—are marshaled as self-evident normative ideals. All of which brush aside the ways in which, say, boundaries and determinations at once constrain and enable—as G.W.F. Hegel long ago expounded and many a historian and anthropologist have since confirmed—depending on the particular historical moments—economic, cultural, political—in which this dialectic concretely plays out. Without critical attention to their conceptual and historical determinations, multiplicity and diversity can be indifferently extended to no end across the political spectrum. What is different, in and of itself, is not better or worse. Revealingly, at the outset of *PPNK* Tully invokes nature to anchor this commitment when he conjures the astonishing forests of the Pacific Northwest and their unity in diversity (*PPNK* I, xiii).[18] Nature, however, is notoriously morally and politically indifferent. One need not be Nietzsche or Lars Von Trier to realize that within its diversity there is also predatory behavior and violence, which is precisely what the beautiful landscape from afar conceals, something that any extended (and truly situated) sojourn within its realms quickly reveals.[19] And while diversity and unity coexist, it is not entirely clear that nature supports one pair of the dichotomy over the other: Tully writes of unity in diversity, but one can equally speak of diversity in unity. Nature's diversity embodies a dialectic of destruction and creation in which both dynamics are deeply intertwined.[20]

Actually, to think of this opposition politically entails recognizing that diversity in unity is precisely what democracy has historically stood for and why it has always entailed a perilous and tragic economy of violence in dealing with the ineluctable imperative to draw enmity lines. Effectively theorizing these aspects of democracy, however, demands a theorization of civic freedom that avows the multiple mediations of bindingness and openness; unity and variegation; identity and difference. Accounting for these pairs equally requires a spatially and temporally differentiated mapping of their concrete historical instantiations. Tully, along with his major interlocutors, however, privileges one pole and disavows the other, thus tilting the architecture of the theory in ways that would become even more important in relation to the relationship between civic freedom, civility, and the dialectic of violence and non-violence (*PPNK* II, 299, 308).

5.

Yet a thinker as erudite and historically minded as Tully surely knows all this. So the question is why he still uncritically idealizes these notions—looseness, fluidity, diversity, and agonism—and bestows upon them an aura of uncontested normativity? One overriding reason already adduced is his choice of theoretical signposts. But that displaces the question to another one—why these theoretical positions are so appealing to Tully the theorist, even if Tully shows that at some level he knows better? Here the Canadian context is crucial to understand this feature of Tully's public philosophy. Similar to the US in its Anglo-American colonialism and the ensuing displacement of indigenous inhabitants, there are, nonetheless, two central points of contrast that are important: on the one hand, extermination was far less thorough than in the US, hence the large presence of indigenous groups, and the obdurate presence of Québec—a large linguistic and cultural community with territorial contiguity and a legitimate sense of proto-national identity within Canada's boundaries; on the other hand, unlike the US, where the founding of the republic and its binding political principles is central to its collective identity and civil religion—as is the Civil War and the amendments to the constitutional settlement of 1787—Canada's historical sense of collective identity has been less confident, lacking a strong political basis. Historically, what defined it politically was negative enough: its refusal of the US's revolutionary war in 1776. Certainly, it is a truism to suggest the lack of any positive political sense of identity for Canada. What is less noticed, however, is the reversal of fortunes that took place in the second half of the twentieth century, when Canada witnessed the emergence of multiculturalism as the predominant marker of its identity. It crystallized under the liberal regime of Pierre Trudeau, and has since become a veritable Canadian achievement and signature of its collective identity.

Echoes of Canadian history resonate in Tully's construction. In a way, his public philosophy can be read as giving a strong political valence to the multicultural experience that defines Canadian identity. Needless to say, the point is not to demote *PPNK* as little but a symptom of Canadian history—since any universal always has a particular point of departure from which it is launched and that it exceeds, even while bearing its traces—but to ask to what extent the foregoing limitations are historical sediments that ought to be more critically interrogated. In the overall vision articulated in *PPNK*, Tully, to be sure, grants the Canadian problematic a political significance that it deserves, but it remains a thin one at that. For the framing and formulation of these political struggles primarily in terms of "struggle over recognition" binds Tully to a conceptual crucible that ultimately undercuts some of the critical and democratic import of his public philosophy. In *PPNK*, for instance, Tully writes admiringly of Trudeau and apropos of the former Prime Minister's civic ethics he poses the central question at the heart of his public philosophy: "Our question today—and everyday—is how can we adapt and apply Trudeau's civic ethics of critical freedom against the currents of the vast concentrations of power that shape, form and carry us along today? Before addressing this question, we need to ascertain the *character* of the big concentrations of power today" (*PPNK* II, 167).

What, then, are those concentrations of power today and how does Tully demarcate their character? Better still, how accurately does the theoretical armature crafted in these volumes capture contemporary predicaments of power? In characterizing these forms of power, Tully offers penetrating accounts of how ideas of constitutional democracy and international law have colluded with the instauration of western imperialism that invite the reader to re-cognize her/his understanding of both imperialism and democracy (*PPNK* II, 127–63, 195–221). In so doing, he contributes to the political literacy that a process of "citizenisation" entails and argues for a form of democratic constitutionalism—all of which remind the reader of similar pleas made by Sheldon S. Wolin and Roberto Unger, both of whom are absent from these pages—as he further insists on how citizenship demands more than just membership in a political community, however important such a recognition is as a precondition for civic freedom and its ensuing actions. But Tully implicitly avows something that *PPNK* fails to systematically thematize: how citizenship and its animating ethos revolve around a way of organizing political power, as its continuous meaningfulness is at once sustained and transformed by a political form that the citizen, in turn, sustains and transforms, either by acting or acquiescing to it.[21] And how contemporary forms of power compromise these attributes. Capitalism, for instance, simultaneously promotes and is nourished by political demobilization. But Tully tends to underestimate the obduracy of these forms of power and debars a realist consideration of their challenge to the forms of civic freedom that he compellingly theorizes. For democratic civic freedom to have political teeth, it needs to avow a form of shared power on a fairly continuous basis, which is the only source for the political education and literacy that is intrinsic to democratic "citizenisation." Equally presupposed in this ideal but not sufficiently theorized are a conception of power as decentralized and a specific account of the precise ways in which current hierarchical forms of power consistently militate against any such decentralization. But to let these questions bear on the architecture of his theory would force Tully to confront some difficult questions, say, how an agonistic conception of freedom confronts forms of power that *PPNK* ultimately misrecognizes.

While Tully has responded with characteristic courtesy and decisiveness to Rainer Forst's objection to his theory, his divorce of a critical ethos from a critical theory dispenses too easily with the problems at stake (this in addition to conflating Habermas with the whole tradition of A critical theory, something that begs the question) (*PPNK* I, 71–131).[22] A critical theory that conceptualizes these forms of power—primarily capitalist and state power, and the different ways in which their collusion is conformed in the present—and the discursive practices and ideological dispositives that are constitutive of liberal–democratic–capitalist hegemony is fundamental for any realist critique of the present.[23] Namely, a critical theory of the present that is at once mediated by a critical ethos and offers the conceptual, historical, and empirical determinations that inform the ethos's critical valences. Without it, a critical ethos remains abstract and its edges are significantly dulled.

Yet it is precisely this possibility—a conceptually bound critical theory—that is foreclosed by the philosophical signposts and theoretical resources underpinning *PPNK*. These lead Tully to underestimate how predicaments of power inaugurate forms of subjection, often finding expression in present-day politicized identities, which in their proto-civic activities presuppose a political identity and form that their current depoliticized politics actively disavows.[24] But Tully's conception of citizenship certainly entails shared power: "Citizenship in a democracy consists in the participation of citizens in the ways in which their conduct is governed by the exercise of political power in any system or practice of governance" (*PPNK* I, 145). Yet for practices of civic freedom to be democratic in substance and form, a corollary sense of political literacy, sobriety, and responsibility needs to be equally affirmed. And for that a critical theory that accurately maps present-day forms of power, the situations conforming the political fields in which new practices of responsibility can unfold, is in order.[25] Otherwise, the temptation is to find silver linings in the present, a temptation to which Tully's account of proto-civic citizenship sometimes yields (*PPNK* II, 226, 292–3, 301–2, 308–9).

Out of Tully's preferred theoretical points of reference, Foucault's account of power provides the most promising point of departure, even if insufficient in its own terms.[26] Indeed, it is by way of a juxtaposition of Foucault and Wolin that Wendy Brown has compellingly articulated some parameters that are instructive here.[27] In her powerful essay "Democracy and Bad Dreams," she has formulated a coruscating account of Wolin's nuanced conception of modern power and the state that speaks directly to the aforementioned questions. Brown's commanding formulation merits lengthy quotation:

> For Wolin, the idea of moving the state or capital out of the picture of modern power is absurd; whatever other forms of power contour and constrain the modern subject, it is corporate capital and the state that vitiate the prospects of democratic citizenship—they monopolize the powers that shape our collective life form, they depoliticize what democracy must politicize, they manage, administer and buy what we need to collectively fashion for ourselves. [...] Wolin's state is a neo-Weberian state, heavy with rationalities and

bureaucratic domination; it is a Marxist-structuralist state, neither identical with nor a simple instrument of capitalism but complexly entwined with it. It is an administrative and penetrative state—those tentacles are everywhere and on everyone, especially the most disempowered; they do not honor public/private distinctions, political/economic distinctions, or even legal/extra-legal distinctions. Wolin does not need to eschew the state to "cut off the king's head in political theory" because—despite his attribution of enormous arbitrary power to the presidency—formal sovereignty is not the aspect of the state that most impedes democratic life. Rather, the contemporary state is a complex amalgam of political, economic, administrative and discursive powers, at once concentrated and decentralized, that saturates the social body with its strategies and ends, and orders subjects according to them. […] modern political power is extraordinary in its range and reach precisely because it is so relentlessly intermixed with daily life, so intimate with us where we are most needy and vulnerable, so without scruple in producing and incorporating these needs as part of its own expansion.[28]

These encagements of political life—its caging, to borrow the expression of the neo-Weberian sociologist of power, Michael Mann, by capitalist, state, and bureaucratic power—are not just out of the purview of Tully's public philosophy, but their theorization would curb the looseness of the agonistic conception of freedom that he advances. Conversely, the violence—ordered, structural, and withheld—of these processes remains mostly at the edges of Tully's thematization of the present.[29] But for civic freedom to be meaningful, it demands a head-on confrontation with the encagement and *incorporation* of democracy and democratic life by these forms of power. Brown does so by bringing into a single field of vision a Wolinian theory of modern and postmodern state power, along with her original theorization, peppered by Foucauldian motifs, of the practices of freedom and subjection that constitute it. She thus carefully maps these determinations to concretely discern the ways in which a politics of freedom and equality can erode them and reconstitute political life along the lines of conceptual and political determinations that foster democratic practices of power.

Of course, Tully sees things differently. He has eloquently argued against the theoretical erasure of the everyday practices of resistance that regularly occur in the contemporary world and how most accounts of the present fail to register these and misrecognize how "another world is actual" (*PPNK* II, 301).[30] In these already actual practices and relationships, he goes on to argue, one finds forms of proto-citizenship that can be activated—for "we are always and everywhere proto-active citizens"—by processes of "civicisation" and "citizenisation": "To civicise governance relationships is—*eo ipso*—to 'democratise' them, for one of the oldest and most ordinary meanings of 'democracy' is that people always have an effective say in and over the relationships (rules) to which they are subject" (*PPNK* II, 279, 281).[31] These governance relationships rely on "participatory diversity [which] involves the redistribution of access to political power so that the oppressed and excluded minorities and women may participate equally" (*PPNK* I, 153).

How exactly is this to be accomplished? Tully speaks of electoral reforms and proportional representation as some of the measures that can bring new governance relationships about. But these, needless to say, have to be forced in the agenda and doing so requires a confrontation with the aforementioned forms of power and their violent imperatives. Tully takes up this challenge somewhat circuitously. After an evocative reading of Euripides's *The Phoenician Women*, he offers a striking statement on the content of civic freedom: "It is the proto-civic and civic freedom of negotiating and democratising in and over the always less-than-ideal relationships in which we live and breathe and become who we are. The only guarantee of freedom and democracy is, not surprisingly, the daily cooperative practices of democratic freedom on webs of relationships and on the fields of possibilities they disclose" (*PPNK* I, 283). The attractiveness of this evocative conception of democracy and freedom is beyond question. What remains in question, however, is whether or not a politics of agonistic freedom can sustain it, let alone bring it about. Tully seeks to further address this question by identifying sources of "civicisation"—unions and other "collective bargaining associations" are identified as historical "agents of such sporadic civicisation of institutions"—and forms of action to enact civic freedom in the present. He then writes:

> The final aspect of citizenship arises when citizens run up against unjustifiable limits to the civic activities in citizen/governance and citizen relations that we have been discussing. In any of these activities, there is always a vast ensemble of relationships that are not open to negotiation in the course of the activities. These background non-negotiable relationships "structure" and limit the foreground field of possible action in citizen/governance and citizen relationships (*PPNK* II, 196).

Again, to his credit, out of all contemporary theorists of "ethos" and "agonistic" politics, Tully stands out by attending to these background conditions. But notice Tully's use of scare quotes to denote structure and the uneasiness with this obdurate aspect of contemporary predicaments of power. Even if he distinguishes with great subtlety the denunciation of structures of domination that impair democratic civic freedom from a rejection of structures *tout court*, he offers a rather labile characterization of these structural relations:

> What holds structural relations of domination in place and integrates both civic negotiations *and* confrontations into an on-going global organization is neither a functional property of a world system nor hidden hand, as it appears from the theoretical gaze. Rather, it is the actual contingent exercise by humans of all the considerable means available to the hegemonic partners in the layers of informal imperial networks that encircle the globe (*PPNK* II, 299).

Yes and no. That is, here one can only partly assent to Tully's formulation and that only with a demurrer. These structures are contingent insofar as these are the outcomes of historical processes that were neither providential, nor foreordained. But that is as far as contingency goes here. Structures, say, capitalist relations, are contingent in their origins, but systematically operate with their own internal imperatives of reproduction that often take the aura of necessity, however tacitly it is expressed. To point out their contingency hardly means anything in this context. One needs to map these structural relationships and how these *structure* different fields of power. Yes, these are produced and reproduced in practices, but in their obduracy these are either explicitly presented as necessary, or tacitly allowed to set the limits of how freedom can be conceptualized. If in doubt, just consider the treatment of capitalism in these pages and how nowhere in *PPNK* one finds an explicit plea for a horizon beyond it as a precondition of democratic, civic freedom, let alone a systematic theorization of how civic freedom effectively confronts it in order to transcend it.[32] What is at stake here is hardly whether or not Tully theorizes these background conditions, but how effectively he does it.

Tully's characterizations of today's forms of power thus betray a blind spot in his tendency to misrecognize the force of the structural imperatives that define the contemporary dynamics of the capitalist political economy, which are intrinsic to contemporary imperial forms, by overemphasizing the pliability of its networks while underestimating their obduracy (*PPNK* II, 89–90, 172–3). Not so with other aspects of imperialism, however. In his characterization of today's powers, Tully sharply dissects central aspects of the nature of the American empire. Its empire is informal and, primarily, has an economic role: the coordination of the defense and perpetuation of the capitalist global order, for which its veritable empire of bases plays a not negligible role. Yet the question is not whether or not *PPNK* registers the constitutive role of capitalism in contemporary forms of imperialism, but whether or not it offers a realistic characterization of this peculiar modality of concentrated power, especially when it is so central to present-day forms of imperialism (*PPNK* II, 141–2). Still, anti-imperialism, not anti-capitalism, is the prevalent leitmotif in Tully's reflections. But a reckoning with one without an adequate theorization of the other, especially when nowadays these collude more than ever before, remains inadequate and, ultimately, misrecognizes the forms of power binding the present.

Analogously, Tully occasionally tends to underestimate the ways in which the immediate playing fields of politics are structurally uneven and how the rules of the game are often historically sedimented and backed up by awesome forms of power that entrench these to the disadvantage of the have nots, even if the latter can creatively resist them. But when the players go to the arena, the stadium and the rules of the political game are stacked against the many. For it is the few who had the resources to tilt the playing field to begin with. Rigged parliamentary and electoral systems, no less than market arrangements are examples of this. Yet when Tully speaks of the relationship between governors and governed an uncharacteristic evasiveness is found:

The governed partner is thus always an active agent—an apprentice player who must learn how to navigate and negotiate his or her way around the field and how to play the game through acting and interacting with the governing partner. The governor is always an interactive partner to some extent, drawn into the game of giving further instructions, answering questions, correcting conduct, responding to seemingly untoward rule-following and so on. Humans are always unavoidably *homo ludens*, creative game players and prototypical civic citizens in the dialogical relationships of their cultures and civilizations before and *as* they take on any other identities (*PPNK* II, 277).

Homo ludens may well be an anthropological feature of humanity as a species, but this appeal to natural history has to account for the ways in which this creativity is already mediated (and sometimes truncated or compromised) by a dialectic of structural imperatives and the entrenchment of what Pierre Bourdieu memorably called their sustaining forms of *habitus*. But anchoring civic citizenship on this anthropological feature is a tacit admission of the difficulty of theorizing its political anchorage: resistance is not insignificant, but it cannot be conflated with political freedom.[33] Again, one of the consequences of this argument is to underestimate the obstacles to meaningful civic citizenship, as well as finding silver linings that come close to conflating acts of resistance with concerted political action. What if the governor does not want to play? Does s/he then have to be forced? If so, how and by what means? Agonistic freedom and a principled—thus abstract—commitment to non-violence can hardly pay this bill. For some "governors" and other elites entrenched in asymmetrical and hierarchical relations of power are hardly more yielding and responsive than the inhabitants of Atlantis in one of Bertolt Brecht's most memorable poems: "Even in fabled Atlantis/ The night the ocean engulf it/The drowning still bawled for their slaves."[34] Tully's characterization of the "governor" presupposes what it is supposed to instill; namely, a democratic temperament already embedded in a culture that is responsive to the questions asked, the grievances voiced.[35] Indigenous peoples, as Tully rightly asserts, have exercised "arts of resistance and survived centuries of imperialisation" but the situation of discrimination and dispossession in which these peoples are mostly found across the western hemisphere is precisely proof of why resistance—never to be discounted—is not political freedom. That resistance can feed a "citizenisation" process goes without saying: it intimates a desire for freedom that could *potentiate* practices of political freedom. Yet it cannot be conflated with them, especially when the structuring of the social formation in question remains unaltered and political conflicts are almost exclusively framed in terms of "the grammar of recognition."[36] While Tully eloquently emphasizes the importance of avoiding misrecognizing current forms of proto-civic freedom, he seems to misrecognize the *character* of contemporary forms of power.

6.

In his response to an earlier round of criticism in the pages of *Political Theory*, Tully has forcefully restated his case and shown a more decisive account of the obduracy of the forms of structural violence inherited from imperialism. In responding to David Armitage's penetrating essay, Tully writes:

> The great powers imposed strong colonial administrations with coercive and regulatory power to open the labour and resources of the global South to rapid social and economic development and exploitation. These processes of dispossession, primitive accumulation, centralized state building, militarization, economic exploitation, and ecological destruction were continued after decolonization by dependent elites in the former colonies and the successive developmental policies of the great powers and the Bretton Woods institutions of global governance. Despite some advances since decolonization, the legacies of inequality and indebtedness are greater now than one hundred years ago.[37]

Indeed. But despite the wink at Marx ("primitive accumulation") these sentences debar a consideration of capitalism, the form of global power that nowadays thoroughly mediates these problems, even if all of them cannot be reduced to it.[38] Once again, civic freedom's foe is imperialism, not capitalism, as if the two could be separated in present-day empires. An obvious question thus reemerges: how can a mapping of contemporary imperial powers dispense with a conceptualization of capitalism, when the current empire, and its surrogates, precisely operates to protect it in a postmodern variation of the Concert of Powers?[39]

And yet, after laying the historical obduracy of these challenges, Tully lays out a rather labile rehearsal of the concluding sections of *PPNK*: the politics to confront these orders is one based on "cooperative, community-based, ecological and non-violent traditions of self-reliance of Mahatma Gandhi, Muhamed Yunus, Vandana Shiva and many others in the global South."[40] Again, this is not to say that these forms of organizing collective life lack democratic import. But are these enough to *attain* and *sustain* a meaningful share of political power that substantive democratic equality and freedom presuppose and demand? Tully's response hardly addresses the full force of Armitage's essay. For what Armitage objected to is analogous to one of the foregoing critiques presented in this essay: the extent to which Tully's account of freedom presupposes a degree of commonality that is hardly attainable within its own terms. The last clause is not present in Armitage's essay, but the first is eloquently voiced: "The practice of civic freedom implies, at the very least, the existence of a *civitas* within which all agents may conduct themselves as *cives*. What, more broadly, are the implied background conditions that are necessary to what Tully calls 'challenging yet rewarding civic relationships'?"[41] This is the crucible of Tully's anti-Statist stance, even if the stability and non-violent politics that civic freedom presupposes have yet to be attained outside of a State form, with its forms of centralization and monopoly of legitimate violence.[42]

There are glimpses of a more forceful way of casting these background conditions and their structuring in *PPNK*, but these lack ascendancy in its theoretical armature. At different moments, Tully tentatively avers the obduracy of the ways in which the political field is structured and the economy of violence historically needed to change them: "There are always asymmetries in power, knowledge, influence and argumentative skills that block the most oppressed from getting to negotiations in the first place and then structuring the negotiations if they do;" he also emphasizes the need "to understand dialogical interactions" beyond the commonplace model of communication: "The field of study is the full range of strategic, communicative, deliberative, negotiated and decision-making interactions, from Intifada-like strategic bargaining by recourse to armed struggle at one end through to the idealised, calm and non-strategic exchange of an agreed-upon range of public reasons on which political philosophers tend to focus" (*PPNK* I, 306, 308–9).

These formulations come in the context of Tully's coruscating discussion of the politics involved in struggles "over," as opposed to just "for," recognition. While he does not directly engage with the terms of the exchange between Nancy Fraser and Axel Honneth on the intersections between recognition and redistribution, his rendering of these intersections echoes the terms of their debate. On the one hand, Tully is closer to Honneth in his tendency to subsume struggles of redistribution in the thickness of struggles over recognition; on the other hand, despite this tilt, he acknowledges the irreducibility of one to the other, and thus comes close to Fraser's position in that regard.[43] But what is clear is that for him recognition is the point of departure and the more central category. What Fraser's account opens the door for—a sharp analytical distinction between the two that allows for the contextual and political demarcation of democratic enmity lines—is mostly eschewed by Tully. If it is not entirely so, it is because he does understand the importance of political confrontation, which is cast in terms of imperialism and anti-imperialism: civic freedom against present-day empires and imperial practices. That is why Gandhi's non-violence is so central in the concluding pages of *PPNK*.

At this point one can return to Tully's momentarily avowal of "armed struggle"—which is absent from the rest of the account and the ensuing discussion of non-violence—and consider the implications it has on his overriding affirmation of non-violence. Revealingly, this momentary avowal happened in reference to the Intifada. In the Palestinian intifadas there has been something akin to an economy of violence, especially in the first—there are important differences between the first (1987–93) and second (2001–05) intifadas and the forms of struggle entailed, and the combinations of violence and non-violence found in each, even if the opposition is not as stark as non-violence in the first and full blown armed struggle in the second. An economy of violence certainly bound the first, which the escalation of violence—a spiral of action and reaction in which Israel shares responsibility—led to the prominence of armed struggle, suicide bombing, and the tragic eclipse of the politics of civility that characterized the second.[44] Tully, however, does not do justice to this insight. Moreover, the need for a politics of civility, and a political theory of violence, are most compellingly theorized by Étienne Balibar, another kindred spirit who, like Wolin, nowhere figures in *PPNK*. Yet both the form and the content of Balibar's theorization of violence and civility are central to Tully's concerns: Balibar offers a realistic charting of the planetary cartographies of violence and cruelty, and the roles of capitalism, racism, and war in them—all of which are cast politically.[45] The absence of Balibar and Wolin from Tully's otherwise encompassing references could be due to their lack of any liberal leanings and, more so in the case of Balibar, the strong presence of a Marxist heritage that complicates the picture of the present laid out in *PPNK*: the absences, along with others—Unger and, to a lesser extent, Brown—can either be symptomatic of Tully's lack of affinity to these theoretical languages and traditions (Wolin is a political theorist, not a political philosopher), or reveal the ideological *litmus test* in and how a subterranean liberalism ultimately binds Tully's thematic. Be that as it may, it is the anti-imperial and anti-colonial nature of the Palestinian struggle that prompted Tully to temporarily permit violence into his discussion, and not capitalism.

Admittedly, Tully's purpose is to foster alternatives to violent confrontations which reconcile "conflicts over recognition" that effectively "unsettle the prejudices and alter the outlooks of the most powerful groups," while breaking with the exclusions that reduce these alternatives and impose "violent resistance" as one among them (*PPNK* I, 309, 314–15). That these are framed as struggles over recognition and emphasis is placed on "prejudice" and "outlook" not only runs the risk of simplification, in which recognition becomes an undifferentiated placeholder for political struggle, but also comes perilously close to the discredited, liberal rhetorical strategy of reducing structural injustices to individual prejudice, a depoliticizing gesture that tends to silence the texture of complex cultural, economic and political processes, in their discursive *and* structural mediations, which constitute present-day predicaments of power. The latter tendency *PPNK* mostly rebuffs, even if it remains somewhat compromised by the first. Yet the way in which "uncompromising non-violent confrontation" is abstractly imposed, forecloses an intrinsic component in the history of anti-imperial struggles that were the relevant context for Gandhi's strategy, and its inheritance by Martin Luther King Jr, as well as sidelines its antinomies.[46]

7.

Apropos to the contemporary cartographies of violence and cruelty, Balibar once wrote about how "the gates of 'communication' sometimes have to be opened by force, sometimes in a violent matter, or they will remain locked forever."[47] This is hardly an avowal of violence *tout court*, but a sober and politically literate acknowledgment of how "a politics of civility … can no more identify itself with non-violence than with the counterviolence that 'prevents' violence or resists it. This also means that a politics of civility cannot coincide (in any case uniquely or completely) with the imperative of peace."[48] This also holds for a politics of civic freedom. In Isaac Deutscher's memorable words to an American audience in 1966: "To preach non-violence to those always the object of violence may even be false."[49]

It is, of course, equally imperative to recognize that its pernicious effects can hardly be overestimated, something that Deutscher equally emphasized to his audience. In both its trenchancy and ambivalence the advice is hardly negligible. Violence is never an abstract "either or" proposition, as commonplace characterizations of it tend to portray it. Nor is it undifferentiated. It is partly due to the disavowal of these insights that has often led proponents of non-violence to antinomian positions whose political consequences are everything but benign. What Tully's account of civic freedom lacks and needs is a conceptualization of violence and the different modalities—structural and subjective—that constitutes contemporary predicaments of power and that impair freedom and democracy. In *PPNK* non-violence runs the risk of becoming an undifferentiated placeholder for Tully's account of civic freedom. But the dialectic between structural and subjective forms of violence needs to be avowed for the ethic of conviction to yield to a political ethic of responsibility, in the tradition of Thucydides, Machiavelli, Weber, Gramsci, and Weil, which is what Tully's public philosophy presupposes but neglects to theorize.[50] Yet theorizing such a political ethic, and its imbrication of both realism and utopia, is hardly attainable within the theoretical and political terms privileged by Tully in *PPNK*.

Enmity, power, and violence—these constitutive aspects of the present remain at the edges of Tully's public philosophy. The displacement of these concepts, and the overemphasis on the agonistic dimension of citizenship, ultimately lessen the democratic import of his conception of civil freedom. When the gates of communication are closed and the "pile of debris," to invoke Benjamin's image, reaches the boiling point, democratic lines of enmity ought to be drawn. Confronting violent predicaments of power has historically demanded lines of enmity and democracy is not exempt from this necessity, nor is it exempted from articulating an economy of violence. And a democratic "public philosophy in a new key" lacks the necessary critical and political edge without properly conceptualizing these predicaments. Even so, what Tully's masterful work provides is a novel way to think through one of the most pressing political questions today—the practice of freedom. It also offers a powerful reminder about how neither enmity lines, nor violence, can ever be hypostatized, let alone idealized. In its non-hypostatized versions, the advice is sound.

Notes

1 While philosophical and moral doctrines are listed as sources of diversities, religion is overwhelmingly at the center of his account. For the salience of religious strife in Rawls's thinking, see Bernard G. Prusak, "Politics, Religion, and the Public Good: An Interview with Philosopher John Rawls," *Commonweal*, 25 September 1998, pp. 12–17.

See also John Rawls, *Political Liberalism*, New York: Columbia University Press, 2005 [1993], p. xxiv.
2 Étienne Balibar, "Toward a Diasporic Citizen? From Internationalism to Cosmopolitanism," in *The Creolization of Theory*, ed. Françoise Lionnet and Shu-mei Shih, Durham: Duke University Press, 2011, p. 212.
3 James Tully, *Public Philosophy in a New Key: Volume I, Democracy and Civic Freedom* and *Public Philosophy in a New Key: Volume II, Imperialism and Civic Freedom*, Cambridge: Cambridge University Press, 2008, hereafter referred to as *PPNK*.
4 To gather the strength of Tully's argument, one has just to compare it with Sankar Muthu's rather disingenuous account of Kant and imperialism in *Enlightenment Against Empire*, Princeton: Princeton University Press, 2003, pp. 122–209.
5 Cf. Michael Mann, *The Sources of Social Power: Vol. 1, A History of Power from the Beginning to AD 1760*, Cambridge: Cambridge University Press, 1986, passim.
6 In his account of the imperial forms of the present, for instance, Tully provides a breath of fresh air from the sanctimonies and euphemisms involved by most theoretical characterizations of it. Just compare his account of contemporary American empire with that of Pagden, or of Habermas, for that matter. See *PPNK* II, 127–42; 153–65; 260–7. Cf. Anthony Pagden, "Imperialism, Liberalism, and the Quest for Perpetual Peace," *Daedalus* 134, 2005, pp. 56–7; Jürgen Habermas, *The Divided West*, ed. and trans. Ciaran Cronin, Cambridge: Polity Press, 2006, p. 28 and *Europe: The Faltering Project*, trans. Ciaran Cronin, Cambridge: Polity Press, 2009, p. 100.
7 It is Arendt's account of freedom and action in texts like *The Human Condition*, *Between Past and Future*, and *On Revolution* that is central for Tully's project, not her perceptively sharp, historical-driven conceptualization of imperialism in the second part of *Origins of Totalitarianism*. For an excellent reading of this aspect of Arendt, see Karuna Mantena, "Genealogies of Catastrophe: Arendt on the Logic and Legacy of Imperialism," *Politics in Dark Times*, ed. Seyla Benhabib, Cambridge: Cambridge University Press, 2010, pp. 83–112.
8 Raia Prokhovnik, "An Interview with Quentin Skinner," *Contemporary Political Theory* 10, 2011, p. 275.
9 For a compelling critique of Skinner apropos to these concerns in relation to his *Hobbes and Republican Liberty* (2008), see Ellen Meiksins Wood, "Why it Matters," *London Review of Books*, 25 September 2008, pp. 3–6.
10 See Prokhovnik, "An Interview with Quentin Skinner," pp. 276–7.
11 Skinner's political interventions have sought to fetch "a third concept of liberty," a neo-Roman conception of liberty, cast as the road-not-taken from the past, that is ultimately innocent to social and economic history. While Pocock's intellectual project is often more ethereal in its discursive bent and the ensuing divorce from social history, his work shares with Skinner's the ability to offer powerful readings characterized by delicacy and rigor. Pocock, however, is the more politically minded figure. A quick comparison of their respective essays in the *LRB* records the gulf between the two, which goes beyond intellectual idiosyncrasy and writing style. Compare Skinner's essays, "A Third Concept of Liberty," *London Review of Books* (2 April 2002), pp. 16–18 and "What does it Mean to be a Free Person," *London Review of Books* (22 May 2008), pp. 16–18 with Pocock's trenchant essay "Deconstructing Europe," *London Review of Books* (19 December 1991), pp. 6–10.
12 See also *PPNK* I, 141.
13 This is particularly acute in the US and no other contemporary thinker has done more to illuminate this question than Sheldon S. Wolin. Tully's idea of civic freedom resonates with Wolin's fugitive democracy, arguably in both their appeal and limits, despite the conceptual and political differences between the two: say, while Tully has a historically richer account of US Empire than Wolin's, whose periodizations

sometimes equivocate, Tully's mapping of its collusion with capitalism and postmodern forms of power is thinner. See *PPNK* II, 89–90. Perhaps symptomatically, while "power relations" figures in the index of volume one, power vanishes entirely from volume two. Still the best account of Wolin's idea of "fugitive democracy" is found in Nicholas Xenos, "Momentary Democracy," *Democracy and Vision*, ed. Aryeh Botwinick and William E. Connolly, Princeton: Princeton University Press, 2001, pp. 25–38.

14 Ludwig Wittgenstein, *Philosophical Investigations*, trans. G.E.M. Anscombe, Oxford: Blackwell, 2001, p. 42. The conservative tenor of this formulation echoes a passage from his influential *Remarks on Frazer's Golden Bough*: "We can only describe and say, human life is like that." See Ludwig Wittgenstein, *Remarks on Frazer's Golden Bough*, trans. Rush Rhees, Norfolk: Brynmill Press, 1987, p. 3. In the context of England, however, this paradox became symptomatic of a contradiction of its intellectual and ideological milieu: in the words of Perry Anderson "the assiduous praise of ordinary language and aversion for technical concepts paradoxically produced a purely technical philosophy, entirely dissociated from the ordinary concerns of social life." See Perry Anderson, *English Questions*, London and New York: Verso, 1992, p. 68.

15 Cf. Patchen Markell, "The Rule of the People: Arendt, Archê, and Democracy," *American Political Science Review* 100, 2006, 2n.5, pp. 5–6.

16 I have offered a critical discussion of Connolly's liberalism and its lack of democratic import with reference to his reduction of democracy to an agonistic ethos in Antonio Y. Vázquez-Arroyo, "Agonized Liberalism: The Liberal Theory of William E. Connolly," *Radical Philosophy* 127, 2004, pp. 8–19. For a defense of Connolly and a contribution in its own right, see Stephen K. White, *The Ethos of the Late Modern Citizen*, Cambridge: Harvard University Press, 2009, 97ff.

17 See, inter alia, *PPNK* II, 244ff. For an initial attempt at formulating what is conceptually at stake in dealing with these questions, which draws on Adorno and Benjamin, see Antonio Y. Vázquez-Arroyo, "Universal History Disavowed," *Postcolonial Studies* 11, 2008, pp. 451–73.

18 Repeated in *PPNK* II, xiii.

19 Cf. Bonnie Honig, "[Un]Dazzled by the Ideal?," *Political Theory* 39, 2011, pp. 138–44, esp. p. 142. Honig's suggestive essay, however marred by its "agonistic" conceit and Connolly's fatuous imperative of "contestability," correctly points out not only how nature is not the peaceful template that Tully's reference to the Pacific North West conveys, but how *PPNK* disavows the tragic element of political life, which must be conceived not along the lines she proposes, but more so along the lines of Simone Weil, Isaac Deutscher, Raymond Williams and Terry Eagleton. Incidentally, in his response to Honig, Tully reveals a more nuanced, dare I say dialectical, rendering of this relationship between reason and violence that could be productively extended to rectify his account of universality. See James Tully, "Dialogue," *Political Theory* 39, 2011, pp. 145–60, esp. pp. 156–7.

20 Cf. Perry Anderson, *The New Old World*, London and New York: Verso, 2009, pp. 527–8.

21 Two formulations found in Sheldon S. Wolin's writings are apposite here. In *The Presence of the Past* he writes about how the identity of a collectivity, the content of its political form, is "made known through the constitutionally sanctioned actions of public officials and the response, or lack thereof, of the collectivity to those actions." Almost 20 years later, the tone is mordant, but the political import of the message remains: "concentrated power, whether of a Leviathan, a benevolent despot, or a superpower, is impossible without the support of a complicitous citizenry that willingly signs on to the covenant, or clicks the 'mute button.'" See, respectively, Sheldon S. Wolin, *The Presence of the Past*, Baltimore: The Johns Hopkins University Press, 1989, p. 12; and *Democracy Incorporated: Managed Democracy and the Specter of Inverted Totalitarianism*, Princeton:

Princeton University Press, 2008, p. 81. From Unger, see Roberto Mangabeira Unger, *Democracy Realized*, London and New York: Verso, 1998, passim.
22 For his response to critics, including his response to Rainer Forst, see Tully, "Dialogue," pp. 146–51.
23 See, *inter alia*, the work of Wendy Brown: *States of Injury*, Princeton: Princeton University Press, 1995, passim; *Regulating Aversion*, Princeton: Princeton University Press, 2006, passim; and *Walled States, Waning Sovereignty*, Cambridge, MA: Zone, 2010, passim. Even if sporadically mentioned, direct engagement with Brown's work is conspicuously absent from *PPNK*.
24 On the idea of "depoliticized politics," see Wang Hui, *The End of the Revolution*, London: Verso, 2008, pp. 3–18; and Wang Hui, *The Politics of Imagining Asia*, ed. Theodore Huters, Cambridge, MA: Harvard University Press, 2011, pp. 34–6, 41. Also of interest is Kenneth Surin, *Freedom Not Yet*, Durham: Duke University Press, 2009, pp. 65–93. Cf. Josep Ramoneda, *Después de la pasión política*, Madrid: Taurus, 1999, passim.
25 This vision of critical theory and its implications are developed at greater length in Antonio Y. Vázquez-Arroyo, *Scenes of Responsibility* (in preparation).
26 In the midst of preference for the "ethical" Foucault, Tully's sober if oblique assessment is exemplary: the realm of "relationships of trust, conviviality, or solidarity and civic friendship across identity related differences and disagreements" is that of "civic freedom as *isegoria*, citizens speaking to each other in equal relationships about their common concerns, rather than *parrhesia*, speaking to their governors in unequal relationships" (*PPNK* II, 290–1). The best argument for the political import of Foucault's late writings is found in Nancy Luxon, "Ethics and Subjectivity: Practices of Self-Governance in the Late Lectures of Michel Foucault," *Political Theory* 36, 2008, pp. 377–402.
27 See, *inter alia*, Wendy Brown, *States of Injury* and *Regulating Aversion*. See also her essay "Power After Foucault," in *The Oxford Handbook of Political Theory*, ed. John S. Dryzek, Bonnie Honig, and Ann Philips, Oxford: Oxford University Press, 2006, pp. 61–84.
28 Wendy Brown, "Democracy and Bad Dreams," *Theory & Event* 10, 2007, para. #11.
29 See Ariella Azoulay and Adi Ophir, "The Order of Violence," in *The Power of Inclusive Exclusion*, ed. Adi Ophir, Michal Givoni, and Sari Hanfi, New York: Zone Books, 2009, 99–140.
30 See also, *PPNK* I, 159.
31 Earlier on, Tully had established the importance of shared power in this theorization: "Citizens participate by 'having a say' and 'negotiating' how power is exercised and who exercises it" (*PPNK* I, 145). Presupposed in this formulation is, of course, a sense of political equality that is undertheorized by Tully.
32 But see *PPNK* II, 251–2, for Tully's acknowledgment of how capitalism impairs civic freedom.
33 For a penetrating rendering of this question, see Brown, *States of Injury*, esp. chs 1–2. These insights are suggestively developed in Marlene Duprey, *Bioislas*, San Juan: Ediciones Callejón, 2010, pp. 149–66.
34 Bertolt Brecht, *Poems: 1913–1953*, ed. John Willett and Ralph Manheim, London: Methuen, 2000, p. 252.
35 Cf. Sheldon S. Wolin, "Democracy, Difference, and Re-cognition," *Political Theory* 21, 1993, pp. 464–83, esp. the comments found at p. 480.
36 See Patchen Markell, "The Recognition of Politics," *Constellations* 7, 2000, pp. 502–4. This critique is forcefully developed in Patchen Markell, *Bound by Recognition*, Princeton, NJ: Princeton University Press, 2003, passim. For critical discussion of Markell's book, see the essays by Joan Cocks, Falguni A. Sheth, and Antonio Y. Vázquez-Arroyo, as well as Markell's rejoinder, in *Polity* 38, 2006, pp. 3–39.
37 Tully, "Dialogue," p. 153.

38 Formidable treatments of the recent travails of capitalism with clear conceptual demarcations and richness of empirical and statistical detail are found in Robert Brenner, *The Boom and the Bubble*, London and New York: Verso, 2002; *The Economics of Global Turbulence*, London and New York: Verso, 2006. Amidst a proliferation of works on "the financial crisis," see the excellent account found in Gopal Balakrishnan, "The Convolution of Capitalism," in *Business as Usual*, ed. Craig Calhoun and Georgi Derluguian, New York: New York University Press, 2011, pp. 211–29. Balakrishnan's essay takes Brenner's account as its point of departure.
39 See Perry Anderson, "Jottings on the Conjuncture," *New Left Review* 48, 2007, pp. 5–37.
40 Tully, "Dialogue," pp. 153–4; *PPNK* II, 300ff.
41 David Armitage, "Probing the Foundations of Tully's Public Philosophy," *Political Theory* 39, 2011, pp. 124–30. See p. 127.
42 Not incidentally, when Tully discusses how the "reasonable" in "reasonable disagreement" is also open to contestation he comes close of theorizing the need to contest the background conditions that frame the field of contestation, but cuts the discussion short by focusing on procedures of argumentation. Wittgenstein abides. See *PPNK* I, 308. Again, unsurprisingly, the context of the discussion is "struggles over recognition." For a thoughtful critique of Tully's earlier formulation that highlights how "the grammar of recognition" may well be more disabling to civic freedom and democratically shared power than he acknowledges, see Markell, "The Recognition of Politics," pp. 496–506.
43 Nancy Fraser and Axel Honneth, *Redistribution or Recognition?: A Political–Philosophical Exchange*, London and New York: Verso, 2003.
44 For a very thoughtful recent discussion, prompted by the revolts in the Arab world that started this spring (2011), see Adam Shatz, "Is Palestine Next?, *London Review of Books*, 14 July 2011, pp. 8–14.
45 See, *inter alia*, Étienne Balibar, *Politics and the Other Scene*, trans. Christine Jones, James Swenson, and Chris Turner, London and New York: Verso, 2002, pp. 1–55, 105–45; *We, The People of Europe?*, trans. James Swenson, Princeton, NJ: Princeton University Press, 2003, pp. 31–50, 115–54; "Violence and Civility: On the Limits of Political Anthropology," *differences* 20, 2009, 9–35; *La proposition de l'égaliberté*, Paris: Presses Universitaires de France, 2011, pp. 11–52, 281–315; *Violence et civilité: Wellek Library Lectures et autres essais de philosophie politique*, Paris: Editions Galilée, 2010, passim.
46 For a trenchant discussion of non-violence that contextualizes historically and captures its antinomies, see Domenico Losurdo, *La non-violenza*, Roma-Bari: Editori Laterza, 2010, esp. pp. 25–185. A précis of his overall argument is available in English: see Domenico Losurdo, "Moral Dilemmas and Broken Promises," *Historical Materialism* 18, 2010, pp. 85–134. King, for instance, began to confront these antinomies at the end of the 1960s' apropos of Vietnam. A fine account of the radical history of civil rights is found in Nikhil Pal Singh, *Black is a Country*, Cambridge, MA: Harvard University Press, 2005, passim.
47 Balibar, *We, the People of Europe?*, p. 131.
48 Balibar, "Violence and Civility," p. 28.
49 Isaac Deutscher, *Marxism, Wars, and Revolutions*, ed. Tamara Deutscher, London and New York: Verso, 1984, pp. 261-2.
50 For a discussion of this tradition, see Antonio Y. Vázquez-Arroyo, "Responsibility, Violence, and Catastrophe" *Constellations* 15, 2008, pp. 98–125.

Chapter 5

"[Un]Dazzled by the Ideal?"— James Tully and New Realism[1]

Bonnie Honig

"If we wish to do justice to the conflicts that surround us and lead to one tragedy after another, we can do *no better* than to keep the example of *Antigone* constantly in mind," says James Tully, in his fabulous book, *Strange Multiplicity* (1995).[2] But it is not Sophocles's lamenting title character that draws Tully, nor is it the playwright's tragic message. It is Haemon, the character commonly seen as the reasonable mediator, cast by Tully as an "exemplary citizen of the intercultural common ground."[3] The son of Creon sees the justice of Antigone's claim and pleads with his father to exercise restraint. Haemon reasons with his father as Tully reasons with his readers throughout his work: Both observe how our investments in certain concepts and imperatives prevent us from seeing how seemingly intractable conflicts can nonetheless be negotiated.

Sophocles's play is unmentioned in the two volumes of *Public Philosophy in a New Key* (2008).[4] But Haemon is still here. Like Haemon, Tully positions himself between the worlds of dissidence and governance, speaking to the powerful in soft reasonable tones on behalf of subaltern subjects, and showing political theorists how, if we look past the abstractions and grand narratives that often bedazzle us, we could be usefully informed by the startlingly diverse array of freedom-oriented practices on the "rough ground" of politics. Directing our attention away from concepts and toward the real, Tully seems to echo Raymond Geuss's recent call to realism in political theory. But Tully departs from Geuss by focusing not on stability but freedom as the first principle of politics, not on *modus vivendi* settlements but on justice, not on the state as the central political institution but on diverse civic practices, and not on the decision as the essence of politics but on the plural real practices and freedoms that make up daily political and civic life. Tully calls his position agonism but given his call to attend to the real, engage actual practices, and resist abstract or essentialist categories including many that surface in Geuss's own realism, Tully might well be seen as a New Realist.[5]

Like Haemon, Tully seeks to dispel dogmatism by recourse to actuality and reasonable moderation. But Tully may not take full account of the power politics of reasonableness, while Haemon, by contrast, beckons us beyond the reasonable or more deeply into its dark recesses. He does not only reason with his father. He also tries to kill him and then finally kills himself. Does Haemon's violence betray his reasonableness or give alternative expression to it?[6] On behalf of the latter possibility, we may note that in all his actions, Haemon seeks parity or equality with his father, first through calm deliberative reasoning, then through violence and finally by way of mimicry or usurpation.[7] Reasoning and stabbing are arguably two ways to kill the father, and a third way is by stepping into his shoes, as Haemon tries to do when he marries Antigone in death. Creon responds to Haemon's claims of equality by infantilizing his son. Haemon tries to fight back but he is impotent against his father. His reasoning fails, his brandished weapon fails, and his effort to become a male adult by marrying fails (the bride is dead).

Sometimes the spell of the father can be broken, as it must be—this is what real psychological and political maturation entail. Arendt understood this when she described political action as a rebirth while insisting on its non-violent possibility. But the father is not easily dispensed with. As Freud knew, even a successful parricide heightens, it does not diminish, the power of the father. Tully understands the problem and enters into it, releasing us from the grip of pictures that, in Wittgenstein's phrase, hold us captive. Tully breaks the spell of a colonial history that positions Aboriginals on lower rungs of civilizational development than their white European "fathers" (so-called in the US colonial context): He turns for inspiration not only to the philosophers of Europe but also and more fundamentally to the native vision of a circle of life and he highlights the costs and not just the benefits of a civil liberties focus that demotes civic participatory practices and offers in their place grand narratives of progress. When he historicizes universalisms that present themselves to us as transcendental or rational, and exposes their contingent, historical character, he locates them *in* the agon they seek to transcend.[8] Discussing the problem of integration in the new Europe, Tully says we should privilege the often messy and plural practical knowledges of civic life that would make for a union that does not bring "its demos into being at the end of the day but one that brought itself into a conversation of reciprocal elucidation and co-articulation with the demoi who have been there since daybreak" (*PPNK* II, 242). The practices of these demoi may not conform to the abstract rational demands of "legal juridification, governmental planification, and corporate commodification" by which politics is often guided these days. But that is not a problem since such abstract rationalities tend to serve imperial or impositional aims, Tully argues. Rather than focus on formal law, state institutions, and corporate charters, Tully looks at movements for native sovereignty, NGO anti-globalization activists, and local actors who live otherwise than in accordance with the demands of global state sovereignties and market efficiencies. These are all models of what freedom can and should be.

Throughout, Tully is as reasonable as he thinks Haemon is. But Tully is not only reasonable; or rather, in so being he is implicated, whether he knows it or not, in something like the attempted parricide he obscures when he reads Haemon as a reasonable intercultural mediator. That reasonableness is part of and not an alternative to power politics is a point to which Tully is not as attuned as one might think he would be given his agonism. To recur to one of Tully's examples: if some Euro-Canadians today respond unreasonably to Aboriginal claims of sovereignty that is not simply because Euro-Canadians' understandings are "distorted" (*PPNK* I, 141), though that is what Tully says in the Habermasian voice he slides into on more than one occasion in these pages (his powerful Foucauldian critique of Habermas in Volume I notwithstanding). Rather, Euro-Canadians sense, not wrongly, that their maintenance of privilege in a new Canada-form is at stake. Their responses to new claims are premised on their awareness that their privilege is in jeopardy. Some may respond to such moments of transition with admirable openness and presumptive generosity and it is to them that Tully's arguments may seem most persuasive, but others will be less available. They may be charged with being unreasonable but that tactic deprives them of what they need to overcome their Creon-like insistence on their privileges. What they need is not just a Haemon-like reasonableness but also an Antigonean capacity to articulate their sense of injustice and lament their losses, which are real. Such difficulties may arise even for those Euro-Canadians who are open to the new petitioners' "internal reasons" of self-worth (*PPNK* II, 179) because no matter how good the Aboriginals' reasons and no matter how meritorious their claims, their full membership in the new public and private formation of Canadian federalism will have wider and perceived deleterious effects on those who currently enjoy the privileges of majority status. Without a way to thematize their losses (and maybe even with one), Euro-Canadians may feel resentment that the new association to which they now belong feels "alien" and "imposed" (*PPNK* I, 165, 179). If they go along with the new Canada-form, and though the new form may well win out, acquiescence or battle fatigue, not persuasion and consent, may be the most accurate terms to describe their submission and may best account for the alienation, resentments, and backlash that are likely to surface from time to time.

Tully does not address this problem, however. Although in *Strange Multiplicity* he saw politics as often tragic, here in these two volumes he would rather re-orient us toward broader ways of conceiving public goods and shared fates than attend to (and perhaps risk contributing thereby to the enhancement of) the zero-sumness of politics. He seems reluctant to take up the issue of woundedness, resentment and loss. He does so only with regard to human use of nature or animal life, noting that in Aboriginal practices worthy of emulation "the harmony and balance among all living things is sustained by a chain of benevolence and gratitude" (*PPNK* I, 244). Even with regard to Aboriginals who could make deep claims of wrong here, Tully keeps the focus not on the trail of tears but on the history of treaty-making (*PPNK* I, 239), as if they could be prized apart, as if in the reality he claims to bring to theory, the tears and the treaties are not inextricably intertwined. Tully does not explain why he approaches the issue this way. For him, these people have a claim to be free and sovereign now not because they have suffered at European hands, though they have, but because they were free and sovereign at the moment of first encounter. Perhaps he believes that claims premised on sovereignty and equality avoid the predicaments of identity politics and wounded attachments.[9] Contextualizing Aboriginal claims in a narrative of sovereignty, mutuality, and equality, Tully dignifies both sides of the conflict. Euro-Canadians are not cast as the heirs of violent dominators and Aboriginals are not merely their victims. But he leaves unaddressed the losses and resentments that also percolate in our politics.

Tully's reasonableness is compelling but it displaces from the realm of politics forces of fantasy, inequality, exploitation, rage, resentment and violence that might bedevil and may even help promote his quest for "justice in a post colonial age" (*PPNK* I, 229). Progressive political victories often depend on both pacifism and protest, reasonable argument and extremism, not just on the former.[10] Moreover, his occupation of the reasonable leaves Tully with little to say to those who claim injustice when the outcome of fair processes goes against them, as it must always do against some of those taking part. We may take some comfort in having accessed open procedures and having been given a fair hearing, but sometimes the sense of injustice is, contra Tully (and Habermas) greater, not lesser, when participation is high and costly. Tully does note the possibility of a "backlash" but he responds by calling for a renewal of the very thing that is both solution and problem: treaty negotiations. When Tully hears Haemon reasoning with his father but does not see the force of the son's later violence against the father; when he champions treaty-making as an intercultural practice of mutuality but does not insist that it also operated as a force of assimilation and conquest (though he cites Taiaiake Alfred on this point); when he insists that alienation can be overcome through participation and not also exacerbated by it; when he claims that "consent can *replace* coercion and conflict" (*PPNK* I, 239, italics added) and goes on to re-narrate the history of European and Aboriginal relations in a way reminiscent of Habermas's own effort to find authorization of his principles in events too complicated to support such claims and which need to be reduced or elevated to what Habermas refers to as their "rational trace,"[11] this agonistic new realist seems to be a bit dazzled by the deliberative ideal.

Either that or Tully has chosen to narrate and emplot in a particular, contestable way. After all, Tully understands all too well the mutual implication of violence and reason in his theoretical chapters (chapters 1–3, volume I); indeed, he insists on it, siding with Foucault against the proclaimed wonders of a power-free Habermasian consensus (e.g. *PPNK* I, 143). So when he recurs to the real in a way that takes full advantage of what we might think as the radical empiricism of Nietzsche, Wittgenstein and Foucault, what is he doing? Stop and look; don't *think*, he says. If we move theory closer to "actual struggles," we will see historical practices of mutuality in colonial relations, and we will see daily practices of freedom today throughout Europe, beneath and alongside forces of modernization, rationalization and globalization. His examples do shake up dominant assumptions about the larger powers that govern and constitute life in late modern (post) colonial democracies. But Tully does not attend to the politics or the essential contestability of the real. He comes closest when he says: "What is needed is neither a theory of the [language] game in question (which is another game with signs) nor an explanation of an underlying structure that determines the play, but a perspicuous representation of the physiognomy of the game itself; what the players do and how they do it" (*PPNK* I, 137). But which representations are perspicuous?

Here Tully is returned to the fact that a great deal of political life involves assessing, judging, or promoting contending representations as perspicuous over others that are not. For example: What were Iranians doing in June, July and then again in December of 2009, when they took to the streets and rooftops of their cities and towns? Protesting against Islamism? Demanding that democratic votes be counted? Irresponsibly destabilizing a legitimate regime? Being modern? Being Persian? Being republican? Being Muslim? Simply describing what they did is part of what Arendt calls storytelling but it also involves selection and genred emplotment, as Hayden White points out. When Tully describes early practices of treaty-making between Aboriginals and settlers as practices of mutuality and recognition out of which current constitutionalism may be seen to arise, he does not merely describe. He emplots and advances a particular perspicuous representation as an essentially contestable contender for historiographic authority and democratic inspiration. But Tully advances that representation as an activist rather than as a theorist. The task of the latter is not merely to advance it, I would argue, but also to highlight its essential contestability.

That said, part of the power of Tully's account is his framing of it as mere (re-) description. He exposes globalization's ongoing resistibility by showing that the alternatives it supposedly destroys still exist. If we fail to see them, that is because our modernist ideologies tell us they are lingering remnants of a premodern past. But they may also be signs of alternative modernities. If some see in them backward economies that need to be made efficient by new markets and incentives, others rightly see in them alternative forms of trade that may bespeak a future not a past. The same practices that look like survivals are cast by Tully as promising new force fields of civic possibility— born of the pressured encounter between global forces and local citizenship, out of which arises something new, something Tully champions as glocal citizenship.

Such possibilities remain even in the context of the grand communicative *habitus* that constitutes late modern life which, Tully argues, "is the characteristic form of subjectivity of network imperialism" (*PPNK* II, 178). Fortunately, this form is just "one (non-omnipotent) form among many that we bear as subjects," Tully says, "and we are not passive recipients of it." In the plurality of our constitutedness and in our resistance to constitution (two key elements of Foucault's project), we find the remaining promise of human freedom. But, Tully concedes in a footnote, "If human consciousness and embodiment are as deeply wired into communication technology as [Arthur] Kroker claims, then the tempered democratic communicative action I recommend ... is too little too late" (*PPNK* II, 177 n. 21). How should we read this concession? As a moment of disarming honesty? It may be. But it is also telling in a different way. For in the very concession of the possible belatedness of his own project, Tully emplots his narrative as a humanistic tale. This is not the rational humanism of sovereign agency celebrated by Enlightenment philosophers. It is the *fingers on the edge of the cliff clinging to some semblance of human life against all odds* humanism of the tragedians, existentialism and some post-humanists. Foucault thought he saw signs of it in Iran in 1979 when Iranians rose up again the Shah and the Savak that terrorized them and before they settled into the theocratic regime that came next. It is the humanism of *the spark of possibility in a world overdetermined by fate or mechanization or other totalizing powers*. Like a realist, Tully sees the expansion of power, governance, violence everywhere, but like a humanist he insists nonetheless on hoping against hope for the human miracle against it. He does not just worship the indomitable human spirit in abstract terms. He tracks the remaining possibilities of freedom in the rifts and fissures of modern subject-constitution. He situates his humanism in a contestatory force field where freedom—a new realist's documentable freedom—endures, against all odds. His humanist emplotment solicits his readers into engagement on freedom's behalf. But as inspired as we must surely be by Tully's narration, we may find ourselves a bit unprepared by him for some aspects of the struggles ahead.

In his acknowledgments, Tully thanks the old forests of the Pacific Northwest for inspiring him with "their magnificent unity in diversity" during a trying time of new imperial aggression. His vision of the trees sustains Tully for political engagement. But it is oddly un-agonistic and ill-attuned to the diverse realities of arboreal life: When plural trees live together in harmony we miss the productivity of an arboreal agonism to which the reasonable, but never only reasonable, Haemon alerts us when he says to his father: "You've seen trees by a raging winter torrent, how many sway with the flood and salvage every twig, but not the stubborn—they're ripped out, roots and all. Bend or break." Haemon's trees demonstrate not what Tully sees in the Pacific Northwest—"a pacific way of being" (which Tully calls for again, citing Gandhi, at the end of Volume II)—but rather an agonistic struggle for life. Tully's trees inspire us with their timeless pacifism but they cannot train us to struggle when that is needful. By contrast, Haemon's trees, just like Haemon himself, do not know how *not* to struggle. Like many of us, they are beset by events, uprooted by storms they never see coming. Haemon's trees teach us to adapt and, if necessary, resist violently when our survival is at stake. Tully's trees might teach Haemon and his heirs how to enter into maturity not just through overt parricide but through contemplation, wisdom, acceptance, indifference or "passing-by" (as Nietzsche called it). That is why we need them both.[12]

Notes

1 This essay's title is from Wittgenstein: we "should call [a game with vagueness in the rules] a game, only we are dazzled by the ideal and therefore fail to see the actual use of the word 'game' clearly" (PI 100 quoted in *PPNK*, I, 140.
2 James Tully, *Strange Multiplicity*, Cambridge: Cambridge University Press, 1995, p. 174.
3 Ibid., p. 23.
4 James Tully, *Public Philosophy in a New Key: Volume I, Democracy and Civic Freedom* and *Public Philosophy in a New Key: Volume II, Imperialism and Civic Freedom*, Cambridge: Cambridge University Press, 2008, hereafter referred to as *PPNK*.

5 On new realism, see Bonnie Honig and Marc Stears, "The New Realism: From Modus Vivendi to Justice," in *History versus Political Philosophy*, eds, Jonathan Floyd and Marc Stears. Cambridge: Cambridge University Press, 2011.
6 I am indebted to Mark Philp on this point. Not just Tully but also Martha Nussbaum and many others focus on Haemon's aptitude for moral reasoning and neglect his violence.
7 For a more detailed account of these themes in the play, see my "Antigone's Two Laws: Greek Tragedy and the Politics of Humanism," *New Literary History* 41(1), 2010, pp. 1–33.
8 Similarly he argues against constitutional democracy, which sets the terrain for democratic activity, and for democratic constitutionalism, in which "the constitution and the democratic [re]negotiation of it are equally basic" (*PPNK* I, 4).
9 On the problem of "wounded attachments," see Wendy Brown, *States of Injury*, Princeton, NJ: Princeton University Press, 1995.
10 On this point, see Marc Stears, *Demanding Democracy*, Princeton, NJ: Princeton University Press, 2010.
11 I discuss in detail Habermas's references to "Paris and Philadelphia" in Chapter 1 of *Emergency Politics*, Princeton, NJ: Princeton University Press, 2009.
12 As well as the anti-arboreal, rhizome perspective advocated by Deleuze, William Connolly, and others.

Part II

In Dialogue with the Past

Chapter 6

Vattel, Internal Colonialism, and the Rights of Indigenous Peoples

Antony Anghie

Introduction

Many of us who style ourselves "post-colonial" scholars, or else, more specifically, adherents to "Third World Approaches to International Law" (TWAIL), feel a particular appreciation for the work of James Tully. Throughout his long and distinguished career, Tully has been exemplary in his concern to understand how the works of the great political theorists of the West, such as Locke, were implicated in the great project of European colonialism, and how many of these scholars, embodiments of cosmopolitan ideals and authors of theories of justice that purported to be universally applicable, served in various complex ways to justify what were essentially imperial projects.[1] The issue of imperialism then, has been central to Tully's work at a number of different levels, ranging from his authoritative scholarship on Locke (which is how, as an undergraduate, I first encountered his writings) to his ongoing concern, from the beginnings of his career, for the rights of Indigenous peoples in his native Canada. Needless to say, these two strands of his work are closely intertwined.

In his pioneering work, *Public Philosophy in a New Key*,[2] James Tully outlines a new approach to thinking about global citizenship and global justice. In advancing this ambitious project he re-conceptualizes the relationship between political theory and praxis, and offers a far-ranging examination of the character and structure of power in a globalized world.

In this chapter I seek to connect two aspects of Tully's work: his long-standing concern with the rights and predicament of Indigenous peoples (which is elaborated in the first volume of *PPNK*); and his exploration of the enduring character of imperialism in the modern international system (which is explored in detail in the second volume). He focuses in particular on the concept of "internal colonization," a category that is crucially important for an understanding of the plight of minorities and Indigenous peoples. In a passage that exemplifies his approach to intellectual history, he asks:

> [...] in what way does Western political theory contribute to the colonization of Indigenous peoples? Western political theories written within the larger

language of political self-understanding and self-reflection of Western societies in general serve either to legitimize or to delegitimize the colonization of Indigenous peoples and their territories (*PPNK* I, 266).

In this chapter I attempt to use Tully's approach to explore the ways in which Emer de Vattel, perhaps more an international lawyer than a political theorist—but the distinction has been, historically, difficult to maintain[3]—contributed to the "colonization of Indigenous peoples." Vattel's great work, *The Law of Nations*, first published in 1758, is arguably the most influential book ever written on the subject of international law.[4] I attempt to place his views on what we now call "Indigenous peoples" within the framework of his broader jurisprudence, and in particular, his writings on colonialism and sovereignty. My interest in Vattel also lies in exploring the connections between his work and contemporary debates about the rights and status of Indigenous peoples. My approach, therefore, is to sketch the outlines of Vattel's jurisprudence, and suggest some of the ways in which his work can be seen as corresponding with, and relevant to, modern debates and issues about Indigenous peoples and colonialism more broadly. These debates have to do, in particular, with issues regarding internal colonization, the different ways in which the non-European world has been conceptualized, and the relationship between development and self-determination in the modern, post-colonial world. It is within this constellation of issues that we might locate the enduring significance of Vattel's work, and the efforts of contemporary international law to challenge and adapt some of the doctrines and principles he was initially so influential in formulating. My further interest lies in suggesting some of the ways in which Tully's analysis, his model of constitutionalism, may contribute to these debates which are to be found, not only in traditional settler colonies such as Canada, the United States and Australia, but in the post-colonial world as well.

Internal colonization, self-determination and Indigenous peoples

For Tully, the concept of "internal colonization" refers to the relationship between established and developed Western societies, and the Indigenous societies that live within the same territories (*PPNK* I, 259). In this chapter, I seek to extend the idea of "internal colonization" to include, in particular, post-colonial states—the states of Africa, Asia and Latin America—which acquired independence by exercising their right to self-determination, and which were then confronted with the challenge of addressing the concerns and demands of minorities and Indigenous peoples within their territory.[5] It is the plight of these peoples—the Indigenous peoples of Central and Latin America and the tribes of India, for instance—that I attempt to explore.[6] Crucial to this task is an understanding of the relationship between sovereignty doctrine, as it has been articulated over the centuries by international lawyers, and Indigenous peoples. The basic problem confronting many

Indigenous peoples is as follows: In its efforts to promote the cause of decolonization in the post-World War period, the United Nations asserted that "peoples had a right to self-determination." The term "people" was never decisively defined, and because of this, hundreds of ethnic communities around the world asserted that they were a "people" entitled to the right to self-determination, the exercise of which would result in their emergence as sovereign states.[7] The new states of Asia and Africa were especially alarmed at this prospect, given the many communities that resided within borders—or sometimes across the borders—that had been drawn by colonial powers. This problem was particularly acute in Africa, as the Berlin Conference of 1884–85, and subsequent treaties between European powers, basically divided up the continent according to European bargains and dictates with no regard to the political and ethnic realities within the continent. Consequently, and somewhat ironically, it was precisely the newly independent African and Asian states who insisted that colonial boundaries were sacrosanct, and that the "people" entitled to self-determination were the "people" who were natives of a particular colonial territory. In this way, it was the "territory" that defined the "people" rather than *vice versa*. Post-colonial states, intent on their own preservation, and extremely mindful of the tragic fate of India where division preceded independence, asserted that "self-determination" was a singular and final event. Once a particular territory became an independent sovereign state, no other entities within that state were entitled to secede by claiming that they too were a "people" and entitled to self-determination. Minorities and indigenous people within a post-colonial state were characterized as lacking any right to secede. International law is essentially conservative, and intent on maintaining the state system and the integrity of the sovereign state. As such, it does not explicitly endorse secession. This situation poses an immense problem to many of these minority and indigenous communities, which argued that they were now subject to a different but equally forceful form of alien rule, this time by the majority community of the new state rather than the previous European colonial power. The claims of indigenous peoples to have a right to self-determination arise directly from this predicament. Indigenous peoples from all parts of the globe have therefore been engaged, over the last several decades, to win recognition and advance their cause under international law. That long campaign culminated in 2007 with the passing, by the General Assembly of the United Nations, of the Declaration of the Rights of Indigenous Peoples. Among the most important of the many important Articles in that Declaration is Article 3, which recognized the right of Indigenous peoples to self-determination.[8]

But the reasons why "Indigenous peoples"[9] have been characterized, almost since their identification as a distinct category in Western legal and political thought, and indeed, by the post-colonial state itself, as lacking sovereignty can be traced back, in important respects, to the work of Vattel and his vision of the Law of Nations.

Emer de Vattel and the Law of Nations

Vattel's role in the formulation of the category that, after various complex transformations, we now call "Indigenous peoples" can only be understood, of course, in the context of his broader vision of imperialism, sovereignty, and the global political order.[10] Any attempt to examine the relationship between Vattel and colonialism is confronted with something of a paradox. His great and profoundly influential work, *The Law of Nations*,[11] does not examine the issue of imperialism in any sustained or comprehensive way, and in this regard it differs from Vitoria's writing on *Des Indis*[12] or Grotius's *The Free Sea*,[13] both of which addressed legal problems arising directly from the expansion of European empires.[14] Vattel's writing, on the other hand, deals only in passing with imperialism. Nevertheless, the passages in which Vattel does explicitly focus on colonial issues have been frequently cited, much commented upon and, indeed, have created ways of thinking and categories of classification that have permanently structured the conceptualization of relations between European and non-European peoples. Vattel is a complex figure because he seems to perceive himself as anti-imperial (like many of his forbears, such as Vitoria) and, indeed, he is powerful in condemning various forms of imperialism. Despite this, his work points to a particular species of colonialism that has a unique character and whose dynamics demand a particular attention.

The passage for which Vattel is perhaps most famous, in relation to colonial issues, needs to be quoted at length:

> The cultivation of the soil deserves the attention of the government, not only on account of the invaluable advantages that flow from it, but from its being an obligation imposed by nature on mankind. The whole earth is destined to feed its inhabitants, but this it would be incapable of doing if it were uncultivated. Every nation is then obliged by the law of nature to cultivate the land that has fallen to its share; and it has no right to enlarge its boundaries, or to have recourse to the assistance of other nations, but in proportion as the land in its possession is incapable of furnishing it with necessaries. Those nations (such as the ancient Germans and some modern Tartars) who inhabit fertile countries but disdain to cultivate their lands, and choose rather to live by plunder, are wanting to themselves, are injurious to all their neighbours, and deserve to be extirpated as savages and pernicious beasts. There are others, who, to avoid labour, choose to live only by hunting and their flocks. This might, doubtless, be allowed in the first ages of the world when the earth, without cultivation, produced more than was sufficient to feed its small number of inhabitants. But at present, when the human race is so greatly multiplied, it could not subsist if all nations were disposed to live in that manner. Those who still pursue this idle mode of life usurp more extensive territories than, with a reasonable share of labour, they would have occasion for, and have, therefore, no reason to complain, if other nations,

more industrious and closely confined, come to take possession of a part of those lands. Thus, although the conquest of the civilized empires of Peru and Mexico was a notorious usurpation, the establishment of many colonies on the continent of North America might, on their confining themselves within just bounds, be extremely lawful. The people of those extensive tracts ranged through rather than inhabited them.[15]

This complex passage occurs in Book I, "Of Nations Considered in Themselves." The preceding chapters in the book broadly consist of discussions of the character, rights and responsibilities of sovereignty and need to be understood in the context of his broader vision of international law, which entails at least an examination of his vision of sovereignty and its relationship to natural law—a natural law which contains the striking principle that people who do not cultivate the soil may be dispossessed of their land—the very land which is the indispensable foundation of sovereignty, as Vattel himself later asserts. It is notable that, in this passage, Vattel seems to identify at least three different forms of nations: nations that "live by plunder" and nations that are not so self-evidently dangerous, but which "choose to live by hunting and their flocks." What these two otherwise very different types of nations have in common is that they do not cultivate the soil. It is especially striking that the former—and the reference to plundering Tartars inevitably invokes images of Mongol hordes and the like—are placed in the same category as the latter, those who pose a threat, not because of their iconically violent behavior, but because they are "idle."[16] Both these types of people have no grounds for complaint if others, "more industrious," take possession of their lands. A third category of peoples, those parts of the "civilized empires of Peru and Mexico," have rights that have been violated by European states—in particular, the Spanish. As this passage alone suggests, Vattel was both imperial and anti-imperial. And it is only by attempting to understand Vattel's broader vision of international law that we might acquire some sense of the peculiar and unique character of Vattel's taxonomy and all that follows from it.

For Vattel, "*The Law of Nations is the science which teaches the rights subsisting between nations or states, and the obligations correspondent to those rights.*"[17] In presenting the relationship between rights and obligations, Vattel elaborates, "We shall examine the Obligations of a people, as well towards themselves as other nations; and by that means we shall discover the *Rights* which result from those obligations."[18] Equally important to Vattel, it is nature that confers these rights among nations, this in order to enable them to perform their duties. Consequently, "We must therefore apply to nations the rules of the law of nature, in order to discover what their obligations are, what their rights: consequently, the law of Nations is originally no other than the law of Nature applied to Nations."[19]

Much of Vattel's work is haunted by the classic tension regarding sovereignty. On the one hand, states are naturally interdependent and must observe the rules that are essential for their coexistence and prosperity; indeed, states cannot fulfill themselves, achieve their goals, without interacting with other states. Whatever the demands of sociability and interdependence, however, the right of self-preservation is central to Vattel's natural law scheme:

> Now all men and all states have a perfect right to those things that are necessary for their preservation, since that right corresponds to an indispensable obligation. All nations have therefore a right to resort to forcible means for the purpose of repressing any one particular nation who openly violates the laws of the society which Nature has established between them, or who directly attacks the welfare and safety of that society.[20]

The implications of this passage are disconcerting, for if sovereigns have a completely unchecked right to judge what is "necessary for their preservation" and to "resort to forcible means" to ensure this, then powerful states which, for whatever reason, suffer from profound insecurities are granted an enormous degree of latitude to resort to force. At the same time, Vattel attempts to establish some element of balance in the scheme, by suggesting that the wrong committed—albeit, presumably, against a particular state—must be a wrong against "the laws of society," a larger entity than a single nation.[21]

It is notable, furthermore, that Vattel characterizes the right to use force against a state that violates the laws of Nations as something akin to a right *erga omnes*; that is, it would seem that *any* state can use force against an offender of the fundamental rules of society, even if the state using force has not itself been directly injured by the offending act. Vattel had previously condemned Grotius for giving states license to use force to remedy a wrong against natural law, pointing to the ways in which the Grotian position may be used as a justification for imperialism. In a passage notable for its anti-imperial attitude and its critical approach to intervention in the name of civilization, Vattel argues:

> But though a nation may be obliged to promote, as far as lies in its power, the perfection of others, it is not entitled forcibly to obtrude these good offices on them. Such an attempt would be a violation of their natural liberty. In order to compel any one to receive a kindness, we must have authority over him; but nations are absolutely free and independent. Those ambitious Europeans who attacked the American nations, and subjected them to their greedy dominion, in order, as they pretended, to civilize them, and cause them to be instructed in the true religion—those usurpers, I say, grounded themselves on a pretext equally unjust and ridiculous. It is strange to hear the learned Grotius assert that a sovereign may justly take up arms and chastise nations which are guilty of enormous transgressions of the laws of nature, *which treat their parents with inhumanity like the Sogdians which eat human flesh as the ancient Gauls &c.* What led him into this error, was, his attributing to every sovereign, an odd kind of right to punish faults which involve an enormous violation of the laws of nature, though they do not affect either his rights or his safety. But we have shewn […] that men derive the right of punishment solely from their

right to provide for their own safety; and consequently they cannot claim it except against those by whom they have been injured. Could it escape Grotius, that notwithstanding all the precautions added by him in the following paragraphs, his opinions open a door to all the ravages of enthusiasm and fanaticism, and furnishes ambition with numberless pretexts. Mahomet and his successors have desolated and subdued Asia to avenge the indignity done to the unity of the Godhead; all of whom they termed associators or idolators fell victim to their devout fury.[22]

This passage is striking for its denunciation of imperialism and its clear recognition of the manner in which principles of natural law and punishment may be abused to justify conquest in the name of civilization and an abstract idea of injury. Further, Vattel seeks to distinguish himself from Grotius and what he regards as a dangerous principle that would justify the use of force in a number of circumstances. Interestingly, Vattel points to the manner in which the principle has been abused by both Christian and Islamic states. Vattel sees himself instead as confining the recourse to force by granting the right to use force only to those who have been injured, rather than providing a right for all parties seeking to remedy a violation committed to some principle of natural law. Nevertheless, of course, the effect of such a limitation depends on his definition of an "injury"; and, since he argues that any act which threatens a nation's right to self-preservation justifies force, his attempt at restricting the use of force appears fragile. Whereas Grotius outlines a number of principles whose violation may justify the resort to war,[23] Vattel instead seems to provide sovereign states which are accountable only to their own conscience and that have complete freedom to make their own judgments, a broad discretion to use force in an effort to exercise their right of self-preservation, a right which only they can assess for themselves. It is uncertain as to whether Vattel's approach is more or less effective in confining the use of force than Grotius's. It is arguable that Vattel expands enormously the right to use force by adopting this approach, as opposed to the narrower approach which prescribes that a state can only take action against another state when the latter state's actions have directly violated the rights of the victim state. It is understandable, then, that Vattel could be seen as being more akin to Grotius than he would at first appear. Kant's famous denunciation, which includes Vattel together with Grotius and Pufendorff, in his illustrious list of "sorry comforters," "who are still dutifully quoted in justification of military aggression," appears completely justified.[24]

Vattel, colonialism and economic sovereignty

It is against this background of Vattel's broader vision of international law, of the rights of the sovereign and its obligations to the international community, that Vattel's famous passages on colonialism must be examined. The crucial question becomes, in the context of his overall jurisprudence: what is essential for self-preservation, and what are the international rules, according to Vattel, that regulate this question? The issue is vital, as a violation of such rules justifies dispossession and even war. My argument here is that Vattel's particular vision of imperialism is best understood, not only in terms of the classical issue of conquest and war (Vitoria asserts, for instance, that the Spanish rule over the Indies can be best understood in terms of doctrines of war) but equally prominently, and originally, in terms of his vision of commerce and its role in the international system. He elaborates on this system by providing some analytic principles that illuminate his distinctive approach to colonial issues.[25] The importance of the concept of commerce in Vattel's work has been widely recognized.[26]

In a searching examination of Vattel's attempt to resolve the tension between sociability and interdependence, and sovereign independence, Isaac Nakhimovsky presents a detailed argument about how this is managed through Vattel's vision of the balance of power as best achieved "through a process of commercial preferences and restrictions."[27] As a consequence of this vision, Nakhimovsky argues, "Vattel held out the hope that a great power could be brought down to size justly and peacefully through trade wars and trading blocs rather than land wars and military alliances."[28] Vattel's vision of international law and the international system, then, saw commerce as an alternative to force and conquest. This was a powerful argument that was espoused by many other thinkers of the time, including Adam Smith, Kant and Ricardo.[29]

My argument is that Vattel's ideas of relations between European and non-European peoples is similarly informed by a vision of commerce—a vision that encompasses not only trade, production and other such economic activities, but foundational ideas of property and possession. Commerce could take place between nations only after those nations had properly come into existence; and, for this it was necessary for a "nation" to take possession of the land.

What is striking about Vattel's approach to non-settler peoples is the distinction he makes between conquest—which he condemns several times—and the dispossession of native peoples, which he characterizes as somehow belonging to a different logic and system of order. Conquest is illegal, but "dispossession" has a different character because, Vattel later suggests, it is not even dispossession because the natives did not properly own the land in any event. He argues in relation to nomadic nations that, "Their unsettled habitation in those immense regions cannot be accounted a true and legal possession."[30]

Vattel's idea of "self-preservation" is intimately connected, of course, with his foundational concept of sovereignty. The entirety of Book I is concerned with the issue "Of Nations Considered in Themselves." Here, Vattel considers a series of broad issues including "General Principles of the Duties of a Nation Towards Herself," the character of National Constitutions, the rights and obligations of the sovereign ("he ought to know the nation"), and the different types of states ("elective, successive, hereditary"). Chapter VI of Book I deals more broadly with the Principal Objects of good government—that being to "provide for the Necessities of the Nation." What is quite prominent in the transitions that take place in Vattel's lengthy analysis of the characteristics of states is its shift from the legal and constitutional discussion of sovereignty, to an elaboration of the sovereign as an economic actor, and the legal implications that follow from this. In this respect, Vattel's work is far more developed and comprehensive than, for instance, the work of Vitoria or Grotius. What is also quite remarkable about this part of Vattel's work is that it operates on the powerful and sweeping assumption—all the more powerful because it seems to be so unquestioningly assumed—that even the most intimate details of a state's political and economic practices are properly subject to the scrutiny of international law, natural law. In this respect, Vattel is still very much closer to Vitoria than the jurists of the nineteenth century, who made a sharp distinction between internal and external sovereignty, the former being completely excluded from the operations of international law.

Vattel's emphasis on the economic dimensions of sovereignty are evident from the fact that, for him, the principal object of government is to "provide for the necessities of the nation."[31] This entails for instance, rewarding workmen, promoting industries, and preventing useful workmen from leaving the country.[32] Further, and very importantly, it involves "cultivating the soil": "Of all the arts, tillage or agriculture, is doubtless, the most useful and necessary, as being the source when the nation derives its subsistence. The cultivation of the soil causes it to produce an infinite increase; it forms the surest resource, and the most solid fund of riches and commerce, for a nation that enjoys a happy climate."[33] Having provided a detailed set of principles relating to agriculture, Vattel's attention then turns to commerce, both domestic and foreign. Once again, he approaches this issue by focusing on what a nation needs in order to survive and flourish: "For the same reason, drawn from the welfare of the state and also to procure for the citizens every thing they want, a nation is obliged to promote and to carry on foreign trade."[34] Included among the laws of nature applicable to trade is Vattel's argument, which appears quite incongruous given his reputation as a promoter of commerce,[35] that the curtailment of trade is legal. While acknowledging all the virtues of trade, Vattel—in complete contrast to scholars such as Vitoria and Grotius—argues emphatically that no state has a right of "selling" and that "Every state has consequently a right to prohibit the entrance of foreign *merchandize*; and the nations that are affected have no right to complain of it; as if they had been refused an office of humanity."[36] Grotius, by contrast, argued that the right to trade was something akin to a *jus cogens*.[37] For Vattel, the right to buy something is an imperfect right in that the prospective buyer cannot compel the prospective seller to part with his goods. Vattel asserts that in general a nation should sell, at a fair price, the goods of which it has no use. While acknowledging that nations can by treaty create among themselves rights to trade, however, Vattel makes it clear that lacking any such treaty, foreigners are allowed to trade only at the discretion of the host sovereign.[38] Significantly, furthermore, Vattel asserts that:

> If one nation finds herself in such circumstances, that she thinks foreign commerce dangerous to the state, she may renounce and prohibit it. This the Chinese have done for a long time together. But again, it is only for very serious

and important reasons that her duty to herself should dictate such a reserve; otherwise, she could not refuse to comply with the general duties of humanity.[39]

The passage is remarkable—given the events that led to the Opium Wars and the Treaty of Nanking that followed—in upholding, in however qualified a form, the basic Chinese position. What is equally remarkable, if this passage is to be contrasted with nineteenth-century writers such as Westlake, is the completely natural and unproblematic way in which China is understood to be a member of the "family of nations." This, then, is the period in which Asian states were treated as equal, at least legally, and which has led authorities such as Alexandrowicz to reflect nostalgically on the golden era of naturalism, before nineteenth-century positivism justified the most blatant imperialist aggression.[40]

This concept of commerce, then, is sensitive to the needs of sovereignty, and a sovereign state can properly refuse to engage in trade precisely in order to maintain its own independence. For Grotius, sovereigns were subject to the right to trade; for Vattel, the issue of production was so central that nations which failed in their duties to cultivate the soil could be seen as violating a perfect right, causing real injury to other nations.[41] This enormous emphasis on having a general duty to produce seems startling; it is more than simply saying that the land was not really in anyone's possession.

It is in his passages on the cultivation of the soil, however, that Vattel's arguments have had particular far-reaching consequences. Vattel's insistence on the use of land to its maximum advantage, led him to formulate a number of rules. Importantly, Vattel's pre-occupation with this principle extends well beyond its significance for imperial expansion. A sovereign could not allow large plots of land to remain uncultivated; laws that prevented the owners from making maximum use of their land for cultivation were "inimical to the welfare of the state, and ought to be suppressed, or reduced to just bounds."[42] Vattel's argument about maximization, indeed, went so far as to prevail even against property rights.[43] Further, he criticizes the states where the profession of agriculture is disdained by industry and singles out China for having preserved the dignity of agriculture: "Hence China is the best cultivated country in the world; it feeds an immense multitude of inhabitants who at first sight appear to the traveler too numerous for the space they occupy."[44] But if the whole point of this regime was to provide for everyone on earth, then it must surely be accompanied by some theory of re-distribution by which rich nations are under an obligation to provide for poor nations. Vattel offers no such developed theory. Rather, it seems the most that can be done is to urge the sovereign to remember its broader international duties that are still not international obligations.

Vattel elaborates on his views on the relationship between agriculture and sovereignty:

> We have already observed (#81), in establishing the obligation to cultivate the earth, that those nations cannot exclusively appropriate to themselves

more land than they have occasion for, or more than they are able to settle and cultivate. Their unsettled habitation in those immense regions cannot be accounted a true and legal possession; and the people of Europe, too closely pent up at home, finding land of which the savage stood in no particular need, and of which they made no actual and constant use, were lawfully entitled to take possession of it and settle it with colonies. The earth, as we have already observed, belongs to mankind in general, and was designed to furnish them with subsistence: if each nation had, from the beginning, resolved to appropriate to itself a vast country, that the people might live only by hunting, fishing, and wild fruits, our globe would not be sufficient to maintain a tenth part of its present inhabitants. We do not, therefore, deviate from the views of nature in confining the Indians within narrower limits. However, we cannot help praising the moderation of the English puritans who first settled in New England; who, notwithstanding their being furnished with a charter from their sovereign, purchased of the Indians the land of which they intended to take possession. This laudable example was followed by William Penn, and the colony of quakers that he conducted to Pennsylvania.[45]

For Vattel, the criticism of these "wandering tribes" appears twofold: first, they offend against natural laws that prescribe the cultivation of the land; secondly, in any event, unless they cultivate the land, they are not in possession of it. This means, of course, that this land may be properly appropriated by other societies; and, for Vattel it was inevitable that "those [wandering] tribes should fix themselves somewhere and appropriate to themselves portions of land in order that they might … apply themselves to render those lands fertile, and thence derive their subsistence."[46] As Sankar Muthu points out, in this regard, Vattel belonged to a group of European thinkers who based their idea of society and legal personality on the practices of agriculture by those societies.[47]

The idea that native people who did not properly use their territory could be dispossessed of it was also developed, among international lawyers such as Grotius, as Richard Tuck points out.[48] Further, Vattel's work reproduces many of the ideas of John Locke for his own ideas of political society and sovereignty. If, as in the case of Locke's arguments, only those peoples who engaged in agriculture constituted a "political society"[49]; and, further, if only particular forms of land use—agriculture—gave people unassailable rights to their land, then those peoples who differed from these norms were vulnerable to dispossession.[50] This process of dispossessing these peoples from their lands, of course, was one aspect of the larger phenomenon of "primitive accumulation."[51]

Vattel and the historical characterization of non-European societies

As I have argued elsewhere, the characterization of non-European peoples by European jurists has played a crucial role in the formulation of doctrines by those jurists and European states that have been devised to account for relations between the European and non-European worlds. Thus, in his seminal lecture, *On the Indians Lately Discovered*, the sixteenth-century jurist and theologian, Francisco de Vitoria, examined the validity of Spanish claims to the New World by considering the Indians to be, variously, slaves, inanimate objects, animals, children, or human beings. Vitoria considered the Indians to be human beings who were bound by a universal natural law. Crucially, furthermore, he argued that they had a right to property that had to be respected by the Spanish. Further, the existence of such a right was intimately connected with the recognition of Indians as being human. Interestingly, he also asserted that even heretics had a right to property, thus suggesting that the Pope's jurisdiction—a crucial issue at this time—did not extend over issues of property in this setting. Importantly, however, Vitoria provides no theory as to how the Indians acquired rights over property.

By the time of the late nineteenth century, the apogee of imperialism, European international lawyers propounded a stark division between civilized and non-civilized states. The division was based on the basic premise that European culture and institutions were definitively superior and in a nominal sense universal—it was the culture that all other cultures were striving to become. Furthermore, civilized states were deemed to be sovereign and uncivilized states lacked sovereignty. Consequently, these uncivilized states lacked legal personality in international law and were unable to participate in the international system. The distinction between civilized and uncivilized states, however, was easier to assert than maintain. Thus, even in the nineteenth century, African and Asian societies were opportunistically deemed to be "quasi-sovereign"—this in order to validate treaties entered into between these societies and European states. Further, African societies were sometimes characterized as "primitive" whereas Asian societies were characterized as "civilized" in their own fashion, but uncivilized in that they were different from Western societies. By the time of the United Nations, this distinction between civilized and uncivilized was abolished as racist.

It is as seen against this background that Vattel's view of non-European societies is illuminating. Significantly, he makes no distinction between "civilized" and "uncivilized" states. Indeed, he presents China as a model state, whereas by the nineteenth century, China was dismissed as "uncivilized." It is in this respect that he can be thought of as being anti-imperial. Importantly, however, the crucial distinctions he makes do not involve so explicitly the categories of race and culture—which nineteenth-century international law relied upon—but instead, the concepts of commerce and economy. These, indeed, were the forces that drove imperialism in the nineteenth century. The East India Company, beginning as a purely commercial venture, which purported to repudiate imperial rule, became itself a conquering power. Imperial rule took place, not only through explicit colonial annexation, but through "indirect rule," which involved effectively controlling native leaders, and insisting on the enforcement of unequal treaties which provided European trading companies with enormous benefits for which they had to give little in return. As Tully puts it when describing the character of "imperial right":

the imperial right of European states and their companies to trade freely in non-European societies and the duty to civilize non-European peoples, together with the correlative duty of hospitality of non-European peoples to open themselves to trade and civilization (*PPNK* II, 210).

If native peoples resisted, they would be compelled by European force to comply with these imperatives, through colonization if necessary. This is the broad and powerful framework established by numerous prominent political theorists, against which we might better understand Vattel's assertion that certain fundamental economic "natural laws" relating to agriculture and production must be adhered to, and societies that do not comply can be properly sanctioned. My broad argument here is that while the international system has abolished the racial and cultural divisions that structured international law for many centuries, economic distinctions still play an important role at a number of different levels of the international system. The division of the world according to economic rather than cultural terms became more prominent in the time of the League of Nations. The Mandate system, created by the League to protect the inhabitants of former German and Ottoman territories, made a distinction between "advanced" and "backward" societies, a distinction that was elaborated and developed using economic criteria. Indeed, in many ways, the Mandate system's concerted attempt to make native labor more productive was directed at remedying the entity that Vattel had so powerfully condemned—the lazy native who failed to make his land more fruitful.[52] The distinction between "advanced" and "backward" societies became further entrenched, particularly in the period immediately following the creation of the United Nations, as the division between the "developed" and the "developing." The idea of "development," which rendered all the social, political and cultural realities of a society in economic terms, was gradually elaborated, in the international sphere by the Mandate system of the League of Nations. What is especially ironic here is that it was the newly independent states, the former colonized territories themselves that completely internalized the division between advanced and backward, developed and developing, even as they vehemently rejected any remaining suggestion of civilizational inferiority. Indeed, the newly independent states of Asia and Africa were so preoccupied with the issue of development that they called themselves "developing states" and proceeded, both in their external and internal policies, to do everything they could to promote economic development. Indeed, what is notable is that both "socialist" and "capitalist" developing countries, whatever their other profound differences, whether adherents to "dependency theory" or "modernization theory," both regarded the achievement of economic development as the defining, fundamental task of the newly emergent nations.

In the international legal and institutional sphere, this resulted in the creation of a complex and comprehensive body of law that could be broadly called "the law of development" on the one hand, while international economic institutions such as the World Bank made the furtherance of development one of its principal goals.

Simply and crudely put, then, the post-colonial states basically reproduced in their own way the system of thought, the operating distinctions, that Vattel had so powerfully articulated in the eighteenth century. The "development state" resembled the more primordial "economic state" that Vattel had been intent on elaborating.[53] The policies of the "development state" have been, on the whole, profoundly detrimental to the Indigenous peoples, as their vision of the land as a part of their being has not been able to resist easily the demands of economic development. To the extent that development is understood to require dams, roads, and other massive infrastructure projects, it is very often the peasants, and Indigenous and tribal peoples whose traditional lifestyles have been massively disrupted—as suggested, for example, by the dislocation and furor surrounding the building of the Narmada dam in India.[54] Vattel's arguments about the right to dispossess societies that did not practice agriculture powerfully and directly justified the actions of settler societies in the late eighteenth century and early nineteenth century. But his conceptualization of the distinction between economic development and Indigenous peoples is replicated at a number of levels by post-colonial states themselves; this, combined with the reluctance of international law to prohibit secession, has placed Indigenous peoples in a precarious and difficult position.

I have argued that Vattel's approach to imperialism is dual; he condemns the imperialism that Grotius justified—while justifying, in essence, what might be called "settler colonialism." But the significance of his ideas endures. Formerly colonized states themselves have in some ways adopted the same classifications and structures of thought articulated by Vattel. Vattel's insistence that land must be made productive has corresponded with the drive of many of these post-colonial states to achieve "development"; and it is in the name of development that Indigenous and tribal peoples, invariably characterized as backward and ignorant, have been deprived, systematically, of their lands. While Canada, Australia, New Zealand and the United States were notorious for their opposition to the Declaration on Indigenous Peoples, Asian and African states have in their own different ways hindered the furtherance of the rights of Indigenous peoples. Asian states have denied the existence of "Indigenous peoples" within their territories. African states have contested the meaning of the term "Indigenous peoples" and have treated Indigenous peoples in ways that disconcertingly resemble the treatment meted out to these peoples by colonial powers.[55] Once again, furthermore, it is the land rights of these people that are most clearly endangered, as their dispossession now continues under the auspices of the post-colonial state itself.[56] Encouragingly, however, after numerous consultations and negotiations, an overwhelming majority of African states accepted the Declaration on the Rights of Indigenous Peoples.[57] Further, institutions within the post-colonial world have handed down decisions, which recognize the land rights of Indigenous peoples— the *Awas Tingi* Case handed down by the Inter-American Court of Human Rights being among the most significant.[58]

The negation of the legal personality of what we might now term "Indigenous peoples" is one of the most enduring aspects of Vattel's thinking on colonial matters. Thus it is hardly surprising that many eminent scholars in the field of Indigenous peoples have discussed his ideas. Understandably, furthermore, one of the central—and most controversial—aspects of the Declaration of the Rights of Indigenous Peoples had to do precisely with their recognition as "peoples" and their corresponding right, under international law, to self-determination.[59] Developments in the concept of self-determination, furthermore, have meant that self-determination is conceptualized not as secession alone, but in terms of "internal self-determination"—that is, some form of autonomy or effective participation within the sphere of government that would enable Indigenous peoples to protect their rights. In writing of the relationship between the Aboriginal peoples of Canada and non-Aboriginal peoples, Tully asserts:

> Once mutual recognition is achieved, they engage in intercultural negotiations with the aim of reaching agreements on how they will address past injustices and associate together in the future (*PPNK* I, 229).

It is precisely this development, the legal recognition of the personality of Indigenous peoples implied by the Declaration of the Rights of Indigenous Peoples that may lead to a similar situation globally, one in which Indigenous peoples may engage meaningfully in protecting their own rights and determining their own future. This is an especially important task given the combination of factors that have now served to reproduce, in various ways, Vattel's animating obsession regarding scarcity and land. The legitimacy of many developing states, including India and China in particular, depends most notably on the achievement of economic growth rates. It is understandable then, that Indigenous peoples themselves have adopted the rhetoric of development—and assert their right to development as an essential aspect of self-determination.[60]

But these governments are now confronted with a new and powerful challenge that has emerged as a result of rising food prices and the fusion of energy and agricultural markets. A recent World Bank report notes that the 2007–08 boom in food prices has led to a "'rediscovery' of the agricultural sector by different types of investors and a wave of interest in land acquisitions in developing countries."[61] This has led to the dramatic emergence of issues of food security, and a drive to secure resources that has led some observers to assert that there is now occurring a second "Scramble for Africa." Almost inevitably, it is the small land-holding peasants and Indigenous peoples of Africa and other developing countries that have suffered most prominently as a result of the return, in this new and formidable manner, of Vattel's preoccupation with scarcity, agriculture and the uses of land.[62] It is especially disquieting and yet instructive that a modern version of Vattel's preoccupations are now being furthered by many developing countries which previously had been victims of the dispossessions resulting from them. It is these governments, working with various international actors such as sovereign wealth funds and large corporations, that are now dispossessing their own peoples—often using the argument of "increasing productivity" to justify such actions.[63]

It is in this setting then, that James Tully's far-reaching analysis of modern forms of imperialism, and ethical approaches to the resolution of these fundamental problems—these are the preoccupations of the closing chapters of volume 1—may contribute in vital ways to debates which are now taking place, not only in traditional settler societies such as Canada, the United States and Australia, but now, in this new dispensation, the post-colonial world, which engages in its own forms of internal colonialism.

Notes

1 For a recent important assessment of the relationship between contemporary political theory and Empire, see Jennifer Pitts. Interestingly, Pitts notes that "Political theory has come slowly and late to the study of empire, relative to other disciplines." See Jennifer Pitts, "Political Theory of Empire and Imperialism," *Annual Review of Political Science* 13, 2010, pp. 211–35, at p. 212.
2 James Tully, *Public Philosophy in a New Key: Volume I, Democracy and Civic Freedom* and *Public Philosophy in a New Key: Volume II, Imperialism and Civic Freedom*, Cambridge: Cambridge University Press, 2008, hereafter referred to as *PPNK*.
3 Richard Tuck, for instance, includes Vattel in his discussion of the rights of war and peace: *The Rights of War and Peace: Political Thought and the International Order from Grotius to Kant*, Oxford: Oxford University Press, 1999. Tully's own definition of "political theory" is equally capacious as it includes "political, legal and social theories, and reasoned legal decisions and legislative and policy documents written …" (*PPNK* I, 258). Further, this political theory is "the language of both political self-understanding and self-reflection of these societies and their non-Indigenous members … It is not the self-understanding and self-reflection of Indigenous peoples, even though they are constrained to use it" (*PPNK* I, 258).
4 For instance, both Franklin and Jefferson read Vattel very closely—his work acted as an important guide to a new sovereign state intent on establishing itself in the international system. See David Armitage, *The Declaration of Independence*, Cambridge, MA: Harvard University Press, 2007.
5 Many Asian countries attempt to resolve the issue by denying the existence of "indigenous peoples" within their territories. See Benedict Kingsbury, "Indigenous Peoples in International Law: A Constructivist Approach to the Asian Controversy," *Am.J.I.L.* 92, 1998, pp. 414–47, at pp. 417–18.
6 See e.g. Gerardo J. Munarriz, "Rhetoric and Reality: The World Bank Development Policies, Mining Corporations and Indigenous Communities in Latin America," *International Community Law Review* 10, 2008, pp. 431–43. The indigenous peoples of Peru and Guatemala have suffered massively and disproportionately in the civil wars that afflicted those countries.
7 It was for this reason that Woodrow Wilson, who was in many ways the champion of the modern doctrine of self-determination, was criticized by many, including his own colleagues and lawyers.
8 *United Nations Declaration on the Rights of Indigenous Peoples*, GA Resolution 61/295, 13 September 2007. Article 3 states: "Indigenous peoples have the right to self-determination. By virtue of that right they freely determine their political status and freely pursue their economic, social and cultural development." It should be noted that the Declaration does not create binding legal obligations.
9 There is no strict, legally binding definition of the term "Indigenous peoples" in international law. A definition that has been widely accepted, however, is provided by Jose

Martinez Cobo, who was appointed Special Rapporteur of a United Nations study of discrimination against Indigenous peoples. Cobo used a "working definition" of Indigenous peoples defined as:

> Those which, having a historical continuity with pre-invasion and pre-colonial societies...[who] consider themselves distinct from other sectors of the societies now prevailing in those territories, or parts of them. They form at present non-dominant sectors of society and are determined to preserve, develop and transmit to future generations their ancestral territories, and their ethnic identity, as the basis of their continued existence as a people, in accordance with their own cultural patterns, social institutions and legal systems.

Jose Martinez Cobo, Special Rapporteur, *Study of the Problem of Discrimination Against Indigenous Populations—Volume 5: Conclusions, Proposals and Recommendations*, UN Doc E/CN.4/Sub.2/1986/7/Add.4 (March 1987).

10 Here I draw upon an earlier essay on Vattel, Antony Anghie, "Vattel and Colonialism: Some Preliminary Observations," in *Vattel's International Law in a XXIst Century Perspective*, eds, Vincent Chetail and Peter Haggenmacher, Leiden: Martinus Nijhoff, 2011, pp. 237–55.
11 Emer de Vattel, *The Law of Nations* or *"Principles of the Law of Nature Applied to the Conduct of Nations and Sovereigns,"* trans. Joseph Chitty (Sixth American Edition), Oxford: Oxford University Press, 1844 [1758].
12 Francisco de Vitoria, *De Indis et de Ivre Belli Relectiones*, ed. Ernest Nys, trans. John Pawley Bate, Washington DC: Carnegie Institute of International Law, 1916.
13 Hugo Grotius, *The Free Sea*, ed. David Armitage, Indianapolis, IN: Liberty Fund Publications, 2004.
14 Recent scholarship has shown, furthermore, how much this early writing influenced the great work for which Grotius is best known, *The Rights of War and Peace*, Indianapolis, IN: Liberty Fund Publications, 2005. See Edward Keene; and, Richard Tuck.
15 Vattel, Bk. I. VII #81
16 For a detailed study of the economy of these types of peoples, see Marshall Sahlins, *Stone Age Economics*, London: Tavistock Publications, 1972, esp. Ch. 1.
17 Vattel, Preliminaries, #3 (italics in original).
18 Vattel, Preliminaries, #3; further, "since rights arises from obligation, as we have just observed, the nation possesses also the same rights which nature has conferred among men in order to perform their duties", Preliminaries, #5.
19 Vattel, Preliminaries, #5.
20 Vattel, Preliminaries, #22. I attempt to explore Vattel's concept of "perfect right" in Antony Anghie, "Vattel and Colonialism: Some Preliminary Inquiries."
21 On the whole, Vattel uses the terms "state" and "nation" interchangeably.
22 Vattel, Book II, Ch. 1 #7.
23 See particularly, Hugo Grotius, *The Rights of War and Peace*, Book II, pp. 389–918.
24 Kant, "Perpetual Peace," in *Kant: Political Writings*, ed. Hans Reiss, Cambridge: Cambridge University Press, 1991, p. 103.
25 For a superb study of the role of commerce in the thinking of Grotius, see Ileana Porras, "Constructing International Law in the East Indian Seas: Property, Sovereignty, Commerce and War in Hogu Grotius' de Iure Praedae—The Law of Prize and Booty, or on How to Distinguish Merchants from Pirates," *Brooklyn Journal of International Law*, Vol. 31, Issue 3 (2006): 741–804.
26 See Benedict Kingsbury and Benjamin Strauman, "The State of Nature and Commercial Sociability in Early Modern Thought," *New York University Public Law and Legal Theory Working Papers* (2011), Paper 258.
27 Isaac Nakhimovsky, "Vattel's Theory of the International Order: Commerce and the

Balance of Power in the Law of Nations," *History of European Ideas* 33, 2007, pp. 157–73, at p. 159.
28 Ibid., p. 165.
29 For an overview of this theme in Western political theory, see Brett Bowden, *The Empire of Civilization: The Evolution of an Imperial Ideal*, Chicago: University of Chicago Press, 2009, pp. 83–6. For a sharp rejoinder to this theory, see for instance, Ileana Porras, op cit., p. 25.
30 Vattel, I, XVIII, 209.
31 Vattel, Book I, Chapter VI; by contrast, the issue of self-defense, the major preoccupation of Grotius and others—understandably, given the contexts in which they wrote—is relegated to Chapter XIV. On these issues, see F.S. Ruddy, *International Law in the Enlightenment: The Background of Emmerich de Vattel's Le Droit des Gens*, New York: Oceana Publications, 1975, esp. Ch. 5.
32 Vattel, Book I, Ch. VI, #74–6.
33 Vattel, Book I, Ch. VII, #77.
34 Vattel, Bk I Ch. 9, #87.
35 See generally, F.S. Ruddy, pp.176–8.
36 Vattel, Bk I Ch. 9, #90.
37 At least in the free sea, see Hugo Grotius, *The Free Sea*, p. 11.
38 "… if one nation has for a time permitted another to come and trade in the country, she is at liberty, whenever she thinks proper, to prohibit that commerce—to restrain it—to subject it to certain regulations; and the people who before carried it on cannot complain of injustice." Vattel, Bk I, Ch. 9, #94.
39 Vattel, Book I, Ch. 9, #94. Similarly, Kant affirmed and approved the same Chinese practice.
40 C.H. Alexandrowicz, *An Introduction to the History of the Law of Nations in the East Indies*, Oxford: Clarendon Press, 1967.
41 It is not clear as to what rights states could exercise against recognizably "civilized" Western states that, while possessing all the institutions necessary to satisfy Vattel's idea of a proper state, still do not make the most productive use of their lands.
42 Vattel, Book I, Ch. VII, #78
43 "Notwithstanding the introduction of private property among the citizens, the nation still has a right to take the most effectual measures to cause the aggregate soil of the country to produce the greatest and most advantageous revenue possible." Vattel, Book I, Ch. VII, #78.
44 Vattel, Book I, Ch. VII, #80.
45 Vattel, Book I, Ch. XVIII, # 209.
46 Vattel, Book I, Ch. XVIII, #203.
47 See Sankar Muthu, *Enlightenment Against Empire*, Princeton, NJ: Princeton University Press, 2003, pp. 276–7. Muthu's work is valuable in pointing to the anti-imperial dimensions of thinkers such as Kant, Herder and Diderot, who questioned whether it was possible to make the sorts of cross-cultural judgments that play such a crucial role in Vattel's thinking. See Muthu, op. cit. Muthu argues that while these thinkers believed in moral universalism, on the one hand, they also recognize the existence of "culturally varying norms, practices and institutions, on the other, as complexly intertwined" (Muthu, 278). As Muthu points out, however, this way of thinking was a "marginalized philosophical viewpoint" by the 1830s.
48 See Tuck, esp. Ch. 3. Grotius's ideas about property were profoundly shaped by his role as lawyer for the Dutch East India Company, and, in particular, his concern to establish the status of "The Free Sea," Tuck, pp. 90 ff.
49 I am here indebted to the work of James Tully, *An Approach to Political Philosophy: Locke in Contexts*, esp. Ch. 5, "Rediscovering America: The Two Treatises and Aboriginal Rights," Cambridge: Cambridge University Press, 1993.

50 See Tully, pp. 138–43.
51 Referring to various imperial atrocities, the Spanish conquest of America, the looting of the East Indies and the exploitation of Africa, Marx sarcastically asserts "These idyllic proceedings are the chief momenta of primitive accumulation," Marx, *Capital*, Vol. 1, Ch. 31. As Tully notes, "Approximately 80 per cent of the Indigenous population, which was larger than Europe's in 1492, was exterminated by 1900" (*PPNK* II, 211).
52 While praising America and the manner in which Indian lands were acquired through treaty rather than brute force, Vattel fails to make any mention of the fact that American prosperity was achieved principally through slave labor.
53 It is notable, however, that Vattel did not have a clearly formulated set of ideas regarding "stages of economic development," the broad structure that is such a powerful feature of thinkers of political economy as diverse as Adam Smith and Karl Marx and Walt Rostow. Further, while Vattel wrote on the virtues of commerce broadly, he focused particularly intensely on the importance of agriculture—and had far less to say on issues such as manufacturing, a marked contrast with Smith.
54 See e.g. Balakrishnan Rajagopal, "The Role of Law in Counterhegemonic Globalization and Global Pluralism: The Case of the Narmada Valley Struggle in India," *Leiden Journal of International Law* 18, 2005, 345–87.
55 See Willem van Genugten, "Protection of Indigenous Peoples on the African Continent: Concepts, Position Seeking and the Interaction of Legal Systems," *Am.J.I.L* 104(1), 2010, pp. 29–65, at p. 30.
56 Genugten, citing the African Commission of Human Rights, "Dispossession of land and natural resources is a major human rights problem for indigenous peoples. They have in so many cases been pushed out of their traditional areas to give way for the economic interests of other more dominant groups and large-scale development initiatives that tend to destroy their lives and cultures rather than improve their situation," Genugten, p. 33.
57 Three African states abstained: Burundi, Kenya and Nigeria, Genugten, p. 48. Nigeria expressed its concern that the Declaration could be interpreted in ways that would interfere with national development policy.
58 *The Mayagna (Sumo) Awas Tingni Community v. Nicaragua*. This case and its importance is extensively discussed in S. James Anaya, *International Human Rights and Indigenous Peoples*, New York: Wolters Kluwer [Aspen Publishers], 2009, pp. 264 ff.
59 *United Nations Declaration on the Rights of Indigenous Peoples*, GA Resolution 61/295, 13 September 2007. See particularly Article 3: "Indigenous peoples have the right to self-determination. By virtue of that right they freely determine their political status and freely pursue their economic, social and cultural development." It should be noted that the Declaration does not create binding legal obligations.
60 The "right to development" is mentioned in the preamble of the Declaration; further, Article 23 asserts that "Indigenous peoples have the right to determine and develop priorities and strategies for exercising their right to development."
61 Klaus Deininger and Derek Byerlee et al., *Rising Global Interest in Farmland: Can it Yield Sustainable and Equitable Benefits?*, Washington DC: The World Bank, 2011. For an important recent work that studies the relationship between Indigenous Peoples and development, see Karen Engle, *The Elusive Promise of Indigenous Development*, Durham, NC: Duke University Press, 2010.
62 Olivier de Schutter, "The Green Rush: The Global Race for Farm Lands and the Rights of Land Users," *Harvard International Law Journal* 52, 2011, p. 502. It is notable that de Schutter is the UN Special Rapporteur on "The Right to Food" (2011). De Schutter characterizes this as a "global enclosure movement."
63 De Schutter, pp. 520–1.

Chapter 7

On the Moral Justification of Reparation for New World Slavery

David Scott

> History is a tale of unrequited justice. Treaties have been broken, communities wiped out, cultures plundered or destroyed, innocent people betrayed, slaughtered, enslaved, robbed, and exploited, and no recompense has ever been made to victims or their descendants. Historical injustices cast a long shadow. Their effects can linger long after the perpetrators and their victims are dead. They haunt the memories of descendants, blight the history of peoples, and poison relations between communities. They are the root cause of many existing inequities. Historical grievances have provided people with a justification for enmity, a reason for seeking revenge. They are at the heart of some of the bloodiest struggles and deeds in both historical and contemporary times. For many of the descendants and successors of those who were wronged, they are a motivation for seeking justice—the focus of demands for reparation.
>
> Janna Thompson

Public philosophy in the shadow of historical injustice

At least as I have come to understand and appreciate it, the project in which James Tully has been engaged over the last many years is that of fundamentally re-formulating the character and tasks of moral–political philosophy in such a way as to draw it more meaningfully, more productively, into an agonistic dialogue with the varied political demands of the present. Since *An Approach to Political Philosophy: Locke in Contexts* (1993) (in which liberalism's autobiography, its self-understanding of the arts and practice of government, is questioned and recast), and *Strange Multiplicity: Constitutionalism in an Age of Diversity* (1995) (in which modern—Western—constitutionalism is challenged for its ability to recognize and accommodate cultural difference), he has been taking aim at the normative story of political order by which we (moderns) have been governed and through which we (moderns) have governed ourselves.[1] This revisionist project, it seems to me, has only become methodologically more self-conscious and explicit and precise in the two magisterial volumes that comprise *Public Philosophy in a New Key* (2008).[2] Again, at least as far as I have come to understand its motivations and its aspirations, the concern in this project is, broadly speaking, to take aim at the *whole* way of conducting political–philosophic work in order to comprehensively transform it.

Notably, however, Tully's concern in this project is not to generate a new systematic political theory, but rather to develop a new *style* of critical thinking as well as to cultivate a new *ethos* of democratic sensibility, in which the way political philosophy addresses itself to the world, on the one hand, and recognizes the world within itself, on the other, is altered. Tully of course takes the idea of "ethos" from Michel Foucault's late reformulation of "critique" in relation to the Enlightenment, but his uses of it are almost more Bakhtinian than Foucauldian, inasmuch as the alteration he seeks to perform on philosophy's attitude to itself in the world is *dialogical* in process and direction.[3] Philosophy's questions, Tully urges, ought to be seen as growing out of what he calls "pedagogical relationships of reciprocal elucidation between academic research and the civic activities of fellow citizens" (*PPNK* I, 3). Indeed, one might say that what Tully is after here is less an academic than a public philosophic voice, a voice that has relevance and resonance in the agonistic multiplicity of the public realm. In this view, a public philosophy is a strategy of intervention that, as a mode of *listening* as much as a mode of *engagement*, a mode of giving that is also a mode of receiving, seeks to unlearn the presumption of entitlement of scholarly intellectual work by re-situating it as *one* among other reflective civic practices.[4] What characterizes this revisionist idea of the activity of criticism is a continuous dialogical loop: the professional philosopher is hailed by a world of ongoing civic struggles, seeking to throw a critical, historicizing light upon them; and these civic struggles in turn, through their own internal languages of self-understanding and practices of political action, test the yield and limits of the philosopher's conceptual frames of reference. There is no end to this recursive, reflective movement. And what is at stake in traversing this hermeneutic circle, obviously enough, is not the hope of a universal, monological Truth of how things should be, but rather, pragmatically, the *best* truths we can collectively imagine for improving the moral–political relationships by which we are governed and by which we govern ourselves.[5]

Noticeably, then, Tully's ethos of political thinking is not articulated in the register of radical *subversion*; nor is his the style of the knowing *ironist*.[6] Tully is too democratic a thinker to adopt the external or distancing attitudes these modes of theoretical address sometimes imply—too committed to hearing and worrying through the ordinary languages of freedom and equity in which popular struggles articulate their discontent and indignation. This is why, perhaps unsurprisingly, Tully defines the critical task of public philosophy in terms of a response to powers of domination, namely as the task of reflecting on "practices of governance" that are experienced as oppressive and are called into question by those subject to them. And this is also why Tully's public philosophy is not interested in developing something like a normative theory as the metaphysical lens through which to construct the horizon of a new ideal way of being governed, say, on the model of Rawls's theory of justice or Habermas's theory of discourse ethics.[7] For

Tully, these are versions of a neo-Kantian tradition of theorizing oriented toward "discovering and prescribing limits" rather than "testing and going beyond" them (*PPNK* I, 18). It is this latter orientation that characterizes the *skeptical* tradition that animates Tully's public philosophy—the work of Wittgenstein, Foucault, and Skinner, being perhaps the central (though by no means the only) inspirations.[8] One could say that two principal strategies activate the mode of operation of this political philosophy. In the first, the aim is to *disclose* the contingent conditions of the languages and practices of prevailing regimes of norm and power so as to grasp the varied ways in which problems and their solutions present, and have historically presented, themselves to determinate actors. In the second, the aim is to *re-describe* these norms and powers in such a way as to enable and encourage those subjected to their rule to envisage possibilities for governing themselves *differently*.

Why, though, is this project of philosophic criticism so attractive and so important, *now*? What contemporary moral–political demand does it answer? What conundrums does it help us re-formulate and address? What discursive space does it prise open? It should not be too difficult to discern, I think, the general contours of the cognitive–political problem-space to which Tully's public philosophy responds. We inhabit, after all, a global political present marked by a seeming exhaustion of the older languages of political criticism, and by a loss, or anyway a claustrophobic sense of the closure, of any acceptable alternative based on freedom and equity to the new imperial dispensation. Eschewing as he does the facile "either/or" of much current theorizing, and refusing to be held hostage to the familiar pieties of academic discipline, Tully seeks to activate a mode of critical inquiry that depends on a distinctive labor of *rehistoricizing* the present— namely (to use a turn of phrase he would doubtlessly recognize), one that alters not the specific answers already offered to the roster of familiar questions, but the very language game of questions and answers in which remembered pasts are connected to inhabited presents and anticipated futures. And this seems to me to have the potential of opening up new arenas for political thinking or of re-describing older ones so as to inscribe them with new possibilities.

One arena in which some of these questions about the re-configured temporalities of past, present, and future come together in an especially acute and significant way is around the issue of unrequited historical injustices and the moral–politics of redress and reparation that seeks to respond to them.[9] During the last decade or so of the twentieth century—with the collapse of the Soviet communist project and the end of the ideological antagonisms of the Cold War, the ascension of a triumphant and globally aggressive neo-liberalism underwritten by a new US imperial agenda—there emerged a novel complex of ideas and concepts that aimed to describe and theorize the problem of settling the persisting effects of past wrongs and atrocities, in particular those perpetrated by states or at least with their sanction. These ideas and concepts—among them, trauma, memory, apology, truth, forgiveness, and reconciliation—now constitute a family of sorts gathered together under the notion of "reparatory" justice (as opposed to "criminal" and "distributive" justice), itself a dimension of the wider project of international human rights. Indeed the transformation of the discourse of human rights was one condition of the story of reparatory justice.[10] Significantly, this was a period of widespread demands for state apology for various historical injustices—and in some instances these were successful campaigns (as, for example, President Clinton's apology for US violation of Hawaiian sovereignty, and Prime Minister Tony Blair's apology for British policy during the Irish potato famine).[11] There was also, importantly, the restitution settlements made by the United States and Canadian governments, respectively, to Japanese-Americans and Japanese-Canadians, for their wrongful re-location and internment during World War II; and there were settlements made to Holocaust survivors by governments and banks and firms in Germany, Switzerland, and Austria.[12] Moreover, an idea of reparatory justice animates discussions about "transitional" justice, that is, the institutional framework (for example, of non-judicial truth-telling) required to mediate so-called transitions from illiberal or authoritarian rule.[13] In short, reparatory justice has come to name a wide swathe of historical instances drawn together it seems by the new context of validation of the past, and memory as a fundamental source of moral–political demands. Now, for some the rise of demands for apology and reparation for historical injustice marks an *ethical* turn—a turn toward morality and human rights—in global politics. Elazar Barkan, for example, has argued that a neo-Enlightenment "threshold of morality" has emerged in international politics since the end of the 1990s, obliging states to be more "self-reflexive" about their actions towards citizens—self-reflexivity he calls the "guilt of nations."[14] There may be empirical as well as conceptual grounds on which to doubt the purchase of this picture of the present. In any case John Torpey seems to me to capture more promisingly the curious historical conjuncture of reparatory justice when he suggests that its rise corresponds to the demise of the politics of emancipation; the rise of a concern to rectify past injustices corresponds to the end of a politics of overcoming the legacies of the past in the present.[15]

There is much that I am going to bracket out here concerning the current debate about "coming to terms with the past," in order to focus my attention principally on the work of Janna Thompson, and her book *Taking Responsibility for the Past* (2002) in particular.[16] The main reason for this is that, like me, Thompson is solely interested in thinking through the *moral justification* for repairing the past; neither she nor I is principally interested in the legal and political question *whether* or to what extent claims for repair meet with success, or *how* they might do so. What holds our attention is the following moral question: what conceptions of harm and wrong and justice, and what considerations of past and memory, and identity and community, govern understandings of redress and support their demands? Moreover, of interest to me is that Thompson is especially interested in what has seemed in recent years the most *intractable* of reparations cases, that of reparation for the injustice of New World slavery. In the wake of the relative success of redress demands (symbolic and material) of other groups—Jews for the Holocaust, for example, or Japanese-Americans for wrongful internment during World War II—it remains a curious fact that the repair of so indisputable a wrong as that of slavery has been unable to gain much moral traction.[17] The concrete reasons for this failure may of course not themselves be moral ones, specifically or entirely, but rather the relative political strength of the organized demands. But it is, nevertheless, important to reflect on how best to understand the moral relation between the distinctive historical injury of slavery and the distinctive obligation to make reparation for its perpetration. Thompson and I, then, are concerned with the moral argument that links past harms to present demands for reparation: if we are to take seriously the view that New World slavery constituted an unspeakable wrong perpetrated on Africans and peoples of African descent for several hundred years, then we are obliged to take seriously the demand that this wrong be redressed.

In this context, however, Thompson is also interesting to think with because her style of philosophic inquiry has much in it that bears comparison with Tully's. To begin with, like Tully she is a methodologically self-conscious skeptic, forever testing the conceptual yield and limits of the arguments she, or her opponent, employs. She is, it is true, less explicitly indebted to Tully's trio of Wittgenstein, Foucault, and Skinner, but she is, like him, involved in a debate with Habermas's "discourse ethics," one that highlights the plural, chronically conflict-ridden character of ethical conversation.[18] Thompson, for example, does not disparage collective agreement but she believes we can do better than a *modus vivendi*: for her, moral reasoning can construct agreement, but such agreement is always contingent and therefore vulnerable to controversy. Connectedly, Thompson like Tully is suspicious of rights-oriented moral–philosophical argument that privileges the rights-bearing, property-owning liberal individual as the proper starting point and ultimate horizon of any discussion of harms and justice. If she seems at times weary of some of the implications of Alasdair MacIntyre's tradition-based theory of the self, she nevertheless draws close to conceptions of moral personality that see it as never-not *situated* in an ongoing collective narrative of embodied identity.[19] It will be easy to see, then, that Thompson like Tully takes the past seriously, not least as a dense source of historical injustice connected to the deep legacy of European empire. For neither of them is the past a neutral, impartial time; the past, rather, is a burdensome time that lays on us unavoidable moral obligations as well as moral entitlements.

Against this background I pursue the following itinerary in the remainder of this essay: First, I sketch in outline the central thread of Thompson's moral defense of a claim for African American reparation, highlighting her concern to make slavery itself (rather than the systematic discrimination that follows in its wake) the source of the injury that justifies the demand of redress. Second, I raise some questions about the background theory she employs to support aspects of her argument. We will see that there are instances in which her assumptions, though well motivated, are not always as persuasive as she might think. And third, in closing, I return to Tully's public philosophy to briefly underline some contrasts between ways of pursuing a political philosophy of the contemporary problem of slavery reparations.

Responsibility for the injustice of slavery

In a catalytic moment in May 1969, the revolutionary black activist James Forman marched into Riverside Church in New York City and delivered to its astonished congregation the substantive demands of his "Black Manifesto," namely that $500 million be paid by Christian white churches and Jewish synagogues in reparation for the centuries of exploitation and oppression which they have inflicted on black people around the world.[20] The wider public response to Forman's demand was, so it seems, lukewarm at best, but there were at least two thoughtful *philosophical* responses to it, the frameworks of which still shape the contemporary debate in many ways. The first of these responses was Bernard Boxill's 1972 essay, "The Morality of Reparation."[21] In this insightful little essay Boxill is especially concerned to demonstrate a distinction between two modes of repair that follow from different kinds of injury and that therefore satisfy different requirements of justice. On the one hand, there is *compensation*, which stems from situations in which no prior injustice need necessarily have occurred. Here justice requires equity to balance or re-balance advantage. On the other hand, there is *reparation*, which stems from a situation in which some injustice has been deliberately perpetrated (as in the systematic enslavement of people), and which therefore requires *redress* as a condition for answering the matter of equity. Central to Boxill's argument for reparation specifically—as correcting an injustice done to a person's right to pursue or acquire what they value—is the idea that the transgressor owes the victim an *acknowledgment* that the reparation is required *in virtue of the prior wrong*. "This concession is required," Boxill maintains, "by the premise that every person is equal in worth and dignity. Without the acknowledgement of error, the injurer implies that the injured has been treated in a manner that befits him; hence, he cannot feel that the injured party is his equal."[22] Injustice involves not only material dispossession or physical harm, but also—and crucially—*disrespect*; therefore, justice entails the repair of that relation between perpetrator and victim such that the worth and dignity of the harmed is recognized and restored.[23]

Boris Bittker takes a very different view in his 1973 book, *The Case for Black Reparations*, a closely argued inquiry into constitutional considerations.[24] For Bittker, reparations are principally about the redress of legally enforced inequalities, and therefore he has a different target than Boxill did. Bittker takes the view that it is not plausible for African Americans to demand reparation for the injustice of slavery. This is because slavery happened "too long ago" for it to be the injustice responsible for the disadvantages they now suffer. More recent inequities have to be implicated. In his view, the period of Reconstruction signaled the possibility that a genuine post-slave society of equal citizens might be brought into being in the US. The reason this did not happen, he argues, is that Reconstruction was aborted by white supremacists and complicit governments and was replaced by a regime of systematic oppression and segregation, namely, Jim Crow. It is to *this* system of institutionalized racial discrimination, and not to the original injustice of slavery, Bittker maintains, that the harms of contemporary African

Americans should be attributed.[25] And therefore it is these harms specifically that morally justify the demand for reparation.[26]

Between the waning revolutionary years of the early 1970s and the Reagan-transformed years of the late 1980s, the demand for black reparation seems to have become somewhat muted. But in the immediate aftermath of the Japanese-American success with the Civil Liberties Act of 1988, a slow momentum began to gather once again.[27] This was enabled no doubt by US Congressman John Conyers's proposed legislation (H.R. 40) to institute a commission to study the legacy of slavery and segregation on African Americans, and to explore the case for remedies.[28] One important contribution to this renewed debate came from the publication in 2000 of Randall Robinson's widely discussed book, *The Debt: What America Owes to Blacks*.[29] Founder of the lobby organization TransAfrica Forum, Robinson argued with considerable elegance and poignancy that the question of liability for the unpaid debt owed to African Americans lay squarely with the US government. One can read Janna Thompson's *Taking Responsibility for the Past* as, in large part, a philosophical response to Robinson's *The Debt*. In particular, Thompson aims to take seriously Robinson's argument that it is slavery—and not merely Jim Crow—that ought to be regarded as the appropriate target for redress. Whatever equity may demand for the structural disadvantages currently suffered by African Americans, slavery remains the vital, originary injustice. As Robinson puts in a moving passage that clearly shapes Thompson's thinking: "Like slavery, other human rights crimes have resulted in the loss of millions of lives. But only slavery, with its sadistic patience, asphyxiated memory, and smothered cultures, has hulled empty a whole race of people with trans-generational efficiency. Every artifact of the victims' past cultures, every custom, every ritual, every god, every language, every trace element of a people's whole hereditary identity, wrenched from them and ground into a sharp choking dust."[30] This is the picture of slavery's harms that Thompson believes we have a moral responsibility to respond to—it is the source of the moral justification for reparation.

At the centre of Thompson's engagement with the question of past injustice is her conceptualization of "obligation"; she aims to give this familiar moral term special historical *bite*. Historical injustices—that is, moral wrongs committed by "past people,"—accrue obligations of repair. But such obligations are "historical" in a distinctive sense, Thompson says, because those who are responsible for making good in the present (keeping the promise, paying the debt, honoring the contract, repairing the harm) are not the same ones as those who undertook the responsibility or committed the wrong in the past, but their descendants or successors. Indeed it is this seeming gap between the identity of the victims of the wrong and the claimants of the redress that often renders reparation for historical injustice especially fraught. As Thompson says, philosophical arguments about historical obligation typically work through assumptions about "historical title"—that is, assumptions about the privilege of historically acquired rights of property or possession that are passed on to people of succeeding generations (Nozick's work is a classic case in point).[31] In consequence, such arguments have nothing to say about reparative responsibilities that do not involve violations of rights of property, but rather stem from injustices such as murder or torture or enslavement or denigration—violations, as Thompson says, that while less tangible or computational, may in fact loom larger in the minds and memories of victims and their descendants. Moreover, arguments from title tend to look only toward the *restitution* of what is owed; they are "past-oriented" inasmuch as they seek the *restoration* of the *status quo ante*. As opposed to this, Thompson is interested in a model of historical obligation that looks to the future; a model that while not unconcerned with the rightful return of ill-gotten possessions, is more interested in bringing about the reconciliation of the conflict-riven communities (xix).[32]

Thompson's idea of the *historicity* of historical obligation rests on a sociological argument about societies or nations, namely that they constitute "intergenerational communities." For her, an intergenerational community is one whose institutions and moral relationships persist over time and through a succession of generations, and depends for its moral and political integrity on its members accepting trans-generational obligations and honoring trans-generational entitlements (xviii). In this account, members of intergenerational communities make moral demands on their successors, and they think that their successors ought to honor these commitments. The guiding meta-ethical principle here is that "like cases should be treated alike"—in other words, those who impose duties on others must be prepared to accept relevantly similar duties (xviii–xix). Consequently, by imposing obligations on their successors, members of intergenerational communities acquire obligations of their own to fulfill similar responsibilities with respect to the commitments and relationships of *their* predecessors. And of course at times such obligations will entail making reparation for past *failure* to honor commitments or for other injustices that, as Thompson puts it (reflecting Boxill's argument), "demonstrated a lack of respect" for other communities and their entitlements. The idea of obligations connected to intergenerational communities, Thompson argues, though "backward-looking" in its insistence that reparation is owed for *past* injustice, is also "forward-looking" inasmuch as it is predicated on our moral relations with our successors, our moral implication in the future. And this gives her further reason for accepting a "reconciliatory" model of reparation, one that seeks the repair of relations damaged by historical injustices (xix).[33]

Now, in Thompson's account, what makes the case for black reparations distinctive, different from say the Maori case (or that of other "native" peoples for that matter) "is that the people to whom reparation is supposed to be made are individuals—the descendants of the victims of injustice. They are supposed to be entitled to reparation not because they are the members of a wronged nation. Their claims arise from the fact that their forebears were enslaved or suffered other kinds of injustice" (101–2). For Thompson, then, reparations claims classically depend on the political or legal *standing* of those seeking redress; and in her view, African Americans do *not* constitute a bona fide "political community"—that is, a community with the standing of a nation or a corporation. If, as she says, the US government were to pay reparation for slavery, it might conceivably decide to give the money to African American associations—churches and the like—which would then be responsible for using it for the benefit of their communities. But, she says, this would only be a matter of "administrative convenience"; it would not be because these organizations were themselves *owed* reparations as organized victims of the historical wrong. It is, she insists, the descendants of slaves who, as *individuals*, are owed reparation for the enslavement of their forebears (102).

A good deal of the shape and persuasiveness of Thompson's argument depends on this founding premise. It is a "basic principle" of reparative justice, she argues, that obligations and entitlements belong *only* to those who have committed or suffered the wrong (103). So the definitive question for her is: How can African Americans who have never been enslaved demand reparation for the injustice of slavery done to their forebears? This is the question to which she seeks moral–philosophic resources. In Thompson's view, it is illegitimate to argue that enslavement was visited upon individuals *not* as individuals but because they were members of a group—"Africans," say, or "black" people—and consequently that it is proper and right that reparation for slavery should go to current members of that group. As she puts it firmly: "From the fact that people can be persecuted just because they happen to belong to a particular group, it doesn't follow that these wrongs should be regarded as injustices done to their group. Individuals are the ones who are enslaved, denied opportunities, or discriminated against. The harm belongs to them" (103).

But is it so clear, as Thompson assumes, that the harms of slavery "belong" (whatever that might mean) to African Americans as "individuals" rather than as a "group"? What moral–psychological theory of "harms" underwrites this bold assertion? How are we to understand "belongingness" of harms to individuals as opposed to "belongingness" of harms to groups? Or more specifically, what is the theory of the distinctive harms of the "peculiar institution" of racial slavery that supports this view? I come back to this later, but it is surely arguable that it is precisely the regime of slavery, its powers of racial subjection and racial subjectification, racial aggregation and racial collectivization, that invited the construction of a collective memory of trauma and helped to shape a palpable sense of racial solidarity and racial community.

On Thompson's account, since (as she believes she has conclusively shown) African Americans cannot make a claim of reparation "as members of a persecuted group," they are obliged to justify their demands "by demonstrating that the injustices done to their forebears have violated *their* rights or caused *them* unjustified harm" as individuals (104). Two ways of approaching this have suggested themselves, both of which are suggestive, but neither of which are entirely satisfactory to her. The first approach is to argue that slavery is the fundamental harm and root cause of the many disadvantages suffered by African Americans, and consequently they are owed reparation for this original injustice. For Thompson, as I have said, this is a compelling claim—one she associates with Randall Robinson—but it has to get round Boris Bittker's argument that it is not slavery but post-Reconstruction Jim Crow that is the immediate cause of the social and economic conditions of

African American life (105). Thompson's response is to dispute Bittker's disregard of slavery, his focus only on the tangible harms. Collective memory matters: "What happened to their ancestors matters to people; recalling injustices done to their family or community can cause them distress. A history of injustices can be demoralizing, destructive of esteem, or the cause of depression" (106). In this view it can be argued that the disadvantages now suffered by African Americans are part of a history of injustices that began with slavery and encompasses segregation as well as more recent forms of racial discrimination. Still, Thompson is worried by the seeming "communitarian" leanings of this argument. Aware of the tension between the *individualist* tendencies in her own position and what she otherwise takes to be attractive in MacIntyre's thesis, that one's moral identity encompasses the history of one's family or community (107), she wants to put restraints on a strong conception of collective identity. Communal identities, she says, are after all not necessarily uniform—they don't give rise to dependably stable demands. So Thompson says "yes" to an argument from slavery's harms but "no" to a deep commitment to a claim from historical community.

The second approach is the "inheritance" line of argument. In this view, the reparative claims of descendants of victims of injustice—such as present-day African Americans—derive their entitlement from their status as *heirs*. For Thompson this approach has the apparent virtue of hanging entitlement on inheritance rather than on the attribution of harm (where the former seems more concrete than the latter). Of course, the inheritance approach does not, strictly-speaking, make a *reparatory* claim—the entitlement exists by virtue of the descendants being heirs to *possessions* that would have been theirs had the injustice not taken place (107). As Thompson argues, this approach puts limits on the kinds of injustices that can be the subject of claims (typically these will be confined to the demand for the restoration of, or compensation for, expropriated possessions). In this terrain, nothing can be claimed for such violations as murder, torture, enslavement, abduction, however grave these may be to the descendants of victims (108). And certainly for the descendants of slaves these are at least as important as being robbed of the fruit of their labors. But if the "harms" argument runs up against Bittker's ancient wrongs exclusions, the "loss of possessions" argument runs up against Jeremy Waldron's "indeterminacy thesis" that foregrounds the difficulty of determining unambiguously who has more right to a particular property whose past is shrouded in injustice (112).[34] So Thompson commends the idea of an intergenerational mechanism of inheritance but she rejects the refusal to consider intangible harms.

In a certain sense, Thompson is looking for an approach that combines the virtues of both the "group harms" and the "inheritance" strategies but suffers the vices of neither. And this leads her to what she calls the "family lines" approach. In Thompson's view, the family, if not a corporate agent like a nation, can nevertheless be thought of as a ground for what she calls "lifetime-transcending interests," that is, interests constituted around projects, values and concerns that reach beyond the natural lifetimes of individuals. The family is constitutively *intergenerational.* Thompson thinks that grounding a claim of repair in the family will enable her to go a far way in lending moral philosophic support to the sort of argument that Robinson seeks to make about the lingering injury of slavery without falling off the deep end of collective identity. Her argument is that harms that can be traced back to slavery are passed down through family lines; what slavery harmed, above all, and continues to harm, is the black *family* (130). Slavery was an injustice committed against family lines, and it is on this basis that descendants of slaves ought to be able to claim reparation for slavery.

We are of course in deep waters here concerning the historical sociology of the black family in slavery and freedom. But in order to demonstrate the purchase of the family as a ground of injury, Thompson turns, curiously, not to the specificity of slavery, but to the case of the Australian government policy of removing "half-caste" children from their Aboriginal families for purposes of assimilation.[35] How, she asks, should we interpret the wrong in this case? To whom does the harm belong? The principal wrong, she maintains, was neither to the children nor to the parents, but to the *relationship* between them. That is, the harm was done to individuals, but individuals *as* members of family lines. Why is this so? The family, Thompson argues, is the "most important conduit" for passing down, from one generation to the next, things valued by individuals: possessions, projects, responsibilities, values, languages, traditions, and so on (134). Thus the harm caused by removing children from their parents is the injury to the "lifetime-transcending interests" that families have in the continuity of meaningful identity-forming relationships. Therefore, she urges, societies ought to recognize the entitlement of parents to pass on their heritage to their children. And since such an entitlement is not simply something that matters to parents only during their own lifetimes, but rather is bound up with their "lifetime-transcending interests," they are entitled to demand that their *successors* respect their wishes concerning their children in the event of their death (135).

Now recall that for Thompson it is a basic principle of reparatory justice that individuals can claim reparation only for injustices that harm *them*; and the fact that they are members of a racial or religious group against which injustices were directed does not give them a reparatory entitlement so long as the harm done to these groups has to be understood as harms done to the *individuals* in them. The idea of family lines solves this dilemma for her. For on this view, an injustice to family lines cannot be reduced to harms done to particular individuals. Such injustices harm *relationships* between parents and children or between forebears and descendants—they harm individuals *as* members of family lines.

But aren't we entitled to ask why this argument about the inheritance of valued goods cannot be made about other *relationships*, say, relationships that constitute *cultural*—as opposed to familial—groups? Is there an ideological *naturalization* of the family at work here, akin to the earlier naturalization of the "nation?"

By analogy with this case of abducted Aboriginal children, at any rate, the question for black reparation is whether slavery can be shown to count as an injustice to family lines. In a succinct statement of what an injustice to family lines entails, Thompson writes: "An injustice to family lines is committed when the perpetrators seek to disrupt family relationships or wipe out family lines, keep members of family lines in perpetual slavery or submission, or attempt to prevent individuals from maintaining family relationships, carrying out family obligations, or receiving their inheritance as members of a family" (137). And of course on this view it can very plausibly be argued that the regime of slavery in the US was directed precisely *against* family lines. It is a familiar story that slave owners in the Americas systematically broke up families—husbands were separated from wives and children from parents—and parents were prevented from educating children in their cultural traditions. Indeed, this regime of slavery was directed against any continuity in cultural traditions passed down through the generations. Moreover, at the same time that slavery worked to fundamentally disrupt the integrity of families, it paradoxically *depended* on families inasmuch as it perpetuated itself *through* the enslavement precisely of families: "The children of slaves were also slaves. Once enslaved, a family was meant to remain in subjugation down through the generations" (137). Therefore, Thompson argues, when Randall Robinson insists that African Americans continue to suffer from the legacy of slavery, "he can be interpreted as saying that they suffer harms as members of family lines. According to his argument, they have been deprived by slavery and other injustices of their African heritage, and denied a positive, affirmative place in American history" (137–8). And individuals can only suffer these deprivations, Thompson argues, *because* they are related to the past through their family lines.

Harms, collective memories, reparation

To my mind, Janna Thompson has offered a very neat and intriguing, and moreover intricately structured argument in support of reparation for US slavery. By recasting obligation as an intergenerational duty and making the family the concrete vehicle for the transmission of expectations and entitlements she frames a discussion of moral responsibility that gets round some of the dilemmas about title, on the one hand, and harms, on the other, and gives robust shape to reparative claims against historical injustice. Attractively, she aims to take seriously, rather than evade, the insistence that the central moral issue for black redress is the fundamental wrong of racial enslavement, not the racial discriminations that are instituted in its wake; and therefore, that black reparation is not primarily a claim about equity but a claim about justice, a claim about making right an historical wrong. Perhaps not since Bernard Boxill's essay "The Morality of Reparation" has there been so sustained a philosophical inquiry into the moral justification of reparation for slavery. There is clearly much in the direction of her argument that seems to me persuasive, indeed enabling. Still I want to wonder out loud about certain of her formulations and assumptions that are less than convincing or at least not uncontroversial, and therefore worth further exploration.

To begin with I want to think about Thompson's assertion that African Americans are not entitled to reparation in virtue of being members of a "wronged nation," but *only* insofar as they are *individual* descendants of slaves or belong (again *as* individuals) to families that descended from slaves. Recall that this view is *foundational* for Thompson. African Americans are not like the Maori who are, on her description, "a structured, intergenerational community" capable, as a collective political agent, "of making and keeping transgenerational commitments" (xix). Nations, she says flatly, are the *norm* of this kind of community, and the Maori are self-evidently a nation. As such they are entitled to reparation for past injustices done to their "community"—acts of aggression, expropriation of communal lands, violations of sovereignty or of treaties, and so on. By contrast, she says, African Americans do *not* constitute a collective of this sort. So that when, for example, a philosopher like Bernard Boxill maintains that descendants of slaves have an historical entitlement to reparation, he cannot, she asserts, be making a claim on behalf of the African American "nation" because: "There is no such thing. The claim depends on the fact that African Americans are descendants of slaves" (xix).[36] There is something curiously arbitrary about this stipulation.[37] In urging this distinction between the Maori and African Americans, Thompson sees no need to expend much time *establishing* it or *arguing* it out: it is, to her, clear and uncontroversial. But *should* it be? What is it that naturally makes the Maori a "nation?" What is the political *theory* that authorizes this "nationhood" and the norm that enforces its salience? What is the political *history* that brings it into being? Why is "nation" the only mode of political sovereignty she recognizes? Thompson seems to suggest that it is the historical fact that the Maori signed a treaty with the colonial powers that signals to us their prior and continued entitlement to being called a "nation." So does this mean that it is the colonial powers that, in signing a treaty, called their status as a "nation" into being with all the warrants that Thompson thinks are implied? Thompson feels no need to inquire into the colonial ethnography through which descriptions of the political identity of the Maori were variously construed and how the Maori came to be thought of, and came to think of themselves, in the idiom of "nation." (Indeed, the entire first part of Thompson's book could be subjected to criticism for its colonial assumptions.) Consequently, there is perhaps no good reason *not* to believe that the identification of the Maori as a "nation" was, in part at least, an *artifact* of the modern colonial encounter.

On the other side, the denial to African Americans of a properly *political* identity seems equally arbitrary, and certainly to simplify a story more historically complicated than Thompson allows. Thompson agrees, remember, that people like African Americans can be persecuted *because* they belong to a particular group. But she says that it does not follow from this that "these wrongs should be regarded as injustices done to their group," because it is *individuals* who were enslaved or otherwise mistreated: "The harm belongs to them" (103). African Americans may be a group in some sense but the wrongs they suffered were *individually* suffered, and suffered *as* individuals. I come back at the end to the theory of harms implicit here but I first want to notice the conception of collective identity that supports this argument. Undoubtedly it is individuals who were captured, chained in coffles, sold as slaves, and transported to the New World across the Middle Passage. However, leaving aside the complex question of the structure of slave trading among African people that brought those coffles to the slave forts along the coast, surely Thompson does not believe that Europeans *bought* or *captured* these individuals into slavery *because* they happened to be the particular individuals they were. Surely they were bought or captured into slavery because they belonged to a group of people—namely black Africans—identified by the colonial powers as distinctly and distinctively *enslavable*. New World slavery imposed (or certainly came very early in its career to impose) equivalence or near equivalence between "African" and "enslavable."[38] This is obviously a crucial chapter in the story of race, or rather, in the story of *racialization*, a process that partly involved, remember, the *collectivization* of individual identity. Consequently, among the descendants of slaves in the Americas the respective narratives of individual and collective identity may not be so easily disentangled from each other as Thompson would have us believe. Or to put it the other way around, the story of whiteness is partly the story of the *naturalization* of race and color such that the white person can appear as preeminently an *individual* rather than as a member or representative of a collective.

Moreover, it was a condition of the form of subjugation embodied in New World plantation slavery that if it allowed the elaboration and expression of *cultural* personality in some constrained measure, it precisely denied *political* personality. The slave was anything *but* a political subject—as also, of course, the ex-slave of post-Reconstruction. The *denial* of political community to African Americans is a constitutive part of the history of enslavement and its aftermaths. This is why the political history of African America—that is, the history of the construction of a self-conscious collective identity, is routed through the narration of a founding trauma, namely slavery; and why this history is partly the history of the claim to a distinctive *political* identity based on *overcoming* that historical injury and injustice (one way of characterizing the legendary antagonism between W.E.B. Du Bois and Booker T. Washington is to think of it as an elaboration of just this tension).[39]

The second dimension of Thompson's argument that seems to me less well thought out than it might be is that concerning the idea of "family lines." To a considerable degree, the overall coherence of her argument (as well as the *end* toward which it tends) hangs on this ingenious idea. Indeed, it is not hard to see how it neatly resolves the dilemma that Thompson sets up: since "nation" has been ruled out as the collective ground of the African American reparation claim, she needs some alternative relational domain that plays the role of identity formation, and that attends simultaneously to the harms of individuals and their inheritance down through the generations. The dimension of "family" enables her, in effect, to foreground *relationships* while retaining an accent on *individuals*. It is as members of families that individuals are harmed, not say, as members of cultures. In this scheme, the family plays the role of a sort of mediating unit between the thinly connected individuals of liberals like Waldron and the thickly constituted individuals of communitarians like MacIntyre. Intriguing as this argument is, however, it is noticeable that Thompson has to rely on a familiar—indeed a conventional and uninterrogated—sociology of the family in general, and of the African American family in particular: the family as the site of injury, the source of identity-forming values, and the locus of the intergenerational transmission of possessions and attachments and heritage. In a curious way, much as with her treatment of the nation, the family is imagined as a *naturalized* form of social organization. (As with slavery and race, Thompson bypasses the entire critical discussion of the family and the powers through which it polices, regulates, disciplines, and so on.) Thompson seems to think that the danger in accounts of moral identity such as MacIntyre's (to which she obviously feels some sympathy) is that they are too tightly scripted: "One trouble with this idea is that communal identities are by no means universal or have uniform implications" (107). By contrast, she thinks that her account of the "lifetime-transcending interests" of family lines does not commit her to a single script of identity or belonging. But what social theory authorizes this? It is far from clear that there is much to distinguish her "family" from a strong conception of community, especially since she commits herself to so internally systemic and integrated an idea of the family as the guardian and transmitter of culture.

In this regard, the conventionality of Thompson's sociological theory of the family is underlined by her unsubstantiated assumptions about the specificity of slavery and the African American family. Anyone marginally acquainted with the topic will know, if nothing else, that the historical sociology of the African American family (as indeed of the New World post-emancipation black family in general) is a densely controversial domain. From the early work of W.E.B. Du Bois and E. Franklin Frazier through the Moynihan Report and the later revisionist work of Herbert Gutmann and Eugene Genovese to the dissenting work of Orlando Patterson, just how slavery harmed or did not harm black families and how black families harm or do not harm black children (especially male children) is a subject of considerable and continuing debate.[40] Therefore, whether or to what extent one can draw such straightforward conclusions as Thompson does about moral harms and the black family is open to pervasive doubt.

Finally it seems to me that part of the *general* problem with Thompson's argument is that while she admirably wants to defend an argument from *slavery* harms (as opposed to Bittker's discrimination harms) in order to keep our focus on *reparative* justice rather than redistributive justice or equity, her conception of the distinctive *harms* of slavery is not completely convincing. The harms of the regime of New World slavery, it seems to me, cannot be adequately described by analogy to the abduction and forced assimilation of Aboriginal children—dreadful as that history clearly was. While there were obviously elements of both, the institution of slavery in the Americas can hardly be reduced to a mechanism of abduction and assimilation. It was this and *more*. Here, I think, Thompson loses sight of the force of Randall Robinson's description of slavery as a systematic and relentless dehumanization—a description that comes closest, perhaps, to Orlando Patterson's well-known idea of slavery as an institutional form of domination that produced and perpetuated a distinctive mode of systemic violence that resulted in the "natal alienation" and "social death" of the slave.[41] Agree or not with the detail of Patterson's theory of the nature of slave domination, the point is that the kind of argument Thompson wishes to make depends on a picture of the distinctive powers of slave-owning regimes and the distinctive harms suffered by slaves. Here again race is not a dispensable category. After all, New World slavery was characterized by a racialization *both* of the powers of subjection and of the "natal alienation" that was its effect. So while Thompson elides its role in her description of slavery harms, race is certainly central to the narrative of the collective memory of injury, and to traditions of African American political identity and political solidarity, and therefore ought perhaps to be more central to the discussion of what the work of redress aims to meet. In this sense, then, an account of the moral justification of reparation for New World slavery has to rest on a more complex argument about the nature of the harms of slavery than Thompson has provided.[42]

In this sense, then, an account of the moral justification of reparation of New World slavery has to rest on a more complex argument about the nature of the harms of slavery than Thompson has provided.

Janna Thompson is after a kind of moral philosophy that, like Tully's, seeks to respond appropriately to public issues by attending, as she says, to "what is being demanded" by those who have suffered historical injustice: "Moral reflection on responsibilities with respect to the past would be appropriate even if concern about historical injustices was not so widespread or politically influential. The fact that demands based on history have become so prevalent merely makes the inquiry more urgent" (ix). She too, in other words, is after a "practical morality," one that can be continually tested by the light of the world. Perhaps, though, one can already discern some points of divergence between the mode of reflection on civic matters that Tully commends and Thompson's approach to public philosophy. For all her careful attention to pertinence and coherence, Thompson's approach to the question of "taking responsibility for the past" operates through a familiar *attitude* or *ethos* of philosophic reflection. Notice that, in her view of a "practical morality" the urgency of moral inquiry is *enhanced* by the prevalence of historically based demands in the public sphere. But, for Thompson, these demands are no more than the *occasion* for philosophic reflection; as with Randall Robinson's argument about the debt owed to African Americans generated by the history of enslavement, they signal something of the stakes and significance of philosophic intervention. But, notably, in Thompson's approach, there is no interest in determining, for example, the languages of comprehension through which the rival accounts that constitute the contemporary debate about reparations for slavery are constructed—the languages of problematization, the styles of reasoning, the rhetorics of rationality, the question/answer complexes, that shape and constrain the discursive arena of her intervention. So there is no means of *disclosing* (to use Tully's term of art here) the distinctive conceptual-ideological shape of the present as a *question* for philosophic reflection. Further there is no interest in a genealogy of the practices and discourses and institutions and powers of subjectification through which the present state of affairs of black life in the US has been made what it is. So there is no ground from which to discern the contingency of the powers of subjection and of testing the adequacy of African American idioms of freedom now being brought to bear on them, and thus of potentially re-describing their relation to the past in the present. The reason is that, for Thompson, philosophic discourse is not *one* moment in an ongoing *dialogical* conversation with reflective citizens, a reciprocal exchange, about how best to be governed and how best to govern ourselves; rather, it is a mode of giving the best philosophic account of what is just. For Tully by contrast, philosophic discourse is precisely a mode of giving that is at once a mode of receiving in an ongoing exchange with engaged citizens—a reciprocal generosity in which the preoccupation with what is just is itself folded into a horizon of reflection concerned with how to be free.

Notes

1 James Tully, *An Approach to Political Philosophy: Locke in Contexts*, Cambridge: Cambridge University Press, 1993, and *Strange Multiplicity: Constitutionalism in an Age of Diversity*, Cambridge: Cambridge University Press, 1995.
2 James Tully, *Public Philosophy in a New Key: Volume I, Democracy and Civic Freedom* and *Public Philosophy in a New Key: Volume II, Imperialism and Civic Freedom*, Cambridge: Cambridge University Press, 2008, hereafter referred to as *PPNK*.
3 There is a good deal that could be said here about *style* and *ethos* in respect of Tully's idea of political criticism, much of which I lack space to develop. But take *style* to begin with. Tully evokes it by way of analogy with musicians to explain the *improvisatory* "new key" in which his philosophical intervention is staged. But "style" might offer richer possibilities as a way of registering aspects of the rationality of a critical orientation, as for example in Ian Hacking's use of the idea of "styles of reasoning." See Hacking, "Language, Truth, and Reason" in *Rationality and Relativism*, eds, Martin Hollis and Steven Lukes, Oxford: Blackwell, 1982, pp. 48–66. (Indeed, the work of Ian Hacking is a very curious absence in Tully's otherwise capaciously inclusive list of interlocutors.) On *ethos*, the source in Foucault is of course "What is Enlightenment?" in Michel Foucault, *Ethics: Subjectivity and Truth, Essential Works of Foucault, 1954–1984, Volume I*, ed. Paul Rabinow, New York: New Press, 1997, p. 319. But my suggestion is that it would be hard to read Foucault's idea in this essay of a "critical ontology of ourselves" in terms of the sort of *dialogical* exercise Tully urges. The style, if you like, is not Foucault's. More helpful here, I think, is the use of the idea of the "dialogical" in Mikhail Bakhtin, *The Dialogical Imagination: Four Essays*, Austin: University of Texas Press, 1982. In other ways Tully's use of the idea of *ethos* reminds one of the work of William Connolly, especially, *The Ethos of Pluralization*, Minneapolis: University of Minnesota Press, 1995—also curiously unmentioned in his assembly of sources.
4 In this regard Tully's practice reminds me of Stuart Hall's mode of intellectual engagement, the reciprocal giving and receiving that shapes its worldliness. For some discussion in these terms, see David Scott, "Stuart Hall's Ethics," *Small Axe* 17, 2007, pp. 1–16. On the idea of "reciprocal generosity" in critical thinking see Romand Coles, *Rethinking Generosity: Critical Theory and the Politics of Caritas*, Ithaca: Cornell University Press, 1997.
5 Interestingly, in articulating what he means by a public philosophy Tully does not mention Michael Sandel who also describes his work in these terms. See especially, Sandel, *Public Philosophy: Essays on Morality in Politics*, Cambridge: Harvard University Press,

2006. True, Sandel does not advocate the sort of *dialogical* ethos that Tully commends, but still there is much in his critique of Rawls and more generally of the liberalism that supports the "procedural republic" that would seem to comport with Tully's project. See Sandel, *Liberalism and the Limits of Justice*, Cambridge: Cambridge University Press, 1982, and *Democracy's Discontent: America in Search of a Public Philosophy*, Cambridge: Belknap Press, 1998.

6 It is hard not to see the trace of Richard Rorty all over Tully's work and indeed Tully acknowledges it. See Tully, "Public Philosophy and Civic Freedom," *PPNK* I, 3–11 at 9. But Rorty was (with almost mischievously subversive intent) an ironist, more explicitly so admittedly in the later than in the earlier work. Perhaps the work of Rorty most useful to Tully's project is *Philosophy and the Mirror of Nature*, Princeton: Princeton University Press, 1979, more so than the Rorty of *Contingency, Irony, Solidarity*, Cambridge: Cambridge University Press, 1989.

7 Contrast Tully's project in *Public Philosophy in a New Key*, for example, with Thomas McCarthy's *Race, Empire, and the Idea of Development*, Cambridge: Cambridge University Press, 2009, a work that strenuously seeks to recuperate a neo-Kantian perspective and to extend it to a consideration of a "neo-racist" and "neo-imperialist" context. For some discussion of this book, see David Scott, "The Traditions of Historical Others" a symposium on Thomas McCarthy's *Race, Empire and the Idea of Human Development* in *Symposium on Gender Race and Philosophy* 8(1)(Winter 2012), available at http://web.mit.edu/~sgrp/2012/no1/Scott0412.pdf (last accessed 28 December 2013).

8 Tully is of course a systematizer and synthesizer and this is one of his great strengths. But it may be wondered just how all the varied thinkers he names in the list of his interlocutors (from Rousseau to Edward Said by way of Nietzsche, Gadamer, Arendt, Collingwood, Skinner, Wittgenstein, Foucault, and so on) add up to an intellectual "tradition"—a term he uses. It would seem to me, however, that the kind of project Tully is engaged in stands in need *precisely* of a robust conception of an intellectual tradition, one that is able to articulate the principle of *continuity* and *discontinuity* between thinkers and between generations of thinkers, he takes to be a condition of his thought. Here, of course, Gadamer is crucial, but so is the work of Alasdair MacIntyre, especially *Three Rival Versions of Moral Enquiry: Encyclopaedia, Genealogy, and Tradition*, Notre Dame: University of Notre Dame Press, 1991. Moreover, given Tully's aim to open political philosophy to non-European or "postcolonial" voices (represented in his list by the lone figure of Edward Said) it will be important *both* to reconstruct the question/answer complexes of the traditions of those voices (as he does so effortlessly and fruitfully for the Western thinkers and traditions he is more familiar with), *and* to extend his idea of what a "dialogue" is so as to enable it to apprehend a "reciprocal elucidation" *among* geopolitically dispersed intellectual traditions.

9 One can of course read Tully's *Strange Multiplicity* as a contribution to this discussion about just ways to respond to historical injustices. It is interesting, then, that in *Public Philosophy in a New Key*, Tully privileges *freedom* before justice. As he argues, it is has been in political philosophies oriented around "the activity of developing comprehensive theories" that "questions of politics tend to be taken up as problems of justice." In his view, the dominant answer to the question, "what is political theory?" has been framed in terms of "the just way to recognize free and equal citizens." Tully is skeptical of the stipulative universalisms that typically drive these theories. Against this orientation he maintains that for the "subaltern school" to which he attaches himself "questions of politics are approached as questions of freedom." See Tully, "Public Philosophy as a Critical Activity," *PPNK* I, 38. How we articulate the problem of justice to the problem of freedom remains an open question.

10 On the ideological history of human rights see Samuel Moyn, *The Last Utopia: Human Rights in History*, Cambridge: Belknap Press, 2010.

11 On 23 November 1993, President Bill Clinton signed the Federal Apology Bill (United States Public Law 103–50), acknowledging not only the illegal actions committed by the US in the overthrow of the legitimate government of Hawai'i, but also that the Hawaiian people never surrendered their sovereignty. On 2 June 1997, Prime Minister Tony Blair apologized for the British government's failure to act responsibly during the famine years of 1845 to 1849. There are a number of books now on the politics of apology, but see Girma Negash, *Apologia Politica: States and their Apologies by Proxy*, New York: Lexington Books, 2007; Melissa Nobles, *The Politics of Official Apologies*, New York: Cambridge University Press, 2008; and more generally, Nicholas Tavuchis, *Mea Culpa: A Sociology of Apology and Reconciliation*, Stanford: Stanford University Press, 1991.

12 The Civil Liberties Act of 1988 signed into law by President Ronald Reagan granted reparations (in the amount of roughly $20,000) to Japanese-Americans who had been interned by the US government during World War II. On the settlements to Holocaust survivors see http://www.economist.com/node/326811 (last accessed 2 November 2011).

13 On transitional justice see variously, Martha Minow, *Between Vengeance and Forgiveness: Facing History after Genocide and Mass Violence*, Boston: Beacon, 1998; Priscilla Hayner, *Unspeakable Truths: Facing the Challenge of Truth Commissions*, New York: Routledge, 2001; and Ruti Teitel, *Transitional Justice*, New York: Oxford University Press, 2000. For a critical engagement with some of this work, see David Scott, *Omens of Adversity: Tragedy, Time, Memory, Justice*, Durham: Duke University Press, 2014.

14 Elazar Barkan, *The Guilt of Nations: Restitution and Negotiating Historical Injustices*, Baltimore: Johns Hopkins University Press, 2001.

15 Alluding to Barkan's argument, Torpey writes: "Indeed, in contrast to the view that reparations politics amounts to the triumph of Enlightenment modes of thinking, I would argue that the phenomenon is a kind of transitional substitute for the progressive politics associated with the Enlightenment, cut out for an age of diminished political expectations." John Torpey, *Making Whole What Has Been Smashed: On Reparations Politics*, Cambridge: Harvard University Press, 2006, p. 5.

16 Janna Thompson, *Taking Responsibility for the Past: Reparation and Historical Injustice*, Cambridge: Polity, 2002. Hereafter, page references to this book are given in the text.

17 President Clinton, for example, declined to apologize for slavery; and despite expectations that he might, neither did Prime Minister Blair. On Clinton see, "Clinton Opposes Slavery Apology" in Roy L. Brooks, ed., *When Sorry Isn't Enough: The Controversy Over Apologies and Reparations for Human Injustice*, New York: New York University Press, 1999, p. 352. In the run-up to the UN-sponsored conference on racism in Durban, South Africa, in August–September 2001, Human Rights Watch published a document entitled "An Approach to Reparations" that sought to expand the traditional framework of compensation to victims of human rights violations to encompass older wrongs rooted in slavery. See, Human Rights Watch, "An Approach to Reparations," at http://www.hrw.org/campaigns/race/reparations.htm (last viewed on 28 April 2010).

18 See Janna Thompson, *Discourse and Knowledge: Defense of a Collectivist Ethics*, New York: Routledge, 1998.

19 See Alasdair MacIntyre, *After Virtue: A Study in Moral Theory*, Notre Dame: University of Notre Dame Press, 1981.

20 For the "The Black Manifesto" that embodied the demand, see "Black Manifesto" by The Black National Economic Conference, *New York Review of Books* 13(1), 10 July 1969 [accessed through http://www.nybooks.com/articles/archives/1969/jul/10/black-manifesto/ (20 May 2010)]. For an autobiographical account see James Forman, *The Making of Black Revolutionaries: A Personal Account*, New York: Macmillan, 1972, pp. 543–50. See also Arnold Schuchter, *Reparations: The Black Manifesto and its Challenge to*

White America, Philadelphia: Lippincott, 1970; and Torpey, *Making Whole What Has Been Smashed*, pp. 112–14. Memorably, if also incongruously, Hannah Arendt refers to Forman's manifesto as a work of "black racism" in her essay, *On Violence*, New York: Harcourt, 1970, p. 77.

21 Bernard Boxill, "The Morality of Reparation," *Social Theory and Practice* 2, 1972, pp. 113–23.
22 Ibid., p. 118.
23 It is important to bear in mind here that Boxill is writing more than two-and-a-half decades before the rise of reparatory justice and its idiom of forgiveness and reconciliation.
24 Boris Bittker, *The Case for Black Reparations*, Boston: Beacon Press, 2003. It is part of Bittker's project here to make the idea of reparations a perfectly reasonable and legally respectable claim, not merely the raucous demand of black revolutionaries. See helpfully Ewart Guinier's Review, *Yale Law Journal* 82(8), 1973, pp. 1719–24.
25 As Bittker writes: "In these comments on black reparations, I have focused on the wrongs of the recent past, the consequences of which are everywhere to be seen; slavery has figured only because of its continuing influence on black-white relations after the Civil War. As suggested above, had segregation not been enforced by law, the residue of slavery might be hard to identify today" (*The Case for Black Reparations*, p. 28).
26 For a more recent engagement that urges this direction, see McCarthy's *Race, Empire, and the Idea of Development*, Ch. 4, "Coming to Terms with the Past: On the Politics of the Memory of Slavery."
27 For an insightful discussion of the debate, see Jacqueline Bacon, "Reading the Reparations Debate," *Quarterly Journal of Speech* 89(3), 2003, pp. 171–95.
28 See John Conyers, "The Commission to Study Reparations Proposals," in Brooks, *When Sorry Isn't Enough*, pp. 367–9; and Conyers and Jo Ann Nichols Watson, "Reparations: An Idea Whose Time Has Come," in *Should America Pay? Slavery and the Raging Debate on Reparations*, ed., Raymond A. Winbush, New York: Amistad, 2003, pp. 14–21.
29 Randall Robinson, *The Debt: What America Owes to Blacks*, New York: Plume, 2000. See also Robinson's account of his sense of outraged disillusionment with America in *Quitting America: The Departure of a Black Man from His Native Land*, New York: Dutton, 2004.
30 Robinson, *The Debt*, p. 216. Thompson quotes this passage as an epigraph at the beginning of her central Ch. 9: "Reparation and Injustices to Family Lines," *Taking Responsibility for the Past*, p. 130.
31 See Robert Nozick, *Anarchy, State, and Utopia*, New York: Basic Books, 1974.
32 The restitution model is sometimes referred to as the "tort" model, and the reparations model as the "atonement" model. See Roy L. Brooks, *Atonement and Forgiveness: A New Model for Black Reparations*, Berkeley: University of California Press, 2004.
33 More recently, Thompson has developed the idea of intergenerational communities in *Intergenerational Justice*, New York: Routledge, 2009.
34 See Jeremy Waldron, "Superseding Historical Injustice," *Ethics* 103(1), 1992, pp. 4–28.
35 Part of the immediate context of Thompson's writing no doubt was the political controversy in Australia around the "Stolen Generation" and the emergence of the "Sorry Books" campaign in 1998. *Taking Responsibility for the Past* was indeed reviewed in this context when it first appeared. See Kristie Dunn, "A Sorry Challenge: Review of 'Taking Responsibility for the Past: Reparation and Historical Justice' by Janna Thompson," *Australian Book Review* 251, 2003, p. 59.
36 Interestingly, while he makes no mention of African Americans in this regard, Boxill does assert that white Americans "can be regarded as a corporation or company which, as a whole, owes reparation to the sons [sic] of slaves." See Boxill, "The Morality of Reparation," p. 121.

37 As she admits, in an unelaborated aside, it is only in virtue of the state of Israel that Jews count as a nation (see Thompson, *Taking Responsibility for the Past*, p. 102). Thus, on these grounds, is it the case that they would not have been entitled to reparation were it not for the contingent historical fact (itself deeply controversial) of the establishment of a state in their name? If African Americans had been able to command the international support (financial and military) to establish a state of their own in the wake of the Civil War (say by driving their former white owners out of certain southern states), would they then be able to claim an entitlement to reparation as a "wronged nation?" Or what about black Jamaica? Or black Barbados? Surely they constitute "wronged nations" on Thompson's account. If we move the discussion away from the US and to the Caribbean, are we now on more secure ground so far as her argument is concerned?

38 There are of course many ways into this story, but for one elegant history see, Winthrop D. Jordan's classic book, *White Over Black: American Attitudes Toward the Negro, 1550–1812*, Chapel Hill: University of North Carolina Press, 1968.

39 See, interestingly, the work of Jeffrey Alexander and his colleagues on cultural trauma—in particular, Jeffrey Alexander, Ron Eyerman, Bernhard Giesen, Neil J. Smelser and Piotr Sztompka, *Cultural Trauma and Collective Identity*, Berkeley: University of California Press, 2004; and Ron Eyerman, *Cultural Trauma: Slavery and the Formation of African American Identity*, New York: Cambridge University Press, 2001. Recently there has been a call from some African American intellectuals to abandon this narrative. See Charles Johnson, "The End of the Black American Narrative," *American Scholar*, Summer 2008, pp. 32–42; and Henry Louis Gates Jr, "Ending the Blame-Game," *New York Times* op-ed 23 April 2010 (and the responses "Letters: Slavery Reparations? Healing the Wounds of the Past," *New York Times*, 30 April 2010).

40 See W.E.B. Du Bois, ed., *The Negro American Family*, New York: Negro Universities Press, 1969 [1908]; E. Franklin Frazier, *The Negro Family in the United States*, Chicago: University of Chicago Press, 1939; Daniel Patrick Moynihan, *The Negro Family: The Case for National Action*, Washington, DC: US Department of Labor, 1965; Eugene Genovese, *Roll, Jordan, Roll: The World the Slaves Made*, New York: Vintage, 1976; Herbert Gutmann, *The Black Family in Slavery and Freedom, 1750–1925*, New York: Vintage, 1977; and Orlando Patterson, *Rituals of Blood: Consequences of Slavery in Two American Centuries*, Washington DC: Civitas/Counterpoint, 1998. For a recent appraisal, see Wilma Dunaway, *The African–American Family in Slavery and Emancipation*, New York: Cambridge University Press, 2003.

41 See Orlando Patterson, *Slavery and Social Death: A Comparative Study*, Cambridge: Harvard University Press, 1982. For a recent critical discussion see Vincent Brown, "Social Death and Political Life in the Study of Slavery," *American Historical Review* 114, 2009, pp. 1231-49.

42 For a wider discussion of the literature of the injured African American psyche that seems to me relevant to Thompson's concerns, see Daryl Michael Scott, *Contempt and Pity: Social Policy and the Image of the Damaged Black Psyche, 1880–1996*, Chapel Hill: University of North Carolina Press, 1997.

Chapter 8

Postnational Constellations? Political Citizenship and the Modern State

Christian J. Emden

In contrast to political philosophers and legal scholars that have to address the finer theoretical points of deliberative democracy or global citizenship, intellectual historians have a slight advantage—at least at first sight. Examining, for instance, republicanism in Renaissance Italy or Hegel's idea of the state, they seem able to rest assured that much of what they can uncover about the relationship between philosophy and governance has relatively little relevance, if any, for the pressing concerns of the contemporary world of politics. The northern Italian city-states and the German provinces of the early nineteenth century are far removed from the meeting rooms of the European Union or the hallways of the Pentagon. Of course, such an understanding of the task of intellectual history, as far as the latter is concerned with the history of political thought, would be more than shortsighted.

At least one task of intellectual history, then, is indeed to open up a field of investigation that is able to highlight how the present political configurations, at the intersection of political theory and the practices of governance, "reflect a series of choices made at different times between different possible worlds," as Quentin Skinner once put it.[1] It is in this sense that intellectual history entails a "political plea," which is a crucial aspect of James Tully's work, for instance, when he argued for a democratic transformation of the public sphere by renegotiating the vocabulary of the liberal tradition that has been dominant in the history of political theory from Hobbes and Kant to John Rawls and Jürgen Habermas.[2] What comes into view in this encounter between intellectual history and political philosophy is indeed a clearer understanding of the present guided by a "historical and critical approach" (*PPNK* II, 63).[3] In this chapter I shall take up a particularly timely example of such an intersection of political philosophy and intellectual history, namely the relationship between (a) the modern constitutional nation-state as a democratic polity and (b) those civic practices and forms of political citizenship that critically seek to transform the practices of governance within and beyond the nation-state. The questions raised in this context highlight the way in which civic practices, as much as the normative constitutionalism of the Kantian tradition, need to respond to what Raymond Geuss has termed "real politics."[4]

As a specific democratic polity the constitutional nation-state faces problems that are not altogether different from those that are negotiated in postnational or multinational democracies. The presumed decline of the nation-state should not necessarily be taken to mean that the nature of politics as it emerged in the history of the nation-state would cease to be of relevance: indeed the need for political and social integration within the state as well as the state's tendency toward an external projection of power do not become obsolete in a postnational context. Instead, they seem to gain in importance as soon as the nation-state is put into question. On the one hand, this raises the problem of political citizenship in and beyond the nation-state, and on the other, it also raises the problem of what I should like to understand as the imperial challenge which emerges as soon as democratic polities become properly embedded in a postnational constellation. This is particularly the case, as I shall argue, with regard to an emerging European polity. A realist conception of political citizenship has to take into account the many ways in which the state renders such political citizenship possible in the first place.

The limits of cosmopolitanism

Even a merely cursory glance at the history of political thought since the Peace Treaty of Westphalia clearly shows a shift from traditional models of the nation-state as a point of reference for political action to imperial, cosmopolitan and, most recently, postnational forms of political association. The same, of course, can be said of debates in political philosophy and international relations theory after 1945: while Hans Morgenthau's *Politics Among Nations* (1948) at the beginning of the Cold War presented nation-states still as the main political actors, Michael Hardt's and Antonio Negri's *Empire* (2000) as much as Jürgen Habermas's highly influential collection on *The Postnational Constellation* (1998), both written before 9/11, largely sought to come to terms with a political world in which the seemingly traditional nation-state had lost its legitimacy—or at least had come under pressure from a broad range of developments. It is, thus, interesting to see how the history of political thought, especially after the Thirty Years War, increasingly shifted its emphasis towards both imperial structures and the idea of cosmopolitanism, while more recent critical interventions in political philosophy and international relations theory have largely taken the same turn in the aftermath of the Second World War.

The modern nation-state, already at the time of its emergence in the seventeenth century, has always been entangled in the world beyond, either through expansion or through the growing body of international law. One particularly pertinent example for this trend is the way in which the nation-state, almost from the beginning, took part in a discourse of "empire" that sought to project European and, increasingly, North American power both in terms of trade and commerce and in terms of an international legal order that gained shape in the course of the nineteenth century.[5] While the roots of this development can be traced back to the early modern European expansion and settlements in the

Americas, the lesson to be drawn from this "American" experience was that settlement proved a less successful program of expansion than the exploitation of overseas territories: settlements, as in the case of the Americas, could eventually secede as sovereign nation-states.[6]

At the same time, the expansionist tendency of the European nation-states, especially after the failed colonial experiments of the sixteenth and seventeenth centuries, increasingly linked international trade and the projection of a regime of law. This regime of law was grounded either in a belief in the spread of democratic constitutionalism, as in the case of a Victorian "Greater Britain," or it was rooted in a version of international law as a normative philosophical project, as in the case of nineteenth-century Germany, which continued to lack the colonial reach of France and Britain.[7] What has been called the "empire of civilization"—a civilizing process centered on, or emanating from, Europe, which had also featured prominently in the work of Norbert Elias about the "civilizing process"—is intricately linked to the modern nation-state as it emerged after the Thirty Years War.[8] But, as Tully has argued, it is also part of a Kantian version of cosmopolitanism that widened the expansion of European constitutional ideas far beyond their site of origin, transforming, albeit at times unintentionally, constitutional democracy—the democracy of the "moderns"—into a quasi-imperialist endeavor (*PPNK* II, 331–4, 210–16).[9]

Kant's version of cosmopolitanism reflects the complexities of the different models of cosmopolitanism that were in circulation during the later eighteenth century. As such, it is marked by a certain ambiguity: a positive account of the possibility of international rights is coupled with an explicit rejection of a cosmopolitan state.[10] Responding to the reordering of the geopolitical landscape in Europe in the aftermath of the French Revolution, in particular to the peace treaty Prussia and France signed on 5 April 1795 and that made Prussia accept territorial losses, Kant famously argued in *On Perpetual Peace* (1795): "Each nation, for the sake of its own security, can and ought to demand of the others that they should enter along with it into a constitution, similar to the civil one, within which the rights of each could be secured. This would mean establishing a *federation of peoples*."[11] Two years later, in the *Metaphysics of Morals* (1797), at a time when French forces had continued their forays into Prussian and Austrian territory, he noted, on the one hand, that an "international state" was as "incapable of realization" as "*perpetual peace*" itself. On the other hand, even though an "association" of states might be regarded as "dissoluble"—unlike a confederation based on a common political constitution like the US—it remained, in principle, universally normative because nation-states are part of a "community of reciprocal action (*commercium*)" characterized by a set of "constant relations."[12] For Kant, such a community of states, clearly centered on Europe, was also able to extend its legal foundations, for instance, through treaties to the non-European world.[13]

Although he recognized that a cosmopolitan state was impossible, and probably not even desirable, Kant nevertheless accepted the notion of a "*civil union of mankind*" in a "universal *cosmopolitan existence*." Within this framework, international law would be able to realize "a cosmopolitan system of general political security"—what Jürgen Habermas, more than 200 years later, would describe as a "global domestic politics without a world government."[14] For such a system, *pace* Habermas, the nation-state continues to play, however, an important role, mediating between the local and the global, for instance, through its constitutional framework—a framework that needs to be both normative *and* substantive, that is, able to respond to the realities of the political world.

The shift outlined above from the Westphalian nation-state to either empire or cosmopolitanism, or to both at the same time, is also reflected in more recent contributions to political theory, such as Habermas's notion of a "postnational" order of civil society or theories of cosmopolitan democracy as they have been discussed by Ulrich Beck, David Held, and Daniele Archibugi, among others. Held in particular has emphasized that the emergence of global and multinational institutions and relationships, from large-scale corporations and transnational bodies of governance to multilateral trade agreements and the circulation of financial capital, render it inevitable to refocus political theory away from the nation-state.[15] Such theories, one could argue, tend to overlook the historical depth and continuity of an "informal imperialism," that is, the legal and economic structures that have made nineteenth-century imperialism possible and that continue to shape the relationships among nation-states, but also among transnational groups and institutions, in the present (*PPNK* II, 130–7). Is the post-Westphalian world, in other words, really quite as post-Westphalian as often assumed?

Despite such questions, Held contends that dissolving the constitutional nation-state into a cosmopolitan democracy ultimately tends to diffuse the traditional concentration of power among states, thus leading to broader and more fairly distributed forms of political participation and influence—a suggestion that also stands at the center of Archibugi's version of cosmopolitan democracy.[16] For both Held and Archibugi, then, cosmopolitan democracy is a project that becomes manifest on both local and global levels—with overlapping regimes of social practices, legal norms, and political organizations—but particularly in the area of international relations theory, with a focus, for instance, on a reform of existing international law and of the United Nations.[17]

Many of Archibugi's suggestions rest on a historical narrative of justification that, as intellectual historians might note, all too swiftly moves from Hugo Grotius's law of the sea to Woodrow Wilson and the United Nations.[18] Lack of historical contextualization renders Grotius's *De iure belli ac pacis* (1625) or Vattel's *Le Droit de gens* (1758) not as merely anticipating the more recent codification of international law, but indeed often seeks to establish an identity among Grotius, Vattel, and the United Nations. Complex shifts and realignments in the history of political thought, triggered by internal theoretical tensions as much as by seemingly external political or social circumstances, highlight the contingent nature of the history of political thought itself, thus rendering questionable the assumption of a grand theory underlying the stipulations by Held, Archibugi, and others. More importantly, though, the idea that cosmopolitan democracy is a viable enterprise implies a world historical process that, in contrast to Kant's more cautiously formulated notion of a "universal history with cosmopolitan purpose," stipulates an almost linear historical progression and geographic expansion of constitutional democracy that can be observed empirically, and statistically, in the number of states, including Russia, that subscribe, in one way or another, to the principles of democracy.[19] Such a shorthand historical model has to underplay substantial qualitative differences in the nature of democracy among different states, from the realization of constitutional norms to the ability of citizens to factually engage in civic action.[20] Canada, clearly, is a different kind of democratic polity than Russia or Rwanda. At the same time, the premise that democracy is in fact a "universal aspiration" suggests that the meaning of democracy itself is historically not contingent.[21] For Grotius, in other words, democracy essentially bears the same meaning as for Hans Kelsen or within the context of contemporary human rights legislation or in the current efforts to democratize authoritarian regimes in North Africa and the Arab world.[22] Moreover, as a universal aspiration that can be realized only through normative regimes of law, cosmopolitan democracy undermines its own openness to change: universal norms that are not historically contingent cannot be open to negotiation.[23] Cosmopolitan democracy, therefore, does not entail the force of the better argument, but rather tends to withdraw from argument.

Ulrich Beck, on the other hand, sought to criticize precisely the exclusive focus of cosmopolitan democracy on international relations.[24] Instead, he advocated a "cosmopolitan realism" in which "the old differentiations between internal and external, national and international, us and them, lose their validity." The aim here is to achieve what he calls a "trans-national politics" which replaces the perceived simplicity of nation-state structures with an "organized, more or less informal domestic, foreign, interstate and substate politics."[25] It is crucial to point out that Beck clearly does not give up on the function of the state as an organized political and social agent, but rather seeks to integrate and, ultimately, diffuse the latter's responsibilities by linking the state to a network of different forms of associations and institutions reaching beyond the traditional nation-state.

One of Beck's examples for actually existing cosmopolitanism is the response to the question: "Where do you come from?" Such a question would not lead to a clear-cut answer for a French citizen with an English first name and a German sounding last name who grew up in the Alsace but worships at a mosque in Ankara.[26] The question itself suggests that cosmopolitanism correctly places human individuals at the centre of the debate, leaving aside whether such a shift from institutions to individuals is inextricably linked to "moral universalism."[27] Do such examples, however, constitute considerable evidence for a cosmopolitan dissolution of the nation-state? Rather, they might simply be evidence for the complexities of migration. Migration is not necessarily linked to cosmopolitanism, although it can, and often does, play a role in the perception of what counts as cosmopolitanism—a perception that, as Craig Calhoun pointed out, entails an "élite perspective on the world."[28] Neither the Zimbabwean farm worker who flees poverty to South Africa and works on a game reserve, nor the housewife from Guatemala who emigrates to the US to become a domestic worker in Houston, are cosmopolitans strictly speaking—they merely are so in the imagination of theory. Likewise, New Yorkers frequenting Egyptian restaurants while on holiday in Cairo cannot really be regarded as examples of cosmopolitanism, as much as their self-perception might suggest.

Although there are differences between the positions of Held, Beck, and Archibugi, they do have in common the claim that the nation-state is a fundamentally outmoded model of political organization. The question remains, however, whether, for instance, concepts of citizenship traditionally, albeit not exclusively, linked to the nation-state can be replaced with multiple citizenships as an expression of the complexities that cosmopolitanism seeks to reflect. The notion of multiple citizenships makes sense as a metaphor for multilayered social belonging, mutual cultural recognition, and for the way in which many individuals participate in political discourses that are both local and global. But the legal and administrative realities that such a notion of multiple citizenships often has to confront can be daunting.[29]

Nevertheless, as David Owen has perceptively argued, the very notion of citizenship has undergone considerable change since the end of the Second World War toward what reasonably might be called "transpolitical citizenship": a steadily increasing number of nation-states not only accept, or at least tolerate, dual citizenship, but overlapping membership in different, and often very distinct, political communities has become the norm in societies characterized by a relatively high level of migration, both in terms of immigration as much as in terms of emigration.[30] Leaving aside the modalities of such transpolitical citizenship, and leaving aside that citizenship largely continues to be debated within the framework of the nation-state, it is remarkable that the widening acceptance of dual citizenship, for instance, depends less on a growing recognition of normative human rights that provide the kind of protection and individual rights traditionally linked to citizenship as the legal status of membership in a particular nation-state. Rather, it seems in the economic and political interest of nation-states to integrate and enfranchise resident foreigners. Transpolitical citizenship, in other words, is not a manifestation of cosmopolitanism, but rather the outcome of practical considerations and the undeniable pressures, positive and negative, that migration exerts on traditional nation-states. There can be little doubt that citizenship does not need to be based on membership in a nation-state, even if citizenship is reduced to a merely legal status or to a set of rights individuals are in possession of.[31] But such a national citizenship will be dependent more on the practice of governance than on cosmopolitan ideals as highlighted by the example of citizenship in the European Union.[32] It is also in this respect that citizenship cannot be limited to the legal possession of certain rights and duties, but it must also be related to substantive political questions, from solidarity and belonging as contributing factors to social integration in a constitutional democracy to actual participation in political discourse.

Political citizenship and the European polity

In conversation with the notions of cosmopolitan democracy outlined above, Jürgen Habermas has developed a more philosophically oriented model of a postnational civil society. Oriented along the lines of the Kantian tradition of modern political thought, and thus also overlapping with John Rawls's liberalism, he pointed out that cosmopolitanism, strictly speaking, does not constitute a practically achievable goal. Habermas, thus, opted for stressing the procedural norms, or constitutional framework, that would render global governance possible in terms of "a world domestic policy without a world government."[33] At the heart of this proposal stands a procedural concept of democracy that focuses less on substantive political and social issues that require negotiation and more on the norms that enable the achievement of limited rational consensus and that provide the framework within which substantive issues can be negotiated. But it also seems to be the case that, by the late 1990s at least, Habermas appealed not only to the normative import of deliberative democracy and liberal constitutionalism. Rather, he openly linked the normative components of his proposal increasingly to substantive "collective identities" that are able to generate "*civic* solidarity." On an institutional level, such civic solidarity is framed by normative procedures.[34] Habermas, to put it more pointedly, is painfully aware that cosmopolitanism is unlikely to provide the forms of collective identity, social integration, and civic solidarity that should be characteristic of constitutional democracy.

As Habermas noted, it is in the context of the nation-state that such collective identities have been particularly successful in transcending, for instance, the ethnic imagination of traditional nationalisms through an emphasis on "social integration" as it can be found in the German *Sozialstaat*, or social welfare state, marked, among other things, by fairly successful forms of "redistributive taxation."[35] As such, nation-states should not be seen as inherently exclusive polities. Likewise, the administrative function of the state in safeguarding the political integration of diverse communities within a larger polity should not be underestimated. Social justice, then, is to a large extent dependent on the state; it is, more specifically, the nation-state within which both social justice and deliberative forms of democracy have been successful.

Habermas's understanding of the social welfare state is, however, not merely a substantive point of reference for political culture. Its integrative effect is rooted in procedural legitimation.[36] Social justice and deliberative democracy are not only linked, they are, indeed, interdependent. It is with this argument, however, that Habermas detaches the German *Sozialstaat*—as it came into being from the new interventionist models of state administration that appeared in Imperial Germany to the *Sozialvertrag* of the current Federal Republic—from its historical context and universalizes its underlying principles.[37]

Habermas's intertwining of a substantive commitment to specific social values and the latter's normative legitimation is itself already part of the German Basic Law, the *Grundgesetz*. The latter defines the Federal Republic as a federal, democratic, and social *Rechtsstaat*, rendering the German *Sozialstaat* constitutionally as unalienable as the principle of human rights.[38] It is, nevertheless, important to point out that the way in which the Basic Law establishes an equiprimordiality between human rights and social welfare is somewhat unusual. Such equiprimordiality would not be possible in US constitutional law, which gives rights and freedoms in a way that is "often offset by a tendency to grant choices without providing the means for everyone to exercise them."[39] Even the South African constitution, which places much emphasis on its social dimension, makes an indirect distinction between human rights and social rights that can be derived from the former: although the constitution explicitly includes labor relations, housing, healthcare, and social security in its Bill of Rights, later articles that cover the limitation of these rights, and that define states of emergency, specifically exclude such social rights from the list of non-derogable rights.[40] Human rights are non-derogable, while social rights can be abrogated; or, to put it differently, social rights are secondary to human rights—a distinction that is difficult to make under current constitutional law in Germany or with regard to the Charter of Fundamental Rights of the European Union.[41]

As much as the German case, the case of South Africa highlights that constitutional norms often mirror social facts and are thus of a substantive nature: regarding social welfare in terms of human rights is not an economically viable option in South Africa. At the time when the Convention of a Democratic South Africa was successfully negotiating between the ANC and the representatives of the old apartheid regime during the early 1990s, some might have argued that the most rational option for South Africa's future development would be a social-democratic contract between political and labor movements, private business, and state administration that followed the model of post-1945 Germany.[42] But what is rational is not necessarily feasible: any post-apartheid society would have to address unemployment, the existence of an urban underclass as well as widespread rural poverty. Progress on these fronts, however, has been understandably slow and the efficient delivery of social services remains limited[43]—leaving aside the fact that South Africa, ironically as a result of its democratization, bears the hallmarks of a one-party state, while real civic action and the proper negotiation of substantive political questions tends to take place on a more local level. This also means that South Africa, albeit for different reasons, shares America's predicament—that is, the existence of rights without the means to exercise them. In contrast, the structure of the German economy since the later nineteenth century could make the authors of the *Grundgesetz* reasonably expect that after the Second World War social welfare was a distinct possibility, while it was also necessary for political integration. Indeed, the integration of the German state, both after 1945 and after 1991, rests to a considerable degree on the constitutional equiprimordiality of human and social rights.

It is precisely against the background of this specifically German experience that, for Habermas, the procedural, normative and therefore universal legitimation of the social welfare state becomes a decisive figure of thought. Projecting this historically contingent German experience—which certainly has parallels in those other post-1945 European states that are seen as constituting a "core Europe"—into the international arena allows him to normatively deescalate the possibility of conflict over substantive political issues. On this account, global governance consists in the diffusion of conflict through normative procedures. This becomes more obvious if we take into account the geographical perspective Habermas develops, moving from the nation-state to a global perspective. Although he argues, quite correctly, against the idea of a "Nation of Europe" and instead opts for a "European Federation," the latter fundamentally appears as an extension of the nation-state, in particular the *bürgerliche Rechtsstaat* of post-1945 Germany: "The form of civil society that has been limited to the nation-state until now has to spread to include all citizens of the union," so that sovereignty is increasingly transferred to the institutions of the European Union and, finally, to a postnational framework in which political legitimacy is inextricably linked "to the organizational forms of an international negotiation system."[44]

The central issue, of course, is that Habermas's vision of global citizenship and global civil society assumes a primacy of procedural legal norms over substantive issues of conflict and thus seeks to project onto global civil society the norms of the modern constitutional nation-state.[45] From the perspective of global civil society, this means, above all, that "a law may claim legitimacy only if all those possibly affected could consent to it after participating in rational discourses" *and* that "the forms of communication necessary for a reasonable will-formation of the political lawgiver, the conditions that ensure legitimacy, must be legally institutionalized."[46] It is precisely through this legal basis, Habermas holds, that "morality can spread to *all* spheres of action."[47] Of course, the shift from normative legal procedures to morality involves a leap of faith, since there is no necessary link between legality and morality.[48] The reason why Habermas often assumes such a link between legality and morality has much to do with the Kantian framework of procedural democracy: moral action can only develop once autonomous individuals live within civil society and the legal regime that comes along with it. Whether this is historically correct is another matter.

Habermas himself responds to this possible objection by arguing that the "normative content" of democracy, including global civil society, "is partially inscribed in the social facticity of observable political processes"—a social facticity that shows how political processes are governed by the "know-how informing argumentative practices" and that highlights how this "know-how" is "neutral with respect to competing world views and forms of life."[49] Such neutrality, though, as Tully pointed out, seems more suggestive than factual (*PPNK* I, 92). Habermas, however, holds that the reason why it seems as though the value neutrality of political communication conflicts with "real politics," to use Geuss's expression, is that the "constitutional principles" at stake are simply "*insufficiently institutionalized.*"[50] More institutionalization, as it were, shows in an almost Hegelian fashion that reality always already conforms to the norms of reason.[51]

Habermas's position, then, tends to reduce democratic processes and civic practices in the global arena to their institutionalization. It is certainly possible to point out that this "runs the risk of substituting ethics for politics" and unmasks discourse ethics as an ultimately utopian project.[52] In other words, Habermas's position is reasonable as long as he operates in the realm of normativity, but it runs into serious difficulties as soon as he crosses over from the world of norms into the world of facts. It is possible, of course, to point out that already in the realm of normativity, discourse ethics—as laid out, for instance, in the chapters of *Moral Consciousness and Communicative Action* (1983)—fails to address how norms and facts are interrelated. To some extent, Habermas shares this problem with John Rawls and, most interestingly, with Christine Korsgaard, who argued that "the source of normativity of moral claims must be found in the agent's own will," that is, in the "capacity for self-conscious reflection about our actions."[53] But this leaves open the question why one specific substantive political claim (e.g. freedom of expression) should be more normative than another (e.g. censorship of minority opinions). As soon as they enter the realm of real politics, Kantian arguments show that normativity, in a formal sense, is not sufficient.[54]

Habermas sought to avoid the problems sketched out above in *Between Facts and Norms* (1992) by emphasizing that a proceduralist understanding of deliberative democracy necessarily includes both "normative and descriptive components," that is, precisely the two aspects he sought to draw together in the term "constitutional patriotism." On the normative side, "constitutional democracy" is presented as "institutionalizing ... the procedures and communicative presuppositions for a discursive opinion- and will-formation that in turn makes possible ... legitimate lawmaking." On the descriptive side, such institutionalization is "embedded" in the "informal processes of public communication" and in a "lifeworld context shaped by a liberal political culture and corresponding socialization patterns."[55] Although Habermas, thus, argues for the "co-originality" of the normative and descriptive, legal and political, dimensions of deliberative democracy, the relationship is, in fact, oddly one-sided, primarily for two reasons.[56] It is, first of all, only the normative component that guarantees universalism and thus makes it possible to transcend, or overcome, the particularist interests of normal political life. Secondly, the descriptive component assumes, silently, that there are reasons why one would wish to live in a deliberative democracy and partake in liberal public culture, but it is these reasons that can only be found in the normative component—unless, of course, we assume that self-interest, as Hobbes claimed in *Leviathan* (1651), is sufficient, but that would also mean to give up the normative component altogether, as Carl Schmitt did in *Political Theology* (1924).[57] As Tully pointed out, Habermas "presupposes what should be open to testing"—that is, the one thing that cannot be debated in Habermas's model for a global domestic policy is the underlying normative framework itself (*PPNK* I, 97).[58]

To be sure, the argument I have outlined above should not be misunderstood as an argument against constitutional democracy, against the democratic polity, or against the value of institutionalizing law both nationally as well as internationally. To make this more obvious it is necessary to return to the problem of

Europe. It is often argued that the European process of constitutionalization takes place without a state, but it seems difficult to deny that such constitutionalization is one area in which the European Union increasingly has to adopt state-like responsibilities—perhaps even against its own wishes and public rhetoric. But if the European Union becomes more state-like, this certainly raises the question why its citizens, covered by different national and transnational regimes of law, should identify with it, or even regard European integration as a worthwhile social project they wish to take part in. The question that is raised here, of course, is the question of belonging, which the nation-state traditionally answered in a number of ways, some more successful and more reasonable than others, ranging from an ethnically grounded nationalism to a number of civic points of identification, such as contemporary Germany's consensus-driven social contract and the German *Grundgesetz* or Basic Law.

Such points of identification would need to be reflected in Habermas's version of constitutional patriotism, precisely because political discourse is beset with the problem of affect, that is, with an emotional investment that is often relegated to the background in accounts of deliberative democracy.[59] As a result, Calhoun has pointed out that constitutional patriotism, if it is to be relevant at all, needs to entail a form of solidarity that reaches beyond merely procedural norms, while Jan-Werner Müller, occasionally closely following Habermas, argued that constitutional norms, in order to become points of political identification, need to be seen as morally legitimate, that is, as referring back to a civic solidarity defined along the lines of fairness.[60] Such civic solidarity, however, can come under intense pressure; transfer payments and bail-out funds to alleviate the recent European financial crisis highlighted the limits of a European constitutional patriotism.

Within the context of European integration, multiple levels of identification exist in parallel and, most importantly, always in flux and in conflict according to the context and issues at stake in public debate. Nevertheless, at the centre of the debate about European integration stands a tension between different national models of the social contract between governing and governed, and equally different democratic preferences. There is, on the one hand, as Tully has highlighted, a practical form of European integration "in the everyday activities of Europeans"—that is, a "democratic negotiation of norms of integration" beyond official forums and governmental institutions that, despite its integrative tendency, is at the very same time conflict-laden and marks a contested space of politics: "What makes a norm 'democratic' ... is precisely that those subject to it have the right to call it into question here and now, to present reasons for interpreting it in different ways, or, if necessary, for changing it. ... The democratic principle of *audi alteram partem*—always listen to the other side—is applied all the way down so that everyone who speaks for another is held accountable."[61]

On the other hand, it is also necessary to add to this that both the right to call something into question and the democratic principle itself are in most cases safeguarded and successfully framed by the institutions and constitutional arrangements of the nation-states within, or across, which such civic activities are able to take place. In the same way as, for instance, nineteenth-century nationalism—whether in Germany, France or Britain—constituted neither a top-down nor a bottom-up discourse but rather an interlinking of both, European integration inevitably brings both everyday civic practices, many of which are undertaken by the majority of citizens without being aware of them, and constitutional power as well as institutional rule into conversation.[62] Such a conversation inevitably includes conflict, and such conflict occasionally requires mediation, be it through law or through the coercive power of the state.

Political citizenship and governance

Given the European predicament outlined above, what can be witnessed is a "reflexive identity" that emerges not only in the interaction of European citizens and European institutions of governance, but rather constitutes a threefold reflexive relationship between (a) citizens that engage in civic practices within and across nation-states, (b) nation-states that enable, safeguard and, at times, restrict these practices, and (c) a wider European legal and administrative order that has to balance the demands and interests of citizens and nation-states alike.[63] Such a reflexive relationship places great emphasis, as well as considerable stress, on both the idea of what constitutes citizenship and on the relationship between governing and governed far beyond the state of affairs in contemporary Europe. Drawing, to some extent, on Quentin Skinner's republican conception of liberty, Tully, for instance, argued for a notion of citizenship that is centered on the idea of "free citizens"—that is, citizens who achieve, and continuously reactualize, freedom through their active participation in the political process and who seek to transform relationships of power within the democratic polity (*PPNK* I, 135–59, 154–8, 161–6).[64] Such an understanding of citizenship, at first sight, seems to emerge in opposition to a normative definition of citizenship as a legal status that individuals can possess, since it rightly stresses the exercise of practical reason and the unpredictable consequences of political actions. As such, it is also able to reflect the agonistic nature of real politics in which negotiations rarely lead to consensus (*PPNK* I, 163, 181; II, 245). Quite in contrast to the notion of citizenship advanced in the Kantian and liberal traditions, which Tully terms "modern" or "cosmopolitan" citizenship, such a civic citizenship does not assume that it is the normative rule of law which provides the status of citizenship. Rather, citizenship is based on the premise that the normative claims of the rule of law are the context-dependent and ever preliminary outcome of practices of negotiation between different groups—to some extent reversing Habermas's position in that the primacy of norms is replaced by the primacy of substantive political practice.

Seen from this perspective, "citizenship is an identity that members acquire through exchanging reasons in public dialogues and negotiations over how and by whom political power is exercised" (*PPNK* I, 164). But it must also take into account two factors that are crucial for any realist account of political life in the democratic polity. First of all, it needs to take into account Kant's insight, more recently reaffirmed by Calhoun in a more positive vein, that a fair share of the actual citizens in any given state "gladly remain immature for life" and largely do not wish to participate in political processes.[65] Democracy, in other words, cannot be restricted to those who take part in political action, but it must also be recognized as valuable by those who prefer, for one reason or another, not to entertain the kind of civic freedom citizenship demands of them. We might wish that citizens live up to, or at least follow, examples of democratic self-actualization, but in real democratic polities—in multinational states as much as in nation-states—this is more the exception than the norm.

On the one hand, it is certainly important to realize that exemplary forms of political action are able to contribute to a much broader passion for, and commitment to, the democratic process.[66] Gandhi or Nelson Mandela, of course, come to mind. It is nevertheless important to point out that such exemplary forms of political action, at least on a larger scale, are often restricted to periods of dramatic political transition, that is, when former colonies gain independence or authoritarian regimes become democratized. As such, they do not reflect normal political life in advanced democracies. Normal politics in democratic states is far from exemplary; it is tedious and dull, but necessary nonetheless.

On the other hand, virtually all liberal democracies, not only in the West, are characterized by a steady decline in terms of direct political participation since the end of the Second World War. Voter turnout can fluctuate considerably, as in the case of Japan from 74.56 percent in 1980 to 44.50 percent in 1995 and 67.46 percent in 2005, but it can also drop sharply in a relatively short period, as in the case of Britain throughout the 1990s, from 77.7 percent in 1992 to 59.4 percent in 2001.[67] While voter turnout is merely one indicator among many, and perhaps even only a very rough one, it is remarkable that electoral participation among eligible voters in all OECD countries is decreasing slowly.[68] This might not necessarily reflect a declining commitment to democracy. It rather hints at the fact that political action in democratic polities often takes place outside traditional institutions, such as the state or political parties, while political leadership itself has become increasingly dispersed.[69]

Nevertheless, it would be detrimental to any understanding of political citizenship to ignore that public interest in political participation has declined. There are, it seems, primarily four broad reasons for this decline: (a) a growing public recognition of the messy complexity of political decision-making in democracies that often leads to disappointing compromise; (b) a shift in the political decision-making process from citizens' involvement to corporate and commercial actors; (c) a reduction of substantive political questions to economic factors; and (d) the assumption that political actors have a limited capacity to shape increasingly global policy questions.[70] The widespread belief—on both sides of the Atlantic and across the entire political spectrum—that the institutions of the state are inefficient and that political actors have little influence, thus, certainly contributes to an increasing passivity among citizens in advanced democracies. Moreover, the most stable group of active participants in political debate and decision seem to be citizens that are well-educated and relatively affluent.[71] If civic freedom, then, becomes manifest exclusively in a kind of political participation that seeks to question, as much as transform, the relationship between governed and governing, it will have to address the very fact that circumstances, economic and social, might prevent citizens from taking such an active role, and it will also need to take into account that, at times, citizens simply want to be left alone. There is thankfully more to life than civic activism.

The second factor of crucial importance for a realist understanding of political citizenship is in many ways more controversial: it remains open to question whether it is desirable that every member of a given democratic polity should enact his or her civic freedom. Political citizenship, for instance, must be inherently limited if it is to fulfill its obligations, simply because it could otherwise open the door to those who seek to destabilize civic freedom through public dialogue. Violence, in a sense, is not the greatest danger to the democratic polity; it is the latter's uncanny ability to undermine itself. Civic freedom needs to be defensible, and this is perhaps a key lesson that can be taken from the rapid disintegration of the Weimar Republic. The open-endedness of a citizenship along the lines of civic freedom has a tendency to skirt the problem of sovereignty—Carl Schmitt's famous, albeit often misinterpreted, question: "Who decides?"[72] While too great an emphasis on the question of decision has historically threatened democratic polities, as the example of Schmitt shows in the most obvious manner, the diffusion of sovereignty into negotiation, engagement, and preliminary compromise renders it equally difficult to defend the democratic polity. Even though democratic polities can accommodate very different forms of cultural and political diversity, and even though they can provide space for a broad range of struggles for recognition, not all forms of diversity and claims for recognition can be negotiable. To put this point bluntly: democratic polities characterized by negotiating all struggles for recognition might ultimately be unable to recognize those groups that, in their struggle to be recognized, seek to undermine the possibility of mutual recognition.

Much hinges here on what we understand by the "politics of recognition"—that is, the transformation of conflict into a mutual recognition of both differences and commonalities based on respect rather than mere tolerance (*PPNK* I, 166–70).[73] Of course, a politics of recognition can, and should, have limits in the sense that not every claim that demands recognition is necessarily qualified, or justified, to achieve such recognition. It would be difficult, even counterproductive, to apply such a politics of recognition to positions that explicitly seek to undercut the possibility of negotiation in terms of publicly exchanging reasons about substantively relevant political issues.[74] A proper politics of recognition, on this account, could only take place among "free citizens" who seek to transform the relationship between governing and governed while at the same time accepting that it is valuable to have a constitutional framework which is both normative and sufficiently open to integrate the changing real needs of such free citizens. Recognition, after all, affects the distribution of access to resources, and vice versa (*PPNK* I, 297–300). But, as pointed out earlier, such political citizenship is inherently limited. Recognition, then, can only be successful if normative demands are seen to be contextual—that is, inextricably linked to the demands of real politics. It is only against this background that the "forms of recognition" and the "accommodation of identities" that are negotiated in multinational democracies through the practices of free citizens constitute the "shared identity" of these citizens "as citizens of the same association" (*PPNK* I, 181). Political realism, in other words, needs to take into account the limits of recognition.

Furthermore, real political participation also requires contextual expertise of one kind or another—*Bildung*, as Wilhelm von Humboldt would have it, as much as specialized knowledge. There are substantive political questions of considerable importance to all citizens, even to those abstaining from participation in the political process, that cannot reasonably be decided by the governed, as Max Weber once pointed out with regard to "any at all complicated *laws*."[75] The more complex and the more substantive such laws are—for instance, laws concerning immigration, health care, trade agreements, or the regulation of financial markets—the more their discussion in the realm of what Hegel termed "public opinion" tends to be either incoherent or marked by emotional appeals.[76] In this respect, the publicness of civic citizenship also raises the question as to whether publicness can be a value in itself. It might be more reasonable in certain areas, such as foreign policy, that, again as Weber put it, "*conducting things in public*" only has "justification for final *statements* of a standpoint which has been considered carefully in advance."[77]

The two factors of real politics introduced above are certainly connected to the relationship between governing and governed, and as such they are also related to the modern state. The traditional language of government and governance, of course, describes citizens as subjects to be governed (*PPNK* II, 274). Indeed, although both Kant and Hegel, to give merely two examples, sought to address and restructure the relationship between state and citizens on normative grounds, responding in many ways to the French Revolution and its consequences, the language of their respective claims to either a constitutional republic, as in the case of Kant, or constitutional monarchy, as in the case of Hegel, were still indebted to a language that emerged in the context of early modern reason of state theories and that transformed the citizen into the subject of the state.[78] Political citizenship, however, requires a shift from the opposition between state and citizen to their intertwining. While this might be obvious, it is also unconventional. John Locke's assumption, in *Two Treatises of Government* (1690), that "institutionalized forms of government are derived from and perpetually rest upon the prior freedom of the people to exercise political power themselves" is not readily compatible with contemporary liberalism which holds that "political freedom is derived from and rests upon basic institutions and traditions," such as the procedural norms of deliberative democracy outlined in Habermas's *Between Facts and Norms* or the principles of justice as fairness emphasized by Rawls.[79] What emerges here is the same dramatic choice for the constitutional nation-state that Max Weber formulated in 1917 when he was thinking about the future of a democratic German state after the First World War: "There are only two choices: either the mass of citizens is left without freedom or rights in a bureaucratic, 'authoritarian state' which has only the appearance of parliamentary rule, and in which the citizens are administered like a herd of cattle; or the citizens are integrated into the state by making them its *co-rulers*."[80]

The limitations of civic freedom come to the fore as soon as we take into account the nature of real politics in advanced democratic polities. Political citizenship is more dependent on the state than *vice versa*, but a state without political citizenship could not be a democratic polity. On the one hand, the task of governance is "to try to guide … the freedom of the governed in their activities so they disclose and act on the field of possibilities open to them in predictable, utile and productive ways" (*PPNK* II, 276). But in the sense that governance thus presupposes that its constitutive partners are, as it were, free citizens, it is also counter-balanced by the necessary "self-formation" of such free citizens through political participation and, as Tully argues, civic activism (*PPNK* II, 277). It is in this interplay between governing and governed that governance is, first of all, able to revolve around, and to reflect, the "real need" of those who are affected by governance (*PPNK* II, 276). Civic freedom, it is important to point out, does not stand in opposition to either the normative framework of constitutional law in the modern tradition or the regimes of power that characterize the modern constitutional state as a democratic polity. Rather, we are dealing here with a complementary relationship in which these three dimensions of political life are in continuous conversation with each other. This relationship is as relevant in the context of traditional nation-states as it is for postnational democratic polities that transcend the boundaries of the Westphalian nation-state. Indeed, Europe is a particularly interesting example in this respect, precisely because of the way in which it brings together both the traditional nation-state and postnational forms of governance and political action.

The challenge of a European polity

As the only democratic postnational polity properly speaking, the European Union is a complex matter. On the one hand, its current political life is partially marked by a diffusion of sovereignty and its citizens are protected by both their respective national constitutions as well as by European legislation.[81] On the other hand, such overlapping, or "nested," forms of citizenship continue to have clear limitations in favor of national citizenship.[82] This becomes particularly obvious from the perspective of those that, through immigration, become new members of a democratic polity: constitutionally grounded human and social rights continue to be acquired predominantly on the level of the nation-state.[83]

Realistically speaking, then, sovereignty in the European Union is less diffused than commonly assumed and remains with its nation-states.[84] This, it seems, reflects a wider trend. Although the legitimacy of the nation-state has been challenged in recent decades by a number of developments—from the circulation of capital and global policy initiatives to a globalization from below by a broad variety of interest groups and transnational associations—the nation-state continues to be the primary point of reference, for example, for international law. Indeed, as Saskia Sassen pointed out, a "new geography power" might tend to dissolve traditional forms of sovereignty in favor of "corporate economic actors," but we can also observe a tension between "denationalizing economic space and renationalizing political discourse in most developed countries."[85]

Such renationalization, however, can be paradoxical. It certainly seems farfetched to argue, as Étienne Balibar has done, that European citizenship creates yet another level of exclusion, drawing a boundary between inside and outside, between "aliens" and citizens.[86] One could point out that non-citizens already face such exclusion within the context of individual nation-states in the European Union—that is, European citizenship does not fundamentally alter an already existing predicament. For all practical purposes, however, individuals that are not citizens of any EU member state but reside in a member state are covered by a number of central provisions in the European Convention of Human Rights.[87] The complexity of European citizenship, then, might pose more questions than it offers solutions. But it does constitute a form of citizenship in which the sovereignty of the nation-state and the democratic practices of European integration are interlinked—that is, it might be best understood as a postnational citizenship grounded in the right of personhood which enriches, or amends, national citizenship and the constitutional rights connected to the latter.[88] Or, in Bonnie Honig's version: in the European Union "national belonging" is both transcended and resecured at the same time.[89]

Does this mean, however, that the European Union is becoming more like a constitutional nation-state, given that it has already taken over some of the tasks traditionally attributed to the nation-state—from foreign policy coordination and economic regulation to military intervention?[90] If it is to survive, the European Union will need to take a more serious coherent and cohesive response to foreign policy and it will also have to address the obvious and pressing need for greater economic integration and the sharing of financial responsibility.

This, however, leads to a far-reaching, and perhaps uncomfortable, conclusion with regard to the nature of political citizenship and civic freedom. It is certainly the case that the structures of the modern constitutional nation-state do not need to be seen in opposition to those civic practices that put the foundations of the nation-state into question and, at the same time, are able to shift the perspective of governance within the nation-state toward both the local and the global. More importantly, though, in much the same way that nation-states can only be successful in the long term if they are able to integrate civic practices in a meaningful way, civic practices—as the most direct manifestations of political citizenship—ultimately depend on the constitutional and institutional structures of the nation-state to realize their goals in terms of real politics. Citizens by themselves cannot govern in order to alleviate what they might regard as grave injustices, but they can force government to adopt policies of regulation that address such injustices within a constitutional and institutional framework—should they wish to do so, which is far from certain. The realization of civic freedom, it seems, rests above all on a complementarity of state interests and political citizenship. Even the postnational world, then, remains rooted in the world of Westphalian states. Political citizenship is historically grounded—and so are the civic practices that go along with it.

Notes

For comments and questions I am grateful to Antony Anghie, Peter C. Caldwell, and James Tully.

1 Quentin Skinner, *Liberty before Liberalism*, Cambridge: Cambridge University Press, 1997, pp. 116–17.
2 See James Tully, "The Pen is a Mighty Sword: Quentin Skinner's Analysis of Politics," in *Meaning and Context: Quentin Skinner and His Critics*, ed., Tully, Princeton, N.J.: Princeton University Press, 1989, pp. 7–25. For a full account of Tully's critique of the Kantian tradition, see especially "The Kantian Idea of Europe: Critical and Cosmopolitan Perspectives," in *The Idea of Europe: From Antiquity to the European Union* ed., Anthony Pagden, (Cambridge: Cambridge University Press, 2002), pp. 331–58.
3 James Tully, *Public Philosophy in a New Key: Volume I, Democracy and Civic Freedom* and *Public Philosophy in a New Key: Volume II, Imperialism and Civic Freedom*, Cambridge: Cambridge University Press, 2008, hereafter referred to as *PPNK*.
4 See Raymond Geuss, *Philosophy and Real Politics*, Princeton, N.J.: Princeton University Press, 2008.
5 See Martti Koskenniemi, *The Gentle Civilizer of Nations: The Rise and Fall of International Law, 1870–1960*, Cambridge: Cambridge University Press, 2002, pp. 98–178, and Antony Anghie, *Imperialism, Sovereignty and the Making of International Law*, Cambridge: Cambridge University Press, 2005, pp. 32–114.
6 See Anthony Pagden, *Lords of All the World: Ideologies of Empire in Spain, Britain and France, c. 1500–c. 1800*, New Haven, Conn.: Yale University Press, 1995, pp. 126–77, and John H. Elliott, *Empires of the Atlantic World: Britain and Spain in America, 1492–1830*, New Haven, Conn.: Yale University Press, 2006, pp. 325–402.
7 See Duncan Bell, *The Idea of Greater Britain: Empire and the Future of World Order, 1860–1900*, Princeton, N.J.: Princeton University Press, 2007, pp. 31–61 and 92–148, and Koskenniemi, *The Gentle Civilizer of Nations*, pp. 179–264.
8 See Brett Bowden, *The Empire of Civilization: The Evolution of an Imperial Idea*, Chicago: University of Chicago Press, 2009, pp. 26–101, and Norbert Elias, *Über den Prozeß der Zivilisation: Soziogenetische und psychogenetische Untersuchungen*, Frankfurt/M.: Suhrkamp, 1976, vol. II, pp. 434–54.
9 On the different features of "modern" constitutionalism, see also James Tully, *Strange Multiplicity: Constitutionalism in an Age of Diversity*, Cambridge: Cambridge University Press, 1995, pp. 62–70.
10 On Kant's context, see Pauline Kleingeld, "Six Varieties of Cosmopolitanism in Late Eighteenth-Century Germany," *Journal of the History of Ideas* 60, 1999, pp. 505–24.
11 Immanuel Kant, *Perpetual Peace: A Philosophical Sketch*, in *Political Writings*, ed. H.S. Reiss, trans. H.B. Nisbet, 2nd edn, Cambridge: Cambridge University Press, 1991, pp. 93–130: 102. For a fuller account of Kant's project of a federation of states and its underlying philosophical principles, see Pauline Kleingeld, "Approaching Perpetual Peace: Kant's Defence of a League of States and his Ideal of a World Federation," *European Journal of Philosophy* 12, 2004, 304–25.
12 Kant, "The Metaphysics of Morals," in *Political Writings*, pp. 131-75: 171-2. For a full discussion of why such constituional associations are, in Kant's view, universally normative, see Wolfgang Kersting, *Wohlgeordnete Freiheit: Immanuel Kants Rechts-und Staatsphilosophie*, 2nd edn, Frankfurt/M.: Suhrkamp, 1993.

13 Kant, "The Metaphysics of Morals," in *Political Writings*, p. 172.
14 Kant, "Idea for a Universal History with a Cosmopolitan Purpose," in *Political Writings*, pp. 41–53 at 49 and 51, and Jürgen Habermas, "Does the Constitutionalization of International Law Still Have a Chance?" in *The Divided West*, ed. and trans. Ciaran Cronin, Cambridge: Polity Press, 2006, pp. 115–93 at 135-9.
15 See, for instance, David Held, "Democracy and Globalization," in *Re-imagining Political Community: Studies in Cosmopolitan Democracy*, eds, Daniele Archibugi, David Held, and Martin Köhler, Cambridge: Polity Press, 1998, pp. 11–27.
16 See David Held, "Democracy: From City-States to a Cosmopolitan Order?" *Political Studies* 40, 2007, pp. 10–39, and *Democracy and the Global Order: From the Modern State to Cosmopolitan Governance*, Cambridge: Polity Press, 1995, pp. 99–139, 231–8 and 267–86, as well as Daniele Archibugi, *The Global Commonwealth of Citizens: Toward Cosmopolitan Democracy*, Princeton, N.J.: Princeton University Press, 2008, pp. 4-5.
17 See, for instance, Daniele Archibugi and Raffaele Marchetti, "Democratic Ethics and UN Reform," in *The Ethics of Global Governance*, ed., Antonio Franceschet, Boulder, Col.: Lynne Rienner Publishers, 2009, pp. 51–66: 60–4, and Archibugi, "From the United Nations to Cosmopolitan Democracy," in *Cosmopolitan Democracy: An Agenda for a New World Order*, eds, Daniele Archibugi and David Held, Cambridge: Polity Press, 1995, pp. 121–62 at 149–55.
18 See, for instance, Daniele Archibugi, "Principles of Cosmopolitan Democracy," in Archibugi, Held, and Köhler, eds, *Re-imagining Political Community*, pp. 198–228 at 198–9.
19 See Archibugi, "Principles of Cosmopolitan Democracy," pp. 201–3, 209–10.
20 Archibugi is aware of these qualitative differences, but integrates them into an overarching political progress within which they become irrelevant. See ibid., p. 202.
21 Ibid., p. 203.
22 Grotius is a case in point. He uses the term "democracy" only on two occasions, in the context of a discussion of the nature of sovereign power, which refers back to Aristotle. See Hugo Grotius, *De jure belli ac pacis libri tres / The Rights of War and Peace*, trans. Francis W. Kelsey, Oxford: Clarendon Press, 1925, I. iii, 8, 10. Aristotle's notion of democracy is, however, at best ambivalent and should not be equated with what, since the eighteenth century, is understood to be constitutional democracy or, in Aristotle's term, "polity." See Aristotle, *Politics*, trans. T.A. Sinclair, 3rd edn, London: Penguin, 1992, pp. 189–206 (III. 7–11), 243–63 (IV. 4–9).
23 Archibugi, "Principles of Cosmopolitan Democracy," p. 217.
24 Ulrich Beck, *The Cosmopolitan Vision*, trans. Ciaran Cronin, Cambridge: Polity Press, 2006, p. 32.
25 Ibid., pp. 14, 37.
26 See ibid., p. 25. Admittedly, Beck's example is less complex than the one I used.
27 For the argument of cosmopolitanism's emphasis on human individuals as an argument for moral universalism, see Patrick Hayden, *Cosmopolitan Global Politics*, Aldershot: Ashgate, 2005, pp. 11–36.
28 Craig Calhoun, "The Class Consciousness of Frequent Travellers: Towards a Critique of Actually Existing Cosmopolitanism," in *Debating Cosmopolitics*, ed., Daniele Archibugi, London: Verso, 2003, pp. 86–116 at 92.
29 See ibid., p. 95.
30 See David Owen, "Transpolitical Citizenship," in *Prospects of Citizenship*, eds, Gerry Stoker et al., London: Bloomsbury, 2011. I am grateful to David Owen for making a draft of this chapter available.
31 See, for instance, Dora Kostakopoulou, *The Future Governance of Citizenship*, Cambridge: Cambridge University Press, 2008.
32 See Christoph Schönberger, *Unionsbürger: Europas Bürgerrecht in vergleichender Sicht*, Tübingen: Mohr Siebeck, 2005, pp. 275–300.

33 Jürgen Habermas, "The Postnational Constellation and the Future of Democracy," in *The Postnational Constellation: Political Essays*, trans. and ed. Max Pensky, Cambridge, MA: MIT Press, 2001, 58–112 at 110. For a critique of the philosophical foundations of Habermas's position, see Tully, "To Think and Act Differently: Comparing Critical Ethos and Critical Theory," and "The Unfreedom of the Moderns in Comparison to Their Ideals of Constitutional Democracy," both in *Public Philosophy in a New Key*, vol. I, pp. 71–131 at 83–93, and vol. II, pp. 91–123, respectively.

34 Habermas, "The Postnational Constellation and the Future of Democracy," p. 108.

35 Ibid., pp. 65, 76.

36 See, for instance, Jürgen Habermas, *Between Facts and Norms: Contributions to a Discourse Theory of Law and Democracy*, trans. William Rehg, Cambridge, MA: MIT Press, 1996, p. 410.

37 On state intervention through administrative law and economic policy in Imperial Germany and the Weimar Republic, see Toni Pierenkemper and Richard Tilly, *The German Economy during the Nineteenth Century*, New York: Berghahn, 2004, pp. 138–44. On the development and structural problems of the German social welfare model, see Franz-Xaver Kaufmann, *Sozialpolitisches Denken: Die deutsche Tradition*, Frankfurt/M.: Suhrkamp, 2003.

38 See the relationship among the following articles: *Grundgesetz*, ed. Udo di Fabio, 39th edn, Munich: dtv, 2004, Art. 1 § 1, Art. 20 § 1, Art. 28 § 1.1, and Art. 79 § 3.

39 Derek Curtis Bok, *The State of the Nation: Government and the Quest for a Better Society*, Cambridge, MA: Harvard University Press, 1998, p. 375.

40 See *Constitution of the Republic of South Africa: Act 108 of 1996, to Introduce a New Constitution for the Republic of South Africa and to Provide for Matters Incidental Thereto*, Pretoria: Government Printer, 1996, Arts 23, 26–7, and 36–7. The various amendments passed since January 1997 do not affect the way in which social rights are secondary to human rights.

41 See *Charter of Fundamental Rights of the European Union* (2000/C 364/01), Arts 26–38.

42 See Heribert Adam and Kogila Moodley, *The Opening of the Apartheid Mind: Options for the New South Africa*, Berkeley, Calif.: University of California Press, 1993, pp. 210–14.

43 See Aletta J. Norval, *Deconstructing Apartheid Discourse*, London: Verso, 1996, pp. 297–8, and Gerhard Maré, "The State of the State: Contestation and Race Re-assertion in a Neoliberal Terrain," in *The State of the Nation: South Africa, 2003–2004*, eds, John Daniel, Adam Habib and Roger Southall, Cape Town: Human Sciences Research Council, 2003, pp. 25–52 at 43–7.

44 Habermas, "The Postnational Constellation and the Future of Democracy," pp. 99, 109.

45 See Habermas, *Between Facts and Norms*, pp. 118–31, 168–86.

46 Habermas, "The Postnational Constellation and the Future of Democracy," pp. 116–17.

47 Habermas, *Between Facts and Norms*, p. 118.

48 See Rainer Forst, *Contexts of Justice: Political Philosophy Beyond Liberalism and Communitarianism*, trans. John M.M. Farrell, Berkeley, Calif.: University of California Press, 2002, p. 28. As Forst points out, Habermas himself suggests on other occasions that normative procedures and morality respond to very different problems. See Habermas, "Discourse Ethics: Notes on a Program of Philosophical Justification," in *Moral Consciousness and Communicative Action*, trans. Christian Lenhardt and Shierry Weber Nicholsen, intro. Thomas McCarthy, Cambridge, MA: MIT Press, 1993, pp. 43–115.

49 Habermas, *Between Facts and Norms*, pp. 287–8.

50 Ibid., p. 436.

51 With regard to political life, see Georg Wilhelm Friedrich Hegel, *Elements of the Philosophy of Right*, ed. Allen W. Wood, trans. H.B. Nisbet, Cambridge: Cambridge University Press, 1991, p. 20 (preface).

52 Calhoun, "The Class Consciousness of Frequent Travellers," p. 110, and Tully, "To Think and Act Differently," in *PPNK* I, 119–29.
53 Christine M. Korsgaard, *The Sources of Normativity*, ed. Onora O'Neill, Cambridge: Cambridge University Press, 1996, p. 19.
54 T.R.S. Allan, *Constitutional Justice: A Liberal Theory of the Rule of Law*, Oxford: Oxford University Press, 2001, pp. 21–9, discusses this problem with regard to the notion of equality: governments must substantively justify the distinctions they make between citizens, and between citizens and non-citizens.
55 Habermas, *Between Facts and Norms*, p. 437.
56 See ibid., p. 314, and Habermas, "The Postnational Constellation and the Future of Democracy," p. 118.
57 See Thomas Hobbes, *Leviathan, with Selected Variants from the Latin Edition of 1668*, ed. Edwin Curley, Indianapolis, Ind.: Hackett, 1994, pp. 76 (I.xiii.9) and 106 (II.xvii.1), and Carl Schmitt, *Political Theology: Four Chapters on the Concept of Sovereignty*, trans. and introd. George Schwab, foreword Tracy B. Strong, 2nd edn, Chicago: University of Chicago Press, 2005, pp. 16–35.
58 See also Tully, "On the Global Multiplicity of Public Spheres: The Democratic Transformation of the Public Sphere?" in *Beyond Habermas: Democracy, Knowledge, and the Public Sphere*, eds, Christian J. Emden and David Midgley, New York: Berghahn, 2012.
59 See Chantal Mouffe, *On the Political*, London: Routledge, 2005, pp. 24–34.
60 See Craig Calhoun, "Constitutional Patriotism and the Public Sphere: Interests, Identity, and Solidarity in the Integration of Europe," in *Global Ethics and Transnational Politics*, eds, Pablo De Greiff and Ciaran Cronin, Cambridge, MA: MIT Press, 2002, pp. 275–312, and Jan-Werner Müller, *Constitutional Patriotism*, Princeton, N.J.: Princeton University Press, 2007, pp. 46–91.
61 Tully, "A New Kind of Europe? Democratic Integration in the European Union," in *Public Philosophy in a New Key*, vol. II, pp. 225–42 at 226, 229.
62 See, however, ibid., p. 229.
63 This notion of a "reflexive identity" has been suggested by Hans Lindahl and is quoted in Tully, "A New Kind of Europe?" in *PPNK* as the "democratic relation between the people and their governors" (*PPNK* II, 242). See also Hans Lindahl, "Acquiring a Community: The Acquis and the Institution of European Legal Order," *European Law Journal* 9, 2003, 433–50, and "Constituent Power and Reflexive Identity: Towards an Ontology of Collective Selfhood," in *The Paradox of Constitutionalism: Constituent Power and Constitutional Form*, eds, Martin Loughlin and Neil Walker, Oxford: Oxford University Press, 2007, pp. 9–24.
64 Tully draws here on Skinner, *Liberty before Liberalism*, pp. 30 and 74, but this notion of free citizens also has many links to the republican tradition of the Italian city states, a tradition that in many ways lies at the core of the Cambridge School of intellectual history. See Quentin Skinner, "The Republican Ideal of Liberty," in *Machiavelli and Republicanism*, eds, Gisela Brock, Quentin Skinner, and Maurizio Viroli, Cambridge: Cambridge University Press, 1990, pp. 293–308.
65 Kant, "An Answer to the Question: 'What is Enlightenment?'" in *Political Writings*, pp. 54–60 at 54. See also Calhoun, "The Class Consciousness of Frequent Travellers," p. 100.
66 See Aletta J. Norval, *Aversive Democracy: Inheritance and Originality in the Democratic Tradition*, Cambridge: Cambridge University Press, 2007, pp. 187–213.
67 International Institute for Democracy and Electoral Assistance (IDEA), Stockholm, Sweden (http://www.idea.int/vt/), and UK House of Commons Research Papers 01/54, 05/33 and 10/36.
68 See Colin Hay, *Why We Hate Politics*, Cambridge: Polity Press, 2007, pp. 13–14.
69 See the overview in Hans-Dieter Klingemann and Dieter Fuchs, eds, *Citizens and the*

State, Oxford: Oxford University Press, 1995, and John Kane, Haig Patapan and Paul Hart, "Dispersed Democratic Leadership," in *Dispersed Democratic Leadership: Origins, Dynamics, and Implications,* eds, Kane, Patapan and Hart, Oxford: Oxford University Press, 2009, pp. 1–12.
70 See Gerry Stoker, *Why Politics Matters: Making Democracy Work*, New York: Palgrave Macmillan, 2006, p. 10; Colin Crouch, *Post-Democracy*, Cambridge: Polity Press, 2004, pp. 1–30; and Hay, *Why We Hate Politics*, pp. 1–59.
71 Hay, *Why We Hate Politics*, pp. 5, 19–20.
72 See Schmitt, *Political Theology*, pp. 5–15.
73 Tully understands such a "politics of recognition" also in terms of "identity politics," arguing that identities are not stable but shaped by struggles for recognition. See Tully, "The Negotiation of Reconciliation," in *Public Philosophy in a New Key*, vol. I, pp. 223–56 at 229–38.
74 While much can be said for the intrinsic value of recognition as a political principle, it is doubtful that all political struggles really are about recognition: individuals and groups are not necessarily predisposed to mutual recognition, while the central and often underestimated role that power plays in such political struggles might demand a more agonistic understanding of the political. See Patchen Markell, *Bound by Recognition* (Princeton, N.J.: Princeton University Press, 2003) and Lois McNay, *Against Recognition* (Cambridge: Polity Press, 2008). For alternative models of an agonistic democracy, see Mark Wenman, *Agonistic Democracy: Constituent Power in the Era of Globalization* (Cambridge: Cambridge University Press, 2013).
75 Max Weber, "Suffrage and Democracy in Germany," in *Political Writings*, ed. Peter Lassman and Ronald Speirs, Cambridge: Cambridge University Press, 1994, pp. 80–129 at 128.
76 See Hegel, *Elements of the Philosophy of Right*, pp. 353–5 (§§ 317–18). See also Weber, "Parliament and Government in Germany under a New Political Order," in *Political Writings*, pp. 130–271 at 230–1.
77 Weber, "Parliament and Government in Germany under a New Political Order," in *Political Writings*, p. 186.
78 See Kant's discussion of "political right" in *The Metaphysics of Morals*, in *Political Writings*, pp. 136–54, and Hegel's discussion of the state in *Elements of the Philosophy of Right*, pp. 305–59 (§§ 272–319).
79 James Tully, *An Approach to Political Philosophy: Locke in Contexts*, Cambridge: Cambridge University Press, 1993, p. 315, referring to John Locke, *Two Treatises of Government*, ed. Peter Laslett, Cambridge: Cambridge University Press, 1970, pp. 381–2 (II.xv.171). See, in contrast, John Rawls, "Justice as Fairness: Political not Metaphyiscal," *Philosophy and Public Affairs* 14, 1985, 223–52, and Habermas, *Between Facts and Norms*, pp. 287–328.
80 Weber, "Suffrage and Democracy in Germany," in *Political Writings*, p. 129.
81 On the diffusion of sovereignty in the European Union, see, for instance, Michael Keating, *Plurinational Democracy: Stateless Nations in a Post-Sovereignty Era*, Oxford: Oxford University Press, 2001, pp. 134–58. It is questionable, however, whether Keating's account accurately reflects central aspects of common European policy. On the tensions between European and national citizenship, see J.H.H. Weiler, *The Constitution of Europe*, Cambridge: Cambridge University Press, 1999, pp. 324–56.
82 On such "nested" citizenship and its problems, see Owen, "Transpolitical Citizenship"; Rainer Bauböck, "Why European Citizenship? Normative Approaches to Supranational Union," *Theoretical Inquiries in Law* 8, 2007, 452–88; Peter Kivisto and Thomas Faist, *Beyond a Border: The Causes and Consequences of Contemporary Immigration*, Thousand Oaks, Calif.: Sage, 2010, pp. 245–54; Thomas Faist, "Social Citizenship in the European Union: Nested Membership," *Journal of Common Market Research* 39, 2001, 37–58.
83 See Kivisto and Faist, *Beyond a Border*, p. 256.

84 This is the case even in the context of the failed draft treaty for a European Constitution. See Clive H. Church and David Phinnemore, *Understanding the European Constitution: An Introduction to the EU Constitutional Treaty*, London: Routledge, 2006, pp. 129–30.
85 Saskia Sassen, *Losing Control? Sovereignty in an Age of Globalization*, New York: Columbia University Press, 1996, pp. xiv, 1–29.
86 See Étienne Balibar, *We, the People of Europe?* Princeton, N.J.: Princeton University Press, 2003, p. 122. For a philosophically and legally more sophisticated analysis of the inevitability of complex, interrelated boundaries, see Hans Lindahl, "A-legality: Postnationalism and the Question of Legal Boundaries," *The Modern Law Review* 73, 2010, pp. 30–56. I am grateful to Hans Lindahl for making this article available to me before publication.
87 See Francis G. Jacobs and Robin C.A. White, *The European Convention on Human Rights*, 2nd edn, Oxford: Clarendon Press, 1996, pp. 278–83. Freedom of movement is also extended to those non-citizens of EU member states that do not reside in the EU lawfully, provided that they are not in conflict with criminal law. Nevertheless, despite this extension of the freedom of movement, individual deportation is possible, while any "collective expulsion of aliens is prohibited."
88 See Carlos Closa, "National Plurality within a Single Statehood in the European Union," in Ferran Requejo ed., *Democracy and National Pluralism*, London: Routledge, 2001, pp. 105–27 at 106–9. See also Vito Breda, "A European Constitution in a Multinational Europe or a Multinational Constitution for Europe?" *European Law Journal* 12, 2006, 330–44. The current state of European Union citizenship law, and its implications within a multilevel European polity, are discussed in Jo Shaw, *The Transformation of Citizenship in the European Union: Electoral Rights and the Restructuring of Political Space*, Cambridge: Cambridge University Press, 2007, pp. 18–50.
89 See Bonnie Honig, "Another Cosmopolitanism? Law and Politics in the New Europe," in Seyla Benhabib, *Another Cosmopolitanism, with Jeremy Waldron, Bonnie Honig, and Will Kymlicka*, ed. Robert Post, Oxford: Oxford University Press, 2006, pp. 102–27 at 114.
90 See Ulrich K. Preuß, "Europa als politische Gemeinschaft," in *Europawissenschaft*, eds, Gunnar Folke Schuppert, Ingolf Pernice and Ulrich Haltern, Baden-Baden: Nomos, 2005, pp. 489–539 at 499–502, 519–21.

Part III

Re-Imagining Civic Freedom Today

Chapter 9

Spaces of Freedom, Citizenship and State in the Context of Globalization: South Africa and Bolivia

Eunice N. Sahle

James Tully's work offers a deeper understanding of the intellectual, political and economic developments that have historically, and in the contemporary epoch, shaped our political, economic, ecological and social worlds. The breadth of his work – ranging from debates concerning social recognition to citizenship, imperialism, freedom and democracy and many other themes – makes it impossible to engage with all dimensions of his scholarship. Thus, this chapter limits its efforts to an examination of one of the keywords[1] in Tully's two volumes on public philosophy: globalization.[2] The underlying premise of the chapter is that Tully's complex approach to processes of neoliberal globalization (NG) greatly enriches our understanding of freedom, citizenship-making, and state reconfiguration that have emerged in the contemporary era. The discussion evolves in three sections with the first teasing out core elements of Tully's complex approach to NG. Drawing on insights from this approach, sections two and three discuss case studies from South Africa and Bolivia.

Tully on contemporary globalization

In the last three decades, globalization has emerged as a keyword in discussions about political, economic and cultural processes. The purpose of the discussion that follows is not to engage in the expansive and contentious debates about the meaning and implications of contemporary globalization. Rather its objective is to tease out core elements of what it considers as Tully's complex approach to some constitutive features of NG. These elements are domination, spatiality, state and contestation.

In various parts of his two volumes on public philosophy, Tully pays close attention to structures of domination in different historical epochs. In doing so, he focuses on ideas and practices underpinning historical and contemporary modes of imperialism and their social and political consequences. For example, he explores the internal colonialism that has characterized relations between indigenous peoples in Canada and the state apparatus. Overall, his concern with the question of domination sees him examining the role of political theory, constitutional democracy and public law in imperial projects. In his studies of current structures of domination, he conceptualizes globalization under neoliberal conditions as forming one such structure. From Tully's perspective, policies underpinning NG are manifestations of contemporary informal imperialism. At the core of Tully's discussion of imperialism in the era of NG is the analytical insight that the end of formal imperialism did not mark the end of imperial strategies and relations. Elaborating on this idea, he states that 'in the course of my research on globalization and freedom ... I came to see that the languages in which the global order was disclosed ... were useful and necessary, yet ultimately limited and inadequate to expose fully the deep-seated global relationships of oppression' which emerged in the era of 'formal Western imperialism' (*PPNK* II, 127). According to Tully, these earlier structures of domination 'survived decolonisation' projects and have 'intensified' in the era of NG (*ibid.*). His complex approach challenges political and other theories that ignore how the ideological, political and economic processes underpinning NG are enabling the reproduction of vestiges of imperialism and related forms of domination.

Features of NG as a structure of domination are for instance embedded in the political and economic modalities of institutions of global governance, mainly the World Trade Organization, the World Bank and the International Monetary Fund. To begin with, the policies of these institutions escape the democratic controls that states are subjected to in a democratic national setting. For Tully, the constitutional orders governing their emergence and practices 'do not pass through and are not subject to the democratic deliberation of the humans who are subject to them' (*PPNK* II, 101). While this form of constitutionalism has 'gained priority' in sites of global governance, its undemocratic character renders it 'illegitimate' (ibid.). Second, these institutions promote policies aimed at the reconfiguration of local economic policies and the role of the state in economic processes, without paying attention to the social and economic consequences of such a shift. The undemocratic character of the constitutional order governing these institutions and their neoliberal ideology has, for example, seen the push towards privatization of public goods and the dismantling of social protections in the name of promoting efficiency, economic development and the growth of the global economy. Overall, processes of NG and their attendant constitutional order are facilitating the penetration and control of local economies by undemocratic global forces such as multinational corporations and institutions of global governance.

Tully's framing of NG as a structure of domination is important to our understanding of its processes, ideas, policies, and social agents, and their role in the emergence of contemporary practices of imperialism. Nonetheless, it is important to note that NG is not the only structure of domination in the contemporary era. Tully's work highlights how other spaces of power, such as states, can be sources of domination. In general, state forms are premier structures of domination not only because of their 'monopoly of the legitimate use of physical force' to borrow from Max Weber,[3] but also because of their distinctive ideologies, policies and historical developments. Overall, while Tully is cognizant of the powerful effects of NG and its informal imperial strategies, his global and local – '*glocal*' (*PPNK* II) – approach to political and economic developments moves us away from a global gaze as the sole structure of domination. As such, his work signals a more complex approach to geographies of structures of domination.

For some time now, the question of spatiality has dominated debates in social theory and geography.[4] A central question in these debates is the privileging of history at the expense of spatial processes. As Michel Foucault suggests, in such analysis 'space' is 'treated as the dead, the fixed, the undialectical, the immobile' while 'time' (or history) has been associated with 'richness, fecundity, life, dialectic'.[5] Geographers such as Edward Soja have commented extensively on the aspatiality in most disciplines and the privileging of history in scholarly works. According to Soja, 'thinking historically about society and social relations is more familiar and has tended to be seen as potentially if not inherently more revealing and insightful than thinking spatially or geographically'. Yet, in his view, 'space, time, along with their more concrete and socially constructed extensions as geography and history, are the most fundamental and encompassing qualities of the physical and social worlds in which we live'. Thus a 'rebalancing of spatial and historical perspectives' is much needed given the neglect of the centrality of space in social, political, economic and other scholarly analysis.[6]

While Tully does not situate his work in debates on spatiality, engagement with his work indicates that spatial thinking is a constitutive feature of his examination of globalization, citizenship, democracy and governance in the contemporary conjuncture. Overall, his spatial sensitivity departs from orthodox perspectives of NG that tend to ignore the spatiality of globalization processes.[7] For Tully, place-making and other geographical processes are intertwined with social and historical processes, thus they influence the manner in which practices of NG translate in a given scale. Two examples of Tully's spatial thinking will suffice here. First, he does not approach globalization as 'a singular' process, rather he suggests that it is 'a cluster of uneven, hierarchical and unpredictable processes of interregional networks and of interaction and exchange' (*PPNK* II, 58). Thus, although he takes seriously the powerful effects of global forces underpinning NG such as multinational corporations, metropolitan states and institutions of global governance, his analytical lens is not solely focused on the global scale. For Tully, processes of NG are constituted and translated in a range of geographical scales: global, regional, national level and other scales. His discussion of the multi-layered character of modes of governance in the context of an unequal world order underpinned by mechanisms of informal imperialism is an example of his multi-scalar approach to NG. Further, his multi-scalar perspective on governance under NG disrupts the view that it is only states that are involved in governance. According to Tully, social movements and non-governmental organizations can be fruitfully conceptualized as spaces of governance in the contemporary era.

Second, processes of NG are implicated in the production of space, albeit differently at each scale depending on the nature of the 'ever shifting geometry of social/power relations'[8] such as imperial practices 'based on the control of peoples and markets by indirect, infrastructural control' (*PPNK* II, 58). Tully's spatial approach indicates that processes of NG are contributing to the production and reconfiguration of political, cultural and economic space.[9] For him, the production of space under NG is influenced by existing spatial relations, socio-economic conditions and historical developments, including the unequal power relations that have underpinned what Walter Mignolo has termed the 'modern/colonial world system'.[10] As such, the reconfiguration of state space[11] under NG in Canada, for instance, will be different than in South Africa and Bolivia.

Another feature of Tully's complex approach to processes of NG is his perspective on the intersection between these processes and state forms. Advocates of neoliberalism have pushed for the restructuring of the role of the state in the economy and other sectors. Proponents of these processes claim that they will lead to efficiency, rational allocation of scarce government resources, economic growth and prosperity. In the context of Africa[12] and other geographies in the global South, these tenets of NG are constructed as policy tools that will curtail rent-seeking activities, waste and corruption. Furthermore, they will lead to the emergence of an entrepreneurial class that is committed to the ethos of market-led development. The discourse of rolling back the state under NG has led scholars to contend that states are retreating[13] from their traditional roles as the logic of the market has emerged as the new common sense.[14] Overall, while in practice the private sector and key social agents of NG such as international banks are dependent on functioning state forms for their economic and political activities, neoliberal theorists call for market-led development and consider a minimalist state the best way to expand conditions for economic and political freedom.[15]

While acknowledging that as a structure of domination NG has influenced political and economic practices of the state, Tully's complex approach makes an important contribution to our understanding of the interplay between processes of NG and state forms. It indicates that states have mediated these processes, thus they have not been their passive victims. To be sure, processes linked to NG such as privatization, budget cuts and liberalization of trade have contributed to the reconfiguration of states' administrative and economic space and have generated unjust social conditions in both the global North and South. However, as Tully argues, states have not surrendered their power and legitimate authority to make policies to a naturalized 'external agent, a deus ex machina'[16] called globalization. Commenting on the case of Canada, he states that 'there is little in global economic processes that now impede, say, job creation policies. Only traditional constraints on representative will-formation impede such policies, and the rise of social-democratic governments in Europe has shown that these can be overcome' (*PPNK* II, 60).

Tully's approach to the intersection of globalization and state power has significant analytical merit. This approach departs from the 'hyper-globalizers' (*ibid.*) who represent NG as a development that is leading to the decline of state forms rather than contributing to processes of reconfiguration of state space. Further, conceptualizing NG as a mediated process diverges from the dominant perspective that tends to represent the global scale as the only influence on modalities of state power and practices. Such an approach opens the possibility of exploring other possible sources of state transformation in countries such as Bolivia and elsewhere. Tully's approach leads one to think of state processes in the plural, for while taking seriously the conditioning role of global variables such as NG, it considers specific historical, spatial and political developments as important influences on such processes.

Finally, Tully's work makes clear the contested nature of NG. Rapid flows of capital, technological transformation, informal imperialism and other markers of NG do not encounter empty local geographies that are effortlessly steamrolled by external developments. Rather, through 'strategies of freedom' (*PPNK* II, 65), citizens challenge the social and political effects generated by NG in various parts of the world. As Tully powerfully reminds us, strategies or 'practices of freedom' (*PPNK* I, 23) by those who are subjects of power are a central feature of practices of government. Practices of government are characterized by 'techniques of government, strategies of freedom and modes of conduct' (*PPNK* II, 65). Thus, powerful as they may be, practices of government, neoliberal or otherwise, do not exist in a vacuum devoid of political agency of citizens. From the perspective of those who are subjects of power, the 'exercise of power' (*PPNK* I, 23) by local or global agents 'opens up ... ways of thinking and acting in response' (ibid.). Furthermore, it is through engaging in practices of freedom, such as 'acting otherwise within the rules of game' or bringing forward issues for 'negotiation, deliberation, problem-solving and reform with the aim of modifying' them, that we become citizens (*PPNK* I, 24). Consequently, processes of 'citizen formation',[17] or what Tully calls 'citizenisation' (*PPNK* I, 311), are possible even under structures of domination such as those that characterize NG. As Tully argues:

> One comes to acquire an identity as a citizen through participation in the practices and institutions of one's society, through having a say in them and over the ways one is governed. In complex contemporary political, legal, cultural and economic associations, one of the fundamental ways that this process of citizenisation occurs is through participation in the very activities in which the norms of mutual recognition in any subsystem are discussed, negotiated, modified, reviewed and questioned again. (ibid.)

Tully's emphasis on the possibility of practices of freedom has implications for debates concerning citizenship and political imaginaries in the context of conditions of domination generated by NG. In terms of citizenship, Tully's work on freedom embodies an active conceptualization of citizenship, in contrast with the passive one embedded in the neoliberal political globalization project that promotes 'low-intensity democracy' (*PPNK* II, 156) in the global South and elsewhere. According to the latter, the duty of citizens in a democracy is solely to 'produce a government'.[18] In this elitist democracy formulation, once citizens have elected their political representatives their participation in the political arena ends, for, in

Schumpeter's view, 'political action' is the responsibility of politicians.[19] Citizens are expected to return to their apolitical everyday life until the next electoral cycle, the only time Schumpeter considers their political agency relevant. Tully's active mode of citizenship enables us to understand the practices of freedom that have characterized public discourses and political developments in South Africa, Argentina, Greece, Britain, Bolivia and other countries in the era of NG. At the level of political imaginaries, Tully's work on practices of freedom contributes to a politics of realist hope because it pushes us to focus on emerging politics of citizenship and reconfiguring of state spaces even under NG as a structure of domination.

The preceding discussion has highlighted several key elements of Tully's critical approach to NG. His framing of NG as a structure of domination sheds light on its role in generating practices of informal imperialism in the contemporary era. Further, his spatial thinking alerts us to the multi-scalar processes of globalization, and the role of these processes in the production and reconfiguration of political, economic and state spaces. In addition, his work challenges studies that neglect the role of states in processes of NG. Moreover, his conceptualization of NG as a contested process contributes to our understanding of practices of freedom that have emerged in the NG epoch. Overall, one of things that I find very inspiring and at the same time challenging is the dialectical tension between structures of domination and democratic freedom in Tully's studies of historical, political, economic and social orders. I suggest that this tension offers an analytical lens that facilitates an exploration and understanding of the emergence of spaces of freedom, citizenisation and a politics of realist hope in the context of NG. I illuminate some of the insights from the preceding discussion in the next section drawing on empirical examples from South Africa and Bolivia.

SPACES OF FREEDOM AND CITIZENIZATION IN POST-APARTHEID SOUTH AFRICA

1994 marked an important historical turn for South Africans. After decades of political struggles in response to centuries of social, spatial, political and economic oppression of the majority African population, the country held its first multi-racial democratic elections in that year. The African National Congress (ANC) won the elections, paving the way for Nelson Mandela to become the President of democratic South Africa. However, from the late 1990s to this writing in 2012, popular protests against the state at various geographical scales have replaced the euphoria that characterized the country's public squares in the events leading to the founding elections and the early days of Mandela's presidency. While not the sole determinant of these protests, the deepening of neoliberal ideas in the formation and implementation of public policy has influenced their rise and evolution. This section focuses on practices of freedom by citizens under neoliberal conditions in post-apartheid South Africa and proposes that their rise demonstrates that global or national hegemonic projects, whether under NG or other political-economic conditions, are never complete.[20] In order to contextualize the discussion on practices of freedom by citizens, this section begins with a brief discussion of the deepening adoption of neoliberalism by the state following the transition to multi-racial democratic politics. The discussion indicates that, like in other political geographies, the state mediated the embedding of neoliberal policies in South Africa. It is then followed by highlights of practices of freedom by citizens involved in social movements in response to practices of the state; a process that I suggest represents spaces of citizenization and the emergence of social movement spaces of governance in the context of a neoliberal project in South Africa.

State and neoliberalism in South Africa

During the liberation struggle, the idea that the social needs of all South Africans should be at the centre of the country's economic policy formed the core of the policy platforms of the ANC. Take for instance its 1955 Freedom Charter;[21] in the section on 'wealth', it states that, 'the mineral wealth beneath the soil, the Banks and monopoly industry shall be transferred to the ownership of the people as a whole. All other industry and trade shall be controlled to assist the wellbeing of the people'.[22] Yet, what has increasingly occurred since 1994 is a shift of the economic policy of the ANC-led state apparatus from one that places social needs at its centre, to one embracing the logic of the market as the determinant of economic and other policies. The turn to neoliberalism did not occur in a global vacuum, for institutions of global governance and metropolitan states contributed to this process. For instance, 'the International Monetary Fund had set the stage for other neoliberal economic policies – e.g. public sector wage and spending cuts – as a condition for an $850 million loan in December 1993, and the Fund's manager, Michel Camdessus, even compelled Mandela to reappoint the apartheid-era finance minister and central bank governor when the ANC took state power in May 1994'.[23] Thus, institutions of global governance and the neoliberal world order[24] set the global context within which neoliberalism was translated in South Africa in the post-1994 period.

While the structural and political effects of institutions of global governance and other features of NG cannot be ignored, the South African state and social forces closely aligned to it mediated the embedding of neoliberalism as an economic idea and practice in the country. For example, like in Britain under the governance of Prime Minister Margaret Thatcher, leading South African elites claimed there was no alternative to neoliberalism and the institutions pushing for it. As one of them declared, 'we don't oppose the WTO. We'd never join a call to abolish it, or to abolish the World Bank or the IMF ... There is no organizational alternative, no real policy alternative to what we're doing'.[25]

In terms of economic policy in the immediate post-apartheid period, the Reconstruction and Development Programme (RDP) formed the foundation of the state's national economic agenda. Ideas framing the RDP were articulated in the White Paper on Reconstruction and Development issued in November 1994. While not a duplicate copy of the ANC's 1955 Charter, RDP goals shared some of its aims. For example, it declared a commitment to 'alleviate the poverty, low wages and extreme inequalities in wages and wealth generated by the apartheid system to meet basic needs, and thus ensure that every South African has a decent living standard and economic security' and to 'democratise the economy and empower the historically oppressed, particularly the workers and their organisations, by encouraging broader participation in decisions about the economy in both the private and public sector'. Furthermore, it indicated that the state's economic policies would 'remain ... people-driven'.[26] In its short period of existence, the RDP lead to the implementation of important projects such as public works in 'older townships and the extension of basic municipal services to newer informal settlements' and publically funded health care services to young children and expectant mothers.[27]

Yet two years following the 1994 turn to multi-racial democracy, the state introduced 'a more orthodox' neoliberal economic project under its 'Growth, Employment and Redistribution' (GEAR) economic development framework.[28] With this policy turn, emphasis was placed on 'reducing the budget deficit ... bringing down inflation ... opening the economy to international competition and securing access to new markets'.[29] This is not to say that poverty and other social sector issues that were part of the RDP economic framework were excluded in GEAR. Indeed, 'a redistribution of income and opportunities in favour of the poor' was one of the latter's goals. Nonetheless, there was a significant difference in the manner in which these issues were articulated in GEAR, with the language of the market and other features of NG taking centre stage.

For instance, GEAR promoted core tenets of NG such as the privatization of public goods. The privatization, and expansive restructuring of 'trade and investment' sectors[30] indicates a deeper turn to a neoliberal economic policy at the national level, a process that has led to an erasure of ANC's historical commitment to social equality. Furthermore, in terms of the state's labour regime, while for historical and political reasons it has adopted a 'two-tier'[31] labour regime which provides some protection for workers with permanent status, overall what has emerged is the casualization of labour and the deepening of 'precarious' labour conditions, especially for black workers.[32] In general, in post-1994 South Africa, neoliberal policies have been adopted at the national and other governing scales such as cities.[33] However, these developments have been highly contested by citizens through their strategies of freedom, including those deployed by members of the Treatment Action Campaign (TAC).

TAC and the neoliberalizing state

As previously mentioned, rolling back the role of the state has been a constitutive feature of NG's ideas and practices. Yet, while the reconstitution of the state along neoliberal lines has been a central element of NG, citizens involved in social movements and other civil society groups have contested neoliberal 'practices of government' (*PPNK* II, 65), including those enacted by multinational corporations. Tully outlines a range of practices of freedom that citizens utilize in their 'struggles of and for democratic freedom' (*PPNK* II, 113). According to him, through practices of freedom citizens 'seek' by way of 'tradition and new forms of deliberation and negotiation, to challenge and modify the non-democratic ways they are governed' (ibid.). Other practices include 'strategies of struggle' such as popular protests that have characterized processes of 'globalisation from below' (*PPNK* I) and the political projects of the diverse social movements linked to the World Social Forum.[34]

In South Africa, while the post-apartheid period has seen the deepening of a neoliberal project and its attendant social effects, citizens have contested its various manifestations. For example, in the city of Durban, neighborhood organizations such as the Westcliff Flat Residents Association (WFRA) have challenged Durban municipal government's neoliberal policies on social housing, water, policing and electricity. Through strategies of freedom such as civil disobedience, petitions and community-based research, and inspired by historical memories of racial and social class oppression,[35] as well as experiences of neoliberal structural violence, members of WRFA have contested the neoliberalization of local spaces and the violations of their rights as citizens of the city of Durban.[36] Further, social movements such as Johannesburg's Anti-Privatization Forum,[37] which emerged in 2000 have contested the privatization of basic services such as electricity and water.[38]

The Treatment Action Campaign (TAC) is another social movement that emerged under increasingly neoliberal state policy in South Africa.[39] Zackie Achmat and his colleagues formed TAC on Human Rights Day in 1998. The formation of TAC on that specific date was significant for a social movement that uses human rights philosophy as a master frame[40] in its struggle for the provision of affordable and publically accessible treatment for South Africans who are HIV positive. TAC's strategies of freedom emerged in the context of the World Trade Organization's (WTO) trading regime which is underpinned by a commodification logic[41] in its approach to the production of goods and services, including those in the health sector. In its democratic struggle for access to HIV/AIDS treatment, TAC has utilized various strategies of freedom, including collaborating with the state and mobilizing citizens against state policies in the context of NG.[42] The discussion that follows illuminates two of TAC's practices of freedom and its contributions to processes of citizenization and new scales of governance in post-apartheid South Africa.

To begin with, until 2002 when President Thabo Mbeki claimed that he was retreating from discussions about the 'science of HIV/AIDS',[43] the state's social policy on HIV/AIDS was one of denialism. This position claimed that there was no link between the HIV virus and AIDS as a disease.[44] Analysis of the state's denialist perspective suggests that 'the impact of poverty on the course of the epidemic,' and an attempt by the state to hide the 'poverty sustaining' role of its neoliberal policies, contributed to its position on HIV/AIDS. In addition, 'the history of constructions of the African as the inherently diseased racial and sexual other in both colonial and post-colonial times' provided legitimacy to the state's policy.[45]

TAC utilized various strategies of freedom such as street protests, civil disobedience and the mobilization of local and global networks to contest the state's denialist policy.[46] For TAC, the human rights framework underpinning the democratic constitution was a significant local background condition (*PPNK* II), for it acted as a source of inspiration and as a strategic tool in TAC's framing of its social grievances against the state's denial of much needed HIV/AIDS treatment to South Africans who were HIV positive. As Mark Heywood posits, 'the intention of the founders of TAC was to popularize and enforce what was loosely described as 'the right of access to treatment' through a combination of protest, mobilization, and legal action'.[47] Informed by its human rights master frame, TAC contended that the state's denialist position was irresponsible and unethical given that the provision of HIV/AIDS treatment would prevent the suffering of those dealing with the debilitating virus. In the words of one of the founders of TAC, 'it is sad that the leader of our government is presiding over a holocaust of poor people and he is doing nothing about it. The AIDS issue has become more than a health issue, much more than a prevention issue. It has actually become a test of governance'.[48]

The post-apartheid state's approach to nevirapine provided another site of contestation for TAC. Nevirapine is a drug that contributes to the reduction of mother-to-child transmission of the virus that causes AIDS. In South Africa, the state restricted access to nevirapine in every province to two public hospitals – one rural and the other urban. The state's position was that more research on the safety of nevirapine was needed even though South Africa's Medicines Control Council deemed it safe and 'effective'.[49] From TAC's perspective, the state's policy on nevirapine was unacceptable, for it had unnecessary and harmful effects on women and children in the context of a growing HIV/AIDS crisis. In response, TAC not only took the state to court, but also engaged in other strategies of freedom such as street protests and the creation of solidarity networks with powerful allies such as the Congress of South African Trade Unions (COSATU).[50]

In its petition to the court, TAC wondered 'what is to happen to those mothers and their babies who cannot afford access to private health care and do not have access to research and training sites?'[51] Furthermore, given that the provision of a 'single dose of Nevirapine (a dose to each mother during delivery and to her newborn)' was an effective strategy in preventing mother to child transmission of the HIV virus,[52] expanding public access to nevirapine was, from TAC's perspective, an urgent health and social issue. In addition, the neoliberal argument against government social spending made no sense in the immediate future because the manufacturer of the drug was willing to offer it free for five years.[53] Leaving aside this offer, TAC's view was that the state had an ethical obligation to provide the drug to its citizens as per the human rights framework underpinning the country's post-1994 democratic constitutional order. As section 27 of the constitution stipulates, 'Everyone has the right to have access to (a) health care services, including reproductive health care' and 'the state must take reasonable legislative and other measures, within its available resources, to achieve the progressive realisation of each of these rights'.[54] For TAC, the state had a positive duty to ensure these rights to health were promoted and protected.[55] Following appeals by the state after the High Court ruled in favour of TAC in 2001, the Constitutional Court declared in July 2002 that the state had failed to uphold its constitutional responsibility under section 27 of the constitution and ordered the state to make nevirapine available in all public hospitals.[56] While it took another year for the state to declare that it would 'rollout'[57] a national anti-retroviral treatment programme in 2004, the ruling by the Constitutional Court was a major victory for pregnant women who were HIV positive, as well as for their children and for citizens' rights in post-apartheid South Africa. Further, it was a major gain for TAC in its struggle to have the state provide treatment for HIV positive South Africans.[58]

TAC's strategies of freedom and relations with the neoliberalizing state apparatus are multiple and complex. Thus while the movement has contested state policies pertaining to HIV/AIDS, it has also emerged as an ally of the state in struggles against other institutions involved in the neoliberal governance of HIV/AIDS treatment. For example, TAC aligned itself with the state in the latter's 2001 court battle against the Pharmaceutical Manufacturer's Association (PMA). PMA, an organization representing 41 national and global pharmaceutical firms filed a suit against the South African state contesting the amendment of section 33 of the Medicines and Related Substances Control Amendment Act (the ACT). The state considered the amendment an important policy measure in the treatment of HIV/AIDS, for it would make anti-retroviral drugs available in the country cheaply. From PMA's perspective, the ACT was a breach of the international arrangements on patents, especially the WTO's Trade-Related Aspects of Intellectual Property Rights (TRIPS) framework governing patents and intellectual property.[59] The PMA was not alone in arguing that the ACT violated TRIPS;[60] American pharmaceutical companies and the US state made similar claims. Overall, in terms of global health issues, Thomas Pogge argues that the TRIPS framework 'discourage[s], impede[s], and delay[s] the manufacture of generic medicines ... through restrictions on and political pressures against the effective use of compulsory licenses'.[61] For Pogge, this framework is 'morally deeply problematic,' a 'fact' that 'has come to be more widely understood in the wake of the AIDS crisis, which pits the vital needs of poor patients against the need of pharmaceutical companies to recoup their investments in research and development'.[62]

TAC considered PMA's position a violation of the human rights underpinning South Africa's constitution.[63] Through its practices of freedom, TAC played a central role in the struggle against PMA and its WTO informed supporters. For example, in 2000 TAC led a popular protest following the death of Christopher Moraka, who had the HIV virus and worked for TAC.[64] Its mobilizing strategy invoked historical memories of democratic struggles such as the 1952 Defiance Campaigns against unjust laws under the apartheid system.[65] According to TAC, the availability of HIV/AIDS medication in state hospitals would have improved Moraka's life chances. The negative publicity resulting from the Moraka Defiance Campaign contributed to the PMA withdrawing its challenge to the ACT, a development that opened the possibility for the state to cheaply provide much needed treatment for HIV positive South Africans.[66]

Beyond joining the state in litigation against PMA, TAC has also emerged as a strategic collaborator in the governing of HIV/AIDS treatment in South Africa. For example, when the state announced that it would roll out a plan for the provision of anti-retroviral drugs, TAC remained actively involved in the process.[67] In recent years, through its promotion of 'treatment literacy' in publications such as 'Equal Treatment',[68] TAC has continued to contribute to the governance of HIV/AIDS. Further, TAC has been involved in the formulation of South Africa's health policy. For instance, in 2007–11 it was involved in the emergence of the 'National Strategic Plan' (NSP), with which TAC later aligned its 'vision, mission and strategic approach'.[69] Indeed, one of its objectives is to enable the success of NSP through initiatives such as 'model districts' which offer 'comprehensive treatment'.[70] In addition to its collaboration with the state, TAC is involved in programmes tackling TB/HIV issues through its partnerships with 'Médecins Sans Frontières (MSF), the City of Cape Town, and the Western Cape Province Department of Health'.[71]

To conclude here, TAC's strategies of freedom indicate the mediated and contested nature of processes of NG. Further, these strategies demonstrate the possibility for citizenization in the context of structures of domination by the state and other institutions such as the WTO trading regime and multinational pharmaceutical firms. As Tully reminds us, we become citizens when we engage in strategies of freedom with other citizens in democratic struggles over the governance of a range of spheres in our societies. Since 1998, members of TAC have contributed to processes of citizenization in the struggle for HIV/AIDS treatment in South Africa. TAC's strategies of freedom demonstrate that active forms of citizenship are possible even in the context of NG and the state as structures of domination. Further, as Tully's work suggests, these strategies illustrate the emergence of social movements spaces as sites of governance in the era of NG. Overall, the emergence and evolution of TAC indicates the possibility of spaces of freedom, citizen-making and state policy-making in the context of a constraining neoliberal world order. The discussion now turns to an exploration of the reconfiguration of state space under conditions of NG in Bolivia.

SPACES OF STATE RECONFIGURATION IN BOLIVIA

As conceptual insights from Tully's work remind us, NG is a structure of domination that has generated powerful political, social and economic effects in the uneven geographies comprising the contemporary world order. Nonetheless, Tully's complex approach to globalization indicates that other socio-political worlds are possible even in the context of the constraints generated by NG and other structures of domination. In the case of Bolivia, one significant development in the last decade has been the emergence of a state form with decolonizing tendencies. The rise of this state form is of course the result of numerous historical, cultural, spatial and politico-economic developments. The main aim of this section is to highlight two key developments in the era of neoliberalism that, in different but complementary ways, contributed to the emergence of a state form with decolonizing logics. These developments are the expansion of political space and the de-legitimization of the Bolivian neoliberal project. The discussion begins with highlights of these developments followed by brief examples of practices of the post-2005 Bolivian state that indicate a decolonizing state form and the tensions underpinning them.

The expansion of political space and the de-legitimization of neoliberalism

The expansion of political space in the 1990s, particularly for indigenous peoples, is an important development in the making of a decolonizing state apparatus in contemporary Bolivia. The political and economic marginalization of indigenous peoples in the country began with colonial projects and, following independence, continued into the era of informal imperialism including the period of neoliberal globalization.[72] Nonetheless, as the work of Laura Gotkowitz and other scholars demonstrates, indigenous peoples have for centuries mobilized against exploitation and social and political exclusion.[73] This tradition has characterized the era of neoliberalism as strategies of freedom by citizens resulted in the expansion of political spaces in the country. For example, in 1991 a neoliberalizing state[74] adopted the 1989 International Labour Organization's Convention No. 169 (the Convention) following 'The Indigenous March for Territory and Dignity in 1990'.[75] This march was 'led by lowland indigenous movements from the department of Beni in the northern Amazon' and included a call for the establishment of a 'constituent assembly'.[76]

In terms of expanding political space, the Convention provided an opening for the ongoing struggles for political and social recognition by indigenous communities in Bolivia. Overall, the Convention offers an opportunity for 'self-management and the right of indigenous and tribal peoples to decide their priorities' and futures.[77] Further, while declaring that states 'have the duty to protect the rights of indigenous and tribal peoples' the Convention also posits that they fulfil this responsibility 'in consultation with, and with the participation of, indigenous and tribal peoples'.[78] In Bolivia, the Convention generated a significant political opportunity that enabled members of indigenous social movements and organizations to engage in strategies of freedom in their struggles for political and social recognition. For example, the Bolivian Confederation of Indigenous Peoples 'proposed a national indigenous law, the *Proyecto de Ley Indígena*' (PLI), based on the Convention.[79] The proposed law 'called for the recognition of the juridical personality of indigenous peoples and protected their collective rights, forms of government and social organization, and legal systems'.[80] The evolution of the PLI saw the circulation of indigenous discourses into the wider political landscape and the emergence of a multicultural discourse 'that challenged the homogenizing nature of the republican and postrevolutionary regimes of citizenship'.[81]

Legal reforms in the 1990s further contributed to the expansion of political space. President Gonzalo Sánchez de Lozada, who came to power in 1993, appointed Víctor Hugo Cárdenas, an indigenous public intellectual and leader of the *Katarismo*[82] party, as Vice-President. Cárdenas' appointment marked an important development for indigenous peoples in the struggle for political inclusion and recognition. During Lozada's administration, the state instituted other reforms that expanded space for political participation. One of these reforms was the introduction of a decentralization process under the Law of Popular Participation (LPP). While decentralization in the country occurred in the context of a state-led neoliberal project and was supported by global neoliberal institutions and regional elites in the Department of Santa Cruz,[83] it also had indigenous roots. As Nancy Grey Postero argues, the Indigenous Peoples Law proposed by the Indigenous Federation of Eastern Bolivia (CIDOB) and the Fundamental Agrarian Law proposed by United Confederation of Peasant Workers of Bolivia called for 'autonomy at the local level'.[84] Overall, the LPP provided an important political opening for indigenous and popular social forces whose participation in the public sphere had historically been marginalized. As part of the LPP, the state 'recognized community organizations including urban neighbourhood associations, pre-Hispanic indigenous groups and modern *campesino* unions',[85] and 'more than 250 new, small and largely indigenous municipalities required thousands of council representatives', a development that expanded the participation of indigenous peoples in local governance.[86]

The reconfiguration of the country's Electoral Law in 1997, which saw the introduction of a German style proportional representation system, is another legal reform that contributed to the expansion of political space in the country. Changes to this law led to increased levels of civic participation of excluded groups at the local level, as 'one-half of representatives' were now to be contested at the district level, rather than at the departmental level which had mainly been driven by party elites in the urban areas.[87] Further, the change in the Electoral Law had significant impact on political party formation in the rural areas. For example, within six years of this Law 'the Chapare coca growers', which began as a rural social movement, emerged as Bolivia's 'second largest political party, winning almost one-quarter of seats in both houses of the national congress'.[88] Clearly, the LLP and the Electoral Law opened up room for popular forces to be engaged in practices of government at the local level. As Kohl and Farthing argue, the decentralization process 'reoriented the direction of much popular resistance to neoliberal programmes, through allocating enough resources to municipalities to attract the attention of local populations while simultaneously redefining the spaces for opposition'.[89] Further, through their involvement in these processes, new political identities would emerge, a factor that would enable social movement mobilizations in the events leading to the emergence of a decolonizing state and the presidency of Evo Morales.

The expansion of political space in the context of other developments, especially the de-legitimization of neoliberalism, generated social and political conditions that heavily contributed to the emergence of a state form with decolonizing tendencies in Bolivia. The effects of neoliberalism were themselves one of major sources of the de-legitimization of the neoliberal project. For example, at the level of state space, neoliberal policies in Bolivia were underpinned by the doctrine of rolling back the state in key sectors of the economy and privatization of public enterprises. Bolivia's privatization policies – which it referred to as Capitalization – saw the state sell off key assets in 'oil and gas, telecommunications, airlines, smelter, power generation and railroad companies'.[90] By the late 1990s the privatization of key sectors of the economy had not led to steady economic growth and the stabilization of the state's material base. On the contrary, the introduction of these policies created financial problems for the state. At the height of the neoliberal privatization agenda, the Bolivian state was losing revenue and could hardly sustain its traditional functions. For example, the *Yacimientos Petrolíferos Fiscales Bolivianos* (YPFB) – the State Oil Corporation – which had between 1985 and 1996 generated 'an average of $350 million annually' for the country – lost this capacity in 1997 while private companies who benefited from the privatization were making profits in the energy sector.[91] Overall, privatization did not emerge as the magic bullet of economic development as proponents of neoliberalism claim. Rather, in addition to its social effects – some of which will be highlighted shortly – this process 'had the perverse effect of creating rising budget deficits ($430 million in 1987 alone) due to shortfalls in revenue', leading to deepening structural dependency as the state became increasingly reliant on 'external aid' in order to meet its obligations such as paying salaries to its workers.[92]

Beyond budgetary and other crises at the level of state space, another development that contributed to the de-legitimization of the neoliberal project was the deepening of social divides, especially along class and racial lines. Massive retrenchment of workers during this period played a role in deepening these divides. With the privatization of the mining sector and the retrenchment of state employees, for example, a significant number of Bolivians lost their livelihoods. According to Hylton and Thompson, the mining and the public service sectors lost 'at least 45,000 jobs' and an additional 35,000 were lost as factories closed.[93] Further, in response to its declining revenue, the state introduced 'energy taxes' which disproportionally affected the poor sectors of Bolivian society.[94] These developments generated human insecurities in the urban areas whereby approximately '60 percent' of the workers become reliant on 'informal activities' for survival and 30 percent of them did not have the resources to buy basic things for human survival such as 'food'.[95] A new labour regime characterized by flexibilization and non-unionized[96] workers also emerged with the privatization of public companies. Like in other labour geographies in the era of neoliberalism, this development contributed to the decline of the labour force[97] and the emergence of a 'precarious' labour regime marked by jobs under 'short-time contracts' and greater job insecurity.[98]

To be sure, oppression in Bolivia, like elsewhere, manifests itself along 'intersecting oppressions'[99] of gender, class and race. The new labour regime for instance had gendered foundations as well as effects, as firms tended to 'increasingly hire female workers with no union experience who ... were more vulnerable to intimidation and sexual harassment'.[100] This development was occurring in the context of legal stipulations banning unionization in firms with less than 'twenty individuals'. Overall, the social assault on workers' well-being under neoliberal conditions was significant. During this period, while the hours of work rose, 'increasingly, workers could obtain only part-time jobs of under forty hours a week, making them ineligible for better social benefits that come with full-time employment' and requiring them to find additional work.[101]

In terms of indigenous communities, their social class exclusion intersected with race, gender and spatial (rural/urban) forms of exclusion. These 'intersecting oppressions' have of course emerged in the context of an evolving imperial order from the high noon of formal Spanish empire in the Andes to the contemporary informal and interactive imperialism that Tully articulates. Overall, these modes of oppression have historically produced the marginalization of indigenous peoples – who are the majority in the country – while Bolivians of Spanish descent (*criollos*) and those of mixed race (*mestizos*) have dominated the country's spaces of social, economic and political power for centuries. This historical development has been reinforced in the age of NG. In many cases, historical socio-cultural and political privilege has opened up avenues for members of these latter communities to consolidate their multiple forms of power during the era of NG. Nowhere is this more evident than in the Department of Santa Cruz, where elites are often able to secure their economic power because of their control of key sectors of the economy, especially in the extractive industries such as hydrocarbons and gas, and in the financial sector. According to Jeffrey Webber, 'between 1985 and 2000, the economy in Santa Cruz was the most dynamic in the country, and the department's agro-industrial, petroleum, and finance capitalists were correspondingly the most influential proponents of the neoliberal model'. As one of them stated, 'We are in favor of globalization. We are in favor of a market economy. We believe that that is the road that nations need to follow in order to develop. We are in complete opposition to the radically distinct vision that dominates the western [indigenous] part of the country'.[102] Meanwhile, as Nancy Grey Postero explains with respect to poverty,

> a World Bank 2005 study showed that 52 percent of Bolivian indigenous people live in extreme poverty. Their condition appears relatively untouched by efforts to combat poverty. For example, between 1997 and 2002, extreme poverty rates began to fall for nonindigenous people (from 31 percent to 27 percent), but they remained constant for indigenous people. Even more

stunning was the finding that in rural areas, poverty actually increased for indigenous peoples (65 percent to 72 percent) while decreasing slightly for nonindigenous people.[103]

The success of broader social movement struggles against the effects of neoliberalism is another significant development that contributed to its de-legitimization and to the emergence of a state with a decolonizing logic. Through their practices of freedom, indigenous and popular movements (IPM) contributed to the resignation of two neoliberal presidents in the period between 2000 and 2005: President Gonzalo Sánchez de Lozada in 2003 and President Carlos Mesa in 2005. Overall, throughout the 1990s and up to 2005, Bolivia's political landscape was characterized by constant resistance against neoliberalism or what social movements referred to as 'the model'.[104] One of the leading struggles by IPM was against water privatization in Cochabamba. The neoliberal roots of the Cochabamba water struggle involved an IMF loan to Bolivia in 1999 conditional upon, among other things, the privatization of the city's water sector.[105] The Bolivian neoliberal state then moved to create a favourable investment climate for capital including the establishment of a legal framework that provided the private sector opportunities 'to manage public water supply systems ... rights to rural water supply sources that had traditionally been under the control of indigenous farmers'.[106] The agreement further 'guaranteed them an average profit of 16 percent for each one of those years, to be financed by the families of Cochabamba'. The results of these developments included the granting of a 40-year concession contract to Bechtel (US) and United Water (UK), and increases on rates for water.[107]

The social, cultural and other implications of the water privatization deal saw the formation of an IPM called the Coalition for the Defense of Water and Life (Coordinadora). The water struggles intensified between January and April 2000 through the occupation of symbolically and historically significant public spaces, in addition to street and highway blockades and strikes that paralysed the cities. By March 2000, calls for the cancellation of the contract were gaining momentum and by this time IPM practices of freedom included the organization of 'a *consulta popular*' by Coordinadora which saw 'activists set up small tables in plazas throughout the Cochabamba valley to survey residents about the rate increases and the water law. More than 60,000 people participated, nearly 10 percent of the valley's population, and 90 percent endorsed cancellation of Bechtel's contract'.[108]

As efforts by Coordinadora gained momentum, the state responded with punitive measures such as arresting members of this movement and suspending constitutional rights. Its use of brutal force intensified, leading to the killing of 'Victor Hugo Daza, an unarmed seventeen-year-old'.[109] As the social unrest spread to most parts of the country, the officials of Bechtel escaped from Bolivia without any notice and the state declared the contract cancelled, saying in a letter to Bechtel's people, 'Given that the directors of your enterprise have left the city of Cochabamba and were not to be found ... said contract is rescinded'.[110] While the state contained efforts by Coordinadora for 'social control' of the city's water system,[111] the political significance of Coordinadora's success nationally and globally in the context of an informal and interactive neoliberal imperial order cannot be underestimated. It is under the preceding context that Bolivians went to the polls in 2005 to elect a president.

The post-2005 Bolivian state

In 2005 Evo Morales and the social movement (turned political party) *Movimiento al Socialism* (MAS) inherited state power in Bolivia, and Morales became the first indigenous President of Bolivia in January 2006.[112] He was re-elected again in 2009. Developments discussed in the previous section contributed not only to the rise of Morales as a political figure but also to processes aimed at the reconfiguration of state space.[113] One of the major processes was the holding of a Constituent Assembly (CA) to reconfigure the judicial foundation of the state and in general its role in society. While underpinned by tensions – some of which will be highlighted shortly – the CA process and its results thus far indicate that the production of a neoliberal state space has not been the only politico-economic project in Bolivia in the era of NG.

The holding of a constituent assembly is one of the processes that IPM increasingly called for from 2003 to reconstitute the constitutional foundation of the state and the relationship between citizens and the state. From IPM's perspective, the majority of Bolivians were historically excluded from dominant political and economic spheres, and the state neglected the needs of the majority of its citizens. The effects of centuries of political, social and economic exclusion and their reproduction in new forms in the era of neoliberalism are some of the factors that led IPM to mobilize for a CA. Their struggle for the holding of the CA can be conceptualized as representing a conjuncture of 'constituent power' in Bolivia. According to Luis Tapia, 'constituent power is formed when projects or forces emerge that seek to change the relationship between the state and civil society, the arenas within them, the subjects involved, the relationships between them, and consequently the political form that society adopts. In this sense, a constituent power is something that emerges at points of crisis, or provokes a political crisis that, among other things, can lead to the reconstitution of a country'.[114]

While the CA was delayed in the immediate election of Morales,[115] it was finally held in 2007. However, important as this development was, processes leading to it were characterized by contradictions. For example, the MAS-led state limited collective representation based on identities with the exception of two forms of identities: gender and region.[116] In its refusal to allow collective representation of indigenous communities in the CA, the state claimed that the interests of these communities were represented by MAS.[117] Overall, the position taken by the state on CA representation resulted in the empowerment of elites in the region of Santa Cruz 'concerning the assembly's structure, conduct, and content' and the further emergence of a 'new political space for the rearticulation of stronger right-wing forces' in the socio-economic geography of Bolivia.[118]

The contradictions and tensions underpinning the CA notwithstanding, its establishment played a key role in the reconfiguration of state space, for it resulted in the emergence of a new constitutional order in 2009. Given the long history of political and social exclusion, the new constitution is an important turning point in Bolivia. While the legitimacy and merits of the constitution are questioned by segments of the citizenry, it nonetheless has laid an important embryonic foundation for the continued reconfiguration of state space in coming decades. As the 'introduction' to the constitution states:

> We left the colonial, republican and neoliberal State in the past. We assumed the historical challenge to collectively build a Social Unitary State of Plurinational Community Law, which integrates and articulates the purposes of advancing towards a Bolivia that is democratic, productive, carrier and inspirer of peace, compromised with the integral development and with the free determination of its people. We, men and women, through the Constitutional Assembly and with the originary power of the people, manifest our compromise with the unity and integrity of the country. Complying with the mandate of our people, with the strength of our Pachamama and giving thanks to God, we refound Bolivia.[119]

To elaborate further, Article 1 of the constitution declares that 'Bolivia is constituted in a Social Unitary State of Plurinational Communitarian Law, free, independent, sovereign, democratic, intercultural, decentralized and with autonomies'. This article redefines state space by departing from a representation of it as being underpinned by a singular cultural and historical development or the adoption of neoliberalism as the only mode of organizing social and economic life. Further, after centuries of dispossession and racialization, it acknowledges indigenous histories as an element of the foundation of the state. As Article 100:1 stipulates, 'it is the patrimony of the indigenous originary farmer nations and peoples, the cosmovisions, the myths, the oral history, the dances, the cultural practices, the knowledge and traditional technologies. This patrimony forms part of the expression and identity of the State'. In addition, Article 9 of the constitution indicates a redefinition of the Bolivian state space for it declares the state's essential purposes and functions as being those constituting 'a just and harmonious society, founded in decolonization, without discrimination or exploitation, with plain social justice' to enable the consolidation of the country's 'plurinational identities'.[120]

Beyond the emergence of a new plurinational state and constitutional order, the decolonial foundation of the contemporary state space as indicated in Article 9 is evident in the emergence of new economic practices by the state. Historical and contemporary forms of marginalization, as well as strategies of freedom by IPM, played a key role in the rise of these practices. In terms of the role of the state in the economy, the new constitution suggests that the state's economic projects ought to generate conditions for Bolivians 'to live well'.[121] The state is to generate such conditions by promoting 'reasonable and planned use of the natural resources' and respecting both individual and collective property.[122] At the level of practice, an example of new economic practices by the state informed by a decolonial logic is its efforts to nationalize the hydrocarbons industry. The state's project to nationalize the hydrocarbons industry emerges out of the long exploitation of Bolivian natural resources by local and global agents beginning with the arrival of Spanish colonial interests, and extending to the era of neoliberalism and responses to it by citizens through their strategies of freedom.

The introduction of a nationalization policy on hydrocarbons – announced by President Morales on May Day through Supreme Decree 28701 titled 'Heroes of the Chaco War Decree'[123] – indicates the decolonial orientation of the post-2005 state. However, the nature of this policy and its evolution greatly departs from discourses that construct the Bolivian state as a hyper-radical state, ignoring the modest nature of the state's decolonial gains so far on the economic front.[124] For instance, while this policy has been important at the level of political symbolism and historical memories, and has generated extra revenue through increased rents from foreign firms, it has not amounted to the total nationalization of the hydrocarbon industry.[125] Arguing along these lines, Kohl and Farthing posit that 'private multinational firms still extract the majority of the country's natural gas and minerals, although the share going to the state has changed dramatically. Income from oil and gas, which now accounts for more than half of state revenues increased from US $173 million in 2002 to more than US $2.2 billion in 2011'.[126]

Overall, although it is characterized by tensions and limitations, the emergence of a decolonial logic as a state philosophy and practice marks an important discursive and political turn in modes of state power in Bolivia. This development acknowledges the historical fact of formal imperialism and the reproduction of imperial practices in the post-independence era, and calls on the state to meet its ethical obligations by engaging in practices of government geared toward decolonization. Further, the redefinition of the Bolivian state as a plurinational country disrupts the imperial projects that privilege the narratives of the conquerors in not only the making of state space but also the consolidation of the national territorial space anchoring it. In addition, this development indicates that processes of state formation and the configuration of territorial space are not static, but rather ongoing political projects[127] which are influenced by local and global developments such as processes of NG and responses to them by citizens and states in specific socio-political geographies. As such, possibilities of reconfiguring state space along more democratic and morally just lines can emerge even in the context of *glocal* structures of domination.

CONCLUSION

This chapter has discussed neoliberal globalization, which is one of the keywords in Tully's extensive work on public philosophy. It has suggested that his complex approach to this keyword enriches our understanding of processes of NG. Drawing on insights from this approach, the chapter has demonstrated the contested and mediated nature of these processes in South Africa and Bolivia. Further, through a discussion of strategies of freedom by TAC and the emergence of a state form with decolonial tendencies in Bolivia, it has shown that while contradictory and constrained, a politics of realist hope and other political-economic projects are possible even in an era in which social forces committed to NG have utilized their extensive ideological and structural power in efforts to consolidate its processes. Overall, Tully's insights from his study of NG offer an important conceptual opening through which to explore the dialectics of freedom and domination in the contemporary period.

Notes

1 I use the concept of keyword in the Raymond Williams sense of the word. For further discussion of the term, see Raymond Williams, *Keywords : A Vocabulary of Culture and Society*, rev. ed. (New York: Oxford University Press, 1985).
2 For more details, see James Tully, *Public Philosophy in a New Key: Volume I, Democracy and Civic Freedom* and *Public Philosophy in a New Key* and *Public Philosophy in a New Key: Volume II, Imperialism and Civic Freedom*, (New York: Cambridge University Press, 2008). (Hereafter cited as *PPNK* I and II.)
3 Max Weber, *Essays on Vocation* (Indianapolis: Hackett, 2004), 33.
4 See, for instance, Derek Gregory, *Geographical Imaginations* (Cambridge, MA: Blackwell, 1994); John Pickles, *A History of Spaces: Cartographic Reason, Mapping, and the Geo-coded World* (London and New York: Routledge, 2004); Neil Brenner and Stuart Elden, 'Henri Lefebvre on State, Space and Territory', *International Political Sociology* 3 (2009): 353–77.
5 Michel Foucault, *Power/Knowledge: Selected Interviews and Other Writings 1972–77*, edited by Colin Gordon and Translated by Colin Gordon, Leo Marshall, John Mepham and Kate Soper (New York: Pantheon Books, 1980), 70. In its chapter titled 'Questions on Geography', this book provides an important discussion on Foucault's thinking about spatiality. Foucault's thinking about spatial questions can also been found in his piece 'Of Other Spaces', in which he contends that 'the great obsession of the nineteenth century was ... history: with its themes of development and of suspension, of crisis and cycle, themes of the ever-accumulating past ... I believe that the anxiety of our era has to do fundamentally with space [for] time probably appears to us only as one of the various distributive operations that are possible for the elements that are spread in space'. For more details on the latter, see Michel Foucault, 'Of Other Spaces', in *Diacritics*, vol. 16, no. 1 (Spring, 1986), 22–7.
6 Edward W. Soja, *Seeking Spatial Justice* (Minneapolis: University of Minnesota Press, 2010), 15.
7 Doreen Massey, *For Space* (Thousand Oaks, California: Sage, 2005).
8 Dorren Massey, *Space, Place and Gender* (Cambridge: Polity Press, 1994), 4.
9 Henri Lefebvre, *The Production of Space* (Oxford: Blackwell, 1991); Massey 1994 and 2005; John Pickles, *A History of Spaces: Cartographic Reason, Mapping, and the Geo-coded World* (London and NY: Routledge, 2004).
10 Walter Mignolo, *Local Histories/Global Designs: Coloniality, Subaltern Knowledges, and Border Thinking* (Princeton: Princeton University Press, 2000), 229.
11 Neil Brenner, Bob Jessop, Martin Jones and Gordon Macleod, eds, *State/Space: A Reader* (Malden: Blackwell, 2003) and Brenner and Elden, 2009, 353–77.
12 For further discussion on social, political and economic developments in the era of

neoliberal globalization, see Thandika P. Mkandawire and Charles C. Soludo, *Our Continent, Our Future: African Perspectives on Structural Adjustment* (Trenton, N.J.: Africa World Press, 1999); Patrick Bond, *Against Global Apartheid: South Africa Meets the World Bank, IMF, and International Finance* (Lansdowne: University of Cape Town Press, 2001); and Eunice N. Sahle, 'Gender, States, and Markets in Africa' in Joseph Mensah, *Neoliberalism and Globalization in Africa: Contestations from the Embattled Continent* (New York: Palgrave Macmillan, 2008).

13 Susan Strange, *The Retreat of the State: The Diffusion of Power in the World Economy* (Cambridge: Cambridge University Press, 1996).
14 Antonio Gramsci, *Selections from the Prison Notebooks* (New York: International Publishers, 1971).
15 For an extended discussion, see Strange 1996; Susan Strange, *Mad Money: When Markets Outgrow Governments* (Ann Arbor: University of Michigan Press, 1998); David Harvey, *A Brief History of Neoliberalism* (New York: Oxford University Press, 2005; Eunice Sahle, *World Orders, Development and Transformation* (Houndmills and New York: Palgrave Macmillan, 2010).
16 Massey 2005, 82.
17 Sallie A. Marston and Katharyne Mitchell, 'Citizens and the State: Citizenship Formations in Space and Time', in Barnett, Clive and Murray Low, eds, *Spaces of Democracy: Geographical Perspectives on Citizenship, Participation and Representation* (London: SAGE, 2004), 95.
18 Joseph Alois Schumpeter, *Capitalism, Socialism and Democracy*, 6th edn (London and Boston: Unwin Paperbacks, 1987), 269.
19 Ibid., 294.
20 *PPNK* I and II and Sahle 2010.
21 The Charter remains an important reference point for South Africans in struggles of justice and equality. For example, between May and July 2012 I had several discussions with Orlean Naidoo, one of the leaders of the Westcliff Flats Residents Association pertaining to historical and contemporary issues in Chatsworth, Durban. Time and time again she invoked the Charter's policies on housing and human security for all in South Africa as inspiration in her long time involvement in struggles for affordable housing and other social needs in Westcliff. For details contained in the Charter see http://www.anc.org.za/show.php?id=72#.
22 Ibid., 1.
23 Patrick Bond, *Against Global Apartheid: South Africa meets the World Bank, IMF and International Finance* (Lansdowne: University of Cape Town Press, 2001), 60. For more on the role of institutions of global governance in the South African state's turn to neoliberalism, see Margaret Hanson and James J. Hentz, 'Neocolonialism and Neoliberalism in South Africa and Zambia', in *Political Science Quarterly*, vol. 114, no. 13, 1999.
24 Sahle 2010.
25 Bond 2001, 29.
26 Government Gazette, vol. 353, Kaapstad 23 November 1994 No. 16085 (Cape Town: 1994), 20. For more details, see http://www.info.gov.za/view/DownloadFileAction?id=70427.
27 Ivan Turok, 'Restructuring or Reconciliation? South Africa's Reconstruction and Development', *International Journal of Urban and Regional Research*, 19 (1995), 311.
28 Jeremy Seekings and Nicoli Nattrass, *Class, Race, and Inequality in South Africa* (Scottsville, University of KwaZulu-Natal, 2006 [originally published by Yale University, 2005]), 349.
29 Government of South Africa, *Growth, Employment and Redistribution, A Macroeconomic Strategy* (Pretoria: Department of Finance, 1996), 1. For ideas and goals of this economic strategy, see http://www.info.gov.za/view/DownloadFileAction?id=70507.

30 Pádraig Carmody, 'Between Globalization and (Post) Apartheid: The Political Economy of Restructuring in South Africa,' *Journal of Southern African Studies*, vol. 28, no. 2 (June 2002): 255–75, 258–9.
31 Ibid., 261.
32 See Franco Barchiesi, *Precarious Liberation : Workers, the State, and Contested Social Citizenship in Postapartheid South Africa* (Albany: State University of New York Press, 2011). For further debates on inequality and wage labour, see Seekings and Nattrass, 2006 and the wage labour and citizenship in the postapartheid period, see Franco Barchiesi, 'Wage Labor and Social Citizenship in the Making of Post-Apartheid South Africa', *Journal of Asian and African Studies*, vol. 42, no. 1 (January 2007): 39–72.
33 David A. McDonald, *World City Syndrome: Neoliberalism and Inequality in Cape Town* (New York: Routledge, 2008).
34 Sahle, 2010.
35 For an extended discussion of these issues, see Eunice N. Sahle, 'Intellectuals, Oppression and Anti-Racist Movements in South Africa', in *Theorizing Anti-Racism: Linkages in Marxism and Critical Race Theories*, Abigail B. Bakan and Enakshi Dua, eds, (Toronto: University of Toronto Press, 2013).
36 I draw these conclusions from current research projects that I am working on which examine urban governance and citizenship in Durban, South Africa and Toronto, Canada.
37 Patrick Bond, *Looting Africa: The Economics of Exploitation* (Scottsville, South Africa: Palgrave Macmillan, 2006), 104.
38 Ibid., and Sahle 2010.
39 For an extensive review of social movements that have emerged in the era of democracy in South Africa, see Richard Ballard, Adam Habid and Imraan Valodia, eds, *Voices of Protest: Social Movements* (Scottsville: University of KwaZulu-Natal, 2006).
40 Suzanne Staggenborg, *Social Movements*, rev. edn. (New York: Oxford University Press, 2011).
41 Karl Polanyi, *The Great Transformation: The Political and Economic Origins of Our Time*, 2nd edn (Boston: Beacon Press, 2001).
42 Extended details on TAC's current campaigns are available at http://www.tac.org.za/community/.
43 H. Schneider and D. Fassin, 'Denial and Defiance: A Socio-political Analysis of AIDS in South Africa, *AIDS* 16 (suppl.): S1–S7, 45.
44 Mandisa Mbali, 'The Treatment Action Campaign and the History of Rights-Based, Patient-Driven Activism in the South', University of KwaZulu-Natal Centre for Civil Society, Research Report No. 29 (2005): http://ccs.ukzn.ac.za/default.asp?2,58,16,70.
45 Ibid., 105.
46 For an extended discussion of the state's position and the struggle by TAC in alliance with global science networks, see Nathan Geffen, *Debunking Delusions: The Inside Story of the Treatment Action Campaign* (Auckland Park, South Africa: Jacana Media, 2010); Pieter Fourie and Melissa Meyer, *The Politics of AIDS Denialism: South Africa's Failure to Respond* (Farnham, Surrey, England: Ashgate Pub., 2010); Steven L. Robins, *From Revolution to Rights in South Africa: Social Movements, NGOs and Popular Politics After Apartheid* (Rochester, New York: James Currey, 2008) and Mandisa Mbali, 'AIDS Discourses and the South Africa State: Government Denialism and Post-Apartheid AIDS Policymaking', *Transformation: Critical Perspectives on Southern Africa* 54 (2004): 104–22.
47 Mark Heywood, 'South Africa's Treatment Action Campaign: Combining Law and Social Mobilization to Realize the Right to Health', *Journal of Human Rights Practice*, vol. 1, no. 1 (March 2009): 14–16 at 15.
48 Zackie Achmat, Kamera: Leva med HIV. SVTV 2 (9 July 2002, Swedish Television)

quoted in S. Peris Jones, 'A Test of Governance: Rights-based Struggles and the Politics of HIV/AIDS Policy in South Africa', *Political Geography* 24 (2005): 419–47 at 420.
49 George J. Annas, 'The Right to Health and the Nevirapine Case in South Africa', in S. Gruskin, ed., *Perspectives on Health and Human Rights* (New York: Routledge, 2005), 499.
50 Jones, 24. COSATU is one of the key allies of the African National Congress, the ruling party since the 1994 general elections. The other ally is the South African Communist Party.
51 Ibid.
52 Hoosen M. Coovadia and Jacquie Hadingham, 'HIV/AIDS: Global Trends, Global Funds and Delivery Bottlenecks', *Globalization and Health* (August 2005), http://www.globalizationandhealth.com/content/pdf/1744-8603-1-13.pdf, 6.
53 Annas, 499.
54 Details of the rights underpinning the post-apartheid democratic constitution are available at http://www.info.gov.za/documents/constitution/1996/96cons2.htm#27.
55 Joan Fitzpatrick and Ron C. Slye, 'Republic of South Africa v. Grootboom and Minister of Health v. Treatment Action Campaign, Case No. CCT 8/02', *American Society of International Law*, vol. 97, no. 3 (July 2003): 669–80.
56 See Alex Tawanda Magaisa, 'Minister of Health and Others v. Treatment Action Campaign and Others', *Journal of African Law*, vol. 47, issue 1 (April 2003): 117–25.
57 Alan Marc Vandormael, *Civil Society and Democracy in Post-Apartheid South Africa: The Treatment Action Campaign, Government, and the Politics of HIV/AIDS* (Saarbrücken: VDM Verlag Dr. Müller, 2007), 45.
58 For more on TAC's challenge to the state on its position on nevirapine, see http://www.lawlib.utoronto.ca/diana/TAC_case_study/MinisterofhealthvTACconst.court.pdf.
59 W.W. Fisher and Cyrill Rigamonti, 'The South African AIDS Controversy: A Case Study in Patent Law and Policy', at http://cyber.law.harvard.edu/people/tfisher/South%20Africa.pdf, 5; Thomas Pogge *World Poverty and Human Rights: Cosmopolitan Responsibilities and Reforms*, 2nd edn (Cambridge: Polity, 2008), 225.
60 Details of the TRIPS Agreement are available at http://www.wto.org/english/docs_e/legal_e/27-trips_01_e.htm.
61 Thomas Pogge, *World Poverty and Human Rights: Cosmopolitan Responsibilities and Reforms* (2nd ed. Cambridge: Polity, 2008), 225.
62 Ibid., 223.
63 Heywood, 14–36.
64 Steven Robins and Bettina von Lieres, 'Remaking Citizenship, Unmaking Marginalization: The Treatment Action Campaign in Post-Apartheid South Africa', *Canadian Association of African Studies* (2004): 575–86.
65 For examples of the 1952 Defiance Campaigns, see http://www.anc.org.za/show.php?id=2591.
66 Robins and von Lieres, 579.
67 Steven Friedman and Shauna Mottiar, 'Seeking the High Ground: The Treatment Action Campaign and the Politics of Morality', in Ballard, Habib and Valodia, eds, *Voices of Protest: Social Movements* (Scottsville: University of KwaZulu-Natal, 2006), 27.
68 For more details, see http://www.tac.org.za/community/about.
69 See Treatment Action Campaign, NSP Quarterly Report (2010), http://www.tac.org.za/sites/default/files/NSP%20Review%201%20March%20-%20May%202010.pdf.
70 Ibid., 3.
71 Ibid., 7.

72 For example, during the General Hugo Banzer administration between 1997 and 2003, the state introduced coca policy which aimed at having 'Zero coc' in five years and in an effort to achieve this goal it embarked on a massive eradication offensive as part of 'Plan Dignity'. See Jim Shultz and Melissa Draper, *Dignity and Defiance: Stories from Bolivia's Challenge to Globalization* (Berkeley: University of California Press, 2008), 191. The state's military apparatus was used in the coca eradication programme leading to human insecurities for indigenous coca growers as the main source of their livelihood went 'up in fire and smoke' during military operations (ibid.). The state-driven coca eradication programme was heavily supported by the US government as part of the latter's 'war on drugs' agenda. The programme was characterized by to extensive human rights violations including 'torture' and death, and generated health problems (ibid., 192) in the context of social crises emerging out of the ongoing neoliberal project. These developments saw the rise of social protests led by indigenous communities and the current Bolivian president was a key actor in the coalition of social movements that challenged the state's coca policy.
73 For detailed explorations of these matters, see Laura Gotkowitz, *A Revolution for Our Rights: Indigenous Struggles for Land and Justice in Bolivia, 1880–1952* (Durham: Duke University Press, 2007).
74 This move by the Bolivian state indicates the contradictory roles and practices of states. While states have been agents of neoliberalism, they have also engaged in practices that challenge neoliberalism and which provide opening for social movements and citizens to articulate and enact other political projects.
75 Nancy Grey Postero, *Now We Are Citizens: Indigenous Politics in Postmulticultural Bolivia* (Stanford: Stanford University Press, 2007), 50. In the era of NG, spatial politics pertaining to territory have emerged as a major development in Bolivia and other Latin American countries. For a discussion of such politics and strategies of freedom by Afro-Colombians, see Arturo Escobar, *Territories of Difference: Place, Movements, Life, Redes* (Durham: Duke University Press, 2008). I am grateful to Professor Escobar for discussions of these matters in Colombia and Latin America in general.
76 Jeffery Webber, *From Rebellion to Reform in Bolivia: Class Struggle, Indigenous Liberation, and the Politics of Evo Morales* (Chicago: Haymarket Books, 2011), 249
77 ILO Convention on Indigenous and Tribal Peoples, 1989 (No. 169): A Manual (Geneva: International Labour Organization, 2003), 9–10.
78 Ibid., 11–12. For an extended discussion, see 'Convention No. 169' at http://www.ilo.org/indigenous/Conventions/no169/lang--en/index.html.
79 Postero, 51. The state nonetheless did institute 'PLI, Indigenous Law Project' as the coordinating organization for indigenous issues.
80 Quoted in Postero, 51.
81 Ibid.
82 This is a political movement/party named after Tupak Katari, a famed indigenous revolutionary during the era of formal imperialism in Bolivia.
83 Webber, 2011.
84 Postero, 128.
85 Benjamin Kohl and Linda Farthing, *Impasse in Bolivia: Neoliberal Hegemony and Popular Resistance* (London and New York: Zed Books, 2006), 132.
86 Ibid., 126.
87 Ibid., 126.
88 Quoted in Kohl and Farthing, 132.
89 Ibid., 143.
90 Ibid., 61.
91 Forrest Hylton and Sinclair Thomson, *Revolutionary Horizons: Past and Present in Bolivian Politics* (London and New York: Verso, 2007), 102.

92 Ibid., 102.
93 Ibid., 96.
94 Ibid., 102.
95 Ibid.
96 Labour unions in Bolivia have played a major part in political and economic processes, especially since the 1952 revolution.
97 See Saskia Sassen, *Globalization and its Discontents: Essays on the New Mobility of People and Money* (New York: New Press, 1998).
98 Webber, 21–3.
99 Patricia Hill Collins, *Black Feminist Thought: Knowledge, Consciousness, and the Politics of Empowerment*, rev. 10th edn (New York: Routledge, 2000), 228.
100 Webber, 23.
101 Ibid.
102 Webber, 59.
103 Postero, 3.
104 Ibid.
105 Karen Bakker, *Privatizing Water: Governance Failure and the World's Urban Water Crisis* (Ithaca: Cornell University Press, 2010), 166.
106 Ibid.
107 Schultz and Draper, 16.
108 Ibid., 22.
109 Ibid., 25.
110 Ibid., 22–6.
111 Bakker, 168.
112 For more details on the evolution of MAS in electoral politics, see Fernando Oviedo Obarrio, translated by Victoria J. Furio, 'Evo Morales and the Altiplano Notes for an Electoral Geography of the Movimiento al Socialismo, 2002–2008' in *Latin American Perspectives*, Issue 172, vol. 37, no. 3 (May 2010): 91–106.
113 See Brenner and Elden.
114 Luis Tapia, 'Constitution and Constitutional Reform in Bolivia', in J. Crabtree and L. Whitehead, eds, *Unresolved Tensions: Bolivia Past and Present* (Pittsburgh: University of Pittsburgh Press, 2008), 163.
115 Webber, 2011.
116 Hylton and Thompson, 140.
117 Ibid., 140.
118 Webber, 71.
119 Unless otherwise stated, references from the 2009 constitution are drawn from a bounded volume of the Constitution produced by the University of North Carolina at Chapel Hill Davis Library. The Constitution is translated by Luis Francisco Valle V and was downloaded from http://www.bolivanconstitution.com/.
120 Ibid.
121 See Art. 8:II.
122 See Art. 10: 6 and Art. 56: 1–11 respectively.
123 Hylton and Thomson, 133.
124 For discussions of the state's project of nationalizing the hydrocarbon sector, see Benjamin Kohl, 'Bolivia under Morales: A Work in Progress' in *Latin American Perspectives*, vol. 37, no. 3 (June 10, 2010): 107–22, and Webber (2011).
125 It is important to note that that while the post-2005 Bolivian state form is underpinned by an economic decolonial logic, this does not mean there has been a total rupture from neoliberalism and other historical economic realities in the last seven years. Such an approach would be ahistorical and myopic for at a minimum it neglects how inherited political, economic and social geographies influence emergent ones. Rather,

given the global context of informal imperialism and the country's economic and political history, what has occurred in spaces of state economic policy formation under MAS is the expansion of economic logics. For further discussion on the complexity, constraints and contradictions charactering the economic practices of the current Bolivian state, see Webber (2011), Filho and Gonçalves (2011), Kohl and Farthing (2012).
126 Kohl and Farthing, 230.
127 Brenner and Elden, 2009.

Chapter 10

'Becoming Black': Acting Otherwise and Re-Imagining Community

Aletta J. Norval

> [Interlocutor:] 'I think you have established some solid lines. You have formed a pact, a certain kind of relationship between yourself and what you want to become towards ...'
> [Krog:] 'In order to move, one needs to know in what direction. How does one know the other side of the pact?'
> [Interlocutor:] 'By listening. To stories, to others.'
> [Krog:] 'Are stories good enough?'
> [Interlocutor:] 'Stories have different characters and threads and plots; they leave space for variety. Stories are boundary crossings, making it possible to move ... no single line holds things together ...' (p. 101, names added)
>
> Antjie Krog in conversation with an interlocutor, *Begging to be Black*[1]

Towards the end of Volume II of *Public Philosophy in a New Key*, Tully raises a question that is crucial to understand the deepening of democratic practices in our contemporary world. He asks how it is possible for 'diverse citizens' to avoid being captivated by a picture of 'one familiar form of national citizenship as the only acceptable form, projecting its hierarchical classifications over others'? How do they exercise their critical faculties and sustain 'a multiplicity of alternative forms of citizenship'? He suggests that the answer is a practical one: that they 'sustain alternative worlds by *acting otherwise*'.[2]

In this chapter I seek to explore further the idea of 'acting otherwise', with a view to fleshing out its relation to the question of creating new forms of belonging that have the potential to bind together citizens in a democratic polity. I start here in agreement with Tully, who questions the idea that citizen identity is generated by the possession of rights and duties, 'or by agreement on substantive or comprehensive common goods, fundamental principles of justice, constitutional essentials, shared values', and so on.[3] Rather, as he suggests, what 'shapes and holds together individuals and groups together as "citizens" and "peoples" is not this or that agreement but the free agonistic activities of participation themselves'.[4] It is through the diversity of these activities, informed by local languages and negotiated practices that novel forms of belonging are fostered and sustained, whilst modern citizenship is de-universalized.[5] If this is indeed the case – if belonging and a sense of citizenship derives from one's participation in the wide array of activities available to citizens in a polity – the question of acting otherwise is posed even more starkly. Under what set of conditions do the possibility of, and the need for, acting otherwise arise? What resources are needed for acting otherwise? What role is played by imagination, by telling stories?

In this chapter, I explore these questions through a reading of Antjie Krog's *Begging to Be Black*, a semi-autobiographical work written in the first decade of this century that deals explicitly with negotiations of identity, difference and belonging from the perspective, not of legal rights narratives, but of the multiplicity of sites and practices in which citizenship is imagined and in the process claimed, exercised and developed. *Begging to be Black* situates these issues in the context of a society that has only recently made the transition to institutional democracy. A work of creative non-fiction[6] that weaves together a range of narratives, it includes accounts of Krog's role in a trial of ANC activists for the murder in 1992 of a local gangster; of the story of an African King, Moshoeshoe, who succeeded in establishing a 'humane space for people to live their lives' in the nineteenth century;[7] of Krog's stay in Berlin as a research fellow; and of her conversations with visiting philosophers, as well as a friend, Bonnini, on the nature of African interconnectedness.[8] Interweaving these stories, Krog sketches out her struggle with the question of belonging in a post-colonial world, of what it might mean for a (white) woman to belong in a majority black society. The text maps the difficult roads to forging community and belonging, the ambiguities and complexities that highlight what Tully calls 'civic diverse citizenship'. Indeed, I also read Krog's text as itself exemplary of the demands such diverse citizenship places on us in a democratic society.

Krog uses a variety of ways to work through what she regards as the demands for transformation, a process without an easy, if indeed any, resolution. *Begging to Be Black* is her account of what it means to live a good life in Africa. It explores different senses of human fulfilment contained in the idea of 'African interconnectedness'.[9] This exploration acts as an exemplary case of a de-universalization of Western, individualistic conceptions of citizenship. Although the issue of an African conception of interconnectedness is obviously crucial here, the aim of this chapter is not primarily to explore the various nuances and interpretation of this conception. (It goes without saying that there is not one, unitary conception of 'Africa', nor of interconnectedness underlying and informing this discussion.) Rather, it is to reflect on the processes through which alternative imaginaries such as that of 'African interconnectedness' may be made available to those for whom it is not already an embedded form of life, as well as to begin to think through the question of the politics of interconnectedness, relevant both to those for whom interconnectedness is already a lived reality, and those for whom it is not.

Begging to be Black is a deeply personal, semi-autobiographical account, with all the attendant difficulties that such accounts entail, and which the author is fully cognizant of. Reflecting on this, Krog notes that everything in the text is filtered through her own memory, culture and subjective interpretation (p. vi), yet this text addresses some of the most pressing, important and difficult issues in our contemporary world.[10] It does not shun those difficulties and is sometimes shockingly forthright. It has drawn fierce comment, with one interlocutor describing Krog's journey as 'identity suicide'. In this sense, the text amply demonstrates the Emersonian suggestion that 'we live lives simultaneously of absolute separateness and endless commonness'.[11] *Begging to Be Black* speaks to the issues of our time: particularly that of belonging in a world of diverse citizenship, a world in which the bonds between citizens cannot be taken from granted, and must be reconfigured and re-imagined anew. This starting-point is crucial for coming to an understanding of Krog's text. The story sets out from and is marked by a deep sense of dislocation, of moral bewilderment and of perplexity, where one is 'lost among the words' (p. 5). The text is explicitly situated in a context where given frameworks of interpretation are experienced as inadequate. As Krog puts it:

> I live in a country that for nearly four centuries was interpreted and organized via Western or European frameworks. Since 1994 I have lived with a black majority that asserts itself more and more confidently. So I find most of my references and many of my frameworks for understanding to be useless and redundant. (p. 93)

It also traverses terrain that foregrounds, and so problematizes, what is often taken for granted in studies on citizenship: the status of the self, individuality conceived as achievement, and its complex relation to community and conceptions of interconnectedness that derive *inter alia* from African, non-Western sources. In so doing, practices of diverse citizenship reconfigure the relation between dominant norms and alternative ways of doing things. To put this in Derridean terms: such practices make visible the violent hierarchies involved in conceptions of modern citizenship; reverse the relation between the dominant and supplementary terms; and reinscribe the marginal terms, thus revaluing them in the process.

Autobiography, examples, conversations

Begging to Be Black is the third volume of a trilogy that was not conceived of as a trilogy from the outset. The first volume, *Country of My Skull* (1998), is a moving and in places disturbing account of Krog's experiences and observations of the hearings of the Truth and Reconciliation Commission. The second volume, *A Change of Tongue* (2003), explores 'the conditions under which identity may transform so that to be an Afrikaner is also to be an *Afrikaan*: a person who is not only in Africa as a displaced European, but also of Africa'.[12] These reflections are developed further in the final volume of the trilogy, with its focus on the question of becoming, of becoming towards another; in this case, 'becoming black'. Before turning to an analysis of this text, seen in the light of issues of belonging and the imagining of acting otherwise, it is important to take cognizance of the structure of the text and the narrative forms deployed therein.

As I have already pointed out, the text weaves together several narratives that are divergent in terms of time, place and voice. It is a mixture of historical materials, recounted largely in fictional form, factual materials, conversations and reflections. Krog notes that the historical part on King Moshoeshoe is not a biography but is focused 'on descriptions of parts of his life that contribute to the conversations' she has tried to trace (p. vii). Her use of Moshoeshoe raises the question of what work the chapters on him do in the text, how they contribute to the conversations she recounts. I shall suggest that Moshoeshoe, although usually invoked as an exceptional figure, captures for Krog something that is exemplary, though for that very reason not exceptional. As a historical figure, he also represents something of a supplement to the imagination, thus addressing Krog's anxieties about the (grounds of the) possibility of knowing others.

The book is structured into three parts, which are entitled 'The Long Conversation: First Perceptions and Un-Hearings'; 'Understandings, Assumed Understandings, and Non-Understandings'; and 'The Long Conversation: Whose Context?' These titles explicitly underline the sense in which any attempt to fashion interconnectedness and belonging are always already marked by the difficulties of reaching understanding and interconnection. The titles also act as markers of the fact that the text does not draw together and refrains from explicitly thematizing and unifying the different narratives. *Begging to Be Black* does not offer an account of sutured identities and communities. Both the structure of the text and its overt arguments, presented in conversational form, leave open the complexities, difficulties and irresolution that accompany the occupation of the position of a 'diverse subject'. This is particularly evident in her reflection, towards the end of the book, on the four figures of sphinxes guarding a bridge in Berlin:

> What is she, I wonder. Is she simply a hybrid, doomed to sit at all crossings, guarding all transits, for ever trapped between two stages? ... For me she is not a hybrid, or a product of rape. She is what she is. Not split, not guarding dichotomies, but presenting beingness as multiple intactness, not with the singular self, but with a bodily akin-ness to the vulnerability of being in and beyond this world. (p. 275)

Before turning to the text in more depth, it is worth reflecting on the use of conversation in this text. Krog makes liberal use of reporting directly her conversations, particularly those with her husband, as well as the more structured presentation of her conversations with 'a philosopher'. These conversations function in different ways in her text. The former recounts intimate arguments, thoughts that may often be regarded as disturbing, a recounting of 'things we say in the privacy of our own homes'. Her husband – J. – often occupies the position of what one could call the voice of 'common sense', relaying the rumours in the community around her involvement in the murder trial, as well as giving expression to commonsensical objections to her sometimes indulgent soul-searching.

By contrast, Krog reflects explicitly on the status of her seven conversations with the philosopher(s), noting the 'patient engagement' and understanding of 'how the conversation texts would be used' in her book (p. ix). In contrast to other chapters, these conversations have titles such as 'Imagining Black' and 'Interconnected with Whom?', reflecting the themes of their engagements during her stay in Berlin. She also notes early on how transcribing a conversation 'makes one acutely aware of how often and how easily people talk past each other, of how a conversation can drift along and then suddenly hit upon a crisp and powerful interactive patch, only to loosen up again, to meander on, as if preparing for the next moment of entanglement' (p. 99). The foregrounding of this conversational structure alerts one to the *processual* quality of conversations and that 'conversations continued or broken constitute or dissolve relations'.[13] The conversational voice thus captures precisely the sense in which Tully refers to our practical identities insofar as they are contrasted with and different from, identities constituted through legislative voices, with all the finality and definiteness associated with them.[14] As he puts it: 'Rather than look on citizenship as a status within an institutional framework backed up by world historical processes and universal norms, the diverse tradition looks on citizenship as *negotiated practices*, as praxis, as actors and activities in context.'

Legal entanglements

Begging to be Black is a book of journeys – 'moral, historical, philosophical and geographical' – exploring 'questions of change and becoming, coherency and connectedness' in the context of a post-apartheid South Africa. Situated firmly in this context the book opens with the recounting of a murder, in 1992, of a gang leader shot dead by an ANC member in Kroonstad, the town in which Krog was living at the time. The murder weapon was hidden on her *stoep* (porch), so linking her into the events surrounding the murder and the trial of the defendants. This first narrative explores the difficulties Krog experiences. As she puts it in her testimony during the trial:

> I had been faced with this terrible choice: if I keep quiet I became an accessory to murder, while one of the reasons why I joined the ANC was precisely because, unlike the apartheid government, it respected everybody's life and not only that of white people. Or I can go to the police and work for the people who are responsible for this tension between Reggie [one of the accused] and the Wheetie [the murdered gang leader]. This was a terrible choice for me. (p. 169)

Some five years after the trial, when Reggie Baartman and Jantjie Petrus appears before the Truth and Reconciliation Commission (TRC) to apply for amnesty, Krog gains access to information that leads her to question her decision to give evidence in the trial.[15] The political contextualization of the Three Million gang, of which the Wheetie was the leader, makes it clear that the gang was used by the security forces as part of its 'counter-insurgency strategy to neutralize and undermine the UDF- and ANC-aligned activism in the mid-1980s' (p. 256).[16] As a result, Krog reaches the conclusion that she made a triple mistake: 'what I did was politically naïve, legally uninformed and morally wrong' (p. 259). Reading the TRC reports, Krog writes, 'is like looking at the same object through different lenses':

> The various frameworks brought together by the amnesty hearing expose a profound moral confusion. Read within the framework of the law during the court case, Jantjie was guilty, because he broke the law. Read within the framework of amnesty, Jantjie was guilty, but deserves amnesty because he killed with a political motive within a political context. Read within a traditional framework, Jantjie was not guilty, because he exercised the will of the community by getting rid of somebody who lived in disregard of the community. Read within the framework of the native white activist, Jantjie was guilty, because he killed somebody, even more guilty because it was a black person. (pp. 257–8)

Given the complexities of the post-apartheid, post-colonial context, the various responses to Krog's participation in the trial are illuminating for they are enlightening not only with respect to the moral quandaries the case raise, but even more so for the light they throw on the question of community and the negotiation of belonging that informs and structures other narratives running throughout the text.

Krog's conversations with her husband on the case revolve largely around the fact that she is torn between the different demands that the various frameworks of interpretation impose on her. She questions whether her qualms are moral at all, or whether they might be the luxuries allowed a white, middle-class woman who can afford to be against murder? (p. 46). To what extent can a moral decision be made in an immoral context? (p. 13). Because of its fractured past, she suggests, South Africans 'have never formed a coherent enough whole to decide what principles we agree on. It was okay to kill blacks, but not whites. It was okay to steal from whites but not from blacks. 'How do we', she asks, 'change that into: It is wrong to kill or steal?' (p. 46).

Her husband contests that there is a moral decision to be made at all. In providing transport to the alleged murderers, he points out that she has broken the law and could be hanged as accessory to murder (p. 13). In contrast to her question as to whether, if the law of the land has no legitimacy, the individual has to take decisions in the light of a 'larger moral framework' (p. 13), he responds with despair, as the voice of common sense, outlining the consequences for them as a family of the actions of the ANC by drawing her into a murder case without obtaining her consent (p. 14).

These fragments of conversations address enormously complex questions, debated in South Africa for decades, and explored in the course of the TRC's hearing into the working of the legal system under apartheid, during its institutional hearings.[17] Here I would like to focus on how these questions are linked to debates and questions of community and belonging. Krog's account foregrounds the difficulties that arise when, in fact, there is *not (yet)* a nation agreeing on the principles informing and shaping its existence. Hence, the absence of shared principles is perhaps first and even foremost a question of the absence of a sense of community and belonging.

These matters are highlighted in her interactions with the defendants after the trial, and in her later conversations with her husband after the surfacing of the evidence of Security Branch activities in support of the Three Million Gang. Here I wish to outline two of these encounters, each of which highlights different aspects of the problem of community, and both of which are relevant for the wider discussion of the issue of 'acting otherwise' explored in this chapter. The first concerns her relation to Reggie, the ANC activist found guilty of 'defeating the ends of justice', who handed her the red T-shirt, worn by the murderer, to dispose of. Being found guilty, in part as a result of her testimony, Reggie's career as a political activist is brought to an end. After the court case, Reggie contacts Krog through a journalist to let her know that he and his wife have forgiven her, even though they were disappointed and shocked by the fact that she was prepared to give evidence against him. She responds:

> I am aghast. *I haven't asked to be forgiven.* In fact I do not even think I am sorry! I feel guilty, but it is a guilt more rooted in confusion than in conviction about wrongdoing. (p. 172, emphasis added)

This response is interesting, as much for what it asserts as what it denies. Krog makes this statement shortly after she has pointed out that the events of the trial and the murder has destroyed 'every small fibre of the sort of non-racial life' that she was trying to create in Kroonstad, a life that tried to 'open up some space to live humanely in this inhumane land' (p. 171). Elsewhere she describes typical 'white' responses to forgiveness, applicable here also to her own response to Reggie:

> I heard whites say: What is going on with these people? Why do they forgive? Some of them forgive even before forgiveness has been asked. What kind of people are these? 'You see, they are not like us; they can't even hate properly.' So their very humaneness is used to describe their inhumanity. (p. 206)

Set in the context of her broader discussion of forgiveness and its role in the transition in South Africa,[18] the fact of having received forgiveness even when one has not asked for it, takes on a new significance for it is precisely this act that does open up the possibility of living humanely in an inhumane land. Whether or not she needed and requested forgiveness, Reggie's act of forgiving could be argued to arise from a sense of community, of interconnectedness that Krog elsewhere describes as standing at the core of African interconnectedness. This is illustrated particularly clearly in her recounting of the response by Cynthia Ngewu, one of the mothers of the Gugulethu Seven,[19] on the prison sentences given to the perpetrators:

> I think that all South African should be committed to the idea of re-accepting these people back into the community. We do not want to return the evil that the perpetrators committed to the nation. We want to demonstrate a humanness [ubuntu] towards them, so that [it] in turn may restore their own humanity. (p. 211)

Reconciliation, Ngewu suggests, means that:

> This perpetrator, this man who has killed [my son] Christopher Piet, if it means he becomes human again, this man, so that I, so that all of us, get our humanity back … then I agree, then I support it all. (p. 211)

Praeg describes Cynthia Ngewu's words here as demonstrating the distance between the discourse of the TRC and 'what she struggles to simply articulate as a self-evident way of being'. While she cannot be sure that words like 'reconciliation' capture her way of being, he argues that it is 'through such equivocations that reconciliation and forgiveness came to stand for an African appreciation of "our shared humanity" and to metonymically represent the meaning of ubuntu'.[20]

The politics of interconnectedness is also at issue in her husband's response to Krog's acknowledgement of her 'triple mistake'. Krog accuses herself of instinctively choosing the safety of the 'Afrikaner government's police' and masking it in moral and legal language because she could not believe 'that the white government was behind it and would go to the trouble of actively putting structures up in a tiny town like Kroonstad in order for black people to kill each other' (p. 259). Her husband picks up on this self-accusation, bringing to light the implicit sense of interconnection at work in it, arguing that:

> I know this is important to you, so let me make another suggestion. You used the word *instinctively*. If you believe, as you always tell me, that Africanness is defined by the idea of being interconnected to one's community, then perhaps you've proved your instinctive Africanness by choosing your own people, however bad and corrupt they were. This is who you are interconnected with. You have proved your Africanness! (p. 259).

He continues to point out that others have cloaked their wars in the language of politics and liberation, to which Krog responds that she is not interested in comparing things, but in living 'a grounded life' and that Africanness, as she understands it, encompasses '*alles* [everything], seen and unseen' (p. 260). Let us now turn to the role that the idea of African interconnectedness plays in Krog's account.

An African gift

> The world will never be able to learn anything from Africa ... we are just something cute, a mask to hang in a television lounge, but we will never be recognized for having contributed something worthwhile to the world. (p. 212)

Interconnectedness is central to Krog's attempt to think through the issue of belonging in the context of diverse citizenship, where there can be no easy assumption of shared values and common languages of morality. Belonging,[21] as is evident from the book's title, for her is a matter of 'becoming black'. These issues are explored in the text in three different narrative contexts: that of her conversations with a philosopher/philosophers in Berlin while on study leave; the recounting of her conversations with a student, Bonnini, concerning African rootedness; and the telling of the Moshoeshoe story, which runs in separate chapters throughout the book. I will deal primarily with the first and the third of these narratives.

Krog's conversations with the philosopher(s) is dispersed throughout the three parts of the text entitled respectively 'The Long Conversation: First Perceptions and Un-Hearings'; 'Understandings, Assumed Understandings, and Non-Understandings'; and 'The Long Conversation: Whose Context?' These titles explicitly underline the sense in which any attempt to fashion interconnectedness is always already marked by the difficulties of reaching understanding and interconnection. Although Krog uses the term almost always as if depicting a singular meaning, these conversations should not be read as nostalgic attempts to recoup a sense of wholeness and of lost unity, or of the authenticity of interconnection promised by 'African interconnectedness'. Rather, as I will argue, in Krog's hands, interconnection is always a matter of becoming – of a 'striving towards' – which can never be achieved unproblematically because, from the outset, it is marked by fissure and the ignobility of origins rather than by authenticity. These fissures arise not only from the outside – from the colonial relationship – but also from the inside.

This is clear, as I have suggested, in the fact that the text arises out of a sense of dislocation and perplexity, a sense that runs deep and remains largely unresolved. In her first conversation with a philosopher, this issue is captured by references to the figure of Robert Mugabe and the responses of African leaders like Mbeki to Mugabe: 'At times when ... Thabo Mbeki, speaks ... I sit like somebody in complete darkness' (p. 94). She is thus unable to understand where he is coming from and from within what logic his position makes sense. Accompanying this sense of perplexity is a questioning of the subject position from which it is possible for her to understand, to 'become "blacker"' (p. 93). In this text, Krog locates her occupation with the question of blackness and whiteness in a moment of dislocation – her participation in the TRC – in which it became apparent to her that most of her references and frameworks of understanding were, if not redundant, at best inadequate (p. 93). Prior to this, she argues, as an active opponent of apartheid, she felt neither white nor black, but 'intensely human' (p. 203). However, her participation in the TRC made her aware of a stronger sense – a new way of making sense of the world, a way of being human that is rooted in blackness (p. 206).[22] She describes it thus:

> [A] radically new way, embedded in an indigenous view of the world, had been put on the table by black people at the end of the twentieth century. I am not saying it is a better way than the post-Second World War approach, but it is a different way of dealing with injustice so that it becomes possible for a country to break out of its cycles of violence. (p. 206)

Before turning to how she portrays this alternative, it is necessary to pause and reflect on the issue of emphasis on 'becoming black'?

An interlude: Begging to the Black

> Arthur Ashe once said it was easier for him to cope with having Aids than it was to cope with being black. Whites can never know what it is to be black. (*A Change of Tongue*, p. 274)

Begging to Be Black is a title that causes unease if viewed from the point of view of a democratic community with a sense of equal citizenship. But perhaps this sense of unease is precisely an indicator of what is not yet achieved.[23] Krog provides little guidance on this. The only reference in the book to the title occurs during her first conversation with a philosopher, when he takes note of a comment on the cover of her manuscript 'bearing the words in bold letters inspired by *The Satanic Verses*: "BEGGING TO BE BLACK." The professor notices my blunt working title and responds somewhat curtly' (p. 93). (He responds, as we will see shortly, by questioning the implicit essentialism of the title.) Both *The Satanic Verses* and *Begging to Be Black* deal with questions of belonging, identity, divided selves and colonialism, and both are multilayered texts providing 'intertexts' that comment on other stories within the text.[24]

However, these structural and thematic similarities do not address the question of 'begging' to become something. Part of the answer to this question may be located in *A Change of Tongue*, where Krog recounts a series of tetchy conversations with activist friends, increasingly foregrounding the question of race and of her whiteness. The question of race infuses the account of the conversation, perhaps not surprisingly, since it takes place at a South African Conference on Racism, at which Krog is also a speaker. While Krog mentions her sense that having (white) friends is now an embarrassment for her (black) friends and former activists, one of her friends – having moved into a formerly white suburb – note how she is 'held accountable for every single thing a black person did'. 'If a black man rapes a child or steals a million, the neighbours of my colleagues want me to explain' (*A Change of Tongue*, p. 272). Her friend continues:

> And if I want to know why it is I never ask *them* to explain when a white farmer shoots a black baby – is it perhaps because I know them well enough? – then they're quick with this ubuntu thing: blacks stick together because of ubuntu, you know? And I can tell you, nothing pisses me off more than whites pretending to understand or even care about African concepts like ubuntu. (*A Change of Tongue*, p. 272)

Krog retorts with an exclamation that 'the only thing we hear is race, race, race. As if my only identity is "white", and I'm not allowed to be more than that!' (*A Change of Tongue*, p. 272) And that race is a trap from which no change is possible.[25]

Instead, Krog suggests she is trying to find a way into – to find her feet with – her friend's definitions of 'African' and 'South Africa', categories that she contends cannot be 'closed off so quickly with skin' (p. 274). While acknowledging the demand for whites to learn to see themselves as African, Krog suggests that there is a further side to this story: one in which she needs to be accepted as an African. 'Who would want to live the life of an unaccepted African?' (p. 274). Here 'African' does not imply 'black' if the latter is taken as a marker of race. For Krog, race narrows things down too quickly and impoverishes lives; for her friends, race is something lived: a life of risk. Her two friends disagree as to whether Krog can become one of them:

> 'The moment you learn to live the black life of risk, you will become one of us.' 'Bullshit,' Mamukwa says sharply to Ghangha. 'She can never become black ... Her people have been living here for generations, surviving, but when we see her, we know she is a kangaroo from elsewhere.' (p. 274)

It is not clear that the term 'black' for either Ghangha or Mamukwa functions simply as a marker of race. For Ghangha, blackness is something that could be 'learnt' insofar as it is lived, whereas for Mamuka blackness seems to be infused with a problematic essentialism, a naturalism of skin and of identity. This conversation captures something of the difficulties in navigating one's way around and avoiding racial essentialism whilst simultaneously capturing something of the lived experience of 'blackness' as well as the complicated politics of 'becoming black'.

Whilst Krog's text is virtually deplete of a political analysis of becoming black, the conversation just recounted, and indeed the titles of both books – *A Change of Tongue* and *Begging to Be Black* – are indicative of what may be seen as important shifts in social imaginary, away from non-racialism as organizing principle, to a concern with race in isolation from that discourse.[26] Of course, this conversation also echoes wider debates on blackness, which hearken back to the black consciousness discourses of the 1970s in South Africa. They should also be set within the context of Mbeki emphasis on an African Renaissance, which has a long history in South Africa.[27] These cannot be elaborated upon here. What is important is the facticity of these difficult conversations, and these attempts to imagine ways of acting otherwise in response to these issues.

A return to 'African interconnectedness'

Krog's conversations with the philosopher traces out her own refining of this sense, from a desire to move towards blackness 'as black South African themselves understand it' (p. 94), to coming to a better understanding of subjectivity, not of philosophy, but of the kind of self one should 'grow into in order to live a caring, useful and informed life – a "good life"' in Southern Africa (p. 95). Hence, whilst these conversations are infused with discussion and a questioning of the assumptions of Western conceptions of individualism and their relation to African philosophy, Krog's aim is not to achieve philosophical clarity, but to come to a better understanding of a life lived in a context infused with a different sense of self and of community, a sense of self that is not limited by an interpretive frame that always already assumes the superiority of dominant Western conceptions of individuality.[28] In this sense, Krog's work echoes that of Tully, in her questioning of what he calls 'imperial right' and the premises of Western superiority (p. 218) of conceptions of self, in favour of a focus on practical identity, a mode of being in the world with others which, as Tully points out, contains a structure of strong evaluations 'in accord with which humans value themselves, find their lives worth living and their actions worth undertaking, and the description under which they require, as a condition of self-worth, that others recognise and respect them'.[29]

It is crucial to Krog's position that this sense of self, of interconnectedness, is not reduced to the familiar too quickly, if at all. That, precisely, is part of the struggle: to find a voice in which one can word this sense which does not already throw it back onto and so reduce it to dominant, available categories of thought. This is evident in her treatment and responses to suggestions by the philosopher who seeks to establish links and similarities between what Krog is struggling to express, and the Western canon of philosophical thinking. He suggests, *inter alia*, that:

> Western philosophy has ample examples of philosophers who emphasized the importance of interconnectedness. Spinoza, Feuerbach, Levinas, Freud … Some would say that Jewish culture has that characteristic. (p. 155)

To which Krog responds:

> There is always a Westerner saying this to me. The West is like a vacuum cleaner, sucking up everything, mauling it to pieces within the debris of its own failures, and then it tells you: But we have already said this. Nothing can be said in the world that the West has not already said. (p. 155)

He retorts with an accusation of exceptionalism, which cuts to the heart of the matter:

> South Africans have been accused of thinking they are always exceptional – encouraged especially by Tutu. African philosophy does not live on an island.

It speaks to Europe and the West out of its lived experience with Europe and the West. So it is always a two-way dialogue. When a non-African tries to understand an African, he or she needs equipment to cross the boundaries between different cultures. Africa's text is being written by Africans, but it is also addressed to a world outside Africa. All of Africa's diasporic voices are entwined with North or South or Arab or Jew, and virtually every European who has a colonial history with Africa. (p. 156)

[Krog]: I think that is precisely what I mean: you don't hear us through our own voice. You keep on hearing us only through *your* voice. (p. 156)

Hence, the interconnectedness that Krog wants to explore is one that must start from a sense of dislocation, also of 'our' familiar ways of making sense of the world, a dislocation that predisposes one to open oneself up to other, foreign possibilities. This is not an easy process. Krog struggles both to articulate precisely what is at stake and to find a way of approaching 'blackness' that is not essentializing, yet that captures a certain sense of specificity.

In all of this, she must also reckon with her own situatedness and what it means for this process. If Krog distances herself very firmly from any identity associated with the term 'whiteness' this is because in her narrative, whiteness is almost always associated with colonialism and her identity, prior to the attempt to think through becoming black, is constituted through discourses of non-racialism rather than whiteness.[30] The sense of specificity she seeks is crucial to her understanding of interconnectedness, as is clear from the above exchange. In response to the question as to what she wants 'to do' with this sense, Krog – like the philosopher – problematizes the idea of exceptionalism, though for reasons that are different from his. Before exploring this, let us turn for a moment to her account of what this interconnectedness entails.

Krog portrays interconnectedness as interconnectedness with a 'wholeness of life' 'religious and secular, spiritual and material, which can never be compartmentalized' (p. 184). It implies a 'cosmological dimension, a human and non-human world that encapsulates plants, animals, a spiritual god and ancestors' (p. 184); a fluid and inclusive sense of community with a 'variety of simultaneous links and networks woven through clanship, cattle, marriage, initiation and rituals' (p. 185). This sense of interconnectedness of the physical, the social and the metaphysical and its relation to becoming is clearly one of the aspects that facilitates the conversation on Deleuze. As the philosopher puts it:

If Deleuze forms the context of our discussion, then we have dealt with essentialism and difference in this sense: plants and animals, inside and outside, and even organic and inorganic, cannot really be told apart. All these things are themselves, yet on another level they are transforming towards one another. Things continue to become the other, while continuing to be what they are, if you understand what I mean. (p. 99)[31]

But this interconnectedness, for Krog, has a specifically African character, one that must be foregrounded but that cannot be thought through the category of exceptionalism.[32] While for the philosopher, exceptionalism must be avoided since it denies the interrelated, entwined character of thought, which does not take place on an island, as he puts it. For Krog, exceptionalism must be avoided since it denies the specifically African rootedness of this sense of interconnectedness.

Let us look at this in more detail. Her argument is that the West (read whites) has treated Mandela and Tutu as figures of exception, and this treatment has led to a separation of their view and their lives from their roots in this sense of African interconnectedness. As she puts it:

> [W]hat makes Nelson Mandela such a special statesman is the fact that his political acumen is embedded in this world view. It is because he, in contrast to the whites, regards white South Africans as part of his interconnectedness. But white people battle to understand that; we treat Mandela as an exception and ignore for convenience's sake that he himself keeps on saying that he is what he is because of others. The same with Tutu. What makes his theology and actions so remarkable is not the Christianity but that his Christianity is embedded in his world view. He redefines Christian community in terms of interconnectedness. (p. 185)

Credit needs to be given to blackness (p. 206). The point is that interconnectedness forms the 'interpretive foundation' of southern African Christianity (211); it is not the case that we are dealing here with exceptional individuals, or simply with mixtures of discourses (of human rights, Christianity and so forth). As Krog puts it: 'To characterise it as such a mixture would misrecognise the sense in which it is rooted in blackness specifically' (p. 206). How precisely one should understand this 'blackness' needs to be explored further. Krog suggests, in the context of the roots of interconnectedness, that this blackness is not a simple Africanness. It is, Krog speculates, rooted in the views of the First Peoples of Southern Africa (rather than, for instance, in North Africa) (p. 184). This, in itself, suggests a de-essentializing view. While much of Krog's texts deploy the term blackness in a seemingly unproblematized fashion – and the philosopher takes her up on this – there are moments in the text where it is not the case; where there is an explicit recognition of the difficulties of filling out the very idea of blackness.

Early on in their conversations the philosopher attempts to clear the issue of essentialism out of the way by drawing on Deleuze. He also warns Krog of the danger of letting blackness 'become a voiceless group' that is defined and observed by her, instead of a 'varied, multiple people'. He tells her not to keep on talking to whites about blacks, but to talk and listen to blacks (p. 123). It is in their penultimate discussion around the xenophobic attacks on foreign workers in South Africa during May 2008[33] that Krog is clearest on the distance between race, blackness and interconnectedness. She warns that conflating race with interconnectedness precludes one from interrogating the question of community, a mistake neither Mandela nor Tutu ever made (p. 237).[34]

Imagining blackness, imagining otherwise

> We also say of people that they are transparent to us. It is, however, important as regards this observation that one human being can be a complete enigma to another. We learn this when we come into a strange country with entirely strange traditions; and, what is more, even given the mastery of the country's language. We do not *understand* (*versteht*) the people. (And not because of not knowing what they are saying to themselves.) We cannot find our feet with them (*Wir können us nicht in sie finden*). (Wittgenstein, *Philosophical Investigations*, p. 190)[35]

> A lot of attention has to be paid to our history if we blacks want to aid each other in our coming into consciousness. We have to rewrite our history and describe in it the heroes that formed the core of resistance to the white invaders. More has to be revealed and stress has to be laid on the successful nation-building attempts by people like Shaka, Moshoeshoe and Hintsa. (Steve Biko, 1978: p. 84)

In one of their early conversations Krog notes that she does not know how to talk about social imaginings. While she can imagine herself scared and ill, she cannot even begin to imagine herself black:

> One stood up against apartheid because one believed that all people shared a common humanity and discrimination was wrong. In other words, I think I can imagine the indignity and hurt and empathize with that, but I can't imagine the being-blackness. (p. 122)

She cannot find her feet with blackness. In the course of trying to think through why that is the case, she suggests that perhaps she just does not *know* enough about being black to imagine it (p. 122), thus drawing an implicit distinction between knowing and imagining. In their final conversation Krog and the philosopher return to the question of imagination. He raises the question as to how 'people's imaginings of what kind of society they want' could function 'when the rites, rituals and stories that sustained their belief systems no longer have a place?' (p. 266). This arises in reference to the alleged experienced redundancy of a sense of interconnected, rooted selfhood and its imagination in the modern world. As just noted, Krog responds by drawing a seemingly sharp opposition between imagination and knowledge, arguing that she does not want to write novels, since that would require giving up a strangeness that is real, captured in the thought of the inability to ever really enter the psyche of another. Hence, in her hands the lives of literary characters become fully known, whereas this is not possible in the actual world, and not writing fiction marks that impossibility. It is important to take a closer look at how she characterises this:

> I simply don't know enough about blackness, or birdness, or mountainness, or even Englishness for that matter, to imagine it in terms other than my exact self or the exotic opposite of myself. A famous Afrikaans poet Eugène Marais visited some Bushmen [sic] researchers during the nineteenth century and said afterwards: The Bushmen could speak lion, they could speak blue crane, they could speak wind. *I want to be this embedded in my world. I want to speak black.* (p. 268, emphasis added)

While what is at issue here is knowledge, or her lack of it, it is not knowledge in the sense of a verificationist conception of knowledge. Rather, the sort of knowledge she strives to obtain is knowledge that is embedded in practical, lived lives; having a sense that allows one to find one's feet with someone else. Imagination, she argues, is simply not up to this task, since it is not 'capable of imagining a reality as – or with – the other' (p. 268). In its place, she suggests – recalling perhaps the earlier conversation with the philosopher – that one observes and listens:

> [T]o imagine black at this stage is to insult black. That is why I stay with non-fiction, listening, engaging, observing, translating, until one can hopefully begin *to sense a thinning of the skin, negotiate possible small openings at places where imaginings can begin to begin.* (p. 268 emphasis added)

However, here again, observation, and this possibility of opening is, as is her whole quest, one of a practical identity, described here as 'a thinning of the skin', and elsewhere as a dissolving of the self into others, a porousness of the body (p. 181), a being part of that arises not 'of some thought-out or yet-to-come imagined space, but part of something that *is*, calibrating hearts' (p. 181). Hence, the sort of imagining for which Krog can see a space arises out of 'small openings' and breaches of barriers, negotiated openings where one can begin to imagine being with another.

Here, I would argue, imagination's work should be conceived of, in Wittgensteinian fashion, 'as an interpretive act through which we, more than simply producing images, see things *as* this or that investment of meaning, *as* this or that means of transcending the present towards something else'.[36] Hence, imagination is 'the capacity for making connections, seeing or realizing possibilities'.[37] On this reading, imagination is not, per definition, opposed to knowledge.[38] As Cavell suggests: 'Imagination is called for, faced with the other, when I have to take the facts in, realize the significance of what is going on, make the behaviour real for myself, make a connection'.[39]

Exemplarity: Moshoeshoe, knowledge and imagination

Motho ke motho ka batho.
A person is a person through other persons.[40]

A key part of the process of observing, listening and engaging through which Krog seeks to open a space where imagination can begin is done through her inclusion of the Moshoeshoe narrative in the text. Ostensibly this narrative functions as a non-fictional narrative, one that provides some of the 'knowledge' she seeks. In this respect the account has the function of 'proving' the existence of exemplary forms of political arrangements on the African continent, so countering the colonial imagination.

The tale of Moshoeshoe is set firmly within the colonial relation.[41] Indeed, Krog uses this exploitative relation to foreground the sense of vulnerability embedded in the African sense of interconnectedness. Making the point more generally Krog argues that:

> On the African continent the dominant framework *is* not Western ... Africa always had a framework accommodating multiple world views, but this very capacity to accommodate becomes the terrible entry point for exploitation, plundering, racism, slavery, etc., by those who tolerate nothing else but their own. (p. 238)

Eugene Casalis' account of Moshoeshoe portrays what Krog sees as a familiar dilemma of colonial representation, one she clearly seeks to circumvent, of 'how to present admirable, worthy ... qualities observed in black people in a way that did not diminish their readiness and urgent need for conversion and civilization?' (p. 19). Casalis, a young French missionary, did this through presenting Moshoeshoe as an exception, an exception to his people; compared to the 'generality of his subjects' he described Moshoeshoe as 'a superior man' (p. 19).

Krog seeks to undercut this account of exceptionality in favour of reading Moshoeshoe as an exemplar of a particular culture, rather than an exception to it. Hence, Moshoeshoe's life is presented as a life that exemplifies the qualities associated with interconnectedness, thus demonstrating an alternative way of being in the world. The key characteristics Krog focuses on are those for which Moshoeshoe is most well known: his attempts to foster a kingdom based on lasting peace and prosperity by uplifting the poor; stabilizing the area through diplomacy, and involve everybody in decisions affecting their lives. (p. 29)

Moshoeshoe was tutored in the arts of government by a neighbouring wise king and old sage, Mohlomi, who inculcated in him the view that a chief's rule would not be able to withstand difficulties of governing if it was not based upon 'peace, justice and "*botho*" (humanness), that "a chief becomes and remains a chief only by means of the people's will, recognition and support"' (p. 24). These principles informed his actions both in relation to his people and to others with whom they came into contact. Krog recounts several examples of how these principles informed Moshoeshoe's governance. For instance, he allowed groups with different cultures (the Amahlapo from Natal and the Amavundle from the Eastern Cape) to keep their language and to practise their cultures, something which continues to be the case in Lesotho today, where there are still groups of Xhosa-speakers (p. 32). In addition to accommodating people and setting up diplomatic relations with other chiefs, Moshoeshoe developed a form of democratic participation consisting of several layers of consultation. Moshoeshoe believed that suppressing people's freedom to express their views would lead to discontent. Hence, he encouraged the formulation in public of 'whatever might be brewing under the surface' (p. 32):

> At the end of the meeting he would sum up what had been said (incorporating the unpopular in a way that both legitimized and defused it), put everything within a specific historical context (it is a Basotho belief that every event is always the son of another event), and then he would make his ruling. (p. 32)

Examples of his leadership and extraordinary ability to embed the principles of governance learnt from Mohlomi in his rulings abound throughout the text, including dealing with cases of cannibalism and other destructive practices in a manner that allowed the cannibals to 'change their habits and earn their place back in the realm of humanity from which their behaviour ... had expelled them' (p. 26).

Running like a thread through these examples is Moshoeshoe's ability imaginatively to draw connections between the narratives of those he came into contact with, and the concerns of his people. Although he refused to be converted, he was able to use the stories from the Bible as retold by Casalis, and confront the missionaries with inconsistencies (p. 80) questioning, for instance, their claims that Jesus had come to bring peace while 'white people were making war'; pointing out that the practice of polygamy condemned by the missionaries was widely present in the Bible (citing the cases of Abraham, Isaac and Jacob). Moshoeshoe on occasion even intervened in favour of Casalis when the latter was questioned. When a member of the audience questioned Casalis' claim that God was the father of them all, Moshoeshoe answered him: 'In my herds are white, red, and spotted cattle; are they not all cattle? do they not come from the same stock, and belong to the same master?' (p. 80). Casalis recorded another case: when faced with white settlers who demanded the drawing of a firm boundary to ensure the demarcation of territory they had invaded, Moshoeshoe recalled the story of the two women in dispute about a baby in front of Solomon, who ordered the child to be cut into half and to which the real mother responded saying she would rather lose her child altogether. Krog notes the other options open to Moshoeshoe. He could have explained, she says, 'how land could be allocated to strangers only through a democratic decision taken at a *pitso*' or how land 'could not and should not be owned' (p. 131). However, he 'chose to tell them *their* story':

He framed his claim to the land in terms of divine providence; he expressed his biological and emotional link to the land by using the image of the mother and child; he played off the real history of greed and appropriation against a biblical history of integrity and willingness to sacrifice.'

With the words, 'You my friends, who are strangers, you think it quite natural that my ground should be cut', Moshoeshoe was stating that this meeting was not merely about a contestation of land, but that 'strangers' were assuming rights they did not have. (p. 131)

The outcome of this story is unknown. However, it illustrated Moshoeshoe's remarkable ability and diplomacy, which was combined with a range of strategies to fight for and 'negotiate ceaselessly to protect his territory and his people' against colonial encroachment[42] (p. 123).

Throughout recounting his story, Krog remains attentive to the colonial framework in which Moshoeshoe was forced to operate and her conclusions are not optimistic. Thus she suggests that:

most of what Moshoeshoe had been saying was misunderstood within the framework of French missionary beliefs, British imperialism and Afrikaner land hunger. He was unable to convince any foreign power that the diversity he had accommodated in his nation was extended to them (at least initially) and that goodness could come into a society when its interconnected humanness was prioritized. (p. 227)

The recognition of this kind of leadership, Krog argues, had to wait. It only dawned:

when the most famous African leader ever, Nelson Mandela, appeared on the political stage. But, like Moshoeshoe, Mandela also had to experience being exceptionalized, extracted as an individual from his people. Although both leaders confirmed on public platforms that they were what they were because of their people (Mandela in his speech opening the first democratic parliament and Moshoeshoe in the idiom for which he is credited: a king is a king through his people), a culture based on individuality could not hear that: the exceptional leader was welcome, his people not. (p. 228)

Begging to Be Black could indeed be read as a plea to recognize this leadership and the importance of interconnectedness in a context in which the world still refuses to learn anything from Africa.

Let us now return to the role the story of Moshoeshoe plays in Krog's text. Moshoeshoe clearly acts as an exemplar of African interconnectedness, with all the attendant difficulties that the living out of such interconnectedness poses in the modern world.[43] Moshoeshoe acts as an exemplar of what an interconnected form of governance might look like. It would be attentive to inclusion of others; sensitive to the diversity of practices that make up a social, cultural and political world and community, and to the connections between the physical and social world; living out a conception of the self that is intimately shaped by its relation to the community, that is rooted and embedded in world from which it arises, yet flexible enough to change and transform itself in the face of challenges and dislocations. Above all, he is an exemplar forged in an *African* context, by an African conception of interconnectedness. Like Mandela and Tutu, he represents, precisely, an excellence that makes a demand upon us.[44] The figure of Moshoeshoe can do this work in Krog's text because he is treated, not as an exception, but as the best instantiation of a particular, specifically African, sense of selfhood and of community.

Exemplars, democracy, citizenship

A human being is a human being *through the otherness* of other human beings.[45]

Krog's work on becoming black precisely is a response to, and then an attempt to think through, the demands that the conception of African interconnectedness places upon those who are open to the possibilities of transformation in post-colonial South Africa. This is not an easy task. This is all too evident in the other responses she encounters and records, for instance, in *A Change of Tongue*, which recounts numerous instances of overtly racist responses to the demands for and of transformation.[46] To the cynical eye, her account may also appear all too idealizing. However, Krog is unflinching in her account, in which she explores that which can and ought to be celebrated, as well as the more difficult and contentious issues. Her treatment of Moshoeshoe equally does not shy away from a number of events showing Moshoeshoe's capacity for violence, acting as reminders of the ignobility of origins. Two of these events are particularly difficult, since they involve the alleged murder of five childhood friends who refused to obey his command, and of his beloved wife, 'Mamohato, who developed an apparently too close relation with a commanding officer in his army. The details of these events do not concern us here. It is crucial that even though Krog deploys Moshoeshoe as an exemplar, she does not collude in the attempts to cover over these deeds (engaged in by the missionaries Casalis and Arbousset's silence, as well as by contemporary researchers).[47] Moshoeshoe, as exemplar, remains marked by those terrible experiences and Krog's textual treatment also signifies the wider significance and necessity of dealing with such events in a thoroughgoing manner. The TRC, of course, stands testament to this. The recounting of these events and Krog's insistence to deal with them openly are also indicative of a particular relation between the exemplar and its 'followers'. The constitution of exemplars in politics is not a matter of consecration. In a democratic context, the need to remain critical, even in following one's exemplars, is crucial. As Owen reminds us in his discussion of the democratic agon in Nietzsche, 'if democracy is to meet its own best aspirations, it requires citizens who cultivate those political virtues (e.g. independence of mind) which are necessary to this task'.[48]

Owen addresses these virtues through a discussion of self-respect, which he links to Tully's emphasis on agonistic deliberation as contestation *within* and *over* the terms of citizenship. He argues that through agonistic engagements 'citizens exercise and develop the capacities and dispositions that compose democratic nobility, i.e. standing to oneself politically as a sovereign individual'.[49] This Nietzsche-inspired account casts self-rule as the non-teleological cultivation of capacities and dispositions that are required 'to extend oneself beyond one's current powers'.[50] It thus operates in a context in which one does not have full control or insight into the trajectory of political life, and in which it is crucial also to create the conditions where others can develop their capacities for self-rule. This account of becoming resonates strongly with Krog's emphasis on becoming, especially her search for capacities and dispositions that would facilitate conversations about the difficult processes of constitution of diverse senses of belonging.

However, her account of belonging also needs to be interrogated further, particularly when placed in the context of diverse citizenship. Krog pays too little attention to the question of plurality, as well as to the complex politics of discourse on 'race' and 'blackness'. This is evident in her somewhat unreflective use of African interconnectedness, as if the latter were a singular and almost self-evident phenomenon. Hence, at least two readings are possible here. As the philosopher suggests in their first conversation, she runs the risk of essentializing 'African interconnectedness', 'blackness', as well as 'whiteness' even as she interrogates these terms. Instead, my alternative reading is one that emphasizes the ongoing character and difficult negotiation of issues of belonging and senses of self, which are problematized and explores though never resolved in the various strands of her texts.

Yet, my reading still does not account adequately for her emphasis on begging to become otherwise. Is 'begging' the appropriate mode of engagement for a democratic citizen? Is it compatible with what is due to the individual *qua* human being, or with 'ubuntu', as proponents of an African sense of interconnectedness may argue? This is a less than robust response to the provocation that she cannot, ever, become black, a response that is difficult to reconcile with democratic equality. These issues may force one to drive a wedge between the emphasis on becoming, with its potentially democratic overtures, and the servility implied in the act of begging. But that, itself, is a matter for debate since one could also read the title as one of *imploring* others, calling upon, to become otherwise from a position that is not yet one in which one can verify equality. There is work to be done.

Acting otherwise

> The block to my vision of the other is not the other's body but my incapacity or unwillingness to interpret or to judge it accurately, to draw the right connections.[51]

We are endlessly separate, for no reason. But then we are answerable for everything that comes between us; if not for causing it, then for continuing it.[52]

Let us now return to the question of 'acting otherwise' with which I opened this discussion. From the foregoing, it is clear that one of the first prerequisites for being able to act otherwise is the condition of dislocation, in which our words no longer appropriately 'word the world', where there is a discrepancy or a disjuncture that needs to be addressed. In Krog's text, this moment is clearly located in her experience of the TRC that made her aware of a different way of being. She only fully comes to realize it at this point, despite the long years she spent determined to live a non-racial life as well as possible. This moment of dislocation is also evident today in our conceptions of citizenship, marked by the introduction of the supplementary term 'diverse citizenship' in Tully's writing.

Yet, such dislocation is only a precondition and not an indication of the direction in which, or even that, we would 'act otherwise'. As Krog puts it in the conversation with Patton quoted at the start of this chapter: 'In order to move, one needs to know in what direction.' For acting otherwise to be accomplished, certain possibilities must be ruled out, whilst others may need to be opened up. In the context in which Krog writes, as in many contemporary societies, for the democratic possibilities of acting otherwise to be realized, closed, given, static forms of identification need to be problematized and possibilities for identification need simultaneously to be pluralized. Krog's work seeks to do so through dealing with an encounter between a dominant conception of individuality, and an alternative account of the relation of the individual and the community, which is at the core of many disputes and conflicts in our contemporary societies. (The substance of this question cannot be settled here, or simply in the abstract.) She seeks to make available to a wider audience, and to work through the implications of an alternative conception of being in the world, whilst challenging the dominance of accepted forms of individuality. Hence, at stake here is not a replacement of a Western conception of individuality with an African conception of some form of 'communalism'. Rather, at issue is a difficult negotiation between different ways of conceiving of individuality in relation to others.

One of the main strengths of Krog's work is that it provides us with multiple ways of approaching the issues of belonging and the constitution of new forms of citizenship. It is no accident that she seeks to draw on a multiplicity of sources to work through these issues. Imagining belonging anew in contemporary societies is a complex matter, requiring engagements that are varied and that can bring to light its many different aspects. A crucial insight gained from Krog's attempt to work through the possibility of being and acting otherwise concerns the respective roles of imagination and knowledge in the development of alternatives. Knowledge, in Krog's text, as I have suggested, has relatively little to do with the 'facts of the case'. Yet she still insists on a sense in which she does not have enough 'knowledge' to imagine being black, to become black, to speak black. When she elaborates on this theme, it quickly becomes clear that what is at stake is an embedded sense of knowledge, of being able to find one's way with another, to become (like) the other, so as to become truly oneself.[53] As Krog puts it, in encountering this sense of African interconnectedness, she 'felt in touch with something' into which she could 'dissolve while simultaneously becoming more what I am' (p. 204). Hence, her quest to 'speak black' is not a case of 'identity suicide' as it has been described by one prominent South African commentator, but a search to become what one is. This difficult task acknowledges the crucial role played by imagination, by the ability to draw connections, to relate to and to stand in the place of another, as if one is standing in one's own shoes. *That* is what becoming black entails. For one can as little stand in another's shoes as in one's own, yet, the struggle to find one's way, with another and so with oneself, is one which is an ongoing task.

Krog's emphasis on becoming is particularly pertinent for thinking about democratic forms of subjectivity and diverse citizenship in our contemporary world. It emphasizes not a given, static conception of self, but a conception of the subject as always underway (*unterwegs*); not towards a fixed destination but working towards and negotiating with the demands that democratic engagements may place upon us. In this sense, *Begging to Be Black* is exemplary of the non-teleological perfectionism also found in Emerson, Nietzsche and Cavell, with its emphasis on work on the self and resistance to dominant norms, coupled with a search for a higher or further self that is always already related to others.[54] It also captures, in the continued foregrounding of the difficulties and tortions of 'becoming black', an ethos of the agonistic struggles through which belonging and citizenship is attained.

It is both interesting and important to take note of the sites in which this work is being done. Tully argues that the work of diverse citizenship takes place in local places and languages. Not simply 'out there', but here, wherever we are.[55] These engagements always carry risks, both positive and negative. The negative risk of engagement with the stories, recalled in *Begging to Be Black* is that we treat them like travel tales of old; something interesting, happening elsewhere, and working to assure us of the superiority of our own positions and senses of self. It is precisely because of this ever-present possibility that the emphasis on dislocation is so important, for it foregrounds the eruption of events, or even just of nagging doubts that may lead us to a willingness to engage with alternative ways of being and acting. Crucially, this also has consequences for the ways we think of democracy, and of belonging in the context of our democracies. If, as Tully suggests, we take democracy to stand for 'any ad hoc assembly of people in negotiation',[56] we will not only have to be able to problematize the specific institutional forms to which we have become accustomed. We should also engage with different visions and imaginations of democratic processes and the character of democratic subjectivities. Imagining alternatives, as *Begging to be Black* so clearly illustrates, is an embedded practice, in which the issue of context itself is problematized. We are required, as a matter of democratic responsibility, to listen to and to learn from the other side. *Audi alteram partem*, as Tully repeatedly reminds us. Exemplars play a crucial educative role in this process. They are not abstract possibilities, but lived embodiments of the possibility of acting otherwise.[57] Possibilities that should not be taken up simply because they are available, but should be evaluated, critically worked through and ruminated upon.[58] This process, of necessity, is one that must take account of the interconnectedness of our worlds, our thinking and our imagination. This intertwining is, itself, also a matter for evaluation. As is clear from Krog's conversations with the philosopher, the establishing and reworking of connections are deeply political just as they are philosophical. Serious engagements requires a decolonization of the imagination just as it asks of us to work deconstructively so as to enable and facilitate finding connections that may help us to find our feet with one another.

Notes

1 In her acknowledgements to the text, Krog notes her conversations with interlocutors in Berlin, and explicitly thanks Paul Patton, Professor of Philosophy at the University of New South Wales. His name does not appear anywhere in the text itself, and not all the comments by the interlocutor can be ascribed to him. There are, nevertheless, conversations, particularly those clearly drawing on Deleuze, which could probably safely be attributed to Patton.
2 James Tully, *Public Philosophy in a New Key, Vol. II, Imperialism and Civic Freedom* (Cambridge: Cambridge University Press, 2008), pp. 268–9.
3 James Tully, *Public Philosophy in a New Key, Vol. I, Democracy and Civic Freedom* (Cambridge: Cambridge University Press, 2008), p. 146.
4 Tully, *Democracy and Civic Freedom*, p.147.
5 Tully, *Imperialism and Civic Freedom*, p. 249.
6 This is the term used to describe her work in the conversation between Antjie Krog and Duncan Brown recorded in 'Creative non-fiction: A conversation', http://www.scribd.com/doc/49492461/Creative-Non- Fiction-Antjie-Krog-in-Conversation-with-Duncan-Brown.
7 According to sources quoted by Krog, his success rested on three basic principles, aiming to achieve lasting peace and prosperity: 'to uplift the poor; to stabilize the area through diplomacy, and to involve everybody in decisions affecting their lives' (p. 29).
8 In line with a work of creative non-fiction, Bonnini, whose relation to Krog I discuss elsewhere, is based upon a real woman, but one 'who cannot form any part of the story', for the cost of reality, Krog suggests, then becomes too high. 'Creative non-fiction: A conversation'.
9 For a discussion of interconnectedness and *ubuntu*, see, *inter alia*, Leonard Praeg, 'An Answer to the Question: What is [ubuntu]?, *South African Journal of Philosophy*, 27(4) (2008); and Johan Cilliers, 'In Search of Meaning between *Ubuntu* and *Into*: Perspectives on Preaching in Post-Apartheid South Africa', Paper delivered at the eighth international conference of *Societas Homiletica*, held in Copenhagen, Denmark, 19–25 July 2008.
10 In the second volume of this trilogy, *A Change of Tongue*, she is even more explicit about this, stating that 'the "I" is seldom me' (p. 369).
11 Stanley Cavell, *A Pitch of Philosophy* (Cambridge, MA: Harvard University Press, 1994), p. vii.
12 Publisher Stephen Johnson describing *A Change of Tongue*, http://zebra.book.co.za/blog/2009/11/11/antjie-krogs-begging-to-be-black-launched-in-cape-town-gallery-and-videos/ (accessed 19 April 2010).

13 Stanley Cavell, *Conditions Handsome and Unhandsome* (Chicago: The University of Chicago Press, 1990), p. xxxii. For a discussion of democracy in processual terms, see David Owen, 'Democracy, Perfectionism and "Undetermined Messianic Hope"', in C. Mouffe and L. Nagel, eds, *The Legacy of Wittgenstein: Pragmatism and Deconstruction* (London: Cornell University Press, 2003), pp. 82–96.
14 Tully, *Imperialism and Civic Freedom*, p. 267.
15 Amnesty applications to the TRC required of applicants to make a full and complete disclosure of their wrongdoings. Amnesty applicants had to provide detailed information pertaining to specific human rights violations; and such acts had to be judged to form part of a wider political event or perpetrated in the name of a political organization.
16 The TRC report concludes in this respect that 'Some 50 per cent of all amnesty applications received from members of the security forces related to incidents that occurred between 1985 and 1989. No applications were received in respect of incidents that occurred in the first decade of the Commission's mandate and few applications were received for the pre-1985 and post-1990 periods. Despite this, evidence received by the Commission shows that the security forces were responsible for the commission of gross human rights violations during both of these periods.' Government of South Africa, *Truth and Reconciliation Commission of South Africa Report*, Vol 6, Sec. 3, Ch. 1, p. 181, http://www.info.gov.za/otherdocs/2003/trc/ (accessed 11 May 2010)
17 In the context of the Truth Commission, the role of the legal profession came under scrutiny in the context of the institutional hearings. For a full account, see *Truth and Reconciliation Commission of South Africa Report*, Vol. 4, Ch. 4 (Institutional Hearings: The Legal Community). See also, David Dyzenhaus, *Judging the Judges, Judging Ourselves* (Oxford: Hart, 1998).
18 There is a significant academic – philosophical and political – literature on the role of forgiveness and its relation to reconciliation in the context of the TRC in South Africa.
19 The Gugulethu Seven is a group of young men – Zandisile Zenith Mjobo, Zola Alfred Swelani, Mandla Simon Mxinwa, Godfrey Jabulani Miya, Themba Mlifi, Zabonke John Konile and Christopher Piet – who were killed in an ambush by the South African apartheid security forces in Gugulethu on 3 March 1986. They were anti-apartheid activists and members of the *Umkhonto we Sizwe* (Spear of the Nation), the armed wing of the ANC.
20 He continues: 'Ironically, for us the distance is augmented by her attempt to reduce it: Cynthia wants to be reassured that what she is, her very way of being is adequately represented by the logic of reconciliation and forgiveness. Yet, she cannot be sure. In her attempt to get certainty, the gulf widens: *This thing called reconciliation ... if I am understanding ... if it means ... if it means ... this man, so that I, so that all of us*'. Praeg, 'An Answer to the Question', p. 375.
21 The theme of belonging is also central to *A Change of Tongue*, where she describes it thus: 'My throat feels thick and ostracized, my chest hurts with the indescribable intimacy of belonging and loss. This is my place. Place that in a way never really wanted me' (p. 36). This sense, depicting belonging as something struggled for but not obtained, runs throughout the text. It is particularly apparent in her account of her participation in the Poetry Caravan to Timbuktu, which is deeply marked by her sense of not belonging, of initially being marked out as a stereotype: 'In the streets, black children run after her with outstretched hands, crying, *"Dollars, s'il vous plait, l'Americaine! Dollar!"* Whereas the Belgian writer is accepted as an African because he is black [sic]. Her whole body pains from it. Is loneliness a kind of desperate non-belonging? An absence of voices to root you?' (p. 300). Note here the equation of 'blackness' with skin colour.
22 These themes are also present in *A Change of Tongue*, where she recounts how deeply aware she is of the extent to which her perception: 'of being in this world is constantly

informed by this Africanness. Black-ness or African-ness, I don't really know, but it is a way of looking at the world that neither I, nor the culture I grew up in, nor the books I have read are able to come up with. I seem to find it only when I sit opposite a black face' (*A Change of Tongue*, p. 259).

23 In a conversation with Paul Patton and Betsy Stoltz at the University of Sydney, they suggested that the reference to begging should be understood as an imploring, an entreating, which arises precisely from a recognition of the difficulties of speaking as a white South African, who cannot demand acceptance.

24 M.D. Fletcher, *Reading Rushdie: Perspectives on the Fiction of Salman Rushdie* (Amsterdam, 1994).

25 'I can change my perspective, my words, my thinking, my body language, but not my skin. Race moves the debate from moral questions – how are you acting? – to narrow, nationalist ones – what colour are you? what group do you belong to?' (*A Change of Tongue*, p. 274).

26 For a discussion of the complex political articulations informing black consciousness in the South African context, see D. Howarth, 'The Difficult Emergence of a Democratic Imaginary: Black Consciousness and Non-Racial Democracy in South Africa', in D. Howarth, A.J. Norval and Y. Stavrakakis, eds, *Discourse Theory and Political Analysis: Identities, Hegemonies and Social Change*, Manchester: Manchester University Press, 2000.

27 The idea of an 'African Renaissance' first surfaced in Thabo Mbeki's speeches in the mid-1990s. It is as a third moment, following decolonization and the outbreak of democracy across the continent in the 1990s. See Thabo Mbeki, 'The African Renaissance, South Africa and the World'. Speech delivered at the United Nations University, 8 April 1998, http://www.unu.edu/unupress/mbeki.html (accessed 10 May 2010).

28 In her discussion of Moshoeshoe, Krog also explicitly addresses this issue, pointing out that Moshoeshoe had spent many hours explaining to missionaries 'the sensible value of customs like polygamy, lobola, initiation and rainmaking in weaving a community together, but he always came up against the whites' inflexible belief that the Western way was the only worthy way of living on earth. Those outside this 'true' way were inferior. They *could* enter the privileged domain through conversion, but black people quickly realised that the conversion made them 'like whites' but never equal to whites' (p. 114).

29 Tully, *Democracy and Civic Freedom*, p. 169.

30 There are a few occasions where whiteness is not immediately associated with colonialism, as when she asks, in the context of residing in Berlin, what is means to have a 'white mind'. Even here, though, the questions are still associated with things 'European': classical music, European literature, the poety of Paul Celan, punctual buses, safe surroundings, trains arriving and departing with regularity (p. 199).

31 Here the relevant text is the discussion of 'Becoming Animal' in G. Deleuze and F. Guattari, *A Thousand Plateaus*, Brian Massumi trans. (Minneapolis: University of Minnesota Press, 1987).

32 Krog already addresses the issue of exceptionalism in *A Change of Tongue*. However, there is a friend of Krog's who draws her attention to it in discussing a rather sharp response from Mandela Krog received in the last public interview Mandela gave as President of South Africa. In that interview, Krog phrased her question to Mandela in terms of his individual achievements. The friend responds to Krog that Mandela abhors this individualistic focus. Through an emphasis on a collective approach, he wishes, instead, 'to impress upon the world that he is not an exception: I am of my people, I am like them. If you are impressed by me, you have to be impressed by them. If I am remarkable, so are they. But whites constantly sing the praises of Mandela, while continuing to treat black people as they did before' (p. 259).

33 There is a long history of xenophobic attacks on foreign workers in South Africa. For a discussion see, *inter alia*, Jonny Steinberg, 'South Africa's xenophobic eruption', Institute for Security Studies, *ISS Occasional Paper* 169, November 2008, http://www.iss.co.za/pgcontent.php?UID=3070 (accessed 3 May 2010).
34 Much here depends, of course, on how precisely one conceives of 'race'.
35 The German expression – '*Wir können uns nicht in sie finden*' – carries interesting overtones missed in the translation. It resonates more closely with the emphasis on the drawing of connections that is necessary here in imaginatively finding our ways with others. See Richard H. Bell, 'Understanding African Philosophy from a Non-African Point of View: An Exercise in Cross-cultural Philosophy', in Emmanuel Chukwudi Eze, ed., *Postcolonial African Philosophy: A Critical Reader* (Oxford: Blackwell, 1997), pp. 197–220.
36 Kirk Pillow, 'Imagination', in *Oxford Handbook of Philosophy and Literature*, ed. Richard Eldrigde (2009), p. 349.
37 Stanley Cavell, *The Claim of Reason* (Oxford: Oxford University Press, 1979), p. 354.
38 Grassi, for instance, argues that *ingenium* ('the viewing of unexpected relations between sensory appearances') is not the other of language, reason or cognition. Rather, it provides the minimal order or logic necessary for the concept. 'Imagination is the condition for thought, knowledge, and judgment', Linda Zerilli, *Feminism and the Abyss of Freedom* (Chicago: University of Chicago Press, 2005), p. 69. See also, Ernesto Grassi, *Rhetoric as Philosophy* (Carbondale: Southern Illinois University Press, 2001), pp. 225–6 on the inventive character of *ingenium*.
39 Cavell, *The Claim of Reason*, p. 354.
40 This is the Sesotho version capturing the spirit of African interconnectedness.
41 As Krog notes, during Moshoeshoe's fifty year rule, the Basotho would systematically be robbed of their land (p. 132).
42 At the height of his power in 1842, Thaba-Bosiu provided safe living for between thirty and forty thousand people (p. 135).
43 This issue is brought to light particularly starkly in Bonnini's account of her own sense of uprootedness when moving from the village where she was born – Semonkong, Lesotho – to Cape Town, South Africa (pp. 214–15).
44 I draw here on Conant's treatment of exemplarity in Nietzsche. See James Conant, 'Nietzsche's Perfectionism: A Reading of *Schopenhauer as Educator*', in Richard Schacht, ed., *Nietzsche's Postmoralism* (Cambridge: Cambridge University Press, 2001).
45 Cilliers, 'In search of meaning between *ubuntu* and *into*', p. 4.
46 Both *Country of My Skull* and *A Change of Tongue* recount numerous instances of overtly racist responses to the demands for and of transformation.
47 Krog (p. 116) notes overhearing a conversation in the archives to the effect of a researcher not wishing to expose these events on national television, so avoiding besmirching the founder of a nation.
48 David Owen, 'Equality, Democracy, and Self-respect: Reflections on Nietzsche's Agonal Perfectionism', *Journal of Nietzsche Studies*, Issue 24, 2002, p. 126.
49 Owen, 'Equality, Democracy and Self-respect', p. 128.
50 Owen, 'Equality, Democracy and Self-respect', p. 118.
51 Cavell, *The Claim of Reason*, p. 368.
52 Cavell, *The Claim of Reason*, p. 369.
53 '"Following" an exemplar is not a matter of following in someone's footsteps (*jemandem nachgehen*), but of regarding someone as an exemplary instance of ... "faithfully following in one's *own* footsteps" (*sich selber treulich nachgehen*)'. (Conant, 'Nietzsche's Perfectionism', p. 206.)
54 As Bates puts it, 'What perfectionism wants is the possibility of self-transformation according to an ideal that is internal to the self's constitution rather than one that comes from without. However, we need to remember that what is "internal" and what comes

from "without" are themselves not fixed and permanent categories. If the transfiguration of any particular state of the self is to be possible, then even these categories will be capable of transformation. Of course, every part of every state of my self is how I relate to the society that has helped to form me.' Stanley Bates, 'Stanley Cavell and Ethics', in Richard Eldrigde, ed., *Stanley Cavell* (Cambridge: Cambridge University Press, 2003), p. 42.
55 These insights resonate with the character of deconstructive interventions as interventions wherever we are. See J. Derrida, *Of Grammatology* (Baltimore: Johns Hopkins University Press, 1976), p. 162.
56 Tully, *Democracy and Civic Freedom*, pp. 155–6.
57 Nietzsche's reading of the Greeks in 'Homer's contest' explicates this sense of exemplarity. See Friedrich Nietzsche, 'Homer's Contest', in J. Lungstrum and E. Sauer, eds, *Agonistics: Arenas of Creative Contest* (New York: State University of New York Press, 1997), pp. 35–45.
58 As Nietzsche suggests, rumination is a crucial part of a self-educative process.

Chapter 11

Accessing Tully: Political Philosophy for the Everyday and the Everyone

Val Napoleon and Hadley Friedland

"Caminando, nos preguntamos"—"Walking, we ask questions." We're all continually discussing and debating effective struggle, effective ways of making change, and our core principles. We don't have fixed answers, but in struggle, in walking, we engage in a process to answer them.[1]

Introduction

As we celebrate and learn from James Tully's wise and generous public philosophizing, our conversations continue to be about how to bring these insights to the everyday struggles, fears and aspirations locally. This chapter explores some of the challenges for doing so. At the local level, we believe that finding ways for citizens to access Tully would allow them to ascribe meaning to their actions, as individuals and as groups, that go beyond the immediate and exhausting struggles, inevitable changes, divisions and even failures that occur in the everyday of life. Reframing local individual and collective struggles as "glocal"[2] (*PPNK* II, 243) practices of citizenship, connection, and cooperation could provide a robust source of strength and encouragement where both are sorely needed.

In his latest treatise, Tully unshackles citizenship from the standard universalizing theories and turns our minds from a grand theory of citizenship to citizenship as negotiated practices of freedom. This empowering shift in turn inspires us to re-imagine and rework the practices of citizenship as an integral part of anti-imperial and decolonizing movements. While Tully de-centers statist political theory by effectively shifting the thinking about citizenship to the glocal, we read him as we continue to be invested in and engaged with the often achingly isolated local, where the unavoidable, the urgent and the dangerous take up inordinate amounts of people's imaginations and most, if not all, of their energy. We continue to examine how we can begin to connect their everyday struggles to global struggles, to struggles "*of* and *for*" freedom?[3] (*PPNK* I, 159). How do we convince the people at the local level to appreciate their everyday practices as practices of citizenship?

We see two particularly challenging yet important local sites of struggle and citizenship where Tully's insights could be applied to build glocal connections. First, we question how individuals who cannot imagine themselves as citizens in any sense, let alone the active citizen-agents that Tully describes, and whose perceptions of powerlessness are continually reinforced through their interactions, can begin to connect their actions to the practices of citizenship.[4]

Second, we examine how diverse individuals, groups and agencies at the local level, who work tirelessly with the individuals just described, can connect with others working in other localities and to contextualize the particular methods they employ to struggle against immediate and urgent local issues within broader practices of freedom. In keeping with our focus on concrete localities, we explore these questions through four brief vignettes offered here.

Four stories

At the local level, on the "rough ground" of civic struggles with and over words (*PPNK* I, 159, n. 3) and in our everyday lives, we often find ourselves confronted with, and *caring* about individuals who cannot imagine themselves as citizens at all. Their lives, often their entire lives, have been experienced at a level of powerlessness where the objective evidence continually reinforces their perception that their existence does not matter.[5]

1. Women at the shelter

> They are safe now. Their children are safe for now. In this wonderful, albeit poorly funded place, they are putting their lives together, piece by painful piece. But this point of refuge is temporary. Vulnerable from the start, now shattered by trauma and betrayal, their tasks are herculean. They must eventually find a place to live, a place they can afford, which will rent to single mothers, and which will hopefully be safe. They must find a way to support themselves and their family, find full-time employment or funding for training, navigate the system of a thousand forms to access any governmental support for income assistance, training, or child-care subsidy, all in the grind of hand to mouth poverty.[6]

> There is no room for mistakes. Just this, while supporting, caring for, and protecting their children. And if they stumble beneath this weight, then the additional burden of "failure to protect" or the label of "neglect" pummels their reality even more. When talking to them, it is often hard to tell if they are depressed, apathetic, confused, ashamed, or simply exhausted.

2. Youth

> When conducting focus groups for an inner city youth housing project with youth who were homeless and/or street entrenched, the youth were highly skeptical. Many, if not all of them, were raised partially or completely within the child welfare system. At a certain point, once they reached the magic age

of sixteen, a social worker decided to close their child welfare file—an action that cut off any realistic hope of being placed in a stable home with adult support.

These file closures were often the last drastic response to either too many failed foster home or group home placements, or too many failures to follow through on "basic" expectations such as attending school or work. The youths' behaviors and their mistakes, which usually involved addictions and addiction-related theft, property damage, or violence, were undeniable. Yet there they were, as of that last fateful birthday and that last discretionary decision, with no home and no adult to fall back on or turn to. They actually verbally identified themselves as "throwaways."

3. One inmate

An inmate's parole hearing is scheduled. He is terrified and with good reason given his past experiences before parole boards. He has never been able to present himself well under stress or before authority. Instead, he becomes inarticulate and stoic, and he involuntary shuts down, withdrawing inside himself. Consequently, over the years, various assessors have concluded that he is antisocial, angry, unemotional, and lacking confidence. He is smart, reads books on alternative economics, social issues, and history, but at this point, he has spent about half of his life incarcerated. This is not a simple matter of a confidence crisis or poor anger management, though these are struggles. He feels the world very deeply. And he is not antisocial.

We read the stack of psychologist assessments and police reports. We look for the positive bits in the overwhelmingly depressing and damning documents. As I encourage him to think about the questions that the parole board put to him, I feel as though I am sinking into a bleak, Kafka-like nightmare of shadows. As an inmate, he has been a part of a massive, entrenched bureaucracy that, from our experience, is monstrous in its lack of accountability, humanity, intelligence, and efficiency. From his perspective, the corrections bureaucracy is ponderous, dull-witted, and suspicious. Distressingly, many of the inmates seem to unconsciously emulate their environment in their behaviors, expectations of life, and relationships. Suggestions and efforts to prepare him for the hearing are deflected by fear, denial, and perhaps an underlying hopelessness.

Despite his extensive reading, he does not have a political analysis within which he can situate himself as an indigenous man in a federal penitentiary in a neoliberal, capitalist nation-state. Without an analytical framework, everything is personal and decontextualized. The psychologist is an asshole. The boss is a shit. The guards are mean bastards although rarely and somewhat inexplicably, they can be good guys too. He believes that any vulnerability and trust that he has ever shown to anyone in the system has been taken advantage of. And, the parole board will be out to get him.

Given the miserable and disheartening reports, he is probably right—the parole board will see him as a potential re-offender. In fact, the parole board will see and judge him on the very behaviors and skills that have enabled him to survive in prison, but they will not make that connection, and instead will judge him as a personal failure for not being properly rehabilitated. He says he sees himself as a citizen, but it is fragile and sometimes impossible to maintain in the power plays he is located in. He primarily understands himself as condemned, as not mattering in the world.

4. Missing and slain indigenous women and girls

In Canada, over the past thirty years, almost 600 indigenous women and girls have gone missing or have been slain.[7] Between 2000 and 2008, there were 153 new cases. Most of the disappearances and deaths occurred in the western provinces in British Columbia, Alberta, Manitoba, and Saskatchewan.[8] The majority of these women and girls were mothers. Some were students. Almost half of these cases remain unsolved. Time and time again they are described as sex trade workers and addicts as if that designation captures them all or somehow explains them away; as if their murders and disappearances were the logical result of poor lifestyle choices.[9] Yet how does being a sex trade worker lessen the importance and tragedy of their suffering and erasure?[10]

A national research group, Sisters in Spirit, found that indigenous women and girls were more likely to be killed by a stranger than other victims of deadly violence.[11] What is so disturbing is that their murders and disappearances seem to have become almost normalized—a part of Canada. It is discussed and dealt with as a budgetary issue. For example, this year, the federal government eliminated the funding for the Sisters in Spirit research initiative, and then allocated ten million dollars over two years to "helping solve the issue of missing and murdered aboriginal women in Canada but it hasn't yet said exactly how the money will be used."[12]

Each of these stories sketches the experiences of citizens who live and die within a living vortex of political power and conflicted relationships. Much of their lives are defined by and reduced to the "wicked problems" they face and embody.[13] The stories reflect the historical and contemporary political dynamics of Canada and form its invisible and ignored underbelly. In making them visible in this discussion regarding citizenship, we explore two sites of challenge and opportunity: First, how can people who do not even see themselves as agents, imagine or recognize themselves as citizens? Second, how can the people committed to supporting or championing this first group of citizens, connect their everyday practices with broader practices of and for freedom?

The first site: imagining/recognizing oneself as a citizen

Tully redefines public political philosophy as an "interlocutory intervention on the side of the oppressed" (*PPNK* I, 17, n. 3).[14] He also persuasively argues that:

> It should not be the burden of the wretched of the earth to refuse to submit and act otherwise, as in the dominant theories of resistance, but of the most powerful and privileged to refuse to comply and engage in the work of glocal citizenship (*PPNK* II, 305, n. 2).

But does this mean the actions of the least privileged and powerful are without purpose or effect? Tully does not call on them to simply wait for glocal networks of negotiation to shift the imperializing forces that have such profound and devastating effects on their lives, and that place such overwhelming limits on their space for acting freely. Instead, Tully emphasizes the agency of the governed in any governance relationship and stresses that there is always freedom to act otherwise within the existing limits—even if that is only at its most basic, in how we think. There is always intellectual space for political theorizing because political philosophy is the purview of being an engaged and thoughtful citizen (*PPNK* I, 29, n. 3).

Here we draw on Foucault to help develop our analysis of citizenship at the local level. Foucault argued against power being described as if it can be held, accumulated, possessed or found:

> [P]ower is not something that is held, but is something that is exercised in relations; relations of power are not exterior to other types of relationships, but are immanent and productive of those relationships; power comes from below and is rooted in the social nexus; power relations are both intentional and non-subjective; and where there is power, there is resistance.[15]

In other words, both the powerless and powerful are produced by the operations of power, and power is less a capacity than a shared process.[16] This is not to suggest an equality of power among all people because as the above stories demonstrate, they are not similarly situated insofar as their ability to act. However, despite the painfully obvious power differentials, all the people in these stories are agents, and the task, according to both Foucault and Tully, is to figure out the citizenry options available to them in their different locations.[17]

Here though, we turn to what we see as a fundamental challenge required for such a task. Can women in a temporary shelter, shattered and faced with the overwhelming tasks for basic survival, identify themselves as citizens? Is there potential for them to be critically engaged in their world and learn to see themselves as public philosophers? What about youth who identify themselves as "throwaways?" The inmate who understands himself as "condemned?" Where do the murdered and missing indigenous women and girls fit? The deep silences regarding these people's social experiences within law, policy circles and political theory is inexcusable but not inexplicable.

At bottom, self-descriptions as "throwaways" or "condemned" reflect what Simone Weil describes as "a state of dumb and ceaseless lamentation," common in those who have "suffered too many blows."[18] Stephen Jay Gould writes about silences from within:

> Few tragedies can be more extensive than the stunting of life, few injustices deeper than the denial of an opportunity to strive or even to hope, by a limit imposed from without, but falsely identified as lying within.[19]

So the woman working as a prostitute who suffers a violent sexual assault on a "bad date" does not bother to report it to the police, or worse, the woman who witnesses the actual butchery of another woman tells friends, but denies even seeing this to police upon questioning, burying that horrific sight, along with everything else, deep under her crack addiction for years afterwards.[20] Even those in such oppressed positions that "still have the power to cry out" tend not to do so nor do they necessarily employ coherent or relevant language.[21] Recall the inmate's descriptions of various authority figures as "assholes," "mean bastards" or "shits." Street entrenched youth sometimes use similar language to describe foster parents who beat them with coat hangers and those who simply refused to let them use drugs in their home—a distinction that obviously must be sorted out. The silencing comes from within and without.

Moving out of these silences and incoherencies is a vital aspect to recognizing agency and understanding oneself as a citizen. We turn to the research of Belenky et al. to explore this further and we extrapolate their findings drawn from empirical research involving women to the people described in our stories.[22] Belenky et al. developed a theory about the necessary link between the concept of self as a knower and the construction of knowledge, which they conceptualize as five stages of knowing.[23] Basically, where women are in relation to these stages is determined by their concept of themselves as learners and creators of knowledge. Significantly, according to this theory women move from a silent, fearful, and reactionary place to that of being an integrated knower with the confidence to be able to draw from both personal experience and information outside themselves to create knowledge. It is the place of silence that is most helpful to us here:

> [S]ilent women have no more confidence in their ability to learn from their own experience than they have in learning from the words that others use. Because the women have relatively underdeveloped representational thought, the ways of knowing available to them are limited to the present (not the past or the future); to the actual (not the imaginary and the metaphorical); to the

concrete (not the deduced or the induced); to the specific (not the generalized or the contextualized); and to behaviors actually enacted (not values and motives entertained).[24]

This inability to find meaning in the words of oneself and others is reflected in relations with authorities. As with the people in the stories, silent women can be passive, reactive, and dependent, seeing "authorities as all-powerful, if not overpowering."[25] When talking to the police or to social workers, one withdraws or shuts down or hangs his or her head, because that is what one does in relationships with authority. As will be explained later, these actions can also be interpreted as acting otherwise and as such, they do have political meanings that can be ascribed to citizenry. But do these actions have to be understood as political and as having meaning by the citizen? Is this political consciousness a necessary part of being a citizen? And how does this local citizenry building happen? How should this work take place and how should it be conducted?

As agents, everyone can interpret and give meaning to their encounters in the world and in doing so they begin to explicitly take up their role as active citizens. All of their actions matter. But interpretation and meaning are generated within the framework of our understanding of the world with us in it. According to James Boyd White, "We are meaning-making creatures. ... This capacity is the deepest nerve of our life, and our instinct to protect it and its freedom at almost any cost is a right one."[26] Given this, the work of citizenship at the local level needs a larger intellectual frame with a critical political analysis of the world. This is reflected in the words of Weil, "No one can love and be just who does not understand the empire of force and know how not to respect it."[27] Citizens need to understand how they matter and how their actions matter.

Fundamentally, then, the shift from internal and external silences, from dumb lamentation or incoherent cries to articulations of agency, begins with the woman working as a sex worker understanding that she and the other women matter. Their suffering and their lives matter. It begins with the inmate understanding that he and all the other inmates matter. He matters and his words and actions matter. What we want for the people described in our stories is an intellectual, political interiority in which they can find inner peace, where they can understand the dynamics of the world, where they can act on their agency and responsibilities, and most importantly, where they can learn that they are not worthless and they are not powerless. We want the inmate, the women and the youth to realize their importance as human beings, and their potential and power as engaged citizens and as public philosophers. We want them to be able to reinterpret their actions of survival and resistance within a larger political framework, which both includes them as citizens and connects their work to the work of other citizens in other localities.

This work of diverse and civic citizenship must include recognizing the ways that indigenous women, inmates, youth and others are already exercising citizenship, and acting otherwise, even in politically inarticulate[28] ways. After all, given the centrality of agency in this discussion and to maintain the diverse citizenship perspective, the "other" cannot be "constructed" all the way down. Tully explains:

> No matter how relentlessly domineering governors try to implant and internalize these role-related abilities without the active interplay of the patients, as if they are blank tablets, in behavioural modification experiments, repetitious advertising and total institutions of colonial and post-colonial discipline (such as internment camps and residential schools), they invariably fail to "construct" the other all the way down. They cannot eliminate completely the interactive and open-ended freedom *of* and *in* the relationship or the room to appear to conform to the public script while thinking and acting otherwise, without reducing the relationship to one of complete immobilization (*PPNK* II, 278, n. 2).

Thus, while keeping one's head down in front of the social worker can come from a place of silence, it can also be reinterpreted or transformed as an action of survival and resistance. The woman at the shelter applying for income assistance or child-care subsidy may hang her head not because that is the only role she can imagine to take in relation to authority, but because, the reality is, that social worker can make her life hell, and adopting the pose may be the most strategic to achieve what is needed for survival. A youth's insistence of extending hospitality to friends or relatives with no place to stay the moment an apartment becomes accessible, can be seen as acting otherwise, as he or she being the change they want to see in the world. Likewise the actions of the inmate when he sticks up for or advises another inmate being unfairly targeted by a guard or a gang, or simply recommends a book, are everyday actions of and for freedom within the limited space for freedom he occupies. Actions of survival and resistance can be seen in the everyday conversations where similarly situated people swap observations and strategies, identify patterns, and have a good laugh about the absurdities they see or are subjected to.

Civic activity emerges when citizens turn away from the *status quo*, imperial and colonial governance relations in which they find themselves to build new diverse, civic citizen relations, ways of acting and exercising political power.[29] The people in our stories must believe that they matter, and recognize their existing actions as actions of and for freedom before embarking on a similar undertaking from the ground up, turning away from the local oppressive *status quo* involving the complex of sexism, racism, consumerism, and addictions. Such a turning away involves the recognition of how the complex of experienced local oppressions is directly connected to the larger imperial, colonial, capitalist systems. Such a turning away must also necessarily include recognition of how each of us is implicated in both the creation and maintenance of oppressive power relations.

We want to be absolutely clear that we are not suggesting victim blaming, but instead are applying Foucault's theory of power dynamics to the examination of local individual and collective behavior.[30] Recognizing the space for thinking and acting otherwise does not, in itself, expand the limited space of freedom that people have to exercise their agency as citizens. It is worth repeating here Tully's admonition that acting otherwise should not be an additional burden on the "wretched of the earth" (*PPNK* I, 305, n. 3). The purpose of recognizing this space is to recognize and use the interactive freedom within relationships of power that does exist. The foregoing discussion leads us directly to the importance of the second local site we have identified—that of the people working directly and in relationship with this first group of citizens.

The second site: connecting between localities and cooperating between practices of freedom

Remaining with the four stories, the second site of challenge and opportunity lies in the lives and practices of the individuals and groups that are most engaged with the citizens described in these stories. Can those who work to provide safe refuge and support to the families in the shelter connect their struggles for safety and stability to global struggles? Can those who work to connect with and respond to the most urgent needs of homeless and street entrenched youth, locate their everyday actions within broader practices of freedom? Do the guards, the parole board members, the psychologists preparing reports, program facilitators, and visiting elders recognize the inmate as a citizen? Can they connect their interactions with him within global networks of acting otherwise? Can the police, social workers and others interacting with and called to respond to the missing and murdered indigenous women and girls see them as citizens rather than merely victims who made bad lifestyle choices?

Every year, across the country, there are marches and rallies and vigils about the missing and slain indigenous women and girls. The internet bristles with sites and ongoing coverage about this issue. There are some shelters, some groups, some services, and some research devoted to ending the deadly violence against indigenous women. On its face, this issue is the best example of our four stories to demonstrate cooperation and connections between localities in action. And yet, the violence against indigenous women and girls continues and they still disappear and are slain. So why is there such an appalling disconnect between these on-the-ground efforts and the continued experiences of indigenous women and girls?

Elizabeth Comack argues that our theoretical approaches not only determine how we define problems, they also determine how we approach the problem (or not as the case may be) and what we think the solutions might be.[31] For example:

> To say that [conservative] functionalists are not well-equipped to handle an analysis of power does not mean that they are unaware of social inequities. Rather, they understand inequality in a particular way, as both *natural* and *functional*. Inequalities are natural in the sense that they emerge out of inherent or innate differences between individuals and groups (like those based on race or sex).[32]

From a conservative functionalist perspective, society remains unexamined while crime is considered a "lower-class phenomenon."[33] The solution is more law and order, and more "getting tough" on crime policies because the sources of crime and instability are not located in the larger society, but rather in the personal failures of individuals. The problem is the "risks that particular individuals pose to social security" and the solution is "the corresponding call for the state to take action to maintain law and order."[34]

Taking this a step further, how might the conservative functionalist approach consider the missing and slain indigenous women and girls? Likely, this issue would be understood as the result of a collective pathological weakness inherent in indigenous societies,[35] and a corresponding pathological weakness on the part of individual indigenous women and girls. The standard conservative response is to call for more law and order as was recently exemplified by the Honorable Rona Ambrose, federal Minister for the Status of Women, when she made the following comment:

> One of the things I hear a lot across the country from women is that they want to feel safe in their communities and homes. That is why I'm proud that our government has done more than any other government in the history of our country to keep women safe. We have introduced new laws to ensure we keep rapists and murderers off the streets and to ensure we protect children from sexual predators. That is what women want.[36]

Indeed. We feel so much safer already.

According to Comack, a standard liberal response would also fail to consider structural inequity and the solutions would likely focus on poor lifestyle choices and the need for more jobs and training.[37] And despite the tough on crime strategies or the various social services approaches over the years, indigenous women and girls are still the target of deadly violence. The hard question is, to what extent do the on-the-ground efforts across the country replicate the standard conservative and liberal approaches by failing to contextualize the local work within a larger political frame and analysis? Arguably, this is often the case. So given this, we must ask a further difficult question, do indigenous women and girls need another rally, march, vigil, or social service?

If we take this approach to the missing and slain indigenous women, then the focus expands beyond confirming the horror and articulating rights,[38] to investigating the creation of political, economic, and legal conditions in which indigenous women and girls are rendered vulnerable and disposable for sexualized and racialized anger and hatred.

Viewed in this light, the situation can seem overwhelming and hopeless, but Tully's work encourages us to see that relations of power and relations of governance are actions that act on "free agents: individuals or groups who always have a limited field of possible ways of thinking and acting in response" (*PPNK* I, 23, n. 3). The way these free agents act on their possibilities are "practices of freedom"

(*PPNK* I, 23, n. 3). We have already discussed the importance we see in being able to access Tully's insights to encourage people to imagine and recognize themselves as citizens—as political philosophers within their limited fields. Now we turn to the importance of Tully's insight that there is a "diverse field of potential ways of thinking and acting in response" (*PPNK* I, 23, n. 3).

In particular, Tully describes three general types of cases where people act on their possibilities. First, individuals and groups may engage in practices of freedom by "'acting otherwise' within the rules of the game" (*PPNK* I, 23, n. 3). Second, individuals and groups may challenge a relation of governance on the ground or raise a problem with a practice by entering into "the available procedures of negotiation, deliberation, problem-solving, and reform with the aim of modifying the practice" (*PPNK* I, 24). Finally, where the procedures for problem-solving and reform are unavailable or fail because those exercising power bypass or subvert the processes, individuals and groups may refuse to be governed, and resist, escape or confront those who exercise power (*PPNK* I, 24). Tully argues that these three complex practices of freedom are always available, even in "the most settled structures of domination" and it is these practices that give human governance "freedom and indeterminacy" (*PPNK* I, 24). Implicit in the complexity and ongoing existence of these practices of freedom through the history of human governance is the possibility to act cooperatively with others exercising diverse practices of freedom.

Human service organizations and practitioners serving marginalized populations also operate themselves within limited fields of freedom. Many, if not most, practitioners have more in common with the people in the four stories than with the elite, primarily affluent and primarily male, decision-makers who create the laws and policies that restrict the ambit of their actions and interventions.[39] The work of care is feminized, chronically undervalued and denigrated as something less than "real work."[40] The majority of human service practitioners are women, as are the majority of service-users.[41] Susan McGrath points out that there "has not only been a feminization of poverty, but a feminization of social problems more generally."[42] Human services practitioners themselves often struggle in a demoralizing poverty or quasi-poverty, and all that goes along with that. While police officers and prison guards typically make a living wage, the youth workers and shelter workers may be living well below the poverty line themselves; the grinding hardship and lack of respect experienced in their day-to-day lives not so removed from that experienced by those they are supporting.

The "knowledge and experience gap between those who make [laws and] policy and those who must live with the consequences is enormous."[43] This yawning chasm means the realities of law and policy often restrict both common sense and empathetic responses of human services practitioners to the human issues before them. Human services are increasingly subject to a "corporate style of management" that divides practitioners and their immediate supervisors from senior managers and policy-makers. Practitioners are "stripped from their professional judgment and discretion and expected to conform to a highly routinized work environment."[44] This bureaucratization has been shown to significantly denigrate and threaten care-work[45] and can create conceptual barriers for care-workers that prevent them from recognizing and acting on the citizenship of the people who access or are dependent on the services and care they provide. As Brian Wharf and Brad McKenzie explain:

> [H]uman services professionals are employed by organizations that not only exclude those who receive services from participation but also transform them from "citizens" to "clients." In a very real way, public sector human services agencies, organized in a hierarchal fashion and enmeshed by rules and regulations, are part of the problem.[46]

Thus a particular challenge for many human services practitioners is being both uncomfortably close to, and at the same time part of, the larger problem affecting the transformation of certain people into *de facto* "second-class citizens."[47] In our opinion, this transformation from "citizen" to "client" is also implicitly perpetuated within academia when it is suggested that there are bright lines between "political theory" and "social work." We emphatically reject the notion that some citizens' lived realities somehow sink below what should be addressed within the field of political theory.

A probation officer, a prison guard, a social worker, the director of the women's shelter, a youth outreach worker, the police who investigate the murder cases of Aboriginal women and girls, all act, at least in their official capacities, within the "rules of the game." As outlined above, these rules are increasingly bureaucratized and constrictive. They also are those of our society at our meanest, actually reinforcing the reasonableness of certain citizens' perceptions of themselves as worthless, "condemned" or "throwaways." As Wharf and McKenzie explain:

> The feeling of loss of citizenship is experienced most acutely by those who are unemployed and who are dependent for a living. This is no wonder, since as a society, we are at our meanest when it comes to dealing with the long term unemployed, with street youth, with single mothers, and with those with addictions.[48]

Yet according to Tully, all of this is not a complete barrier to their engaging in practices of freedom. Rather, their "ongoing conversation and conduct" has the potential to modify practices "in often unnoticed and significant ways" (*PPNK* I, 23, n. 3). The fields of and for freedom for practitioners or allies are not so different from those people in the center of the four stories.

As in the first site, practitioners need to know they and their actions matter, to recognize their current actions as actions of and for freedom, and to critically interrogate their own complicity in power structures that maintain an oppressive *status quo*. What we want for care-workers is to be able to recognize that they and their work matters, despite the chronic practical and rhetorical denigration of their work. We want them to realize their importance as human beings, and their potential and power as engaged citizens and as public philosophers. We want them to understand that their words and actions matter, and to recognize the work of care as a vital, even central, aspect of the citizenship relationship. We want them to be able to reinterpret their actions of care and advocacy within a larger political framework, which includes both them and their service-users as citizens, and connects both with broader practices of freedom across other localities.

Iris Marion Young's work is helpful here to combat traditional conservative and liberal ideologies that so clearly do not touch on the conditions that leave so many citizens so abandoned and desperately vulnerable within our society. In her criticism of the increasing securitization in modern states, she explains and expands on recent feminist arguments "against a model of citizenship that requires each citizen to be independent and self-sufficient in order to be equal and autonomous."[49] These arguments "reject the assumption behind self-sufficient citizenship that a need for social support or care is more exceptional than normal."[50] On this view, the work of social support or care needed by inmates, street youth, or women is normalized and considered an aspect of their citizenship. Young continues:

> People who need care and support ought not to be forced into a position of subordination and obedience in relation to those who provide care and support; not only should they retain the rights of full citizens to choose their own way of life and hold authorities accountable but also they ought to be able to criticize the way in which support comes to them.[51]

If youth workers and shelter workers can reject the prevalent view that their work is an unfortunate necessity due to the inherent weaknesses of individual youth and families, and instead see the support needed and offered as fulfillment of ordinary needs, their work actually becomes central, rather than functionally detrimental, to citizenship.

These arguments lead Young to maintain that proper security measures can be seen as part of the duties of government in a citizenship regime. She argues that "[t]he organization of reasonable measures to protect people from harm and to make people confident that they can move and act relatively safely" can be seen as one of the forms of "generalized care and support" that in modern societies, "ought to be organized and guaranteed through state institutions."[52] This has particular resonance when one considers the plight of inmates within institutions, where violence is notorious, or for the erasure of vulnerable indigenous women. If prison guards or the police in the Vancouver downtown eastside can see their duties as part of a continuum of care and support owed to the citizens, and themselves accountable to these citizens, their everyday actions can be seen as meaningful acts of creation and maintenance of citizenship.

Human service practitioners also have a unique opportunity to continually interrogate their own implication in power structures if they deliberately "think otherwise" from the *de facto* second-class citizenship described above, and view their service-users as full citizens, who retain the right to choose their own way of life and who can provide useful criticism for the services they provide. Again, this is not about heaping further responsibility on people's shoulders that already are often over-burdened. Rather, it is about developing a broader frame of meaning that enables them to connect their everyday practices to other practices of freedom within a larger political project of citizenship. It is this broader frame of meaning that is imperative to generating new possibilities when cooperating between practices of freedom, either with others also working within the rules, or with those engaged in processes of negotiation and reform, or grassroots or political activism.

Conclusion

We began this chapter with the desire to make Tully's work accessible to the struggles at the local level where being a citizen is problematic, and the concept of citizenship is shadowy at best and oppressive at worst (i.e. in the categorization and treatment of the marginalized). We have drawn on Tully to argue that even people who are at the margins have the space to act otherwise as forms of resistance, and that our challenge is to learn to recognize these disparate practices of citizenship in the behaviours and actions of people at the local level. We have also argued that local work must be conceptually and practically connected to a larger political frame to transform local work into the glocal. Finally, we have argued that those in relative positions of power in relation to the marginalized also have the intellectual and practice space to act otherwise in their treatment of oppressed people.

We have reached two other conclusions about citizenship at the local everyday of life. First, implicit acts of resistance must be made explicit in order to contextualize their interpretation and meaning-making. Second, we must critically interrogate and examine the ways that we work, whether through social services, direct political action, or in other capacities, in order to ensure that we are not simply perpetuating the *status quo* systems of oppression. In other words, more of the same (e.g. programs, research, groups, etc.) is not going to make a difference to anyone. The heart of civic citizenship is about transforming citizen/governance relationships (*PPNK* II, 281, n. 2)—and, we argue, transforming all our other power relationships.

Postscript

In his generous response to an early draft of this chapter, James Tully observed that the question of how a person moves from being a passive subject of unjust relations to being an active agent of change in and over that relationship is necessarily case specific (*PPNK* II, 2, n. 4). However, he wisely argues that there is a general response that can be made wherein a person becomes an active agent by being drawn into ethical cooperative work and by participating in three types of activities; ethical practices of the self, practices of negotiation, and cooperative enterprises. According to Tully, ethical cooperative work requires fundamentally decolonizing the colonial relationships so that, "If we want equal relationships then we must treat each other equally in working on unequal relationships" and "If we want democratic relationships, then we must change them by being democratic" (*PPNK* II, 1). Furthermore, for the work to be substantively "ethical," it must be "grounded in ethical practices of the self on the self" (*PPNK* II, 1). In other words, we have to "change ourselves in the course of unjust or oppressive or destructive or unequal relations" (*PPNK* II, 1).

We believe that Tully's suggestions for the development of ethical cooperative working relationships are useful and potentially transformative for all the people in the stories we have shared here. We also believe that the very action of turning one's mind to the questions raised in this chapter, and thoughtfully responding to them, is, in itself, useful and potentially transformative. It is part of re-imagining a different world and ourselves.

Notes

1 Pasha Malla, "The Question Remains," *The Walrus* 7(10), 2010, 37 at p. 39.
2 James Tully, *Public Philosophy in a New Key: Volume I, Democracy and Civic Freedom* and *Public Philosophy in a New Key: Volume II, Imperialism and Civic Freedom*, Cambridge: Cambridge University Press, 2008, hereafter referred to as *PPNK*. Tully weaves together diverse strands of citizenship constructs to combine the local with the global, hence "glocal" citizenship.
3 Tully describes the "free activities of the citizens engaged in [the changes in citizenship and democracy], as struggles *of* and *for* more democratic forms and practices of participation in the games in which we are governed. And these struggles can be seen in turn as manifestations of an impatience for what Arendt and many other citizens call freedom" (*PPNK* I, 159).
4 James Tully, "The Work of Decolonizing Relationships between Indigenous and non-Indigenous People," paper presented at the University of Alberta, 4 November 2010 [unpublished, archived with the author]. Emphasis in original [Tully, "Decolonizing Relationships."] Tully describes the resulting ethos thus: "The relationships between natives and newcomers are in general not only colonial or imperial, but also *unequal* along almost all social and economic indicators, as we know. Moreover, growing up in these relationships can often generate and internalize attitudes and behavior of inferiority and superiority: *inferiority-superiority* complexes that have perverse effects and are difficult to change".
5 We draw on the work of Ron Kraybill who has argued that "people experience powerlessness at various levels, each more debilitating than the previous." These five levels of powerless are: (1) outcome—when one is overruled and does not get his or her way, (2) process—when one is not seriously consulted and the processes are unfair, (3) social esteem—one is excluded from fair decision-making and is not valued or respected as a person, (4) self-esteem—when one feels worthless regardless of other opinions, and (5) existential—when one's existence is inconsequential and does not matter in the universe, when there is a profound loss of meaning and connection. Ron Kraybill

(Summer 1987), "MCS Conciliation Quarterly at 10", reprinted in Jim Stutzman and Carolyn Schrock-Shenk, *Mediation and Facilitation Training Manual: Foundations and Skills for Constructive Conflict Transformation*, 3rd edn, Akron, PA: Mennonite Central Committee, 1995, pp. 96–7.
6 According to Conservative Senator Hugh Segal, it is harder to get welfare today than it was during the great depression and a person on social assistance in Canada has to comply with over 800 rules in order to keep getting their social assistance payments. Interview by Michael Enright, CBC Sunday Edition (19 December 2010) at http://www.cbc.ca/video/news/audioplayer.html. Senator Hugh Segal co-chaired the Senate Committee that authored the 2009 senate report entitled *In From the Margins: Poverty, Housing and Homelessness*. This 300-page report contains over 70 recommendations and has been virtually ignored by the federal government since its release. According to Enright, the report "was sweeping and it was swept right under the carpet."
7 Native Women's Association of Canada, *What Their Stories Tell Us: Research Findings from the Sisters in Spirit Initiative* (2010), http://www.nwac-hq.org/. Over 150 of these women are still missing and over half the total cases remain unsolved (*Sisters in Spirit*).
8 Also see Christine Welsh's important documentary, *Finding Dawn* (2006), National Film Board, and Amnesty International, *Stolen Sisters: A Human Rights Response to Discrimination and Violence Against Indigenous Women in Canada* (2004), http://www.amnesty.ca/stolensisters/. For an international perspective on missing and murdered women and girls, see the *Backyard (El traspatio)*, a movie based on real life events in a Mexico–US border town.
9 There are no national statistics about the number of aboriginal women in the sex trade, but in the prairie provinces, the number of aboriginal women working as prostitutes is disproportionately high. *Sisters in Spirit*, p. 13.
10 We know there are male sex trade workers also working in dangerous and often violent situations, but with this chapter, we are focusing on the missing and murdered aboriginal women and girls.
11 Anne Dempsey, "Native women's group hopes for share of money Ottawa budgeted for cause," (21 April 21, 2010), *Globe and Mail*, http://www.theglobeandmail.com/news/national/.
12 Harris McLeod (12 April 2010) ADMIN, http://hilltimes.com/page/view/aboriginal-women-04-12-2010. More recently, the federal government announced the approval of funding to "78 projects directly supporting more than 24,000 Canadian women … This includes 34 groups that have received funding for the first time." Status of Women News Release (6 May 2010), http://swc-cfc.gc.ca/med/news-nouvelles/2010/0506-eng.html.
13 See the discussion of "wicked problems" in Brad McKenzie and Brian Wharf, *Connecting Policy to Practice in the Human Services*, Toronto: Oxford University Press, 1998, p. 41. "Wicked Problems" are social problems with a number of features: they defy easy definitions, they are essentially unique, and are symptoms of another problem. These wicked problems "have no stopping rule." Rather, they must be "resolved over and over again." At the same time, solutions occur in contexts where there is no room for trial and error, because each solution has an immediate significant impact.
14 We also draw on an earlier draft of this article, James Tully, "Two Meanings of Global Citizenship: Modern and Diverse," 2005, presented at the Meanings of Global Citizenship Conference held at UBC (Tully, Early Draft).
15 Rebecca Johnson, *Taxing Choices: The Intersection of Class, Gender, Parenthood, and the Law*, Vancouver: UBC Press, 2002, p. 8.
16 Ibid.
17 Ibid.
18 Simone Weil, "Human Personality," in *The Simone Weil Reader*, ed. George A. Panichase,

Mt. Kisco, N.Y.: Moyer Bell, 1977, pp. 315–17, as reproduced in James Boyd White, *Living Speech: Resisting the Empire of Force*, New Jersey: Princeton University Press, 2006, pp. 224–6.
19 Stephen Jay Gould, *The Mismeasure of Man*, New York: W.W. Norton & Co, 1996, p. 50.
20 Robert Matas, "Week 21: Witness says she saw Pickton butchering woman," *Globe & Mail*, 30 November 2007, http://v1.theglobeandmail.com/servlet/story/RTGAM.20071130.wpicktonweek21/BNStory/specialPickton/home.
21 Weil, "Human Personality," pp. 224–6.
22 Mary Field Belenky, Blythe McVicker Clinchy, Nancy Rule Goldberger and Jill Mattuck Tarule, *Women's Ways of Knowing: The Development of Self, Voice, and Mind*, HarperCollins Publishers, 1986. Despite a range of criticisms over the years, this has been a fairly enduring book in the social science field especially in adult education and feminist theories. The criticisms are mainly concerned with the limited extent to which the methodology can be replicated, the assumptions about race and racialization, and the hierarchy they organize their five stages of knowing into. Despite the criticisms, the theory resulting from this research can be usefully adapted to other groups of people to explore the cognitive experiences of powerlessness. Furthermore, the stages of knowing or construction of knowledge can be reconceptualized as cyclical and simultaneous rather than sequential and hierarchical (Belenky et al.).
23 Briefly, these are (1) silent knowing: basic survival of external authorities, (2) received knowing: only knowledge outside oneself is trusted, (3) subjective knowing: knowledge is only personal, private, and intuited, (4) procedural knowing: thinking is within systems and objective procedures, and (5) constructing knowing: integration of internal and external information to create knowledge.
24 Ibid., pp. 26–7.
25 Ibid., p. 27.
26 James Boyd White, *Living Speech: Resisting the Empire of Force*, New Jersey: Princeton University Press, 2006, p. 41.
27 Simone Weil, "L'Iliade, ou le poème de la force," in *The Simone Weil Reader*, ed. George A. Panichase, Mt. Kisko, NY.: Moyer Bell, 1977 at 153; cited in James Boyd White, *Living Speech*, at 1.
28 Arguably, the people described in the vignette are very articulate. Calling oneself a "throwaway" is an exquisitely articulate act—if one is listening and able to hear. However, the messages contained in these kinds of statements are usually not understood very far beyond the speaker and so they remain incoherent to the larger world.
29 Ibid., p. 280.
30 Johnson, *Taxing Choices*, p. 8.
31 Elizabeth Comack, "Theoretical Approaches in the Sociology of Law," in Elizabeth Comack, ed. *Locating Law: Race, Class, Gender, Sexuality, Connections*, 2nd edn, Black Point, NS: Fernwood Publishing, 2006, p. 26.
32 Ibid.
33 Ibid., p. 28.
34 Ibid. Comack also provides similar thumbnail critiques of other major political theories such as liberalism, Marxism and various feminisms.
35 Often these conservative perspectives are described in evolutionary terms whereby indigenous societies had not yet evolved to European levels of civilization, or are lacking the western rule of law. Arguably, the work of Tom Flanagan and Francis Widdowson fit this bill. See Tom Flanagan, *First Nations, Second Thoughts*, Montreal: McGill-Queen's University Press, 2000, and Francis Widdowson and Albert Howard, *Disrobing the Aboriginal Industry*, Montreal: McGill-Queen's University Press, 2008.
36 Carol Goar, "This is 'what women want'? Highly unlikely" (14 May 2010) *The Star*, http://www.thestar.com/opinion/editorialopinion/article/809069--goar-this-is-

what-women-want.
37 Comack, "Theoretical Approaches in the Sociology of Law," p. 32.
38 According to Tully, "Rights are neither necessary nor sufficient conditions of citizenship" (*PPNK* II, 371, n. 2).
39 Brad McKenzie and Brian Wharf, *Connecting Police to Practice in the Human Services*, Toronto: Oxford University Press, 1998, p. 5. Policy-makers, legislators and senior bureaucrats who develop laws and policies regarding human services delivery are predominately male, middle-aged, and have usually comfortably lived most of their lives in middle to upper socio-economic brackets. On the other hand, both human services practitioners and those who receive services are predominately female, many living in poverty or quasi-poverty.
40 Deborah Stone, "For Love Nor Money: The Commodification of Care," in *Rethinking Commodification*, Martha M. Ertman and Joan C. Williams, eds, New York: New York University Press, 2005, p. 281.
41 Wharf and McKenzie, *Connecting Police to Practice in the Human Services*, p. 5.
42 Susan McGrath, "Child Poverty Advocacy and the Politics of Influence," in Jane Pulkingham and Gordon Ternowetsky, eds, *Child and Family Policies: Struggles, Strategies and Options*, Halifax: Fernwood Publishing, 1997, p. 81.
43 Wharf and McKenzie, *Connecting Police to Practice in the Human Services*, p. 5.
44 Ibid.
45 Stone, p. 286.
46 Wharf and McKenzie, *Connecting Police to Practice in the Human Services*, p. 6.
47 Ibid.
48 Ibid., p. 7.
49 Iris Marion Young, "The Logic of Masculinist Protection: Reflections on the Current Security State," *Signs* 29, 2003, pp. 1–25 at p. 21.
50 Ibid.
51 Ibid.
52 Ibid.

Part IV

Conclusion

Chapter 12

Responses

James Tully

Introduction

It is a great honour to be invited to respond to the contributions by these outstanding scholars. I would first like to thank Robert Nichols and Jakeet Singh for bringing these scholars together and for asking them to bring their different approaches into a dialogue with my less well-known approach. This dialogue is immensely helpful. It enables us to see the strengths and weaknesses of my specific type of public philosophy in relation to civic freedom and, reciprocally, the strengths and weaknesses of the other approaches in comparison and contrast. The overall effect is to remind us of the complexity of the world of politics and how each approach reveals some aspects of it while concealing others. This in turn shows us that no one approach is comprehensive. If we wish to understand the complexity of our field we need to enter into these types of dialogue and learn from each other's perspectives.[1]

Civil and civic citizenship

My perspective is the following. I seek to disclose the world of politics in languages that enable citizens to see the local and global problems they face and the possible ways of acting effectively in response to them. In *PPNK* I explicate two very general ways of thinking and acting effectively in response to local and global injustices: civil and civic citizenship. These are two overlapping traditions of citizen participation; where 'citizen participation' refers to individual and collective engagement in and over the practices of governance in which humans find themselves. Civil and civic citizenship within states and within the local and global relationships of informal imperialism are studied in *PPNK* I and *PPNK* II respectively.

Civil citizenship discloses the field of global citizenship as constituted by the legal, political and economic rights and duties, institutions and processes of historical development of modern states with representative governments, the international system of states under international law, the institutions of global governance and the traditions of democratic theory that have developed forms of critical reflection on these rights, institutions and processes. Civil citizenship exists within these rights, institutions and processes. Civil citizens participate by exercising their communicative powers in elections, political parties, deliberation in official public spheres and civil disobedience with the hopes of exercising influence power on elected representatives who exercise governmental power through legislative deliberation and lawmaking. The laws are seen as imperatives enforced by coercion that can be justified to citizens or challenged by them in the courts and public spheres. This model is standardly seen as a universal model of citizenship and democracy in the civil tradition.

Civic citizenship discloses the field in a much broader and pluralistic manner, even taking the self-organization of the ecosphere as the commonwealth of all forms of life in which human citizenship has its home. The institutional form of modern representative civil citizenship appears as one type of governor–citizen relationship among many types, and even here civic citizens have a different history and representation of these institutions. From the civic perspective, citizenship comes into being whenever and wherever people who are subject to or affected by practices of governance become active co-agents within them; exercising the powers of having a say (negotiating) and having a hand (powers of self-organization and self-government) in and over the relationships that govern their interaction. 'Civic freedom' is the situated, relational freedom manifest in the countless activities of bringing the relationships of disputation and resolution, recognition and distribution, and action-coordination that comprise practices of governance in this broad sense under the shared democratic agency and authority of those subject to or affected by them.

The primary examples of civic citizenship are everyday practices of grass-roots political, social, economic and ecological democracy where the members discuss and exercise powers of self-organization and self-government themselves (citizen–citizen relationships) prior to any separation of ruler and ruled or governor and citizen in representative practices of government. They become citizens by democratizing or cooperating their relationships of living and working together. These activities of reasoning and acting together provide the ground of civic relationships of representative government in which citizens conditionally delegate some of their powers of self-government to representatives (citizen–governor relationships). These dialogical relationships of representation extend civic practices of democratic governance from the local to the state-centred and global. The relationships within institutions of modern representative government are acceptable insofar as they enable the exercise of civic freedom within and on them. Civic citizenship practices of these two broad types are the means by which cooperative practices of self-government can be brought into being and by which unjust practices of governance can be challenged, reformed and transformed by those who suffer under them, becoming co-agents of them (practices of negotiation).[2]

In the following discussion I devote more time responding to the authors who criticise the limitations of this approach. I devote less time to the authors who present complementary studies of freedom and democracy in an imperial context. The way they complement each other is self-evident and needs little comment. In responding to the criticisms I show that my approach is not quite as limited as the critics characterise it. In addition, I return the favour and point out the limitations of their approaches, especially the priority they accord to violence and institutions. In these two comparative ways, I seek to bring all the chapters into conversation with one another for the edification of readers. You are the best judges of its success.

Anthony Laden

Practical reasoning and acting together

Anthony Laden brings to the dialogue his original analysis of practical reason as the intersubjective activities of conversing and reasoning together in relationships with others. From this perspective, practical reasoning comprises the various ways of relating to and interacting with others, from everyday talking and interacting in conversational norms to the more specialised varieties of reasoning together that he calls engagements. Following Hannah Arendt, this approach focuses more on the activities themselves – and how they transform the participants – than on the specific agreements and disagreements they bring about over time. His account of the 'logic of deliberation' explicates the widespread mode of reasoning and acting together at the centre of everyday practices of civic freedom. The logic of deliberation consists in 'reasoning-with' others: that is, of being responsive to them as free co-agents of dialogical relationships. It is different in kind from violence, manipulation, reasoning-over others (imperatives and commands), and 'negotiation' in his technical sense of bargaining. It is literally the transformative power of reasoning with others.[3]

The only difference between Laden's account of citizens reasoning together and my own is, as he notes, a terminological difference. He draws a distinction between deliberation and negotiation, where 'negotiation' refers to the specific logic of bargaining. I use 'negotiation' in the generic historical sense to refer to the world of human interaction (*negotium* in contrast to *otium*). I then demarcate specific types of negotiation as they come up in particular cases. Deliberative negotiation is surrounded by other types of civic negotiation (in my broad sense) in which humans engage in order to move others into transformative relationships of deliberation. These broader forms of negotiation differ from Laden's contrastive account of the 'logic of negotiation'.

First, genres of negotiation are not oriented to victory over the others, but to bringing them into relationships of deliberation (in Laden's sense) in which they can resolve their differences through dialogue. Second, they exclude relationships of violence and command because these ways of treating others fail to respect their reciprocal civic freedom. Third, like deliberation, these forms of engagement have to be responsive not only to the people with whom one is immediately negotiating. They also have to be responsive to all affected. Those who are affected by the negotiations or the outcome have a say or it is not a 'civic' engagement.[4] I call this broad field of practices of civic freedom nonviolent agonistics.[5] Diverse practices of tough negotiation, bargaining, boycotts, strikes, non-cooperation, nonviolent regime change and so on are all possible under these three civic conditions, as Gandhi and his many followers have shown. These broader types of engagement are clearly different from Laden's contrastive 'logic of bargaining'. They share many features of Laden's 'logic of deliberation', yet they are obviously more instrumental than deliberation. They are the nonviolent means by which violent, commanding, manipulative and bargaining adversaries are moved into the transformative logic of deliberation.

The primary example of citizens reasoning together in these ways is when they are also acting together in exercising powers of self-organisation and self-government with respect to public goods. The prototype of reasoning together in the logic deliberation is participatory democracy (citizen–citizen relationships of cooperative citizenship).[6] That is, civic reasoning is the mode of reasoning that is internally related to what Arendt calls 'acting in concert': citizens with a plurality of views about public goods reasoning and exercising power together. Just as Laden contrasts reasoning with others to commanding and bargaining, Arendt contrasts exercising power with others to exercising violence and power over others.[7] Civic citizens can also bring into being relationships of representation (citizen–governor relationships) and other forms of civic freedom (practices of negotiation and acting otherwise), but these are derivative of relationships of self-organisation and self-government, and accountable to them. In contrast, civil citizenship presupposes the separation of citizens from the exercise of powers of self-government (representative government) and institutions as preconditions of representative participation in the public sphere.[8] Laden's account of practical reasoning as the *praxis* of reasoning in practices in these ways has been immensely helpful to me and I am most grateful to him.

Eduardo Mendieta

Eduardo Mendieta presents a robust formulation and defence of the tradition of civil philosophy and civil citizenship in response to some of the objections I raise to it. He then presents four important questions and asks for further clarifications from me. I have learned an enormous amount from the neo-Kantian tradition in which he writes and, in particular, from the writings of Jürgen Habermas.[9] However, I continue to have concerns with it and I will try to clarify these in response to his questions.

The public sphere and crisis of global citizenship

With respect to the question concerning public spheres and citizenship, I agree with Mendieta's summary of Habermas' evolving work on the European public sphere. Habermas' account of the public sphere is a classic example of a civil theory of the public sphere. It discloses the field of participation as composed of the institutionalised public sphere in relation to western-style representative government and a capitalist market in the private sphere. Citizens participate in the public sphere through the exercise of communicative freedom in accordance with norms of public reason and their public opinions are channelled to voters, elected representatives and policy communities as influence power. The official public sphere is surrounded by subaltern public spheres and the unofficial opinions generated in them are channelled and translated into the official public sphere.

This model takes for granted representative government, citizen participation as the exercise of communicative powers abstracted from the exercise of political power, the ranking of public spheres relative to the official public sphere, and prior institutionalisation of public spheres as the basis of citizen participation. These are constitutive features of the tradition of civil citizenship and civil theories. This model of the public sphere emerged in Europe and has been spread around the world by western imperialism, dispossessing non-European societies of their forms of law, government, economic organization and modes of citizenship. As Habermas pointed out in his earlier work, participation in the official public sphere in order to address local and global problems comes up against limits set by the institutional basis of this form of participation and the legal, political, military and economic institutions that go along with it. These limits give rise to the current 'crisis of global citizenship'. This crisis is the incapacity of active citizens to address effectively the problems of global inequality, environmental destruction, privatization of the commons, and militarization from within these institutions. The problem is that the modern institutions that the official public sphere presupposes are themselves contributing causes of these problems. While the official public sphere enables an important range of participation, it also disables participation that calls their limits into question and tries to find ways to go beyond them in order to address the injustices of the present more directly and effectively.[10]

When citizens run up against these limits to participation, they have three alternatives. They can work to reform the official public sphere and its surrounding institutions from within by the exercise of communicative freedom and limited forms of civil disobedience. Many important advances have been made by reform movements over the last 200 years. However, these civil reform movements have limited success in trying to regulate the activities that cause the major problems of the present through public sphere participation in relation to representative government. The explanation of this is that the module of civil institutions that underpin civil citizenship place the economic and military activities that cause the major problems that now threaten life on earth in the private sphere and thus beyond the democratic participation of the very people who are subject to them and their perverse effects.

The second response to this crisis of global citizenship has been violent revolution and the seizure of state power. However, decolonization and the failure of the Non-Aligned Movement has shown this response, in the post-colonial context of informal imperialism of the former great powers, is so far unable to bring these activities and institutions under the democratic authority of the people who are subject to them.[11]

The third response is the tradition of civic citizenship. Mendieta claims that Habermas' 'communicative freedom is in perfect accord with Tully's definition of what he calls "civic freedom"' and that both conceptions of freedom presuppose institutions. I demur. It is certainly true that civic citizens participate in the official public sphere along with civil citizens. However, they have a different history and understanding of these institutions. From the practice-based civic perspective, public institutions do not precede civic participation. Rather, the rights and institutions of modern participation and representative government are seen as the result of the struggles of civic citizens long before they had either the institutions or rights to participate in struggling for them. This priority of practices of civic engagement to institutionalisation continues today in struggles for new kinds of institutions and rights to address global problems. Moreover, even well-established institutions are never independent containers of the activities that take place within them. Institutions gain their democratic legitimacy not only by enabling participation, as in the official public sphere, but by participants being active agents in gaining a say and a hand in co-articulating the relationships that comprise the institutions themselves. That is, civic citizens democratise or 'civicise' institutions from within, by bringing their relationships of governance under their shared authority.[12]

Civic citizens take the same orientation to human rights. Like Mendieta in the final section of his chapter, civic citizens see many human rights as the product of struggles by the oppressed for women's and children's rights, rights to participate, social and economic rights, minority rights, and the right of self-determination of peoples. However, rights, to be legitimate, go hand in hand with civic democracy. That is, the people who are subject to a regime of rights have an ongoing say over the meaning, implementation, review and re-negotiation of the rights in question for rights and democracy to be equiprimordial, to use Habermas' phrase. If the rights are imposed and declared unilaterally to be the unquestionable precondition of agency, then they fail to meet the ongoing test of democratic acceptability of the civic tradition. Also, it is not enough to speak of rights in general. Rights enable some forms of activity while disabling others. It is always enlightening to examine the history of struggles over specific rights to become aware of what is at stake. The actual social history of human rights at the United Nations since 1947 is scarcely a 'utopia', as Mendieta puts it. It has been an uneven series of struggles in which liberal and neo-liberal types, ordering and interpretation of rights have gained hegemony over more robust forms of participatory rights, social and economic rights, and rights of self-determination argued for by members from the Second, Third and Fourth Worlds.[13]

In addition, as we have seen in the Introduction and Laden's chapter, practices of civic citizenship begin in everyday relationships, from the daycare to global relationships of fair trade, in which the subjects of them have a say in and over them. Civic citizenship does not begin or end in institutions and legality, but in the informal norms of conversation. This is not 'utopian', as Mendieta claims in reference to Foucault, but the mode of reasoning, resolving disputes and acting together that is the phenomenological ground of the more institutionalised forms of power and authority that the civil theorists take as their starting point. Most importantly, civic citizenship is grounded in practices of collective self-organisation and self-government, not in representative institutions and the exercise of communicative powers over general norms in abstraction from the responsible exercise of power together with fellow citizens. On the civic view, citizens become good and effective public reasoners by relating their deliberations to specific experiences of social suffering and working out concrete ways of responding to them, either directly or by means of dialogues of reciprocal elucidation with those suffering the injustice in question. Finally, in the civil tradition, participation is limited to influencing lawmaking. From the civic perspective, a formal legal system is one important form of the power of government, but scarcely the only one or the one into which all others must be translated. Humans exercise powers of self- and representative government in a multiplicity of institutionalised and non-institutionalised practices of governance in different activities and state and non-state civilizations.[14]

Hence, when civic citizens run up against the limits of reform of the official public sphere, they part company with their fellow civil reformers, call these limits into question, and go beyond them by exercising their capacities of civic freedom in practices of civic citizenship. For example, they organise local and global practices of negotiation with powers-that-be responsible for global injustices; cooperative movements that establish democratically-run economic organisations around the world; community-based organizations; and nonviolent revolutions to address directly and more effectively the global problems that we confront today. They also often join hands with civil reformers working within the official institutions in relationships of mutual support and assistance.[15] I hope this brief sketch clarifies the difference and irreducibility of civic freedom and civic citizenship to the institutionalised communicative freedom and civil citizenship of Habermas and Mendieta.

Michel Foucault and Jürgen Habermas

Mendieta argues that Foucault's 'critical ontologies of the present' are 'complementary' to Habermas' 'fallible reconstructions of moral, political and discursive competencies'. I agree with his argument to some extent and with others who have made similar arguments.[16] There is a complementarity between their approaches in that Foucault's historical approach 'tests' the fallibility of Habermas' fallible reconstruction of universal competencies and the universal institutions in which they develop historically. This testing relationship is Foucault's depiction of his approach relative to the Kantian tradition:[17]

But if the Kantian question was that of knowing what limits knowledge must renounce exceeding, it seems to me that the critical question today must be turned back into a positive one: In what is given to us as universal, necessary, obligatory, what place is occupied by whatever is singular, contingent and the product of arbitrary constraints? The point, in brief, is to transform the critique conducted in the form of necessary limitation into a practical critique that takes the form of a possible crossing-over [*franschissement*].

Foucault and many other scholars have argued that the competencies, institutions and processes of modernization that Habermas reconstructs as fallibly universal, necessary and obligatory are singular and contingent. Moreover, they are the product of the arbitrary constraints of building states, markets, representative governments, public spheres and the rule of law in Europe and the interaction between colonial and post-colonial imperialism and anti-imperial responses beyond Europe. The competencies, institutions and processes of 'social progress' have been spread around the world unjustly and with enormous damage to other forms of social and political organization. And, they limit democratic participation in, and transformation of, the very activities that are the major cause of the problems we face today.[18]

Yet, despite the overwhelming body of critical literature in the global north and south, as far as I know Habermas has not responded to these tests of his vindicatory reconstruction of the 'social evolution' of modernity as a 'process of learning'. Like Mendieta, he has acknowledged some of the historical injustices and the unevenness of social evolution. However, he has continued to argue that criticism and reform of this unfinished project must take place within the general framework of these competencies, processes and institutions, and the universal discourses that serve to legitimate them.[19] In *Between Facts and Norms*, he states that they are the basis of any legitimate form of political association and exercise of the right of self-determination of peoples. In *The Divided West*, he states that these processes and institutions, as they are developed in modern states, The European Union and international law should continue to be adopted around the world. This appears to be the same type of historical reconstruction that Kant presents in *Universal History with a Cosmopolitan Purpose* and the guarantee section of Perpetual Peace.[20] It is precisely the form of progressive history that Foucault seeks to test and challenge in the quotation above: that is, to turn the Enlightenment commitment to critique into a test of the unexamined presuppositions of the Enlightenment project.

Two methods: critical theory and critical comparison

Mendieta writes that, 'if there is progress in knowledge, it is because we as a society have learned how to produce better systems of knowledge', and 'history is the field of contingent processes of learning – things could have been different, but we cannot think differently than we presently can precisely because of the competencies we have acquired'. This is partly true. However, a multiplicity of competencies and systems of knowledge are produced in the various societies of the world and by various actors and communities, not by a single 'we' or 'society'. The questions are: which ones are 'better', and better relative to which human needs and aspirations and in what contexts? Privileging a particular set of modern processes, systems of knowledge and competencies forecloses the alternative kind of critical and comparative study of different systems of knowledge in different societies for different purposes and with different normative standards of better and worse.[21] Yet, this alternative, comparative and pluralistic approach to learning might be better suited to address the global problems we face today and to deal with them in a genuinely democratic manner. On the comparative view of human education, we 'can think differently' because the second-order ability to compare and contrast competencies frees us from any particular set.

I hope that Mendieta will open his preferred competencies, systems of knowledge and institutions to this kind of critical engagement with the many alternatives available to us in practice and academic research. There are many aspects of the Kantian civil tradition that are worthy of respect and diffusion across contemporary traditions of political thought, but we can only know what they are if they are submitted to a test of public reason that is external to the tradition, as with any other tradition, including the civic.

In the passage above, Foucault argues that it is possible not only to test the universal claims of the Kantian tradition. It is also possible to 'cross-over' or go beyond them once they are shown to be singular, contingent and arbitrary. This indicates further differences between a broadly Foucaultian approach and the institutional approach of Mendieta and Habermas. The first way to go beyond the limits of the civil tradition is to locate citizenship and freedom in social relationships of contestation and cooperation in all kinds of activities.[22] This is the turn to civic citizenship. Institutionalisation can then be studied from this broader perspective of embeddedness in local communities and cooperatives when addressing the problems of global inequality, rather than taking institutions as the basis of any possible solution. And this leads to the study of the practices of the self that are required to engage in practices of civic freedom in social relationships.[23]

The civic tradition takes the hypothesis that humans are in relationships of cooperation and contestation further than Foucault. Civic citizens see themselves as Gaia citizens in the first instances; in relationships of mutual care with other living beings and the ecology as a living system of relationships in which we live and breathe and have our being. It is then possible to view institutions and social relationships from this broader perspective of the commonwealth of all forms of life. [24] This orientation provides a critical perspective from which we can develop appropriate competencies and systems of knowledge to cope with the ecological crisis and climate change, other than an orientation that treats humans and their institutions in abstraction from the ecological relationships in which they exist and on which they depend. Taking up this relational way of being in the world enables citizens and researchers to see reasoning and acting together from the locales of grass-roots democracy. Being active citizens does not wait on the often coercive imposition of a particular set of institutions. It begins in the multiplicity of normative relationships in which we find ourselves here and now and begin to act. From this perspective, the way humans act as citizens of the world helps to shape the way institutions develop, rather than the other way round.[25]

Public philosophy

Mendieta gives a fine summary of several recent attempts to free political theory from its role in legitimating western imperialism on the one hand and from various disciplinary limitations on the other. I have learned from the important changes he mentions.[26] One could add a number of other important trends. For example, he mentions that Charles Mills and Enrique Dussel work to gain recognition of African Americans and Latin Americans as equal participants in a single modernity. One could compare them with David Scott and Arturo Escobar, who work to gain recognition of African Americans and Latin Americans as members of communities and peoples who inhabit a plural modernity differently. The interdisciplinary scholarship on the persistence of informal imperialism after decolonization is also of fundamental importance in understanding how global governance operates.[27] As well, the engaged research methods of Indigenous, post-colonial and post-development scholars have changed the way many of us think about research.[28]

As Laden, Anghie, Scott, Norval and Napoleon and Friedland mention, reflection on these trends has moved me to transform the way I research and write: from the standard monological critical theory of the world of politics from an epistemic and often legislative perspective above the demos to a dialogical approach within the demos. My kind of public philosophy is academic research oriented to engagement in dialogues with other academic researchers in the global north and south, as well as Indigenous scholars in the Americas, in order to free my limited thought from its disciplinary and imperial biases and open it to ongoing comparative criticism. It also strives to enter into dialogues of mutual elucidation with citizens engaged in various individual and collective practices of citizenship. Their diverse practices of doing democracy are approached as epistemic communities from which researchers can learn. For there can be no global justice without epistemic justice to the multiplicity of actual existing demoi that political theory standardly overlooks. In reciprocity, researchers offer the best available critical research on the history, present configuration and possibilities of the context in which citizens are constrained to organise and act. Citizens learn from the interchange and researchers test their research in relation to practice and improve it accordingly.[29]

Hence, my writings are not the construction of a theory, let alone a critical theory, but, simply perspectival proposals about aspects of the field we inhabit from my situated place and limited knowledge and within webs of interlocution. They strive to be 'experiments in truth' in the sense given by Mahatma Gandhi and Foucault: partial expressions of a way of knowing and being to be critically tested by reciprocal proposals of interlocutors for their limited truthfulness in theory and practice.[30] Public philosophy is an academic way of exercising civic freedom.

I would like to thank Mendieta for his provocative questions. They have stimulated me to modify and reformulate my objections to features of the civil tradition and to address the objections he raises to the civic tradition. I hope these responses provide the clarification he asked for and I look forward to his responses in return. Like him, I believe that these two traditions can learn from and complement each other if they open themselves to the kind of reciprocal testing we have begun in this exchange.

Antonio Y. Vázquez-Arroyo

Antonio Vázquez-Arroyo presents an outstanding interpretation and critique of my approach to the study of politics. It has caused me to reconsider many of my central arguments, to modify them where necessary, and to try to represent them in a better way in response. He opens with an excellent contextualization and summary of the main themes of *Public Philosophy*. He then asks the following three questions (p. 50):

> 'How, and to what extent' can this approach 'effectively conceptualize contemporary predicaments of power and the forms of structural violence that permeate and constitute these political spaces [of civic freedom]'? In particular, can this approach 'dispense with a sustained analysis of capitalism, the forms of state and market power and their respective "cagings" of political life in the present, as well as the ineluctability of enmity lines?' Furthermore, 'does a principled commitment to non-violence fully capture these complexities?'

In a careful reading of *PPNK* and series of arguments he roundly concludes that I fail to answer the questions satisfactorily. His critique consists of four main arguments.

Four objections

First, I fail to conceptualize adequately the 'the question of power and determinations – conceptual, historical and institutional' (p. 51). The 'determinations' that I fail to conceptualize are the forms of power and structural violence of the modern state and capitalism and the way they cage or determine political life in the present (p. 59). There are three main explanations of why I overlook these determinants of modern politics. First, I have fallen under the harmful influence of philosophers, theorists and activists who focus on situated human agency within these structures and thus allegedly overlook the way they determine or cage the field of agency (p. 51). These misguiding mentors include Arendt, Foucault, Skinner and Wittgenstein. Second, I go astray even when I focus on the background determinations because I apparently misrecognize them as too 'indeterminate' and 'pliable' (p. 61). Third, when I do analyse background structures I allegedly focus on the wrong ones; that is, on imperialism rather than capitalism and the state. As a result, '[a]nti-imperialism, not anti-capitalism is the prevalent leitmotif in Tully's reflections. But a reckoning with one without an adequate theorization of the other, especially when nowadays they collude more than ever before, remains inadequate and, ultimately, misrecognizes the forms of power binding in the present' (p. 61). More fatally, my approach is said to 'debar a consideration of capitalism' (p. 63).

Second, Vázquez-Arroyo presents the correct theoretical approach to the study of these modern structures. They should be recognized as determinate structures of domination and conceptualised within a comprehensive 'critical theory of the present' of the state, capitalism and power (p. 58) along the lines set out by Wendy Brown, Michael Mann and Sheldon Wolin. Furthermore, it is also the role of theory to provide a vision of the world beyond capitalism. Without such a high-powered critical theory a 'critical ethos remains abstract and its edges are significantly dulled' (p. 58). For 'civic freedom to be meaningful', he argues, it demands a 'head-on confrontation' with the encagement and incorporation of democracy and democratic life by these forms of power (p. 57). In contrast to this tradition, my approach either fails to recognize or seriously 'under-theorizes' the determinations of modern politics.

Third, as the 'head-on confrontation' quotation above suggests, once the theorist presents such a comprehensive critical theory it is possible to derive the correct form of political action from it. Here again, I apparently fail to 'systematically thematize' collective political action. I do not explain how civic freedom is compromised by state and capitalist power and I give no account of decentralized forms of collective action (p. 57). Even worse, I reject Vázquez-Arroyo's premise that effective political action requires the use of violence and the drawing of lines of enmity. The premise of mainstream modern political theory and practice since Hobbes that violence and friend–enemy relationships are necessary and effective features of politics is not a testable hypothesis, but a necessary truth (p. 65). I am said to know this but refuse to acknowledge it. 'Predatory behavior and violence' are intrinsic to politics as well as to the natural world, where 'nature's diversity embodies dialectic of destruction and creation in which both dynamics are deeply intertwined', as Perry Anderson and Étienne Balibar have apparently shown (pp. 55–56). Once this irreducible dialectic is correctly recognized, it can be seen that democracy 'has always entailed a perilous and tragic economy of violence in dealing with the ineluctable imperative to draw enmity lines': that is, the basic 'dialectic of violence and nonviolence' (p. 56).

Fourth, the cumulative conclusion of these three arguments is that a dialogue approach and the practices of civic freedom outlined in *PPNK* are hopelessly inadequate and ineffective: that is, practices within states and markets (civil and civic working together to reform); practices of nonviolent agonistics to transform them from without (practices of negotiation); and practices of bringing into being cooperative and community-based social, economic and ecological democracies from the grass-roots to the global (practices of acting otherwise) (p. 62). Moreover, nowhere in *PPNK* is there an 'explicit plea for a horizon beyond it [capitalism] as a precondition of democratic civic freedom, let alone a systematic theorization of how civic freedom effectively confronts it in order to transcend it' (p. 61). In conclusion (p. 66):

> Confronting violent predicaments of power has historically demanded lines of enmity and democracy is not exempt from this necessity, nor is it exempted from articulating an economy of violence. And a democratic 'public philosophy in a new key' lacks the necessary critical and political edge without properly conceptualizing these predicaments.

Response

I am grateful to Vázquez-Arroyo for presenting such a well-formulated critique of my approach and re-assertion of the traditional critical theory approach centred on the state, the market and violent political action. This way of disclosing and analysing the present has developed since Marx in non-dialectical opposition to the civil tradition (which is well represented by Mendieta's chapter). I have learned a lot from this Marxist and non-Marxist tradition, including from the contemporary theorists he mentions, but clearly different lessons than he has learned. However, like the authors I draw on and Vázquez-Arroyo criticises, I have gradually worked my way out of a number of basic assumptions of both traditions, especially their imperative language of necessity, ineluctability, preconditions and determinations. Indeed, I announce in the Introduction to *PPNK* that my primary aim is to dissolve their shared transcendent conception of the role of theory above the demos and replace it in the everyday world.[31] I then try to show how valuable elements in both appear as less necessary and determinant from this phenomenological position of being in the world. I will call the tradition of critique, enmity, violence and the transcendence of capitalism that Vázquez-Arroyo presents as the standard by which other approaches are judged as adequate or inadequate the violent critical tradition.[32] In response, I will try to show why and how the civic tradition, which overlaps historically with the violent critical tradition, has, ever since William Thompson, Kropotkin and Gandhi, moved away from it in response to experiences of the last two centuries and now constitutes a distinct tradition of civic freedom.[33]

Informal imperialism, capitalism and the state

One such decisive experience for the civic tradition is the 'tragedy of decolonization'. This is the failure of the violent revolutions of decolonization and the state building of the Non-Aligned Movement to create a third way different from the capitalist and communist models of development, or to hold out against neo-liberalization after the Cold War. The result in many cases has been centralised armed states with dependent political, economic and military elites, rapid economic development, continuing inequality, environmental destruction, indebtedness, the failure of the New International Economic Order in 1974, and low-intensity representative democracy at best (often armed against the majority of their own people). How could this happen when the Non-Aligned Movement had critical theories of the state, capitalism, power and violent revolution, an alliance of the majority of the world's population, armed states after decolonisation, representation at the United Nations and the right of self-determination under international law after Resolution 1516 in 1960?[34]

The working hypothesis of post-colonial theorists, historians of informal imperialism, anthropologists, political economists, critical theorists of international law, political theorists of empire and *PPNK* is worth consideration and testing.[35] Decolonisation, the Cold War and the construction and networkisation of institutions of global governance by the great powers and their multinational corporations marked the triumph of informal imperialism over colonial imperialism.[36] This informal mode of global governance and its global military network has the capacity to govern the development of the subaltern former colonies, to extend and protect multinational corporations and state-owned enterprises of China, to employ massively destructive counter-violence against violent insurrections, and to incorporate them when they temporarily succeed, as we see today.

Contrary to Vázquez-Arroyo in one of his very few misinterpretations, informal imperialism is not a mode of power that I conceptualise as separate from capitalism or the modern state. Rather, informal imperialism *is* the so-called 'processes' that spread and reshape these political, legal and economic institutions and relations around the world and protect them against insurrection. Informal imperialism carries on the project of colonial imperialism of spreading the module of institutions of capitalism and the modern state by violent means, yet in a non-colonial manner, as I lay out in detail.[37] This 'contrapuntal ensemble', as Edward Said called it – of institutions and processes and the multiplicity of interactions in and against its complex parts – co-determines the present to a large extent. Vázquez-Arroyo also recognises that there are internal relationships between capitalism, the modern state and imperialism, yet he does not see that *PPNK* II is a sustained attempt to present a historical and critical account of these dynamic relationships.

Vázquez-Arroyo also claims that I fail to analyse the form of power characteristic of informal imperialism. On the contrary, every chapter of *PPNK* II is given over to how this form of power works globally and locally in a host of cases. One of its defining features is that one hegemonic partner (individual, collective or alliance) is able to govern the salient features of the conduct of the other subaltern partners of the relationship (also, individual, collective or alliance) most of the time through their partly constituted and constrained freedom of action, as Kwane Nkrumah was among the first to recognise.[38] This form of power has spread throughout modern societies, not only in international relations, but also in reshaping the relationships within state and market institutions, especially after the network revolution.[39] This constrained freedom or 'room to maneuver' within many modern power relations is the Achilles' heel of the modern system of local and global governance; the space in which civic freedom emerges (in citizen–citizen or citizen–governor practices).[40] Vázquez-Arroyo states that I fail to theorise the 'precondition' of civic freedom, yet this co-condition is analysed in different contexts in each chapter.

Institutions and agency

Next, if I may return the compliment to Vázquez-Arroyo, his neo-Weberian understanding of the way structures 'determine' human agency misrecognises the interactive internal relation between agency and institutions in our time. The processes and institutions of informal imperialism are certainly structures of violence, dispossession, destruction of the living earth, domination, inequality, exploitation and de-localization, as we both agree. However, they are not structures that 'determine' human agency in the way his neo-Weberian language of theorisation presupposes. They are not 'cages' that are prior to and independent of the activities that take place within them, and thus they are not susceptible to transformation in the way his institution-oriented violent politics of confrontation presupposes, as the decolonisation example illustrates. Rather, they are informed and shaped by the more complex, interactive form of power I describe in detail in *PPNK*.

The concerted activities of unequal agents within and around the institutions are also sometimes activities over the background conditions of the institutions, bringing them into the space of contestation and change in unexpected ways. Institutions are internally related to the activities that take place in and over their background conditions to varying degrees. It is thus perhaps more insightful to study the relationship between various degrees of institutionalisation and various strategies of democratisation by those subject to, subordinated within, or excluded from them, who seek to bring them under their transformative democratic control to some extent. Surely, the last 200 years of creative popular struggles to democratise the institutions of states and markets by civil and civic strategies have not been entirely in vain. Rather, they have changed these institutions significantly, even when these changes are viewed from the grand heights of a critical theory oriented to transcending them. Of course there are background features that are not the target of a particular struggle and remain unchanged, but this is not to say that they 'encage' and 'determine' the struggle or that they in turn are permanently immune from other kinds of interactive strategies of civic freedom.[41] Vázquez-Arroyo acknowledges this when he begins to join me in analysing the interaction of power, institutionalisation and collective agency in terms of 'obduracy' and 'pliability' *vis-à-vis* agency, rather than as independent structures and determinations (p. 61). All I can say in response to this section of his chapter is welcome to the complex world of informal power and civic freedom. And if he and I are to test institutions for their obduracy and pliability, then we have to study them from the side of human agency. Hence the central importance of the philosophers who have taken this revolutionary turn and whom he criticises: Arendt, Foucault, Skinner and Wittgenstein.[42]

Practices of civic citizenship

As I mention in my response to Mendieta, I argue that civic citizens and progressive civil citizens both work to reform the institutions of representative government and capitalism from within, yet each in their distinctive ways. When they try to address local and global problems of inequality and exploitation, ecological destruction, climate change, war and misrecognition, they find that reform within official channels is limited. When civic citizens run up against this incapacitation or crisis of global citizenship, they re-appropriate their delegated powers of self-organisation and self-government and engage in practices of civic freedom beyond the representative channels in three general ways: nonviolent practices of negotiation, confrontation and participatory democracy.

Vázquez-Arroyo dismisses these local and global practices of civic citizenship as ineffective and inadequate. He asks, 'are these enough to attain and sustain a meaningful share of political power that substantive democratic equality and freedom presuppose and demand?' and roundly concludes that they are not (p. 63). Yet, this is a question posed entirely within the shared institutional framework of the civil and violent critical traditions, in which democratic equality and freedom presuppose gaining a meaningful share of established forms of political power (and, in the violent critical tradition, gaining it by head-on confrontation and violence). From the civic perspective, in contrast, the self-organisation and exercise of powers of self-government by people acting in concert brings into being and sustains democratic freedom and equality, whether these activities becomes institutionalised or remain organised in non-institutional associations.[43] He does not even consider this other way of thinking about the power of the people that enables us to see what is going on in civic practices in a completely different light. As he writes earlier, 'Tully ultimately misrecognizes the history and structures of contemporary forms of power and ends up reverting to a quest for silver linings in the present and an antinomian anti-politics of non-violence' (p. 52). Since I have tried to show that I did not completely misrecognise the history and structures of contemporary forms of power, I will now try to show that the practices of civic freedom are more effective and sustainable than he concludes, and a far better alternative to his politics of violence and enmity.

Vázquez-Arroyo suggests that Marx's theory of primitive accumulation should play a more central role in my account of capitalism. The reason I do not disclose the field of political possibilities under Marx's specific explication of primitive accumulation is that it accepts the following processes as unjust yet necessary and universal preconditions of the development of capitalism to communism: the dispossession of Indigenous peoples; the destruction of non-capitalist modes of production; the individuation and commodification of human productive powers into commodities; and the commodification of the earth. The dispossessed are incorporated and constrained to struggle within these unjust determinations to organise, confront and eventually gain state power in order to transcend capitalism. Others forms of political action are judged as inadequate and backward-looking relative to this one form of struggle and the meta-narrative of historical development.[44]

Yet, these monumental injustices are the major causes of the global crisis of inequality, ecological crisis, climate change, and war and militarisation we face today. Marxist regimes that have gained power in accord with this developmental model have not yet made a major difference to these local and global problems or achieved the pan-socialist ideal of 'an association in which the free development of each is the condition for the free development of all'.[45] In contrast, practices of civic freedom throughout the world bring the latter to bear on the former directly. Indigenous peoples have rejected incorporation for centuries and continue to inhabit modernity differently as much as possible. Cooperativists, decentralised socialists and anarchists like Robert Owen, William Morris and Peter Kropotkin at the time, and Gandhi, Karl Polanyi and Fritz Schumacher a century later, rejected this developmental acceptance of present injustices in the name of some predicted future good and addressed the injustices of dispossession and commodification here and now. They built a third tradition to capitalism and state communism by rejecting the commodification of labour and nature; re-appropriating and exercising their social and economic powers in self-governing community-based organisations and cooperatives; and relating to the ecology as a commonwealth of all forms of life on which humans depend and to which they have responsibilities of care. This 'third' way now has over 800 million members worldwide in the United Nations year of cooperatives.[46]

Civic citizens do not require a 'vision' that transcends capitalism as Vázquez-Arroyo claims. They manifest another world here and now in everything they do, as Boaventura de Sousa Santos puts it.[47] They do not share the modernist orientation to some just and peaceful future 'to come' by unjust and violent means. They are oriented to acting justly here and now on the hypothesis that means are not contingently related to ends, as the modern traditions presume, but, rather, constitutive and prefigurative of ends, as a seed to the tree.[48]

The transformative power of nonviolence

This working hypothesis concerning the internal relationship between means and ends is also one of the main reasons that the civic tradition has come to reject violence and enmity and to embrace nonviolence and compassion in the course of the twentieth century. I would like to end by discussing this last difference between us. Since publishing *PPNK* I have been presenting the best arguments of the anti-war and peace movements against the politics of an economy of violence and enmity and for a politics of nonviolence and compassion in hopes that influential critical theorists of violence such as Vázquez-Arroyo and Bonnie Honig will take these arguments more seriously and help to bring them into the mainstream of our discipline. I will attempt to summarise some of these arguments.

International Relations theorists argue that drawing lines of enmity and distrust between oneself and others and preparing for war tends to induce the same response in others. The reciprocal and escalating logic of enmity, war preparation and the exercise of violence among states over the labour and resources of the planet and between states and state-seeking revolutionary and terrorist movements is the dialectic of violence and counter-violence at the centre of the modern world system of armed states and state-seekers. In times of peace it is rational to prepare for war. This security dilemma has given rise to institutions of global governance, a growing global military network, and new forms of violent oppositional networks. In 1969, Arendt summarised four well-supported arguments that it is irrational to continue to prepare for and resolve disputes in this way. These include the argument that drawing enmity lines and dehumanizing the other, the command–obedience relations needed to prepare for the use of violence, and the multiple effects on the societies engaged in the struggles all overwhelm the ends. Moreover, the continuation of this modern world system in the nuclear age tends towards the destruction of life on earth. The irrational system continues, she concluded, because a substitute for enmity and violence has not been found.[49]

By the late nineteenth century the anti-war movement had a perspicuous analysis of the irrationality of the dialectic of violence and counter-violence. They also had the alternative ethics to violence and enmity in nonviolence (thou shall not kill) and always treat the other as you would yourself, with an open hand rather than a closed fist (turn your cheek and love your enemy).[50] However, as William James pointed out, they lacked a nonviolent substitute for violence as the means to resolve disputes and generate solidarity.[51] The techniques of nonviolent organisation, revolution, dispute resolution among political associations and policing only began to be discovered and rediscovered, collected together and tested in practice after the horrors of World War I and Gandhi's experiments in India.[52] Arendt was right to say that these techniques were not yet seen as a complete substitute for the world system of violent states and revolutions. However, they were further along than she acknowledged in the work of Martin Luther King Junior, the anti-war movement, and Malcolm X's realisation that 'bloodless revolutions' were possible after the experience of Vietnam.[53] Invention of and experimentation with the ethics and techniques of nonviolence and compassionate negotiation have increased ever since. This is the reason I say in *PPNK* that the civic tradition is learning the ethical and strategic arts of nonviolent politics and unlearning the politics of violence and enmity.[54]

In contrast, Vázquez-Arroyo and Honig simply assert that violence and enmity are necessary features of politics and democracy. Yet, nonviolent practitioners and theorists have contested this reigning dogma of the left and right for a century.[55] For example, Gene Sharp has shown that nonviolent movements around the world have developed hundreds of techniques of nonviolent agonistics that are capable of converting violent adversaries into actors willing to negotiate their differences nonviolently. He has also shown that techniques of nonviolent civic defence can replace armed forces.[56] Brian Martin has argued that nonviolent strategies are effective against the injustices of capitalism.[57] In their examination of over 300 cases, Erica Chenoweth and Maria Stephan have shown that nonviolent negotiation techniques, backed by broad-based participation, can be effective in transforming small and large unjust regimes backed by violence.[58] The power of nonviolence, they argue, is more powerful than violence. Five theorists of nonviolence have explained in detail the unique transformative power of nonviolent agonistics and shown how it can be used to replace violence across the board: Richard Gregg, H.J.N. Horsburgh, Joan Bondurant, Jonathan Schell and Dustin Howes. The Dalai Lama and Thich Nhat Hahn have explicated the practices of a global ethics of negative and positive nonviolence (non-harm and active compassion) as a comprehensive way of life. The nonviolent movements in the Middle East and Aung San Suu Kyi in Myanmar have furnished yet more examples. These are authors and actors who are scarcely unfamiliar with the reality of violence and counter-violence. Yet, *contra* Vázquez-Arroyo, Honig and the authorities they cite, they are able to free themselves from it in practice and theory; put the ethics and techniques of nonviolence into practice and theory; and test continuously nonviolent ways of being in the world.[59]

I would like to summarise five interconnected practices of the transformative power of nonviolence that are central features of nonviolent agonistics and negotiation. These five civic practices explain why nonviolence is more powerful and transformative than the power of violence and enmity and the command-obedience relationships their exercise requires. We can think of these as comprising education in nonviolent civic citizenship. This is a well-developed field of counter-mainstream civics in communities, social movements, schools and engaged teaching and research universities throughout the world.

The first area of civic education comprises meditative and group meditative practices of care of the self. These practices educate children and adults to deal with their harmful emotions, habits and reactions; to cultivate the four stages of empathy that enable them to attend to and understand the suffering of oneself and others; and to cultivate compassion that moves them to act to alleviate that suffering. They free the self from destructive and hateful self-narratives, and re-orient the participants to be present in the here and now ('to come to their senses') and to care for themselves in preparation for caring for other human and non-human beings. This is the first axis of the transformative power of nonviolence: nonviolent relations of the self to the self (self-compassion). Education and exercise in the transformative, nonviolent practices of the ethics of the self is the ground of all other nonviolent practices: being peace. This is not only the ethical teaching of the great practitioners of nonviolence such as Gandhi, Thich Nhat Hahn, Dalai Lama, Martin Luther King Jr. and Thomas Merton.[60] The same fundamental point concerning the primacy of ethics of the self in relation to practices of freedom in the world of power relations is also made by Michel Foucault:[61]

> If we take the question of power, of political power, situating it in the more general question of governmentality understood as a strategic field of power relations in the broadest and not merely political sense of the term, if we understand by governmentality a strategic field of power relations in their mobility, transformability, and reversibility, then I do not think that reflection on this notion of governmentality can avoid passing through, theoretically and practically, the element of a subject defined by the relationship of self to self ... an ethics of the subject.

The second area of education is civic engagement in self-organizing and self-governing practices of bringing about common goods. These begin in looking after the classroom or hood, growing vegetables, making and cleaning up after meals, making utensils, studying where food, clothing, shelter and funding come from and under what conditions, and how are other humans and the environment affected by what they are doing. These civic communities are extended out to larger constructive programmes through networking with others schools, cooperatives and community-based organisations.[62] This is the second axis of the transformative power of nonviolence: engagement in practices of exercising power in concert.

The third area of civic education is in the arts of cooperation and nonviolent contestation in dialogue. This begins with nonviolent techniques of classroom communication and civic dialogues between teachers and students: questioning what is being taught, how it is being taught and nonviolent practices of disputation and resolution. These civic practices of contestation do not necessarily transform all master–pupil relationships, but they teach students and teachers how to enter into various types of dialogues and to challenge command relationships and demand justifications that they can test and accept or reject. This area comprises education in the wide variety of verbal and non-verbal (performative) types of dialogue available in western and non-western cultures. Moreover, these include the varieties of dialogical relationships among humans and non-human beings as fellow citizens of an ecological commonwealth of all forms of life.[63] This is the third and most familiar axis of the transformative power of nonviolence: the power of receptive, reciprocal and critical dialogues.

The fourth and most difficult area of education is in the types of civic negotiations that involve nonviolent agonistics with violent others. These are oriented to moving violent actors around by nonviolent ways to see the superiority of nonviolent cooperative and contestatory ways of settling disputes through negotiation and dialogue. That is, these are negotiations with actors who have not had the advantage of a civic education. There are over two hundred techniques for different situations. One of the most basic in my opinion is an education in the nonviolent martial arts that enable an individual or collective agent: (1) to discourage a potential attacker from attacking just in the way they comport themselves; (2) to disarm and overthrow violent opponents by using their aggressive behaviour to throw them off balance, into dis-equilibrium and undermine their confidence in the efficacy of violence; (3) to be able to withstand blows and continue to uphold the stance of concern and readiness to settle things by negotiation and compromise; (4) to be willing to die for a negotiable just cause but never to kill (self-suffering); and (5) thereby to implant the suggestion in others that there is a superior ethical and reasonable way to resolve the dispute – by being moved and moving to nonviolent agonistics of types three, two and one above. In all five dimensions, the power of nonviolence is acting on both opponents and bystanders by the experience and sight of an entirely different and ethically superior way of interacting and resolving differences.

This complex logic of nonviolent interaction with violence is the fourth axis of the transformative power of nonviolence. It is often considered the fundamental transformative power of nonviolence since it transforms the opponent and the relationship between them from one mode of being to another. Along with constructive programmes it is at the core of Gandhi's Satyagraha. It is called the jiu-jitsu logic of nonviolence because it uses the movements and dis-equilibrium of the opponent to bring about the transformation. The nonviolent actors are not only offering and suggesting a nonviolent alternative in which they can combine their energy and work together rather than wasting it in futile conflict. They also manifest this alternative in their interaction *and* envelope the violent others in these nonviolent and potentially transformative relationships. They are being peace and making peace at one and the same time. Most of the more complex and mediated techniques and strategies of nonviolent agonistics are derived from and extend the bodily logic of interaction and transformation of this famous phenomenological prototype.[64] It is the nonviolent tradition's alternative to the violent critical tradition's prototype of violence and counter-violence: the means of freeing ourselves from this allegedly inescapable dialectic and weaving ourselves into nonviolent relationships at the same time.[65]

The other technique that is equally important is non-cooperation. The civic tradition claims that unjust regimes rest not on violence or manufactured consensus but on cooperation in the sense of compliance. Therefore, the basic technique of dealing with an unjust regime from Étienne de la Boétie to the Egyptian Spring and nonviolent Intifada is to withdraw cooperation in the everyday reproduction of the unjust system of cooperation.[66] Non-cooperation includes techniques of slowdowns, work-to-rule, absenteeism, strikes, boycotts, complete withdrawal of support, encouraging others to join the campaign (especially the military), civic disobedience practices and so on; as long as these evince concern for the opponents and the readiness to negotiate. That is, non-cooperation campaigns are organized cooperatively in accord with the demands of civic freedom and this spectacle of the high moral ground also helps to undermine the authority and power, and so the support, of the violent regime in contrast.

Research shows that non-cooperation requires the reciprocal support of the other types of civic practice: practices of the self, constructive programmes of community-based organisations and unions that provide the food, shelter and so on that the unjust regime formerly provided, and the negotiation practices towards which non-cooperation aims to move the contest. Community-based organizations provide a nonviolent way of life for supporters and safe haven to which the campaigners can return during the long spells between campaigns and jail terms. They regain their strength, engage in constructive work and discuss strategy.[67] Cooperative non-cooperation is fairly easy to teach in practice and there are hundreds of examples to learn from since the great anti-war movements after World War I.[68] If they are organized at the neighborhood, city, national, regional and international level through the United Nations, such nonviolent networks have the capacity to remove unjust rulers and to deter their rise to power in the first place – as peaceniks from Albert Einstein, Aldous Huxley, Bertrand Russell and Gene Sharp to the millions who research and practice it today have argued against the proponents of war as the means to peace and justice.

The fifth area of nonviolent education is in anti-war research on the global problem of war, violence and hatred. This consists in the history and present of the escalating global system of war, war preparation and arms trading among the states and state-seeking revolutionary and terrorist movements, and the limits of official disarmament talks. It brings into relief the diabolical global complex of war and militarization and how it is mobilized to protect the structural causes of other global problems – of poverty, exploitation, environmental destruction and climate change – from being brought under the democratic authority of the billions who suffer and die under them. This is the fifth axis of the transformative power of nonviolence. This kind of critical education has the capacity to free students from taking the modern political system of violence and counter-violence for granted and being interpolated into it. And it enables them to see the other four transformative practices of a nonviolent way of life as both the replacement for this life-destroying system and the means of replacing it.

Finally, nonviolent movements have a completely different view of victory. They do not see victory as defeating an opponent and taking power. Their aim is the transformation of the world system of violence and power over others that holds inequality, exploitation and environmental injustice in place. They work to convert unjust and violent adversaries to nonviolent dispute resolution and to transform the unjust power relationship between them into one that is open to negotiation by the partners of it. This movement transforms, rather than seizes, power over others into democratic power with others. Moreover, nonviolent actors require the active participation of their opponent in order to test the validity of their claim of justice, which, prior to the negotiations is one-sided and monological. In the course of transforming command–obedience relationships of power into power-with and reasoning-with relationships, the partners come to combine their creative energy in the construction of a new relationship of genuinely shared authority.[69] This is, as Karuna Mantena puts it, 'another realism' from the realism advanced by the defenders of violence.[70]

In conclusion, I hope this brief sketch begins to call into question the deeply ingrained presumption that there is no alternative to violence and enmity and presents a well-supported alternative. My question in return is: where are the counter-arguments from the defenders of the necessity of violence and enmity? I also hope that these responses to Vázquez-Arroyo's objections and to his more familiar approach help to explain public philosophy more clearly and the reasons I believe it discloses aspects of the real world of politics that others conceptualise less well. I look forward to his response and a continuing dialogue of mutual learning over these important issues.

Bonnie Honig

I responded to Bonnie Honig's challenging contribution when it was first published. My response is reprinted below. I also responded to further reflections by her and Marc Stears on violence and nonviolence.[71] Furthermore, my response to Vázquez-Arroyo's defence of the necessity of violence and enmity also responds to some of her arguments. It is a challenge and a pleasure to continue this edifying dialogue with her.

The characteristically original and insightful question Bonnie Honig raises in her reflection on *PPNK* follows from her outstanding work on agonistic democracy and Sophocles' *Antigone* and it is surely central to our whole discussion. Rephrasing the question in the plural, what are the relationships between reason and violence? Is reasonableness an alternative to violence or an alternative expression of it? I cannot imagine a more challenging and important question on which to draw the discussion together and conclude, at least for now. But let me begin with a clarification.

Indigenous peoples

Honig suggests that I 'neglect' the relationship between reason and violence and that, in my study of Indigenous–settler relationships I focus on treaty negotiations to the exclusion of the violence ('the trail of tears'). I am insufficiently 'attuned' to what seems obvious from her Sophoclean and Freudian perspective: 'reasonableness is a part of and not an alternative to power politics' and that violence is a 'necessary' feature of politics. I would like to advance two clarifications in response. First, her suggestion is based primarily on one chapter on Indigenous peoples in *PPNK I* that is concerned with explicating the intersubjective conventions shared by many Indigenous and non-Indigenous peoples. These developed historically to facilitate nonviolent forms of the contestation, negotiation, review and cooperative governance of their relationships of interaction over shared sovereignty, territory, resource use, environmental management, shared powers, and the like. This is the positive critique of treaty relationships. In the following chapter I present the negative critique. This consists in exposing and listing the complex historical relationships among forms of western reason (especially legal and political reason), types of violence and fraud (war, genocide, dispossession, disease, exploitation, marginalisation, discrimination, and so on) and treaty negotiations from first contact to the contemporary treaty processes and court cases.

At the beginning of the chapter I state that these relationships between reason, violence and treaties continually, but not continuously, undermine nonviolent treaty negotiations.[72]

Second, in *PPNK* II I offer a critique of the historically layered relationships between forms of political, legal and economic reason and the violence and deceit of western modernisation and expansion, and the forms of reason, violence and deceit that have been deployed by imperialised peoples in response. The detailed historical study of this complex contrapuntal ensemble of violent modern power politics has been the main negative task of my research since the early 1990s. This includes not only the roles that western political theory plays in explicitly justifying violence and exploitation in the name of civilisation, modernisation, globalisation and democratisation, which we hear every day, but more complex and unnoticed ways that our most prized forms of reason are deeply woven into forms of violence. My two chapters on Indigenous peoples are part of this larger project of understanding western imperialism and the responses to it, both the predominant violence and counter-violence, but also the practices of nonviolent agonistics.

Reason and violence

Turning to the relationship between reason and violence, Honig draws upon Sophocles' *Antigone*, and asks, 'Does Haemon's violence betray his reasonableness or give an alternative expression to it?' She argues that his violence is just an alternative expression of his reasonableness. Reasoning and violence are seen as alternative strategic means to the same end – parricide. Haemon's attempt to convince Creon by reason is an alternative expression of his attempt to kill the father by violence. It is certainly true that reasons are used strategically and violently and that violence always comes cloaked in the finest of reasons and justifications. Yet, are they *always* related to each other as her outstanding work on Sophocles and Freud powerfully suggests? My approach is to ask the opposite yet complementary question to hers. I try to expose a relationship of reason and violence and then ask, 'what kind of nonviolent reason does the recourse to reason-related violence betray?' In my study of the complicity of western forms of political reason in the violence of imperial expansion one close relationship between reason and violence reappears over and over again. This is the assumption that certain institutional conditions must be in place and humans must be subject to them before it is possible to engage in nonviolent reasoning together (cooperating and contesting forms of cooperation). Accordingly, it is irrational to try to reason with another person or people prior to imposing coercively over them a secure structure of law, for only once they have been pacified, civilised or modernised by forceful subjection to a structure of cooperation of some kind or another (military rule, western law, primitive accumulation, labour discipline, markets, state structures, restructuring policies) is it then reasonable to reason nonviolently with them. Thus violence is both reasonable and necessary to establish democracy and peace.

Unfortunately for this thesis of the necessary relation between violence and reason, the others over whom the institutions of forced cooperation are imposed do not submit. They often reason in exactly the reciprocal way in response and resist violence with violence. This security dilemma does not lead to perpetual peace and the kingdom of ends, but to power politics and violent struggles. This familiar outcome is then said by both sides to prove the reasonableness of their premise (humans are naturally antagonistic) and of the conclusion (more coerced cooperation is needed). The violent struggles for existence or justice continue apace.[73] It is not difficult to see that many forms of reason in the humanities and social sciences are deeply implicated in this dogma of the priority of violent agonistics to cooperation, as well as the statements and policies of world leaders and peace prizes recipients.

Strange Multiplicity and *PPNK* are journals of a long and involved journey in search for and discovery of a nonviolent alternative to this deadly nexus of reason and violence called power politics. As I explain in my response to Vázquez-Arroyo, the alternative of a politics of reasonable nonviolent cooperation and agonistics (Satyagraha) was discovered in the twentieth century by William James, Gandhi, Abdul Gaffar Khan, Einstein, Ashley Montagu, Bertrand Russell, Martin Luther King Junior, Thomas Merton, Thich Nhat Hanh, Gene Sharp, Petra Kelly, Johann Galtung and Barbara Deming. They argued that the antagonistic premise of western theories of reasonable violence is false. Nonviolent practices of cooperation, disputation and dispute resolution are more basic and prevalent than violent antagonism. This is a central feature of civic freedom. If this were not true, if violent struggles for existence and wars of all against all were primary, the human species would have perished long ago. Cooperation, not violent antagonism, is the primary factor in evolution, as Kropotkin first responded to Darwin and as many have since tested and substantiated.[74]

Nonviolent webs of human and non-human cooperation and agonistics are the preconditions of peace and reason, not coercively imposed and policed structures of domination. Nonviolent practices of civic freedom transform both the game and game players. This is not parricide by other means, but the opposite. It is the meaning and transformative power of love for and care of the world and every living being in it. In an ancient commonplace, violence begets violence and nonviolence begets nonviolence. The genius of Gandhi and King was not only to see this but to live it. Yes, they were surrounded by a sea of violence and lying. Their brothers and sisters often succumbed to violence or cowardice. Gandhi and King had to work on themselves constantly. They were assassinated and those who pretend to follow in their footsteps often betray them. Yet they changed the world and set an example that millions of civic citizens try to follow.

Honig's unflinching exploration of the complex relations between reason and violence in her interpretation of *Antigone* and elsewhere shows us the difficulty, but not the impossibility, of realising this peaceful way of being in the world, which continues to be our task today and every day. Her insightful depiction of my humanism as 'fingers on the edge of the cliff' has made me see the complexity and importance of the task more clearly than before, and how much work is yet to be done.

Antony Anghie

All of the following chapters in the volume are not critiques of my approach. Rather, they are original explorations of freedom and democracy in an imperial context that relate to my work in complementary ways. It is an honour and a pleasure to see how these scholars have used some of my ideas in their own outstanding work to help to illuminate unfreedom and oppression in the past and the present. I apologize for not saying more in response to the chapters by Anghie and Scott, but I find myself in agreement with their important analyses and thus with nothing further to add except my gratitude.

It is a particular pleasure to see this complementarity in the chapter by Antony Anghie, for his *Imperialism, Sovereignty and the Making of International Law* has been of fundamental importance to me in understanding the history and present of colonial and informal modes of imperialism in relation to international law.[75] He shows how Vattel's arguments were used to dispossess Indigenous peoples of their traditional territories during the colonial period. Of equal importance, he also shows arguments inherited from Vattel continue to be used by the former colonies, not only Canada, Australia and New Zealand, but also Third World post-colonial states to dispossess and incorporate Indigenous peoples, and now to negate their legal personality in response to the United Nations Declaration of the Rights of Indigenous Peoples in 2007. The central argument he brings to our attention is Vattel's claim that a people comprise a nation and possess sovereignty over their territory only if they cultivate the soil, engage in productive commercial agriculture, and have the corresponding forms of private property. Since Indigenous peoples are hunters and gatherers, they fail to meet this standard of true and legal possession and production. Vattel was so insistent on this baseline argument that he deemed the productive commercial cultivation of the soil to the maximum as a perfect duty and the failure to do so the violation of a perfect right. Thus, dispossession and imposition of these institutions over their territories by colonisation is not considered a conquest, but the laying down of the preconditions of nationhood and economic development.

Anghie traces this economic development argument through the nineteenth century and its adoption by the new Third World states after decolonisation. As he mentions, this developmental scheme is a central feature of western political theory. It demarcates developing European-style sovereign states from 'lawless' undeveloped peoples with only 'provisional' rights in the 'state of nature' and thus in need of western law and commerce to establish the basis for competitive development, in the Kantian tradition, and the unjust yet necessary conditions of 'primitive accumulation' and development, in the Marxist tradition.[76] Anghie's careful scholarship complements the critical work on the history of development.[77]

The major point of Anghie's critical history is to throw light on the present moment in which Indigenous peoples are attempting to exercise their declared right of self-determination. On the one hand, Indigenous peoples are demanding a 'right to development', but, in many cases, to development understood in Indigenous ways of knowing and being, and thus a direct challenge to the developmental paradigm.[78] On the other hand, powerful states and multinational corporations are exercising a neo-liberal form of development that seeks to privatize their traditional territories and incorporate their right of self-determination within it.[79] Anghie's critical history helps us and Indigenous people to see the discursive field of development in which they are constrained to discuss and negotiate the exercise of internal self-determination. This kind of knowledge is indispensible if Indigenous peoples are to be prepared and able to enter into effective, nation-to-nation treaty negotiations over self-determination with states and corporations.[80] Like Anghie, I hope that it may lead to a situation 'in which Indigenous Peoples may engage meaningfully in protecting their own rights and determining their own future' (p. 95).[81]

David Scott

I am deeply indebted to the thoughtful and original scholarship of David Scott. His critical work on post-colonial theory and practice and on the relevance of western political theories to this work has been indispensable for my own research.[82] I am thus grateful for this opportunity to comment on his characteristically careful, thoughtful and insightful chapter on reparations for new world slavery.

I appreciate the careful way Scott explicates my dialogical approach so clearly and contrasts it with other contemporary approaches. In addition to its role in the chapter as a whole, this explication can be read as a conversational response to and corrective of Mendieta's discussion of similar themes. This introduction sets the stage for his critical and constructive analysis of Janna Thompson's book on reparation and historical injustice. I would like to comment briefly on two features of this important analysis. The first is his concluding observation that Thompson takes the standard monological stance of the theorist to the demands of African Americans, rather than a dialogical stance. While this stance enables her to generate a sophisticated theoretical language of reparations and insightful conceptual distinctions, it also tends to foreclose two types of critical reflection that a dialogical approach enables: calling into question the languages in which the problem of reparations is formulated and writing a history of them and the practices in which they are based. Why might these two types of reflection provide a deeper understanding of the problem she seeks to resolve with a theory of reparations?

This question is addressed in a second feature of Scott's argument. He points out that the language of description Thompson uses discloses the recipients of reparations as individuals. This may well be appropriate in some cases. However, he argues, this overlooks the possibility – and actuality – that African Americans, however they may be construed in the theoretical literature, understand themselves historically and in the present as members of a cultural community with a 'claim to a distinctive *political* identity based on *overcoming* that historical injury and injustice [of the denial of political personality]'. This lived experience of African Americans as a historical community and the appropriate language of self-understanding of it could be discovered by dialogues of reciprocal elucidation with the historical documents of African Americans in the new world and with African Americans in the present. If researchers do not engage in these two critical reflections, they run the risk of misrecognising the very people to whom they are trying to be just and, in this case, continuing the historical injustice of denying their claim to justice as a community, precisely what reparation and redistribution are supposed to address.[83]

Although I may not be a completely impartial judge, Scott's analysis seems to me to be a decisive argument for the value of a dialogical-genealogical approach, not only for African Americans, but for doing justice to the diversity of struggles over recognition and distribution. Moreover, his specific approach to African American struggles is urgently needed today. From the 1920s to the 1970s African American activists of all stripes made it difficult if not impossible to deny or ignore the African American community and the problems specific to it: such as racism, inequality, and high levels of incarceration, unemployment, and HIV. Yet, in *The Price of the Ticket*, Fredrick Harris argues that from the 1970s to the presidency of Barack Obama the problems and claims of African Americans as a community have been steadily marginalised and denied in a race-neutral politics.[84] I hope Scott's incisive chapter is part of a broader response to this urgent need.

Christian Emden

It is a great pleasure to read Christian Emden's masterful survey of the history and current debates over citizenship in nation states, the European Union and a real or imagined cosmopolis. As he points out, we are both educated in an approach that seeks to bring to bear on contemporary problems a careful analysis of their historical formation. I have benefited immensely from his outstanding scholarship on German intellectual history from Kant and Herder through Nietzsche to Arendt and Habermas. This remarkable chapter draws on that scholarship in order to throw critical light on the conditions and practices of citizenship and the competing theories of them. I have learned a great deal from his critical survey and I find myself in agreement with most of what he says. I would like to clarify one point and then address the two factors he asks me to consider.

I agree with the first section on the limits of cosmopolitanism and especially the conclusion that 'citizenship cannot be limited to the legal possession of certain rights and duties, but it must also be related to substantive political questions, from solidarity and belonging as contributing factors to social integration in constitutional democracy to actual participation in political discourse' (p. 126). As he points out, it is these 'substantive political questions' of solidarity, belonging and participation that I explore under the orientations of civil and civic citizenship throughout *PPNK*.

The principles of constitutionalism and democracy and civil and civic citizenship

I also agree with the second section on political citizenship and the European polity and the conclusion he draws in the last two paragraphs. He concludes that the processes of European integration should be seen as the 'interlocking' of the exercise of constitutional power through institutions and the rule of law on the one hand and practices of democratic participation on the other. Following Rawls and Habermas, I call these two processes constitutionalism (or the rule of law) and democracy (or popular sovereignty). The interlocking of these two processes is 'legitimate' if and only if the principles that legitimate each process are equiprimordial or equally basic in the co-articulation of the European Union by means of these two processes. I interpret the co-equality of these two meta-norms in the following way.[85]

The principle of constitutionalism (or the rule of law) requires that the exercise of political power in the whole and in every part of any *constitutionally* legitimate system of political, social and economic cooperation should be exercised in accordance with and through a general system of principles, formal and informal rules, norms and procedures, including procedures for amending any principle, rule or procedure. The 'constitution' in the narrow sense is the cluster of supreme or 'essential' principles, rules and procedures to which other laws, institutions and governing authorities within the association are subject. In the broader sense 'constitution' includes 'the rule of law' – the systems of laws, rules, norms, conventions and procedures which govern the actions of all those who are subject to them.

The principle of democracy (or popular sovereignty) requires that, although the people or peoples who comprise a political association are subject to the constitutional system, they, or their entrusted representatives, must also be participants in imposing the general system on themselves in order to be sovereign and free, and thus for the association to be *democratically* legitimate. The sovereign people or peoples participate in articulating and reforming a system of rules for and on themselves by means of having a say over the principles, rules and procedures through the exchange of public reasons in democratic practices of deliberation; either directly (in practices of participatory democracy) or indirectly through their representatives (insofar as they are trustworthy, accountable and revocable and the deliberations are public), usually in a piecemeal fashion by taking up and testing some subset of the principles, rules and procedures of the system. These democratic practices of direct and representative deliberation – of having a say and a hand – are themselves rule governed (to be constitutionally legitimate), but the rules must also be open to democratic amendment (to be democratically legitimate).

In summary, a modern political association is legitimate if and only if it is equally constitutional and democratic: that is, the combination of *constitutional* democracy and *democratic* constitutionalism.[86] I restate them here because they are central to Emden's discussion in this and the following sections.

Like many other scholars, I argue that these two principles are not co-equal in the processes of European integration. The principle of the rule of law is clearly prior to, weightier than, and often untested for its legitimacy by, the co-application of the principle of democracy. There is thus a 'democratic deficit' and the European people, including immigrants and refugees, are unfree to the extent that the deficit is not remedied.[87] Emden agrees with this thesis. He also points out that Habermas does not always treat these two principles as equally basic. He tends to position constitutional norms and institutions of the rule of law prior to and containers of democratic participation. Emden ends on the note that the ongoing 'conversation' between the demands of these two principles in practices inevitably involves conflict, 'and such conflict occasionally requires meditation, be it through law or through the coercive power of the state' (p. 132). I do not see this feature as a violation of equiprimordiality as long as the exercise of constitutional power (not necessarily coercive) and the resolution it establishes follow rule of law procedures and are subject to democratic monitoring and review.[88] Moreover, the threefold reflexive relationship he draws between practices of civil and civic engagement, the governmental policies of member states and the actions of the European legal and administrative order makes these principles more difficult to apply, but also more important to the legitimacy of integration processes.

However, after setting out the distinction between civil and civic citizenship at the beginning of the third section, Emden claims that I fall foul of the co-equality condition. He writes that my account of '[civic] citizenship is based on the premise that the normative claims of the rule of law are the context-dependent and ever preliminary outcome of practices of negotiation between different groups – to some extent reversing Habermas' position in that the primacy of norms is replaced by the primacy of substantive political practice' (p. 132). This is a misunderstanding, but one that is my fault. In *PPNK* II I did not clarify the relationship between the two principles of legitimacy in Chapter Four and the two modes of citizenship in Chapter Nine. I will do so now. As we have seen, civil and civic citizenship are two ways of disclosing the field of citizenship, acting in it and studying it. Civil and civic citizenship both appear in the field under the two norms: civil citizenship under constitutional democracy and civic citizenship under democratic constitutionalism.

The local and global organisations of civic citizenship are legitimate if and only if they embody in their organisation the two principles of rule of law and democracy in ways appropriate to their circumstances. They see the way these two norms are articulated and exercised in European-style nation states and the European Union as only one way among many of interpreting and applying these two general norms. And, as Emden points out and Antje Wiener has shown in detail, there is a wide plurality of ways in which these two principles are understood historically in Europe, in the member states and in the institutions of the European Union.[89] Once we see law and democracy from the much broader perspective of the civic tradition, we see that the legal and governmental pluralism within the official institutions of Europe is just one kind of pluralism within a global diversity of *nomoi* and *demoi*.[90] In many respects, the conditions of the co-equality of these two principles in grass-roots democracies are more demanding than the conditions standardly employed in the institutions of modern nation states.[91] Civic citizens learn how to apply the two principles in their own organisations. Over the last 200 years, they have frequently come to the official institutions of the nation state with this know-how, challenged the illegitimacy of the official institutions accordingly, and negotiated the great democratic reforms of them. In these ways, they not only coordinate the two principles in their own organisations, but work with reforming civil citizens to coordinate them in the institutions of the nation state. I hope this clarifies the relationship between the two principles and two traditions of citizenship.

The decline of participation in the official public sphere

The first factor Emden asks me to comment on is the decline of participation in European nation states since World War II and the four reasons he gives for this decline.[92] Emden focuses primarily on the decline of voting and from the state-centred and institutional perspective of the civil tradition from Weber to Habermas. A complementary genealogy of participation in European countries could be given from the practice-based perspective of the civic tradition from Kropotkin to Boaventura de Sousa Santos.[93] This would illuminate the complex phenomenon from the standpoint of the participants and thereby broaden and deepen our understanding of it.[94]

Such a genealogy would show how generations of European civic citizens organised practices of mobilisation and negotiation and struggled for representative governments, party systems, rights and institutions of assembly and participation, electoral reform, and robust social, economic and minority rights of self-government against powerful opposition interests, long before they had the rights or institutions to do so. Civil citizens could not join them in these uncivil and often illegal activities without ceasing to be civil citizens. However, they worked in solidarity from within the narrow official channels open to them to reform from within. These negotiations from within and without 'democratised' the institutions of European nation states. The institutions of a state are not legitimate in themselves. They can be structures of domination, as Emden notes. Institutions always enable certain forms of activity for certain people and disable others. For example, as Emden notes, the neo-liberal rights and institutions of 'market citizenship' enable and disable certain activities, while social, economic and minority rights enable and disable others. The civic and civil modes of active negotiation of the existing norms of inclusion and exclusion, recognition and non-recognition, and distribution and non-distribution bring the democratic principle to bear on them, co-articulating degrees of institutionalisation with degrees of democratisation.[95]

At some point in the post-war period generations came along that assumed they had successfully institutionalised their rights of participation and the social, economic and minority rights that enable their effective exercise. They thought that these institutions 'guaranteed' these rights. Hence, it was no longer necessary to fight for them or even to mobilise and exercise the ones they inherited. That is, these generations accepted the ascendency of the civil perspective that institutions are the preconditions and guarantee of democratic participation. The old struggles of civic citizenship for them were no longer seen as the living ground of their hard-won civic and civil freedoms, but as pre-civil means contingently related to the institutions they brought about. Next, the opponents of participatory representative democracy set about remodelling voting systems and downsizing rights of participation and the social, economic and minority rights that enable their exercise. This was complemented by the promotion of an image of the successful life as a life of consumption. Participation declined accordingly, and also for the reasons Emden mentions.

However, civic participation did not decline. New generations turned to and expanded significantly the traditional civic practices of citizenship that often provide the grass-roots of electoral participation: community-based organisations, cooperatives, unions, networks, human rights NGOs and new organisations 'without borders' to confront the growing global crisis of inequality, environmental destruction, immigration, racism, neo-imperial wars and climate change. However, these were not well coordinated with participation in and reform of official institutions and government policy.[96] The financial crisis of 2009 changed all this in ways no one predicted. In response, Europeans protested by means of traditional and new practices of civic and civic citizenship inside and outside European public spheres. The *indignados* in Portugal and Spain, the *beni comuni* (common goods) movement in Italy, the occupy movements in the north, and European-wide the protests movements against corruption and the neo-liberal austerity programmes revived old ways and invented new ways to participate.[97]

In short, what we see from this perspective is a complex history of struggle over every aspect of voting systems in the OECD countries for over a century. It is possible to re-learn two lessons from this civic perspective on the decline of official participation and the renewal of both civil and civic participation. The first is that participation in and reform of the official institutions of modern nation states on the one hand and participation in practices of civic citizenship around them on the other hand can be mutually supportive.[98] The second is the oldest civics lesson of all. Institutions do not guarantee democratic freedom. The only guarantee of democratic freedom is the practice of it. Organisation, mobilisation and exercise give rise to democratic institutions and rights, not the other way round (*usus* gives rise to *ius*, not *vice versa*).[99] Since Emden mentions Gandhi and Mandela with approval, I would add that they taught Indians and South Africans these two lessons by their exemplary conduct.[100]

Is robust democratic participation desirable and does it have limits?

The second factor Emden asks me to consider is whether or not robust democratic participation and struggles over rights of recognition and distribution are desirable? (p. 134). Well, it is not desirable for ordo-liberals who would like to reduce participation to elections, market citizenship and controlled labour mobility. And it is equally undesirable for the parties of the right that seek unilaterally to exclude immigrants and refugees, refuse to listen to the demands for recognition of various kinds of minorities, and draw lines of enmity rather than fraternity within Europe. I would argue that these two movements violate the two norms of legitimacy in different ways and harm public goods of the European Union and its member states.

In contrast, I argue that robust forms of civil and civic participation are desirable. Because one of the basic norms of both civil and civic participation is to take into account public goods and 'all affected', through processes of consultation (*audi alteram partem*), civil and civic participation is good for both those who participate and those who do not. I argue that these forms of participation create the 'civic solidarity' Habermas and others call for, even in cases when the participants do not win a particular struggle for recognition or distribution.[101] Moreover, the particular contribution of cooperative practices of civic citizenship is that they solve Humboldt's problem of the Bildung or character formation necessary for participation in complex societies.[102] As we have seen, practices of civic participation and the development of the corresponding forms of knowledge about public goods and the skills to present them in public and negotiate with others begin in everyday civic conversations, the daycare, school and neighbourhood.[103] As Emden nicely puts it, these practices could be called 'everyday Mandelaism'.

Finally, Emden asks if there are not 'limits to participatory struggles over recognition and distribution'. In the first place, demands for recognition and the reforms of rights (and powers that follow from them) are challenges to the existing institutionalised laws of recognition and distribution of the nation state to which they are addressed. These constitute the existing limits to recognition and distribution. Demands for recognition and distribution are claims that these limits are unjust, either on rule of law or democratic grounds. The civil and civic negotiations in which such demands are taken up, tested for their validity and accepted or rejected are the just means of testing the *de facto* limits to recognition and distribution. They are the democratic means of testing the legitimacy of institutions that purport to be legal and democratic. Of course, there are limits to how many a given state or non-state society can handle at any one time. However, there is no known limit to the number and kind that might be brought forward. Moreover, democratic societies should provide public support to marginalised citizens to formulate and bring forward demands. The reason for this is that political associations are always less than perfect. These negotiations are the most democratic and effective means humans have so far discovered for revealing and addressing imperfections, and, in so doing, integrating all affected in the reformed institutions. These negotiations generate what Rawls calls 'stability for the right reasons'. In contrast, the alternative of setting pre-emptive limits to demands for recognition and distribution is the real cause of destabilisation. It creates polarisation, conflict, lines of enmity, violence, and disintegration or balkanisation.[104]

In conclusion, this is a rather lengthy way of saying that I agree with Emden's conclusion to section three.[105] He ends the chapter with the following statement. 'Even the postnational world, then, remains rooted in the world of Westphalian states. Political citizenship is historically grounded – and so are the civic practices that go along with it' (p. 138). Yes, both civil and civic practices of citizenship in Europe are rooted or grounded in Westphalian states – as well as both older legal–political features these states incorporated and newer transnational feature they are constrained to accept. Yet, it is important not to over interpret 'grounded'. These Westphalian states would be unrecognizable to the Westphalians of 1648. Thus, we might say as well that the democratic *shape* of these Westphalian states is also grounded in the traditions of civic and civil participation.

Eunice Sahle

It is an enormous pleasure to comment on Eunice Sahle's chapter on the spaces of freedom and citizenship in and beyond the state in the context of globalization in South Africa and Bolivia. In her 2010 book, *World Orders, Development and Transformation*, she presents an outstanding analysis of globalisation as a continuation of informal imperialism. It is much more detailed than my earlier analysis in *PPNK*. Like my approach, she analyses globalisation from the perspective of the multiple spaces of freedom available within it and from which it can be criticised, democratised and transformed. Her chapter in *World Orders* on the World Social Forum is a synopsis of this critical perspective.[106] In her chapter for this volume, Sahle goes on to extend this freedom-oriented perspective to detailed analyses of TAC in South Africa and the Indigenous and popular movements (IPM) and the Movement towards Socialism (MAS) in Bolivia. In so doing, she also shows how her analysis of globalisation and of these diverse practices of freedom is complementary to my analysis of informal imperialism and practices of citizenisation (civil and civic citizenship).

I mention in the Introduction that I devote less time to the authors who present complementary studies of freedom and democracy in an imperial context. Sahle's chapter is clearly an instance of this. I am most grateful to her for showing how our two approaches complement each other and I have learned immensely from the dialogue she initiates between us. What strikes me the most is that the examples she presents include just about every type of civil and civic practice of freedom in 'On Local *and* Global Citizenship: an apprenticeship manual' (*PPNK* II.9): the five main types of civic citizenship in Section Four and the six types in Section Five. In addition, they manifest the central features of civic citizenship: praxis, diversity, participatory freedom, citizen–citizen and citizen–govern relationships, legal pluralism, civic goods, and nonviolence. Moreover, they illustrate in creative ways the important feature that I have been studying since *PPNK*. This is the ways in which progressive civil and civic citizens working within the official institutions of participation can join hands and work with civic citizens negotiating and acting otherwise outside the official institutions.[107] This is true of Sahle's analysis of TAC in South Africa and of IMP and MAS in Bolivia.

The case of IMP and MAS in Bolivia is of particular interest in regard to working together. It is illustrative of the creative strategies of civil and civic freedom in alliances under neo-liberal globalisation. Of course, as Arturo Escobar has argued, these kinds of alliances are characteristic of the renaissance of practices of freedom throughout Latin America that have resonated worldwide.[108] However, the IMP and MAS are distinctive. Evo Morales is the first Indigenous person to be elected (and re-elected) as President of a nation state in the Americas. Moreover, Morales came up through the local organisations of Aymara and Quechua peoples and popular movements against the privatisation of water resources by Bechtel in the 1990s. This is a world-historical disruption of 500 years of imperialism and it is seen in this revolutionary light throughout indigenous Americas.[109] The IMP is composed of alliances of Indigenous and non-Indigenous communities and activists working together across gender, race and class differences. The Indigenous Law Project has contributed to legal reforms and the recognition of legal pluralism. The MAS has used state power to begin the difficult task of re-appropriating public goods from privatisation under neo-liberal policies. It held a constituent assembly in 2007, which, as Sahle points out, was criticised by IPM, yet initiated significant constitutional change.

Furthermore, in 2008, President Morales gave his famous speech on the relationship between capitalist development and climate change, 'Save the Planet from Capitalism'. It was updated in 2010 in 'Capitalism is the Main Enemy of the Earth'. In both presentations, he argued that the commodification of the natural world under capitalism is the major cause of climate change and the ecological crisis. In contrast, he argued, as Indigenous peoples have for millennia, the earth is our mother. It does not belong to us, as private property, but, rather, we human beings belong to mother earth, as citizens in and of it, with collective responsibilities of care:[110]

> As long as we do not change the capitalist system for a system based on complementarity, solidarity, and harmony between the people and nature, the measures we adopt will be palliatives that will [be] limited in and precarious in character. For us, what has failed is the model of 'living better', of unlimited development, industrialization without frontiers, of modernity that deprecates history, of increasing accumulation of goods at the expense of others and nature. For that reason we promote the idea of Living Well, in harmony with other human beings and with nature.

The long-term goal of MAS is to bring about this transformation – by means of the multiplicity of strategies of freedom Sahle surveys. This is also the thesis of Gaia citizenship.[111] It is shared by many other activists and scholars. For example, John Bellamy Foster argues that it is at the heart of the deep ecology movement and it should be the ground of movements oriented to social and ecological justice.

And, he continues, transformative movements should draw on Marx's analysis of the human metabolic relation to nature, but also on such exemplary civic citizens as William Morris, Gandhi and Morales.[112]

In these and other ways Sahle's chapter provides concrete examples of how diverse practices of civil and civic freedom can work together in the context of neo-liberal globalisation to make significant changes. They do not look at all like the traditional modernist revolution that claims to go beyond capitalism. Nevertheless, they may be laying the groundwork here and now of another world of 'living well' that has the capacity to transform the injustices of the present in new ways.[113] I am deeply grateful to Sahle for pointing out these spaces and activities of what she calls the 'dialectics of freedom and domination'.

Aletta Norval

In her fascinating chapter Aletta Norval takes up the primary question in our conversation. How does an individual or group move from being a subject to becoming an agent with the motivation, disposition and abilities to begin to act otherwise in the diverse forms of civic practices that we have been discussing? As she poses it: 'Under what set of conditions do the possibility of, and the need for, acting otherwise arise? What resources are needed for acting otherwise? What role is played by imagination, by telling stories?' All our discussion of what happens once people engage in practices of civic citizenship would be radically incomplete if we did not address this prior question of self-transformation.

Becoming a civic citizen

Norval addresses the question of the steps involved in becoming a civic or diverse citizen through one concrete example: it is the autobiographical text *Begging to Be Black* written by Antjie Krog, a white South African woman. Krog discusses her own attempts to approach the possibility of acting otherwise. Norval carefully explicates the text in its own terms: in the language and techniques Krog uses to describe her own experiences and self-practices (events, narratives, dialogues, wrong paths, and so on). We see the text as exercises or attempts to approach, if not to achieve, the lived experience of another way of being in the world – *ubuntu* (interconnectedness).

At the same time, Norval humbly suggests that the reader might also compare and contrast Krog's ways of recounting her attempts at self-change to the concepts and techniques Norval herself has developed to try to explicate the lived experience of becoming and acting otherwise in diverse situations and practices of democratic citizenship (the role of exemplars, imagination, stories and so on). She draws on Nietzsche, Wittgenstein, Cavell, Derrida, Owen and others in developing these concepts and techniques. Yet, she has transformed them in order to address, in her unique way, this primary question of becoming an active citizen. They are set out and explained her ground-breaking text, *Aversive Democracy*.[114]

Thus, the chapter consists in the two exemplary ways of thinking about these processes of self-change of Krog and Norval in a dialogue of reciprocal elucidation, akin to the multiple dialogues in *Begging to Be Black*. It is important to bear in mind as well that Norval is also a white South African women who is also trying to come to terms and connection with the *ubuntu* way of being in the post-apartheid world – to find her feet in it. It is a masterpiece that speaks to us directly without any further commentary. I am tempted to just ask you to listen and hear what these two remarkable authors are saying to each other and to us. I am also tempted to say something in the way of paying tribute to such an exemplary way of addressing this crucial question. So, I will just comment briefly on two features of it as a way of approaching the possibility of entering into the dialogue with them. And bear in mind that I am a white male Canadian male trying to support and come to terms with the decolonization of Indigenous peoples, the dismantling of the Indian Act, truth and reconciliation commissions, and various attempts to act otherwise.

Dislocation, means, direction

Krog tells us that the initial step in this process is to move from a settled identity and sense of belonging to the condition of being unsettled or 'dislocated' from that mode of being. In her case, this consists in the means by which she moved from the self-assurance of the rightness of her testimony at the murder trial as a 'native white activist' to the dislocation that occurred when she read and reflected on the TRC records and realised her 'triple mistake' in her formerly self-assured testimony. It was in retrospect 'politically naïve, legally uninformed and morally wrong'. This experience of radical dislocation was brought out by her reflection on the 'various frameworks brought together by the amnesty hearing'. It was like 'looking at the same object through different lenses' (p. 179). The amnesty hearing, in the context of the broader experiences of the changes from apartheid to post-apartheid, moved her to not only notice the various perspectives and frameworks, but to see and understand the 'same object' from these different perspectives, thereby dislocating her from her former settled perspective as the horizon of her location in the world.

This initial step of dislocation as Krog describes it involves three processes of empathy: the imaginary movement or transposition of herself into the location of the others who see the same object differently; understanding the others as others to her and of her as an other to them; and the correlative ethical perception of self and others as moral persons. The other lenses, frameworks and stories have the effect of dislocation only if they are taken seriously as alternative ways of seeing and experiencing the same 'object'. Transformation in the way one hears and responds to the stories of others hinges on these three processes of perspective-taking and empathetic mutual understanding. They bring about the experience of 'dislocation' and 'expose a profound moral confusion'. If the person is deeply embedded in their own way of belonging, when they hear or read the other frameworks, they disregard, deny or denigrate these alternatives, or they include and subordinate them within the imperious horizon of their given identity. Krog gives examples of each of these monological responses by her fellow white South Africans. What combination of experiences and practices of freeing herself from her self-assured identity (participation in ANC, multiple dialogues, reading and writing, criticism and self-criticism, self-reflection and so on) came together to move her to be open and receptive to the other perspectives in this transformative way is probably impossible to determine.[115]

The next step Krog takes is to try to find a 'direction' for her striving towards another way of being and acting. As Norval points out by means of a contrast with Barack Obama's search for his identity in *Dreams of My Father*, this is not a search for another monological, foundational and authentic identity that simply replaces the earlier one. Krog is 'striving towards' another kind of identity and belonging altogether; one that is true to the diversity of irreconcilable perspectives she experienced in the first step. In this sense, the empathetic processes of perspective-taking involved in dislocation prefigure the 'direction' of her search for a way of being and acting otherwise in two ways. First, they prefigure the means by which she explores possibilities. The dialogues, narratives and stories through which she thinks writes and acts carry on the perspectival world that opened up to her in the processes of dislocation. I suggest, therefore, in response to Norval's question, that dialogues and stories are constitutive features of becoming able to act otherwise.

Second, Krog was fortunate to have before her another way of being and acting that embodies the difficult dialogical diversity and empathetic interconnectedness that she was thrown into in step one and carries on in her techniques of moving forward. This is the Indigenous African *ubuntu* mode of being in the world with others. *Ubuntu* is the basic ontological category of the Bantu-speaking peoples. It emerged in the 1970s in South Africa and became the ascendant post-apartheid and post-colonial pan-African worldview in the following decades. The prefix *ubu* stands for a mode of being or becoming and *ntu* for the person as the realization of *ubu*. The process of becoming a human being takes places in internal relationships of interdependency or inter-becoming with other human beings. In the IsiZulu phrase, *umuntu umuntu ngabantu*, a person becomes a person through, by and with other persons. The very possibility of becoming a person at all is to be in community relationships with others, and, as Norval notes, this is a dynamic and ongoing process of 'striving towards' or 'becoming-with'; not an end-state. *Ubuntu* is seen as a way of being equal in status to western modernity and superior to it in practice; a way of freeing Africa from the imperial stages of historical development horizon in which it is placed in modernist narratives and policies.[116] Moreover, Krog has three exemplary human beings who embody this dialogical, diverse and interdependent way of becoming in the world with others: the Basotho leader Moshoeshoe, Nelson Mandela and Bishop Tutu. Indeed, she highlights the way Moshoeshoe lives and acts in an interconnected pluriverse, rather than a western universe, and negotiates the diverse perspectives of his interdependent partners.

A second dislocation and transformation

I think that finding one's feet in *ubuntu* for Krog, and for settlers more generally, presents an even greater challenge and dislocation than the first dislocation. If I am beginning to understand *ubuntu* partially, then it discloses underneath the empathetic recognition of others as moral persons with differing perspectives an even more basic dimension of being human. The ground of our becoming persons is interdependent relationships of mutual concern, care and well-being in, by and through which we co-develop, co-determine and co-operate together. The well-being of each is dependent on the well-being of all. Compassion (the rational and emotional disposition to sense and care for self and others together), often translated as solidarity, therefore, is even more basic than empathy for our reciprocal distinctiveness, and the ground of it. Conflict, when it arises, does so as a deviation from this background. Justice consists in reconciling and re-embedding the parties involved into the background social relationships of interdependency.[117]

Ubuntu presents a radical challenge even to settlers who have gone through the first dislocation and realise that the other is the bearer of another mode of being in the world – *ubuntu* – and are trying to understand it. The colonial settlers in Africa (and elsewhere) brought with them a system of property, economics and politics in which individuals, classes, races and states are taken to be independent of one another and in competitive struggles for existence and development with higher and lower types. Thus, the basis of cooperation has to be coercively imposed to control the competition and begin the cultivation of sociability, empathy and finally compassion at the highest stage of development, against the underlying grain of independence and antagonism. But, any such imposition is part of the competition and conflict, not above it, and so the cycles of violence continue, through the scramble for Africa, decolonization and beyond. To try to free oneself from this modern western mode of being and move around to see the world from the perspective of *ubuntu* is to see the underlying injustice of colonisation: the imposition of an independent and competitive way of life over an interdependent and cooperative one, and the near destruction and assimilation of the latter. This is an injustice that post-Apartheid South Africa or any other post-colonial country has yet to address.[118] Krog has the astonishing courage to see the situation in this light and thus the need to strive towards *ubuntu*. She says she is drawn to *ubuntu* and its three exemplars because it is 'a different way of dealing with injustice so that it becomes possible for a country to break out of its cycles of violence' (p. 183).

Yet, she wrestles with another factor throughout the text that seems to block the way forward through this second dislocation. This is the factor of 'blackness'. On my provisional interpretation, from the outside and from my experience of struggling with Indigenity here, Krog is struggling with the idea that any route to *ubuntu* is through blackness: that is, one has to '*be* black' to become *ubuntu*. But being accepted by blacks as one of them would seem to require, given the history, some kind of supplication or 'servility' (as Norval puts it); a practice of 'begging' for acceptance, and thus, a reversal of the master–servant relationship rather than transcending it. From this 'perspective', blackness is seen as a continuation of the African positive nativism that helped to give Africans the solidarity and empowerment to free themselves from the inferiority–superiority complex of colonialism and struggle for independence; yet which often has been used in oppressive ways in post-colonial Africa.

On the other hand, if one fails to take blackness seriously and simply tries to bypass the fact that *ubuntu* is an Indigenous creation, then *ubuntu* for white South Africans becomes little more than a kind of 'thin' diversity 'beyond blackness'. Indeed, it becomes a dissimulative way of appearing to go through the first processes of empathic transformation in order to appropriate *ubuntu* and then criticise Indigenous Africans for a 'too thick' attachment to their blackness to respect the diversity of their white partners. They bypass the second and deeper dislocation altogether. The master–servant relationship remains in place, but with a new post-colonial patina. This is the new face of post-colonial imperialism. It is important to see that this is what Krog warns us about in her discussion of Moshoeshoe. He was a master of negotiating with others in the relationships of interdependency and diversity of *ubuntu*. Yet, as Krog and Norval point out, the imperialists, with their monological and competitive mode of being, were able to manipulate the negotiations, dispossess him of the land of his people and impose the property, economic and political institutions of another way of life. When the World Bank, multinational corporations and the state-owned enterprises of China dress their policies in the language of *ubuntu* today, we see this process of dispossession and assimilation taking place in front of our eyes, and not only in Africa.

I would like to suggest that Krog is struggling to find a way towards *ubuntu* that avoids the dead end of begging to be black and refuses the neo-colonialism finesse of the Indigenous bringing into being and carrying on of *ubuntu*. This would be some way of becoming interconnected that would pay the appropriate recognition and respect to the central place of blackness in *ubuntu*, yet would also enable her to 'inhabit *ubuntu* differently', to use David Scott's phrase; a way that black African partners could reciprocally endorse from their perspectives. Steven Biko, Tutu and Mandela are exemplars of blacks who reach out to join hands with white South Africans as interdependent partners from within a black *ubuntu* way of interacting. In so doing, they offer Krog a way forward that is neither servile nor non-transformative and to which she is manifestly drawn. But, the actual way can be imagined or known only by going through the embodied *praxis* of striving towards interconnection in a respectful way, and testing and revising that way in dialogues with diverse and interdependent others, as Krog and Norval argue. This is not the achievement of *being* interconnected but the proto-*ubuntu* way of 'striving towards' becoming interconnected we have seen in each step. And, as the exemplars show in their lives, and the morphology of *ubuntu* indicates, the *way* is constitutive of the end.

Norval's anti-imperial method

In her dialogues with Paul Patton, Krog raises objections to the way westerners approach Africa in order to understand it. I would like to suggest that Norval's method is a response to her objections. Bear in mind in what follows that Paul Patton, in addition to being a scholar of Foucault and Deleuze, is also a white male Australian, working with Aboriginal Australians and Torres Strait Islanders to find a way to act otherwise in his decolonizing context.

When Krog tries to explain her understanding of *ubuntu* to Patton he replies that there are western philosophies of interconnectedness as well. Krog replies that this is the standard imperious western response. Whatever the other says has already been said by the west and thus the west presumes it can understand African *ubuntu* through the lens of western philosophy. But this is precisely the monological stance that forecloses understanding of the other. As Boaventura de Sousa Santos puts this point, there is no global understanding and justice without epistemic justice: without understanding the other's ways of being and knowing. Patton responds with the accusation of exceptionalism. He then says that the way to come to an understanding is through a 'two-way dialogue'. 'When a non-African tries to understand an African he or she needs *equipment* to cross the boundaries between different cultures'. And he ends with a reference to the intermixing of African and non-African civilizations over time. Krog responds, 'you don't hear us through our own voice. You keep on hearing us only through your voice'.

Norval comments that Krog's objection is that this evocation of a two-way dialogue fails to see the difficulty of genuine cross-civilization dialogue and understanding. To enter into such a dialogue one must become dislocated from one's embodied self-understanding in a deeper sense than Patton seems to realize. He sounds to Krog like he does not fully appreciate the two dislocative transformations she strives to articulate. The 'equipment' he brings with him is the familiar western philosophies of interdependency and the path to understanding is already laid down by the diaspora of Africans in the west and *vice versa*. So the imperial imposition of western ways of knowing continue even in the context of a two-way dialogue. Whether or not this is how Patton meant his comment to be taken, it is certainly a common form of dialogical approaches today.[119]

The method Norval employs presents a radically different mode of two-way dialogue. She lets Krog speak in her own terms and ways, just as Krog lets her interlocutors speak in her text. She then presents her western 'equipment' for understanding self-transformation and acting aversively alongside Krog's as an object of comparison and contrast. It is not a framework or lens in which the text is translated and (mis)understood, but another and perhaps more familiar way of understanding becoming and acting otherwise laid quietly alongside Krog's. Comparing and contrasting Krog's explication with Norval's equipment enables readers to see similarities and dissimilarities and thus to move closer to understanding Krog in her own terms – just as Krog's dialogues over *ubuntu* help us to begin to understand it. Norval's equipment functions as an intermediate case – a stepping stone used to dislocate ourselves from our familiar ways of understanding and open ourselves to moving around (and being moved around) to Krog's perspective on the processes of becoming otherwise and *ubuntu*, by the force of her exemplary text.

This dialogical method is derived from the late Wittgenstein. The way Norval adapts and employs it works to de-imperialise western ways of knowing and open them to the possibility of a post-imperial two-way dialogue. But, as Krog stresses in her responses to Patton, this dialogue is not a philosophical dialogue. The difficult dislocations and transformations on the way to *ubuntu* are not concepts or philosophies. They are embodied practices with others in, by and through which light dawns slowly over the whole. Exemplary texts like Krog's and Norval's remarkable chapter can move us in this direction to some extent, but the next step is to interact and interconnect together.[120]

Val Napoleon and Hadley Friedland

I have learned more from Val Napoleon and Hadley Friedland than I can express in a brief comment on their characteristically generous and enlightening chapter. Indeed, many of my ways of thinking about situated practices of civic agency derive from reflections on their tireless work in Indigenous communities and in the academic world of law. One of their most inspiring projects is to help Indigenous peoples revive and refashion their normative orders of law and governance so they exercise powers of self-determination and deal with their own problems in their own ways. Their revolutionary Indigenous Law Clinic at the University of Victoria is the first of its kind in Canada.

As they mention, I responded to an earlier version of this chapter and they incorporated parts of it into this final version. Thus, I will just add a few comments on this outstanding work of engaged research and public philosophy in the best possible sense. The two questions they raise are the same kind of primary questions as Norval raises in her chapter. (1) How do humans who in situations where they cannot even imagine being active citizens of the world they inhabit become everyday and everywhere citizens? And, (2) how can they connect with others in similar situations or in positions to help? They address these questions in relation to four situations or vignettes and develop their answers in response to them and to relevant academic literature.

Practices of becoming everyday citizens

In response to the first question they say the turning point 'begins with the woman working as a sex worker understanding that she and other women matter. Their suffering and their lives matter. It also begins with an inmate understanding that he and all the others matter' (p. 208). I agree, and particularly with their point that such a transformational turn can take place in silence. What happens in the space of silence is not only that she realises that her life matters to her and others, but that she has found a relationship of 'inner peace' with herself (p. 208). In addition to the unpredictable experiences that often initiate or augment the turn, I am familiar with two ways that this peaceful relationship with oneself can be brought about. The first is through practices of radical narrative therapy, usually with helpful and exemplary others, through which one frees oneself from a violent, abusive, worthless, or disempowering self-narrative such as 'I am a throwaway' or oppressive others are 'overpowering'. Then, positively, practices through which one acquires a peaceful, non-judgmental relationship to oneself as the basis of an empowering self-narrative.[121] A second way in which a peaceful relationship to oneself can be acquired is through meditation practices. In these mindfulness practices one lets go of the narrative self altogether and becomes aware of and experiences the non-judgmental, embodied, sensual immediate self in the here and now. One 'comes to one's senses' and so with one's connections to others and the world. In Indigenous versions of these practices, the practitioners overcome alienation and become attuned to deeper, spiritual relations of interconnectedness with mother earth.[122] These meditative practices of awareness of one's being in the world often combine western psychology and cognitive science with eastern meditation traditions.[123]

In both practices of turning away and turning inward the person takes up a nonviolent, non-judgmental and compassionate relationship to her or himself. One becomes a civic citizen of oneself: being concerned for and taking care of oneself as a person who matters. The care of oneself is, as Amy Allen puts it in agreement with Foucault, the 'politics of our selves'.[124] As I argue in my response to Vázquez-Arroyo, this kind of practice is the first practice of five types of practice of civic citizenship and the ground of them. Letting go of the negative relationships of self-loathing, enmity, violence and worthlessness, making peace within and cultivating self-compassion is 'one of the noblest endeavors you can pursue – for yourself, for others, for the world'.[125] For all the reasons that Laden gives, this relationship cannot be a relationship of self-mastery, for this simply lays the groundwork for the master–servant relationships of command and obedience that dominate contemporary institutions. It has to be a peaceful dialogical relationship of non-harm and compassion; what Laden calls a relationship of connection. This kind of relationship of civic freedom with oneself goes hand-in-hand with the relationships one enacts and negotiates with others.[126]

In their response to the second question Napoleon and Friedland discuss and reject conservative and liberal responses to how health service professionals and others can help people in any of the four situations. In addition, the three types of response they mention from *PPNK* I are clearly insufficient. They draw on the broader survey of practices in *PPNK* II and introduce more of their own. In particular, the development of local, small-scale relationships of mutual assistance among the members of a group and with professional and non-professional helpers seems to me to be among the most important. These close relationships are replications of peaceful and compassionate self-relationships, and they are already involved in practices of narrative therapy and meditation when these practices are carried out with others. They in turn prefigure the relationships of connection one group works to form with others. The discussion of creating interconnectedness through dialogues, stories and interdependent practices of collective action in Norval's chapter is a rich exploration this field of acting otherwise together in widening circles of interconnection.

These types of relationship are what I call citizen–citizen relationships of self-organisation and self-government. They are the basic form of collective civic action: the grass roots out of which healthy representative relationships of citizen–governor relationships grow. Accordingly, the only change I would dare suggest to this incisive and insightful chapter is a slight amendment to the concluding sentence. 'The heart of civic citizenship is about transforming citizen/governance relationships' by means of citizen–citizen relationships with one self and others.

I would like to thank Napoleon and Friedland and all the contributors for commenting on my work, offering constructive criticisms, applying it in ways I never imagined, and showing me its strengths and weaknesses in different contexts and from different perspectives. I am also profoundly grateful to Nichols and Singh who, more than a decade ago, invited me to an ongoing, challenging, transformative dialogue on freedom, democracy and imperialism out of which the very possibility of this volume came to light. This is the kind of critical dialogue that public philosophy aims to promote, especially one that brings public philosophy into the space of questions, shows its usefulness to others, interrogates its limits, and suggests possible ways forward.

Notes

1. See James Tully, *Public Philosophy in a New Key*, vol. I, ch. 1 for this method. Hereafter cited in text as *PPNK*.
2. See *PPNK* II, c.9 and Tully, 'Afterword', in David Owen, ed. *On Global Citizenship* (London: Bloomsbury, 2013).
3. See *PPNK* I, c.9; Anthony Laden, *Reasoning: A Social Picture* (Oxford: Oxford University Press, 2012), and Laden, 'Civic Reasoning: A Democratic Perspective', in Owen, ed. *On Global Citizenship*.
4. See PPNK I, c.4–9.
5. See Tully, 'Dialogue,' *Political Theory*, 39, 1 (February 2011), 145–60.
6. *PPNK* II, c.9, pp. 290–2.
7. Hannah Arendt, *On Violence* (New York: Harcourt, 1970).
8. See *PPNK* II, c.9, pp. 249–56, and my response to Eduardo Mendieta.
9. See *PPNK* I, c.3 and *PPNK* II, c.4.
10. *PPNK* II, c.9, pp. 266–7, 300, and James Tully, 'The Crisis of Global Citizenship', *Radical Politics Today* (July 2009) http://www.spaceofdemocracy.org.
11. See *PPNK* II, c.5, 7 and 9, and my response to Vázquez-Arroyo.
12. This is far from the anti-legalism and anti-institutionalism that Mendieta attributes to the civic tradition. See the civic account of law and institutions in *PPNK* II, pp. 281–90 and my response to Vázquez-Arroyo and Emden.
13. See James Tully, 'Rethinking Human Rights and the Enlightenment: A View from the Twenty-first Century,' in Kate E. Tunstall, ed., *Self-Evident Truths? Human Rights and the Enlightenment* (London: Bloomsbury, 2012), pp. 3–34.

14 *PPNK* II, c.9, pp. 269–81. I discuss civil and civic understandings of the public sphere in more detail in 'On the Multiplicity of Global Public Spheres', in Christian Emden and David Midgley, eds., *Beyond Habermas: Democracy, Knowledge and the Public Sphere* (New York: Berghahn Books, 2012).
15 *PPNK* II, c.9, pp. 300-309, and James Tully, 'Two Ways of Realizing Justice and Democracy: Linking Amartya Sen and Elinor Ostrom,' *Critical Review of International Social and Political Philosophy*, (Autumn 2013).
16 *PPNK* I, c.3. See, for example, Amy Allen, *The Politics of Our Selves: Power, Autonomy and Gender in Contemporary Critical Theory* (New York: Columbia University Press, 2007).
17 Michel Foucault, 'What is Enlightenment?' in *Ethics, Subjectivity and Truth: Essential Works of Foucault, Vol. I*, ed. Paul Rabinow (New York: New Press, 1997), pp. 303–28. For my understanding of Foucault and freedom I am deeply indebted to Robert Nichols' forthcoming book, *Freedom and Historical Ontology in Heidegger and Foucault*.
18 See *PPNK* II, c.5–9 and the chapters by Anghie and Scott in this volume. I fail to see how these institutions and processes can 'domesticate' the violence of imperialism, as Mendieta suggests, when they are the major cause of it.
19 His argument that the basic institutions and processes of western modernization are beyond question and require only interpretation and further development dates from the period of the theory of communicative action. See *PPNK* I, c.2–3.
20 Jürgen Habermas, *Between Facts and Norms: Contributions to a Discourse Theory of Law and Democracy*, trans. William Rehg (Cambridge: MIT Press, 1996) and Habermas, *The Divided West*, trans. Ciaran Cronin (Cambridge: Polity Press, 2006). I have discussed these texts in Tully, 'On the Multiplicity of Global Public Spheres'.
21 The hierarchy of competencies and systems of knowledge is characteristic of the civil tradition while the comparative approach is characteristic of the civic tradition. See *PPNK* II. c.5 and 9.
22 Michel Foucault, 'The Subject and Power' in *Power: The Essential Works of Michel Foucault, Vol. III*, ed. James Baubion (New York: New Press, 1994), pp. 326–48 at 342–6,
23 Michel Foucault, *The Government of Self and Others*, ed. Frederic Gros, tr. Graham Burchell (New York: Palgrave Macmillan, 2008).
24 *PPNK* II, c.9, pp. 293–300.
25 See James Tully, 'Citizenship for the Love of the World', *The Conference on Challenging Citizenship*, CES, University of Coimbra, Coimbra, Portugal, 3–5 June 2011, and my response to Emden in this volume.
26 *PPNK* I, c.1.
27 See Jennifer Pitts, 'Political Theory of Empire and Imperialism', *Annual Review of Political Science*, 13 (2010): 211–35.
28 For a critical survey of these trends to which I am deeply indebted, see Jakeet Singh, *Beyond Free and Equal: Subalternity and the Limits of Liberal-Democracy* (PhD Dissertation, Department of Political Science, University of Toronto, 2012).
29 See *PPNK* I, c.1, and James Tully, 'Deparochializing Political Theory: The Dialogue and Interbeing Approach', *The Conference on Deparochializing Political Theory*, University of Victoria, Victoria, B.C., 2–4 August 2012.
30 For this conception of the 'field', see *PPNK* II, c.9, pp. 243–6.
31 *PPNK* I, c.8–10. Vázquez-Arroyo does not refer to the Introduction.
32 The phrase 'violent critical' tradition is simply meant to capture the ideas that violence and enmity are necessary features of politics and that the use of them by active citizens should be guided by a critical theory of capitalism, the state and power, such as those put forward by the theorists Vázquez-Arroyo cites.
33 One important overlapping continuity is the shared conception of freedom as

practices of 'association in which the free development of each is the condition for the free development of all', yet interpreted and enacted in different ways from Marx and William Morris to Fanon and Gandhi. See, Karl Marx and Frederick Engels, *The Communist Manifesto* (Oxford: Oxford University Press, 2002), p. 26.

34 *PPNK* II, c.5, 7, 9, and Robert Young, *Postcolonialism: An Historical Introduction* (Oxford: Basil Blackwell, 2001).

35 David Scott, *Conscripts of Modernity: The Tragedy of Colonial Enlightenment* (Durham: Duke University Press, 2004); David Scott, 'Norms of Self-Determination: Thinking Sovereignty Through', *Middle East Law and Governance*, Special Issue (Fall 2012): 2–30; Balakrishnan Rajagopal, *International Law from Below: Development, Social Movements and Third World Resistance* (Cambridge: Cambridge University Press, 2003); Vijay Prashad, *The Darker Nations* (New York: The New Press, 2009).

36 Informal imperialism is also called neo-colonialism and imperialism without colonies.

37 *PPNK* II, c.5, 6, 7, 9, and James Tully, 'Lineages of Contemporary Imperialism', in Duncan Kelly, ed. *Lineages of Empire: The Historical Roots of British Imperial Thought* (Oxford: Oxford University Press, 2009), pp. 3–30.

38 Kwane Nkrumah, *Neo-colonialism, the Last Stage of Capitalism* (London: Nelson, 1965).

39 *PPNK* II, c.5–7.

40 *PPNK* II, c.9, pp. 276–9, 300.

41 *PPNK* II, c.3, 4, 9, pp. 296–300, and see my response to Emden.

42 For the difficulty of taking this revolutionary turn to situated agency in disciplines defined by the old institutional and pre-conditions premises, see Hans Joas, *The Creativity of Action* (Chicago: Chicago University Press, 1996) and David Hoy, *Critical Resistance: From Post-structuralism to Post-critique* (Cambridge: MIT Press, 2004).

43 In addition to *PPNK* II, c.3, 4, 9, see Tully, 'Two Ways of Realizing Justice and Democracy'. This is the world Howard Zinn explored.

44 See Marx and Engel's judgment of other progressive movements in the *Communist Manifesto*, pp. 34–7. The theory of primitive accumulation is in Karl Marx, *Capital, Vol I* (London: Penguin, 1990), pp. 873–942. As I mention below, Karl Polanyi, *The Great Transformation: The Political and Economic Origins of Our Time* (Boston: Beacon Press, 2004), ch. 6, give the civic tradition a way of addressing the commodification of labour and nature directly. See Tully, 'Two Ways of Realizing Justice and Democracy'.

45 This is Marx's and Engel's formulation of a relational view of individual and collective freedom. See note 34.

46 See John Restakis, *Humanizing the Economy: Co-operatives in the Age of Capital* (Gabriola: New Society Publishers, 2010); Tully, 'Two Ways of Realizing Justice and Democracy'.

47 Boaventura de Sousa Santos, *The Rise of the Global Left: The World Social Forum and Beyond* (London: Zed Books, 2006).

48 Mahatma Gandhi, *The Essential Writings*, ed. Judith M. Brown (Oxford: Oxford University Press, 2008), p. 58. See Tully, 'Afterword,' *On Global Citizenship*.

49 Arendt, *On Violence*, 1970, pp. 4–10. Perhaps the most influential restatement of these arguments is Jonathan Schell, *The Fate of the Earth* (New York: Knopf, 1982). For a more recent restatement of some of Arendt's arguments, see Chalmers Johnson, *Nemesis: The Last Days of the American Republic* (New York: Henry Holt, 2006).

50 See Mark Kurlansky, *Nonviolence* (New York: Modern Library, 2006), pp. 57–109. For a remarkable argument on these lines, see Friedrich Nietzsche, 'The Means to Real Peace', in *Human All Too Human,* tr. R.J. Hollingdale (Cambridge: Cambridge University Press, 1986), #284, pp. 380–1. He analyses the security dilemma and then calls for unilateral disarmament and the overcoming of fear and hatred of others and of making oneself hated and feared. In the later Gay Science he expands on how to

overcome violence and treat the other with love. Friedrich Nietzsche, *The Gay Science* (Cambridge: Cambridge University Press, 2001), #337, pp. 190–1.
51 William James, 'The Moral Equivalent of War', *McClure's Magazine*, 35 (1910): 463–8. See Gregg and Horsburgh at note 59 for direct responses to James.
52 Michael Randle, *Civil Resistance* (London: Fontana, 1993).
53 Malcolm X gave this famous speech after his return from Mecca and just before he was murdered: Malcolm X, 'Bloodless Revolution', is readily available on Youtube. See, 'The African Sojourner', The Life of Malcolm X, The Malcolm X Project at Columbia University, http://www.edu/cu/ccbh/mxp/africa.html.
54 *PPNK* II, c.9, pp. 294–5.
55 The following subsection is drawn from Tully, 'Response', in David Owen, ed., *On Global Citizenship*.
56 Gene Sharp, *The Politics of Nonviolent Action* (Boston: Porter Sargent, 1973); *Waging Nonviolent Struggle* (Boston: Porter Sargent, 2005); *From Dictatorship to Democracy*, 4th edn (Boston: Albert Einstein Institute, 2010).
57 Brian Martin, *Nonviolence versus Capitalism* (London: War Resisters International, 2001).
58 Erica Chenoweth and Maria J. Stephan, *Why Civil Resistance Works: The Strategic Logic of Nonviolent Conflict* (New York: Columbia University Press, 2011). They examine 323 violent and nonviolent cases. More than 100 cases are nonviolent and roughly three-quarters of these (83 or so) are ranked as partial success or success (pp. 9–11).
59 Richard Gregg, *The Power of Nonviolence* (New York: Schocken Books, 1966); H.J.N. Horsburgh, *Non-Violence and Aggression: A Study of Gandhi's Moral Equivalent of War* (Oxford: Oxford University Press, 1968); Joan Bondurant, *The Conquest of Violence* (Princeton, NJ: Princeton University Press, 1988); Jonathan Schell, *The Unconquerable World: Power, Nonviolence and the Will of the People* (New York: Henry Holt and Co, 2003); Dalai Lama, *Beyond Religion: Ethics for a Whole World* (Toronto: McClelland Stewart, 2011); Thich Nhat Hahn, *Peace is Every Step* (New York: Bantam, 1992); Maria J. Stephan, ed., *Civilian Jihad: Nonviolent Struggle, Democratization and Governance in the Middle East* (New York: Palgrave Macmillan, 2009); Dustin Ellis Howes, *Toward a Credible Pacifism* (Albany: SUNY Press, 2009).
60 See references at note 59 and my response to Napoleon and Friedland.
61 Michel Foucault, *The Hermeneutics of the Subject*, ed. Frederic Gros, tr. Graham Burchell (New York: Picador, 2005), p. 252. For more detail, see Michel Foucault, 'The Ethics of the Concern for Self as a Practice of Freedom', in *Ethics: The Essential Works of Michel Foucault*, pp. 281–302. In a manner somewhat similar to Arendt, Foucault came to conceptualise power independent of and in contrast to violence and force from 1979 to his death in 1984 (see Foucault, 'The Subject and Power', pp. 326–48 at 340–1). I discuss nonviolent practices of the self further in my response to Norval and Napoleon and Friedland.
62 For one approach to this, see Bill Moyer, *Doing Democracy: The MAP Model for Organising Social Movements* (Gabriola Island BC: New Society Publications, 2001).
63 See Anthony Laden, 'Learning to be Equal: Just Schools and Schools of Justice', *Democracy, Education and Justice*, ed. Danielle Allen and Robert Reich (Chicago: University of Chicago Press, 2012). For this broad and deep sense of dialogical human relationships, see Jeffrey Stout, *Democracy and Tradition* (Princeton: Princeton University Press, 2004). For my capacious conception of verbal and non-verbal practices of dialogue, see James Tully, 'Deparochializing Political Theory'.
64 See Gregg, *The Power of Nonviolence*, for the classic presentation of the phenomenological analysis of the transformative jiu-jitsu logic on nonviolence. Gregg studied with Gandhi and then brought this analysis to North America and it was adopted by Martin Luther King Junior. For an excellent example of training in martial arts as a

preparation for and manifestation of peaceful social relationships, see *Thousand Waves Martial Arts and Self-Defense Center*, Chicago, IL, http://www.thousandwaves.org.

65 For the prototype of enmity, violence and counter-violence, see Vázquez-Arroyo's comments on Étienne Balibar.

66 See Étienne de la Boétie, *Discourse on Voluntary Servitude*, tr. James B. Atkinson and David Sices (Indianapolis/Cambridge: Hackett Publishing Co, 2012).

67 For an excellent analysis of the synergy of nonviolent agonistics and community based organizations, see Mary Elizabeth King, *A Quiet Revolution: The Palestinian Intifada and Nonviolent Resistance* (New York: Nation Books, 2007), and Mary Elizabeth King, 'Palestinian Civil Resistance against Israeli Military Occupation' in Maria J. Stephan, ed., *Civilian Jihad*, pp. 131–56. For similar findings in the nonviolent Egyptian revolution, see Tully, 'Legal and Governmental Pluralism: A View from the Demos', *Middle East Law and Governance*, Special Edition (Fall 2012), pp. 31–60.

68 See Peter Ackerman and Jack DuVall, *A Force more Powerful: A Century of Non-Violent Conflict* (London: Palgrave Macmillan, 2001), Chenoweth and Stephan, *Why Civil Resistance Works*, Sharp, *Politics of Nonviolent Action*, and Randle, *Civil Resistance*.

69 For this analysis, see H.J.N. Horsburgh, 'The Distinctiveness of Satyagrah,' *Philosophy East and West*, 19, 2 (April 1969): 171–80; Gregg, *Power of Nonviolence*, pp. 52–66; and Gandhi, *Non-violent Resistance*.

70 See Karuna Mantena, '"Another Realism": The Politics of Gandhian Nonviolence,' *American Political Science Review*, 106, 2 (May 2012): 455–70.

71 Bonnie Honig and Marc Stears, 'The New Realism: From Modus Vivendi to Justice', in Jonathan Floyd and Marc Stears, eds, *History versus Political Philosophy* (Cambridge: Cambridge University Press, 2011).

72 *PPNK* I, c.8. For an outstanding study of the role of violence, see Ned Blackhawk, *Violence over the Land: Indians and Empires in the Early American West* (Cambridge: Harvard University Press, 2006).

73 See also my response to Vázquez-Arroyo.

74 See Randle, *Civil Resistance* and Ackerman and Duvall, *A Force More Powerful*.

75 Antony Anghie, *Imperialism, Sovereignty and the Making of International Law* (Cambridge: Cambridge University Press, 2005).

76 Immanuel Kant, *Metaphysics of Morals*, tr. Mary Gregor (Cambridge: Cambridge University Press, 1991), ##14–16, 41–2, 43–4, 61, and Marx, *Capital*, pp. 873–942.

77 The classic text is Gilbert Rist, *The History of Development: from Western Origins to Global Faith*, tr. Patrick Camiller (London: Zed Books, 1997).

78 See, for example, Taiaiake Alfred, *Wasase: Indigenous Pathways of Action and Freedom* (Peterborough ON: Broadview, 2005).

79 Boaventura de Sousa Santos and César A Rodiquez-Garavito, eds, *Law and Globalization from Below* (Cambridge: Cambridge University Press, 2006).

80 They can also learn important lessons from the history of treaty negotiations and from the failure of Third World negotiations over self-determination and the New International Economic Order in 1974.

81 See also the discussion of Indigenous peoples in Bolivia in Sahle's chapter and my response.

82 David Scott, *Refashioning Futures: Criticism after Postcoloniality* (Princeton: Princeton University Press, 1999) and Scott, *Conscripts of Modernity*.

83 For more on this theme, see David Scott, 'Two Traditions of Historical Others,' *Symposia on Gender, Race and Philosophy*, 8, 1 (Winter 2012), http://web.mit.edu/sgrp.

84 Fredrick Harris, *The Price of the Ticket: Barack Obama and the Rise and Decline of Black Politics* (Oxford: Oxford University Press, 2012).

85 The following two paragraphs are drawn from an updated version of 'The Unfreedom of the Moderns', *PPNK* II, c.4. See Mike Simpson and James Tully, 'The Unfreedom

of the Moderns in the post-9/11 Age of Constitutionalism and Imperialism', *Federalism, Plurinationality and Democratic Constitutionalism*, eds, Ferran Requejo and Miquel Caminal (London: Routledge, 2012), pp. 51–84.
86 In *PPNK* II, c.4, I go on to discuss six conditions of contemporary societies that make it challenging to apply these norms in practice.
87 *PPNK* II, c.4 and 8.
88 *PPNK* I, c.5.
89 Antje Wiener, *The Invisible Constitution of Politics: Contested Norms and International Encounters* (Cambridge: Cambridge University Press, 2008).
90 See Tully, 'On Legal and Governmental Pluralism'.
91 In *PPNK* II, c.9, pp. 267–308, and *PPNK* I, c.6.
92 Emden claims that the decline in participation is also evident throughout the west and beyond but I think the phenomenon is too complex to generalise beyond Europe, or even within Europe in certain cases and, as I argue below, after 2009.
93 See Tully, 'On the Multiplicity of Global Public Spheres' and 'Citizenship for the Love of the World' for sketches of a genealogy.
94 For the importance of dialogical perspective-taking, see Laden, Scott and my response to Mendieta.
95 See my response to Mendieta and Vázquez-Arroyo.
96 See, Tully, 'Crisis of Global Citizenship'.
97 See Saki Bailey and Ugo Mattei, 'Social Movements as Constituent Power: The Italian Struggle for the Commons' (Unpublished MS 2012); Boaventura de Sousa Santos, 'Southern Europe Crises and Resistances,' *The Birkbeck Institute for the Humanities*, University of London (22 November 2012). Of course the renaissance of forms of participation in the Global North was accompanied by similar practices of civic citizenship in the Middle East and the Global South. See the discussion of new strategies of participation in South Africa and Bolivia in Sahle's chapter.
98 See Tully, 'Two Ways of Realizing Justice and Democracy'.
99 This rough sketch is indebted to the meticulous study of the democratic struggles over voting systems of OECD countries over the last century by Dennis M. Pilon, *Wrestling with Democracy: Voting Systems as Politics in the Twentieth-Century West* (Toronto: University of Toronto Press, 2013).
100 For Gandhi and his influence in this context, see David Hardiman, *Gandhi in His Time and Ours: The Global Legacy of His Ideas* (New York: Columbia, 2001).
101 *PPNK* I, c.4–6, 9.
102 This is also known as Rousseau's paradox.
103 See Laden this volume and my response to Mendieta and Vázquez-Arroyo.
104 See *PPNK* I, c.4–6.
105 I have also tried to address his two factors in a way that responds to his 'perhaps uncomfortable conclusion' in the final section.
106 Eunice N. Sahle, *World Orders, Development and Transformation* (Houndmills and New York: Palgrave Macmillan, 2010), pp. 177–93.
107 For this theme of civil and civic citizens joining hands, see my Introduction, discussions with Mendieta, Vázquez-Arroyo, and Emden, and Tully, 'Two Ways of Realising Justice and Democracy'.
108 Arturo Escobar, 'Latin America at a Crossroads,' *Cultural Studies*, 24, 1 (2010): 1–65.
109 See Anthony J. Hall, *Earth in Property: Colonization, Decolonization and Capitalism* (Montreal: McGill-Queens University Press, 2010), pp. 168–70. See also the discussion of Indigenous peoples in Anghie's chapter.
110 Evo Morales, 'Save the Planet from Capitalism', http://links.org.au/node/769, from which the quotation is taken, and Evo Morales, 'Capitalism is the Main Enemy of the

Earth', http://links.org.au/node/1634. Note how close this speech is to the analysis by Anghie in his chapter on the intellectual origins of capitalist development.

111 PNNKII, pp. 293–4. I have discussed it in much the same way as Morales, yet drawing on the analysis of capitalism by Karl Polanyi and Vandana Shiva, in Tully, 'The Crisis of Global Citizenship', 'Two Ways of Realising Justice and Democracy', and 'Citizenship for the Love of the World'.

112 John Bellamy Foster, *The Ecological Revolution: Making Peace with the Planet* (New York: Monthly Review Press, 2009), pp. 35, 276. He also cites the quotation from Morales above. For the tradition of Morris and Gandhi see my response to Vázquez-Arroyo.

113 See *PPNK* II, pp. 296–300, 308–9. For a complementary analysis of the Egyptian Spring along these lines, see Tully, 'Middle East Legal and Governmental Pluralism'.

114 Aletta J. Norval, *Aversive Democracy: Inheritance and Originality in the Democratic Tradition* (Cambridge: Cambridge University Press, 2007).

115 For a powerful exploration of this question of unsettling and dislocating the settler in the Canadian context of decolonization of the internal colonization of Indigenous peoples, see Paulette Regan, *Unsettling the Settler Within* (Vancouver; UBC Press, 2009).

116 See Nkonko Kamwangamalu, '*Ubuntu* in South Africa: A Sociolinguistic Perspective to a Pan-African Concept', *Critical Arts*, 13, 2 (1999): 24–41. The Haida symbol of *The Spirit of Haida Gwaii* plays a somewhat similar role to *ubuntu* in decolonization struggles on the northwest coast.

117 See Drucilla Cornell and Karin Van Marle, 'Exploring ubuntu: Tentative Reflections', *African Human Rights Law Journal*, 5, 2 (2005): 195–220.

118 This is a shared thesis of post-development, post-colonial and modernity/coloniality scholars. See my discussions with Vázquez-Arroyo on informal imperialism, primitive accumulation and violence; with Anghie on development; with Scott on self-determination; Sahle on South Africa and Bolivia; and, for the broader background, Sahle, *World Orders, Development and Transformation*.

119 I do not think Patton meant his comment to be taken in this way.

120 For similar reflections on steps of dislocation and decolonization in the Canadian settler context, see Regan, *Unsettling the Settler Within*, and Stephanie Irlbacher-Fox, *Finding Dahshaa: Self-government, Social Suffering, and Aboriginal Policy in Canada* (Vancouver: UBC Press, 2009).

121 See, for example, Helen O'Grady, *Woman's Relationship to Herself: Gender, Foucault and Therapy* (London: Routledge, 2005), and Patti LaBoucane-Benson, *Reconciliation, Reparation and Reconnection: A Framework for Building Resilience in Canadian Indigenous Families* (PhD Dissertation, Department of Human Ecology, University of Alberta, 2009).

122 For example, Alfred, *Wasase*.

123 For example, Paul Bedson and Ian Gawler, *Meditation: An In-Depth Guide* (New York: Penguin 2011); Steve Flowers and Bob Stahl, *Living with Your Heart Wide Open* (Oakland: Rain Forest Books, 2011).

124 Allen, *The Politics of Our Selves*.

125 Flowers and Stahl, *Living with Your Heart Wide Open*, p. 3

126 Laden, this volume, and *Reasoning: A Social Picture*, pp. 50–78.

Bibliography

Ackerman, Peter and Jack DuVall. *A Force more Powerful: A Century of Non-Violent Conflict.* London: Palgrave Macmillan, 2001.
Adam, Heribert and Kogila Moodley. *The Opening of the Apartheid Mind: Options for the New South Africa.* Berkeley, CA: University of California Press, 1993.
Alexander, Jeffrey, Ron Eyerman, Bernhard Giesen, Neil J. Smelser, and Piotr Sztompka. *Cultural Trauma and Collective Identity.* Berkeley, CA: University of California Press, 2004.
Alexandrowicz, Charles Henry. *An Introduction to the History of the Law of Nations in the East Indies.* Oxford: Clarendon Press, 1967.
Alfred, Taiaiake. *Wasase: Indigenous Pathways of Action and Freedom.* Peterborough, ON: Broadview, 2005.
Allan, T.R.S. *Constitutional Justice: A Liberal Theory of the Rule of Law.* Oxford: Oxford University Press, 2001.
Allen, Amy. *The Politics of Our Selves: Power, Autonomy and Gender in Contemporary Critical Theory.* New York: Columbia University Press, 2007.
Amnesty International. *Stolen Sisters: A Human Rights Response to Discrimination and Violence Against Indigenous Women in Canada* (2004) online: http://www.amnesty.ca/stolensisters/.
Anaya, S. James. *International Human Rights and Indigenous Peoples.* NY: Wolters Kluwer [Aspen Publishers], 2009.
Anderson, Perry. *The New Old World.* London and New York: Verso, 2009.
Anderson, Perry. 'Jottings on the Conjuncture,' *New Left Review* 48 (2007): 5–37.
Anderson, Perry. *English Questions.* London and New York: Verso, 1992.
Anghie, Antony. 'Vattel and Colonialism: Some Preliminary Observations,' in *Vattel's International Law in a XXIst Century Perspective*, eds. Vincent Chetail and Peter Haggenmacher, eds. Leiden: Martinus Nijhoff, 2011, pp. 237–55.
Anghie, Antony. *Imperialism, Sovereignty and the Making of International Law.* Cambridge: Cambridge University Press, 2005.
Annas, George J. 'The Right to Health and the Nevrapine Case in South Africa,' in *Perspectives on Health and Human Rights*, ed., S.Gruskin. NY: Routledge, 2005.
Archibugi, Daniele and Raffaele Marchetti. 'Democratic Ethics and UN Reform,' in *The Ethics of Global Governance*, ed., Antonio Franceschet. Boulder, Col.: Lynne Rienner Publishers, 2009, pp. 51–66.
Archibugi, Daniele. *The Global Commonwealth of Citizens: Toward Cosmopolitan Democracy.* Princeton, NJ: Princeton University Press, 2008.
Archibugi, Daniele. 'From the United Nations to Cosmopolitan Democracy,' in *Cosmopolitan*

Democracy: An Agenda for a New World Order, eds, Daniele Archibugi and David Held. Cambridge: Polity Press, 1995, pp. 121–62.

Archibugi, Daniele. 'Principles of Cosmopolitan Democracy,' in *Re-imagining Political Community: Studies in Cosmopolitan Democracy*, eds, Archibugi, Held and Köhler. Cambridge: Polity Press, 1998, pp. 198–228.

Arendt, Hannah. *On Violence*. New York: Harcourt, 1970.

Aristotle. *Politics*, trans. T.A. Sinclair, 3rd edn. London: Penguin, 1992.

Armitage, David. 'Probing the Foundations of Tully's Public Philosophy,' *Political Theory* 39 (2011): 124–30.

Armitage, David. *The Declaration of Independence*. Cambridge, MA: Harvard University Press, 2007.

Austen, Jane. *Pride and Prejudice*, Oxford World Classics, ed. James Kinsley. Oxford: Oxford University Press, 2008.

Azoulay, Ariella and Adi Ophir. 'The Order of Violence,' in *The Power of Inclusive Exclusion*, ed. Adi Ophir, Michal Givoni and Sari Hanfi. New York: Zone Books, 2009, pp. 99–140.

Bacon, Jacqueline. 'Reading the Reparations Debate,' *Quarterly Journal of Speech* 89.3 (2003): 171–95.

Bailey, Saki and Ugo Mattei. 'Social Movements as Constituent Power: The Italian struggle for the commons' (Unpublished MS 2012).

Bakhtin, Mikhail. *The Dialogical Imagination: Four Essays*. Austin: University of Texas Press, 1982.

Bakker, Karen. *Privatizing Water: Governance Failure and the World's Urban Water Crisis*. Ithaca: Cornell University Press, 2010.

Balakrishnan, Gopal. 'The Convolution of Capitalism,' in *Business as Usual*, ed. Craig Calhoun and Georgi Derluguian. New York: New York University Press, 2011, pp. 211–29.

Balibar, Étienne. *La proposition de l'égaliberté*. Paris: Presses Universitaires de France, 2011.

Balibar, Étienne. 'Toward a Diasporic Citizen? From Internationalism to Cosmopolitanism,' in *The Creolization of Theory*, ed. Françoise Lionnet and Shu-mei Shih. Durham: Duke University Press, 2011.

Balibar, Étienne. *Violence et civilité: Wellek Library Lectures et autres essais de philosophie politique*. Paris: Editions Galilée, 2010.

Balibar, Étienne. 'Violence and Civility: On the Limits of Political Anthropology,' *differences* 20 (2009): 9–35.

Balibar, Étienne. *We, the People of Europe?*, trans. James Swenson. Princeton, NJ: Princeton University Press, 2003.

Balibar, Étienne. *Politics and the Other Scene*, trans. Christine Jones, James Swenson and Chris Turner. London and New York: Verso, 2002.

Ballard, Richard, Adam Habid and Imraan Valodia, eds. *Voices of Protest: Social Movements*. Scottsville: University of KwaZulu-Natal, 2006.

Barchiesi, Franco. *Precarious Liberation : Workers, the State, and Contested Social Citizenship in Postapartheid South Africa*. Albany: State University of New York Press, 2011.

Barchiesi, Franco, 'Wage Labor and Social Citizenship in the Making of Post-Apartheid South Africa', *Journal of Asian and African Studies* 42.1 (January 2007): 39–72.

Barkan, Elazar. *The Guilt of Nations: Restitution and Negotiating Historical Injustices*. Baltimore: Johns Hopkins University Press, 2001.

Bates, Stanley. 'Stanley Cavell and Ethics,' in *Stanley Cavell*, ed., Richard Eldrigde. Cambridge: Cambridge University Press, 2003.
Bauböck, Rainer. 'Why European Citizenship? Normative Approaches to Supranational Union,' *Theoretical Inquiries in Law* 8 (2007): 452–88.
Beck, Ulrich. *The Cosmopolitan Vision*, trans. Ciaran Cronin. Cambridge: Polity Press, 2006.
Bedson, Paul and Ian Gawler. *Meditation: An In-Depth Guide*. New York: Penguin 2011.
Belenky, Mary Field, Blythe McVicker Clinchy, Nancy Rule Goldberger and Jill Mattuck Tarule. *Women's Ways of Knowing: The Development of Self, Voice, and Mind*. New York: HarperCollins Publishers, 1986.
Bell, Duncan. *The Idea of Greater Britain: Empire and the Future of World Order, 1860–1900*. Princeton, NJ: Princeton University Press, 2007.
Bell, Richard H. 'Understanding African Philosophy from a Non-African Point of View: An Exercise in Cross-cultural Philosophy', in *Postcolonial African Philosophy: A Critical Reader*, ed., Emmanuel Chukwudi Eze. Oxford: Blackwell, 1997, pp. 197–220.
Benhabib, Seyla. *Another Cosmopolitanism, with Commentaries by Jeremy Waldron, Bonnie Honig, Will Kymlicka*. New York: Oxford University Press, 2006.
Bittker, Boris. *The Case for Black Reparations*. Boston: Beacon Press, 2003.
Blackhawk, Ned. *Violence Over the Land: Indians and Empires in the Early American West*. Cambridge: Harvard University Press, 2006.
Bloch, Ernst. *Natural Law and Human Dignity*, trans. Dennis J. Schmidt. Cambridge, MA: MIT Press, 1987.
de la Boétie, Étienne. *Discourse on Voluntary Servitude*, trans. James B. Atkinson and David Sices. Indianapolis: Hackett Publishing Co, 2012.
Bok, Derek Curtis. *The State of the Nation: Government and the Quest for a Better Society*. Cambridge, MA: Harvard University Press, 1998.
Bond, Patrick. *Looting Africa: the Economics of Exploitation*. Scottsville, South Africa: Distributed in the USA by Palgrave Macmillan, 2006.
Bond, Patrick. *Against Global Apartheid: South Africa Meets the World Bank, IMF, and International Finance*. Lansdowne: University of Cape Town Press, 2001.
Bondurant, Joan. *The Conquest of Violence*. Princeton, NJ: Princeton University Press, 1988.
Bowden, Brett. *The Empire of Civilization: The Evolution of an Imperial Idea*. Chicago: University of Chicago Press, 2009.
Boxill, Bernard. 'The Morality of Reparation,' *Social Theory and Practice* 2.1 (Spring 1972): 113–123
Brecht, Bertolt. *Poems: 1913–1953*, ed. John Willett and Ralph Manheim. London: Methuen, 2000.
Breda, Vito. 'A European Constitution in a Multinational Europe or a Multinational Constitution for Europe?,' *European Law Journal* 12 (2006): 330–44.
Brenner, Neil and Stuart Elden. 'Henri Lefebvre on State, Space and Territory,' *International Political Sociology* 3 (2009): 353–377.
Brenner, Neil, Bob Jessop, Martin Jones and Gordon Macleod, eds. *State/Space: A Reader*. Malden, MA: Blackwell, 2003.
Brenner, Robert. *The Economics of Global Turbulence*. London and New York: Verso, 2006.
Brenner, Robert. *The Boom and the Bubble*. London and New York: Verso, 2002.
Brooks, Roy L. *Atonement and Forgiveness: A New Model for Black Reparations*. Berkeley, CA: University of California Press, 2004.

Brooks, Roy L., ed. *When Sorry Isn't Enough: The Controversy Over Apologies and Reparations for Human Injustice.* New York: New York University Press, 1999.
Brown, Vincent. 'Social Death and Political Life in the Study of Slavery,' *American Historical Review* 114 (2009): 1231–49.
Brown, Wendy. *Walled States, Waning Sovereignty.* Cambridge, MA: Zone, 2010.
Brown, Wendy. 'Editor's Introduction: We are all democrats now...,' *Theory & Event* 13.2 (2010).
Brown, Wendy. 'Democracy and Bad Dreams,' *Theory & Event* 10.1 (2007).
Brown, Wendy. *Regulating Aversion: Tolerance in an Age of Identity and Empire.* Princeton, NJ: Princeton University Press, 2006.
Brown, Wendy. 'Power After Foucault,' in *The Oxford Handbook of Political Theory*, ed. John S. Dryzek, Bonnie Honig and Ann Philips. Oxford: Oxford University Press, 2006, pp. 61–84.
Brown, Wendy. *States of Injury: Power and Freedom in Late Modernity.* Princeton, NJ: Princeton University Press, 1995.
Cavell, Stanley. *A Pitch of Philosophy.* Cambridge, MA: Harvard University Press, 1994.
Cavell, Stanley. *Conditions Handsome and Unhandsome.* Chicago: The University of Chicago Press, 1990.
Cavell, Stanley. *The Claim of Reason.* Oxford: Oxford University Press, 1979.
Cavell, Stanley. 'The Availability of Wittgenstein's Later Philosophy,' in *Must We Mean What We Say?* New York: Charles Scribner's Sons, 1969.
Calhoun, Craig. 'The Class Consciousness of Frequent Travellers: Towards a Critique of Actually Existing Cosmopolitanism,' in *Debating Cosmopolitics*, ed., Daniele Archibugi. London: Verso, 2003, pp. 86–116.
Calhoun, Craig. 'Constitutional Patriotism and the Public Sphere: Interests, Identity, and Solidarity in the Integration of Europe,' in *Global Ethics and Transnational Politics*, eds, Pablo De Greiff and Ciaran Cronin. Cambridge, MA: MIT Press, 2002, pp. 275–312.
Carmody, Pádraig. 'Between Globalization and (Post) Apartheid: The Political Economy of Restructuring in South Africa,' *Journal of Southern African Studies* 28.2 (June 2002): 255–75.
Charter of Fundamental Rights of the European Union, Official Journal of the European Communities C 364 (2000).
Chenoweth, Erica and Maria J. Stephan. *Why Civil Resistance Works: The Strategic Logic of Nonviolent Conflict.* New York: Columbia University Press, 2011.
Church, Clive H. and David Phinnemore. *Understanding the European Constitution: An Introduction to the EU Constitutional Treaty.* London: Routledge, 2006.
Cilliers, Johan. 'In Search of Meaning Between *Ubuntu* and *Into*: Perspectives on Preaching in Post-Apartheid South Africa,' Paper delivered at the eighth international conference of *Societas Homiletica*, held in Copenhagen, Denmark, 19–25 July 2008.
Closa, Carlos. 'National Plurality within a Single Statehood in the European Union,' in Ferran Requejo ed., *Democracy and National Pluralism.* London: Routledge, 2001, pp. 105–27.
Cobo, Jose Martinez. *Special Rapporteur Report: Study of the Problem of Discrimination Against Indigenous Populations – Volume 5: Conclusions, Proposals and Recommendations*, UN Doc E/CN.4/Sub.2/1986/7/Add.4 (March 1987).
Coles, Romand. *Rethinking Generosity: Critical Theory and the Politics of Caritas.* Ithaca: Cornell University Press, 1997.

Collins, Patricia Hill. *Black Feminist Thought: Knowledge, Consciousness, and the Politics of Empowerment*, rev. 10th edn. New York: Routledge, 2000.
Comack, Elizabeth. 'Theoretical Approaches in the Sociology of Law,' in *Locating Law: Race, Class, Gender, Sexuality, Connections*, ed. Elizabeth Comack, 2nd edn. Black Point, NS: Fernwood Publishing, 2006.
Conant, James. 'Nietzsche's Perfectionism: A Reading of *Schopenhauer as Educator*,' in *Nietzsche's Postmoralism*, ed., Richard Schacht. Cambridge: Cambridge University Press, 2001.
Connolly, William. *The Ethos of Pluralization*. Minneapolis: University of Minnesota Press, 1995.
Constitution of the Republic of South Africa: Act 108 of 1996, to Introduce a New Constitution for the Republic of South Africa and to Provide for Matters Incidental Thereto. Pretoria: Government Printer, 1996.
Conyers, John. 'The Commission to Study Reparations Proposals,' in *When Sorry Isn't Enough: The Controversy Over Apologies and Reparations for Human Injustice*, ed., Roy L. Brooks. New York: New York University Press, 1999, pp. 367–9.
Conyers, John and Jo Ann Nichols Watson. 'Reparations: An Idea Whose Time Has Come,' in *Should America Pay? Slavery and the Raging Debate on Reparations*, ed., Raymond A. Winbush. New York: Amistad, 2003, pp. 14–21.
Cornell, Drucilla and Karin Van Marle. 'Exploring ubuntu: Tentative Reflections,' *African Human Rights Law Journal* 5.2 (2005): 195–220.
Coovadia, Hoosen M. and Jacquie Hadingham. 'HIV/AIDS: Global Trends, Global Funds and Delivery Bottlenecks,' in *Globalization and Health* 1.13 (August 2005).
Crouch, Colin. *Post-Democracy*. Cambridge: Polity Press, 2004.
Dalai Lama. *Beyond Religion: Ethics for a Whole World*. Toronto: McClelland Stewart, 2011.
Deininger, Klaus and Derek Byerlee et al., *Rising Global Interest in Farmland: Can it Yield Sustainable and Equitable Benefits?* Washington DC: The World Bank, 2011.
Deleuze, G. and F. Guattari, *A Thousand Plateaus*, Brian Massumi trans. Minneapolis: University of Minnesota Press, 1987.
Dempsey, Anne. 'Native women's group hopes for share of money Ottawa budgeted for cause,' (21 April 2010), *Globe and Mail*, online: http://www.theglobeandmail.com/news/national/.
Derrida, Jacques. *Of Grammatology*. Baltimore: Johns Hopkins University Press, 1976.
Deutscher, Isaac. *Marxism, Wars, and Revolutions*, ed. Tamara Deutscher. London and New York: Verso, 1984.
Du Bois, W.E.B. *The Negro American Family*. New York: Negro Universities Press, 1969 [1908].
Dunaway, Wilma. *The African–American Family in Slavery and Emancipation*. New York: Cambridge University Press, 2003.
Dunn, Kristie. 'A Sorry Challenge: Review of "Taking Responsibility for the Past: Reparation and Historical Justice" by Janna Thompson,' *Australian Book Review* 251 (2003).
Duprey, Marlene. *Bioislas*. San Juan: Ediciones Callejón, 2010.
Dussel, Enrique. *Twenty Theses on Politics*, Durham, NC: Duke University Press, 2008.
Dussel, Enrique. *Politics of Liberation: A Critical World History*, London: SCM Press, 2011.
Dussel, Enrique. *Ética de la liberación en la edad de la gloablización y la exclusion*. Madrid: Editorial Trotta, 1998.

Dyzenhaus, David. *Judging the Judges, Judging Ourselves.* Oxford: Hart Publishing, 1998.
Elias, Norbert. *Über den Prozeß der Zivilisation: Soziogenetische und psychogenetische Untersuchungen.* Frankfurt/M.: Suhrkamp, 1976.
Elliott, John H. *Empires of the Atlantic World: Britain and Spain in America, 1492–1830.* New Haven, Conn.: Yale University Press, 2006.
Engle, Karen. *The Elusive Promise of Indigenous Development.* Durham, NC: Duke University Press, 2010.
Escobar, Arturo. 'Latin America at a Crossroads,' *Cultural Studies* 24.1 (2010): 1–65.
Escobar, Arturo. *Territories of Difference: Place, Movements, Life, Redes.* Durham: Duke University Press, 2008.
Eyerman, Ron. *Cultural Trauma: Slavery and the Formation of African American Identity.* New York: Cambridge University Press, 2001.
Eze, Emmanuel Chukwudi, ed. *Postcolonial African Philosophy.* Oxford: Blackwell, 1997.
Faist, Thomas. 'Social Citizenship in the European Union: Nested Membership,' *Journal of Common Market Research* 39 (2001): 37–58.
Finlayson, James Gordon and Fabian Freyenhagen, eds, *Habermas and Rawls: Disputing the Political.* New York: Routledge, 2011.
Fisher, W.W. and Cyrill Rigamonti. 'The South African AIDS Controversy: A Case Study in Patent Law and Policy,' at http://cyber.law.harvard.edu/people/tfisher/South%20Africa.pdf.
Fitzpatrick, Joan and Ron C. Slye. 'Republic of South Africa v Grootboom and Minister of Health V. Treatment Action Campaign Case No. CCT 8/02,' *American Society of International Law* 97.3 (July 2003): 669–80.
Flanagan, Tom. *First Nations, Second Thoughts.* Montreal: McGill-Queen's University Press, 2000.
Fletcher, M.D. *Reading Rushdie: Perspectives on the Fiction of Salman Rushdie.* Amsterdam: Rodopi, 1994.
Flowers, Steve and Bob Stahl. *Living with your Heart Wide Open.* Oakland: Rain Forest Books, 2011.
Forman, James. *The Making of Black Revolutionaries: A Personal Account.* New York: Macmillan, 1972.
Forst, Rainer. *The Right to Justification.* New York: Columbia University Press, 2011.
Forst, Rainer. *Contexts of Justice: Political Philosophy Beyond Liberalism and Communitarianism,* trans. John M.M. Farrell. Berkeley, CA: University of California Press, 2002.
Foster, John Bellamy. *The Ecological Revolution: Making Peace with the Planet.* New York: Monthly Review Press, 2009.
Foucault, Michel. *The Government of Self and Others,* ed. Frederic Gros, tr. Graham Burchell. New York: Palgrave Macmillan, 2008.
Foucault, Michel. *The Hermeneutics of the Subject,* ed. Frederic Gros, tr. Graham Burchell. New York: Picador, 2005.
Foucault, Michel. *Ethics, Subjectivity and Truth: Essential Works of Foucault, Vol. I,* ed. Paul Rabinow. New York: New Press, 1997.
Foucault, Michel. *Fearless Speech.* Los Angeles: Semiotext(e), 2001.
Foucault, Michel. *Power: The Essential Works of Michel Foucault, Vol. III,* ed. James Baubion. New York: New Press, 1994.
Foucault, Michel. 'Of Other Spaces,' *Diacritics* 16.1 (Spring, 1986), pp. 22–7.
Foucault, Michel. *Power/Knowledge: Selected Interviews and Other Writings 1972–1977,* ed. Colin

Gordon, transl. Colin Gordon, Leo Marshall, John Mepham and Kate Soper. New York: Pantheon Books, 1980.
Fourie, Pieter and Melissa Meyer, *The Politics of AIDS Denialism: South Africa's Failure to Respond*. Farnham, Surrey, England: Ashgate Pub., 2010.
Fraser, Nancy and Axel Honneth. *Redistribution or Recognition?: A Political–Philosophical Exchange*. London and New York: Verso, 2003.
Fraser, Nancy. *Unruly Practices: Power, Discourse and Gender in Contemporary Social Theory*. Minneapolis: University of Minnesota Press, 1989.
Frazier, E. Franklyn. *The Negro Family in the United States*. Chicago: University of Chicago Press, 1939.
Freeman, Kathleen. *Ancilla to the Pre-Socratic Philosophers: A Complete Translation of the Fragments of Diels*, Fragmente der Vorsokratiker. Cambridge, MA: Harvard University Press, 1983 [1943].
Friedman, Steven and Shauna Mottiar. 'Seeking the High Ground: The Treatment Action Campaign and the Politics of Morality,' in *Voices of Protest: Social Movements*, eds. Ballard, Habib and Valodia. Scottsville: University of KwaZulu-Natal, 2006.
Gandhi, M.K. *The Essential Writings*, ed., Judith M. Brown. Oxford: Oxford University Press, 2008.
Gates Jr., Henry Louis. 'Ending the Blame-Game,' *New York Times*, 23 April 2010.
Geffen, Nathan. *Debunking Delusions: The Inside Story of the Treatment Action Campaign*. Auckland Park, South Africa: Jacana Media, 2010.
Genovese, Eugene. *Roll, Jordan, Roll: The World the Slaves Made*. New York: Vintage, 1976.
Genugten, Willem van. 'Protection of Indigenous Peoples on the African Continent: Concepts, Position Seeking and the Interaction of Legal Systems,' *Am.J.I.L* 104.1 (2010): 29–65.
Geuss, Raymond. *Philosophy and Real Politics*. Princeton, NJ: Princeton University Press, 2008.
Goar, Carol. 'This is "what women want"? Highly unlikely,' *The Star* (14 May 2010), online: http://www.thestar.com/opinion/editorialopinion/article/809069—goar-this-is-what-women-want.
Gotkowitz, Laura. *A Revolution for Our Rights: Indigenous Struggles for Land and Justice in Bolivia, 1880–1952*. Durham: Duke University Press, 2007.
Gould, Stephen Jay. *The Mismeasure of Man*. New York: W.W. Norton & Co, 1996.
Government Gazette, vol. 353, Kaapstad 23 November No. 16085. Cape Town: 1994.
Government of South Africa. *Truth and Reconciliation Commission of South Africa Report*, 6 (2003): http://www.info.gov.za/otherdocs/2003/trc/.
Government of South Africa. *Constitution of the Republic of South Africa: Act 108 of 1996, to Introduce a New Constitution for the Republic of South Africa and to Provide for Matters Incidental Thereto*. Pretoria: Government Printer, 1996.
Government of South Africa. *Growth, Employment and Redistribution, A Macroeconomic Strategy*. Pretoria: Department of Finance, 1996.
Gramsci, Antonio. *Selections from the Prison Notebooks*. NY: International Publishers, 1971.
Grassi, Ernesto. *Rhetoric as Philosophy*. Carbondale: Southern Illinois University Press, 2001.
Gregg, Richard. *The Power of Nonviolence*. New York: Schocken Books, 1966.
Gregory, Derek. *Geographical Imaginations*. Cambridge, MA: Blackwell, 1994.
Grotius, Hugo. *The Rights of War and Peace*. Indianapolis, IN: Liberty Fund Publications, 2005.

Grotius, Hugo. *The Free Sea*, ed. David Armitage. Indianapolis, IN: Liberty Fund Publications, 2004.
Grotius, Hugo. *De jure belli ac pacis libri tres / The Rights of War and Peace*, trans. Francis W. Kelsey. Oxford: Clarendon Press, 1925.
Guinier, Ewart. Review, *Yale Law Journal* 82.8 (1973): 1719–24.
Günther, Klaus. *The Sense of Appropriateness: Application Discourses in Morality and Law*, trans. John Farrell. Albany, NY: SUNY Press, 1993.
Gutmann, Herbert. *The Black Family in Slavery and Freedom, 1750–1925*. New York: Vintage, 1977.
Habermas, Jürgen. 'The Concept of Human Dignity and the Realistic Utopia of Human Rights,' *Metaphilosophy* 41.4 (2010): 464–80.
Habermas, Jürgen. *Europe: The Faltering Project*, trans. Ciaran Cronin. Cambridge: Polity Press, 2009.
Habermas, Jürgen. *The Divided West*, trans. Ciaran Cronin. Cambridge: Polity Press, 2006.
Habermas, Jürgen. 'The Postnational Constellation and the Future of Democracy,' in *The Postnational Constellation: Political Essays*, trans. and ed. Max Pensky. Cambridge, MA: MIT Press, 2001, pp. 58–112.
Habermas, Jürgen. *Between Facts and Norms: Contributions to a Discourse Theory of Law and Democracy*, trans. William Rehg. Cambridge, MA: The MIT Press, 1996.
Habermas, Jürgen. 'Discourse Ethics: Notes on a Program of Philosophical Justification,' in *Moral Consciousness and Communicative Action*, trans. Christian Lenhardt and Shierry Weber Nicholsen, intro. Thomas McCarthy, Cambridge, MA: MIT Press, 1993, pp. 43–115.
Habermas, Jürgen. 'Further Reflections on the Public Sphere,' in *Habermas and the Public Sphere*, ed., Craig Calhoun. Cambridge, MA: The MIT Press, 1992.
Habermas, Jürgen. *Postmetaphysical Thinking: Philosophical Essays*, trans. William Mark Hohengarten. Cambridge, MA: The MIT Press, 1992.
Habermas, Jürgen. *The Structural Transformation of the Public Sphere: An Inquiry into a Category of Bourgeois Society*, trans. Thomas Burger and Frederick Lawrence. Cambridge, MA: The MIT Press, 1989.
Habermas, Jürgen. *The Philosophical Discourse of Modernity: Twelve Lectures*, trans. Frederick Lawrence. Cambridge, MA: The MIT Press, 1987.
Habermas, Jürgen. *The Theory of Communicative Action, 2 Volumes*, trans. Thomas McCarthy. Boston: Beacon Press, 1984–87.
Habermas, Jürgen. *Philosophical–Political Profiles*, trans. Frederick G. Lawrence. Cambridge, MA: The MIT Press, 1983.
Habermas, Jürgen. *Communication and the Evolution of Society*, trans. Thomas McCarthy. Boston: Beacon Press, 1979.
Habermas, Jürgen. *Theory and Practice*, trans. John Viertel. Boston: Beacon Press, 1973.
Habermas, Jürgen. *Knowledge and Human Interests*, trans. Jeremy J. Shapiro. Boston: Beacon Press, 1971.
Hacking, Ian. 'Language, Truth, and Reason', in *Rationality and Relativism*, eds, Martin Hollis and Steven Lukes. Oxford: Blackwell, 1982, pp. 48–66.
Hall, Anthony J. *Earth in Property: Colonization, Decolonization and Capitalism*. Montreal: McGill-Queens University Press, 2010.
Hanson, Margaret and James J. Hentz, 'Neocolonialism and Neoliberalism in South Africa and Zambia', in *Political Science Quarterly* 114.13 (1999).

Hardiman, David. *Gandhi in His Time and Ours: The Global Legacy of His Ideas*. New York: Columbia, 2001.
Harris, Fredrick. *The Price of the Ticket: Barack Obama and the Rise and Decline of Black Politics*. Oxford: Oxford University Press, 2012.
Harvey, David. *A Brief History of Neoliberalism*. New York: Oxford University Press, 2005.
Hay, Colin. *Why We Hate Politics*. Cambridge: Polity Press, 2007.
Hayden, Patrick. *Cosmopolitan Global Politics*. Aldershot: Ashgate, 2005.
Hayner, Priscilla. *Unspeakable Truths: Facing the Challenge of Truth Commissions*. New York: Routledge, 2001.
Hegel, Georg W.F. *Elements of the Philosophy of Right*, ed. Allen W. Wood, trans. H.B. Nisbet. Cambridge: Cambridge University Press, 1991.
Held, David. 'Democracy: From City-States to a Cosmopolitan Order?' *Political Studies* 40 (2007): 10–39.
Held, David. 'Democracy and Globalization,' in *Re-imagining Political Community: Studies in Cosmopolitan Democracy*, eds, Daniele Archibugi, David Held and Martin Köhler. Cambridge: Polity Press, 1998, pp. 11–27.
Held, David. *Democracy and the Global Order: From the Modern State to Cosmopolitan Governance*. Cambridge: Polity Press, 1995.
Heywood, Mark. 'South Africa's Treatment Action Campaign: Combining Law and Social Mobilization to Realize the Right to Health,' *Journal of Human Rights Practice*, 1.1 (March 2009): 14–36.
Hobbes, Thomas. *Leviathan, with Selected Variants from the Latin Edition of 1668*, ed. Edwin Curley. Indianapolis, Ind.: Hackett, 1994.
Honig, Bonnie. '[Un]Dazzled by the Ideal?,' *Political Theory* 39 (2011): 138–44.
Honig, Bonnie and Marc Stears, 'The New Realism: From Modus Vivendi to Justice,' in *History versus Political Philosophy*, eds, Jonathan Floyd and Marc Stears. Cambridge: Cambridge University Press, 2011.
Honig, Bonnie. 'Antigone's Two Laws: Greek Tragedy and the Politics of Humanism,' *New Literary History* 41.1 (2010): 1–33.
Honig, Bonnie. *Emergency Politics*. Princeton, NJ: Princeton University Press, 2009.
Honig, Bonnie. 'Another Cosmopolitanism? Law and Politics in the New Europe,' in Seyla Benhabib, *Another Cosmopolitanism, with Jeremy Waldron, Bonnie Honig, and Will Kymlicka*, ed. Robert Post. Oxford: Oxford University Press, 2006, pp. 102–27.
Horsburgh, H.J.N. 'The Distinctiveness of Satyagraha,' *Philosophy East and West* 19.2 (April 1969): 171–80.
Horsburgh, H.J.N. *Non-Violence and Aggression: A Study of Gandhi's Moral Equivalent of War*. Oxford: Oxford University Press, 1968.
Howarth, David. 'The Difficult Emergence of a Democratic Imaginary: Black Consciousness and Non-Racial Democracy in South Africa,' in *Discourse Theory and Political Analysis: Identities, Hegemonies and Social Change*, eds. D. Howarth, A. J. Norval and Y. Stavrakakis. Manchester: Manchester University Press, 2000.
Howes, Dustin Ellis. *Toward a Credible Pacifism*. Albany: SUNY Press, 2009.
Hoy, David. *Critical Resistance: From Post-structuralism to Post-critique*. Cambridge: MIT Press, 2004.
Hui, Wang. *The End of the Revolution*. London: Verso, 2008.
Hui, Wang. *The Politics of Imagining Asia*, ed. Theodore Huters. Cambridge, MA: Harvard University Press, 2011.

Human Rights Watch, 'An Approach to Reparations,' at http://www.hrw.org/campaigns/race/reparations.html.

Hunt, Lynn. *Inventing Human Rights: A History.* New York: W.W. Norton & Co, 2008.

Hylton, Forrest and Sinclair Thomson, *Revolutionary Horizons: Past and Present in Bolivian Politics.* London and New York: Verso, 2007.

Irlbacher-Fox, Stephanie. *Finding Dahshaa: Self-government, Social Suffering, and Aboriginal Policy in Canada.* Vancouver: UBC Press, 2009.

Ishay, Micheline R. *The History of Human Rights: From Ancient Times to the Globalization Era.* Berkeley, CA: University of California Press, 2004.

Jacobs, Francis G. and Robin C.A. White. *The European Convention on Human Rights*, 2nd edn. Oxford: Clarendon Press, 1996.

James, William. 'The Moral Equivalent of War,' *McClure's Magazine*, 35 (1910): 463–8.

Joas, Hans. *The Creativity of Action.* Chicago: Chicago University Press, 1996.

Jones, S. Peris. 'A Test of Governance: Rights-based Struggles and the Politics of HIV/AIDS Policy in South Africa,' *Political Geography* 24 (2005): 419–47.

Jordan, Winthrop D. *White Over Black: American Attitudes Toward the Negro, 1550–1812.* Chapel Hill: University of North Carolina Press, 1968.

Johnson, Chalmers. *Nemesis: The Last Days of the American Republic.* New York: Henry Holt, 2006.

Johnson, Charles. 'The End of the Black American Narrative,' *American Scholar*, Summer 2008, pp. 32–42.

Johnson, Rebecca. *Taxing Choices: The Intersection of Class, Gender, Parenthood, and the Law.* Vancouver: UBC Press, 2002.

Kamwangamalu, Nkonko. '*Ubuntu* in South Africa: A Sociolinguistic Perspective to a Pan-African Concept,' *Critical Arts* 13.2 (1999): 24–41.

Kane, John, Haig Patapan and Paul Hart, 'Dispersed Democratic Leadership,' in *Dispersed Democratic Leadership: Origins, Dynamics, and Implications*, eds. Kane, Patapan and Hart. Oxford: Oxford University Press, 2009, pp. 1–12.

Kant, Immanuel. *Metaphysics of Morals*, tr. Mary Gregor. Cambridge: Cambridge University Press, 1991.

Kant, Immanuel. *Political Writings*, ed. H.S. Reiss, trans. H.B. Nisbet, 2nd edn. Cambridge: Cambridge University Press, 1991.

Kaufmann, Franz-Xaver. *Sozialpolitisches Denken: Die deutsche Tradition.* Frankfurt/M.: Suhrkamp, 2003.

Keating, Michael. *Plurinational Democracy: Stateless Nations in a Post-Sovereignty Era.* Oxford: Oxford University Press, 2001.

Kersting, Wolfgang. *Wohlgeordnete Freiheit: Immanuel Kants Rechts-und Staatsphilosophie*, 2nd edn. Frankfurt/M.: Suhrkamp, 1993.

King, Mary Elizabeth. *A Quiet Revolution: The Palestinian Intifada and Nonviolent Resistance.* New York: Nation Books, 2007.

King, Mary Elizabeth. 'Palestinian Civil Resistance against Israeli Military Occupation', in *Civilian Jihad: Nonviolent Struggle, Democratization and Governance in the Middle East*, ed., Maria Stephan. New York: Palgrave Macmillan, 2009, pp. 131–56.

Kingsbury, Benedict and Benjamin Strauman. 'The State of Nature and Commercial Sociability in Early Modern Thought,' *New York University Public Law and Legal Theory Working Papers* (2011): Paper 258.

Kingsbury, Benedict. 'Indigenous Peoples in International Law: A Constructivist Approach to the Asian Controversy,' *Am.J.I.L.* 92 (1998): 414–47.
Kivisto, Peter and Thomas Faist. *Beyond a Border: The Causes and Consequences of Contemporary Immigration*. Thousand Oaks, Calif.: Sage, 2010.
Kleingeld, Pauline. 'Approaching Perpetual Peace: Kant's Defence of a League of States and his Ideal of a World Federation,' *European Journal of Philosophy* 12 (2004): 304–25.
Kleingeld, Pauline. 'Six Varieties of Cosmopolitanism in Late Eighteenth-Century Germany,' *Journal of the History of Ideas* 60 (1999): 505–24.
Klingemann, Hans-Dieter and Dieter Fuchs, eds. *Citizens and the State*. Oxford: Oxford University Press, 1995.
Kohl, Benjamin. 'Bolivia under Morales: A Work in Progress,' *Latin American Perspectives*, 37.3 (June 10, 2010).
Kohl, Benjamin and Linda Farthing, *Impasse in Bolivia: Neoliberal Hegemony and Popular Resistance*. London and New York: Zed Books, 2006.
Korsgaard, Christine M. *The Sources of Normativity*, ed. Onora O'Neill. Cambridge: Cambridge University Press, 1996.
Koskenniemi, Martti. *The Gentle Civilizer of Nations: The Rise and Fall of International Law, 1870–1960*. Cambridge: Cambridge University Press, 2002.
Kostakopoulou, Dora. *The Future Governance of Citizenship*. Cambridge: Cambridge University Press, 2008.
Kraybill, Ron. 'MCS Conciliation Quarterly at 10' (Summer 1987). Reprinted in *Mediation and Facilitation Training Manual: Foundations and Skills for Constructive Conflict Transformation*, Jim Stutzman and Carolyn Schrock-Shenk, 3rd edn. Akron, PA: Mennonite Central Committee, 1995.
Krog, Antjie. *A Change of Tongue*. Cape Town, SA: Struik, 2009.
Krog, Antjie. *Begging to Be Black*. Cape Town, SA: Struik, 2009.
Krog, Antjie. *Country of My Skull*. New York: Broadway, 2000.
Kurlansky, Mark. *Nonviolence*. New York: Modern Library, 2006.
LaBoucane-Benson, Patti. *Reconciliation, Reparation and Reconnection: A Framework for Building Resilience in Canadian Indigenous Families*. PhD Dissertation, Department of Human Ecology; University of Alberta, 2009.
Laden, Anthony. 'Learning to be Equal: Just Schools and Schools of Justice,' *Democracy, Education and Justice*, ed. Danielle Allen and Robert Reich. Chicago: University of Chicago Press, 2012.
Laden, Anthony. *Reasoning: A Social Picture*. Oxford: Oxford University Press, 2012.
Laden, Anthony. 'Justice of Justification,' in *Habermas and Rawls: Disputing the Political*, ed. Fabian Frayenhagen and James Gordon Finlayson. New York: Routledge, 2011.
Laden, Anthony. 'Negotiation, Deliberation and the Claims of Politics,' in *Multiculturalism and Political Theory*, ed. Anthony Smon Laden and David Owen. Cambridge: Cambridge University Press, 2007, pp. 198–217.
Laden, Anthony. 'Reasonable Deliberation, Constructive Power and the Struggle for Recognition,' in *Recognition and Power*, ed. Bert van den Brink and David Owen. Cambridge: Cambridge University Press, 2007, pp. 270–89.
Laden, Anthony. *Reasonably Radical*. Ithaca, NY: Cornell University Press, 2001.
Laden, Anthony. 'Outline of a Theory of Reasonable Deliberation,' *Canadian Journal of Philosophy* 30 (2000): 551–80.

Laden, Anthony. 'Civic Reasoning: A Democratic Perspective,' in *On Global Citizenship*, ed. David Owen. London: Bloomsbury 2013.
Lefebvre, Henri. *The Production of Space*. Oxford: Blackwell, 1991.
Lindahl, Hans. 'A-legality: Postnationalism and the Question of Legal Boundaries,' *The Modern Law Review* 73 (2010): 30–56.
Lindahl, Hans. 'Constituent Power and Reflexive Identity: Towards an Ontology of Collective Selfhood,' in *The Paradox of Constitutionalism: Constituent Power and Constitutional Form*, eds. Martin Loughlin and Neil Walker, Oxford: Oxford University Press, 2007, pp. 9–24.
Lindahl, Hans. 'Acquiring a Community: The Acquis and the Institution of European Legal Order,' *European Law Journal* 9 (2003): 433–50.
Locke, John. *Two Treatises of Government*, ed. Peter Laslett. Cambridge: Cambridge University Press, 1970.
Losurdo, Domenico. *La non-violenza*. Roma-Bari: Editori Laterza, 2010.
Losurdo, Domenico. 'Moral Dilemmas and Broken Promises,' *Historical Materialism* 18 (2010): 85–134.
Luxon, Nancy. 'Ethics and Subjectivity: Practices of Self-Governance in the Late Lectures of Michel Foucault,' 36 *Political Theory* (2008): 377–402.
MacIntyre, Alasdair. *Three Rival Versions of Moral Enquiry: Encyclopaedia, Genealogy, and Tradition*. Notre Dame: University of Notre Dame Press, 1991.
MacIntyre, Alasdair. *After Virtue: A Study in Moral Theory*. Notre Dame: University of Notre Dame Press, 1981.
Magaisa, Alex Tawanda. 'Minister of Health and Others v. Treatment Action Campaign and Others', *Journal of African Law* 47.1 (April 2003): 117–25.
Malla, Pasha. 'The Question Remains,' *The Walrus* 7.10 (2010).
Mann, Michael. *The Sources of Social Power: Vol. 1, A History of Power from the Beginning to AD 1760*. Cambridge: Cambridge University Press, 1986.
Mantena, Karuna. 'Genealogies of Catastrophe: Arendt on the Logic and Legacy of Imperialism,' *Politics in Dark Times*, ed. Seyla Benhabib. Cambridge: Cambridge University Press, 2010.
Mantena, Karuna. '"Another Realism" The Politics of Gandhian Nonviolence,' *American Political Science Review* 106.2 (May 2012): 455–70.
Maré, Gerhard. 'The State of the State: Contestation and Race Re-assertion in a Neoliberal Terrain,' in *The State of the Nation: South Africa, 2003–2004*, eds, John Daniel, Adam Habib, and Roger Southall. Cape Town: Human Sciences Research Council, 2003, pp. 25–52.
Markell, Patchen. 'The Rule of the People: Arendt, Archê, and Democracy,' *American Political Science Review*, 100.1 (February 2006): 1–14.
Markell, Patchen. *Bound by Recognition*. Princeton, NJ: Princeton University Press, 2003.
Markell, Patchen. 'The Recognition of Politics,' *Constellations* 7 (2000): 496–506.
Marston, Sallie A. and Katharyne Mitchell, 'Citizens and the State: Citizenship Formations in *Spaces of Democracy: Geographical Perspectives on Citizenship, Participation and Representation*, eds, Space and Time', in Barnett, Clive and Murray Low. London: Sage, 2004.
Martin, Brian. *Nonviolence versus Capitalism*. London: War Resisters International, 2001.
Marx, Karl and Frederick Engels. *The Communist Manifesto*. Oxford: Oxford University Press, 2002.
Marx, Karl. *Capital, Volume I*. London: Penguin, 1990.

Massey, Doreen. *For Space*. Thousand Oaks, California: Sage, 2005.
Massey, Dorren. *Space, Place and Gender*. Cambridge: Polity Press, 1994.
Matas, Robert. 'Week 21: Witness says she saw Pickton butchering woman,' *Globe & Mail*, 30 November 2007, online: http://v1.theglobeandmail.com/servlet/story/RTGAM.20071130.wpicktonweek21/BNStory/specialPickton/home.
Mbali, Mandisa. 'The Treatment Action Campaign and the History of Rights-Based, Patient-Driven Activism in the South,' University of KwaZulu-Natal Centre for Civil Society, Research Report No. 29 (2005).
Mbali, Mandisa. 'AIDS Discourses and the South Africa State: Government Denialism and Post-Apartheid AIDS Policy-Making,' *Transformation: Critical Perspectives on Southern Africa* 54 (2004): 104–122.
Mbeki, Thabo. 'The African Renaissance, South Africa and the World.' Speech delivered at the United Nations University, 8 April 1998, online http://www.unu.edu/unupress/mbeki.html.
McCarthy, Thomas. *Race, Empire, and the Idea of Human Development*. Cambridge: Cambridge University Press, 2009.
McDonald, David A. *World City Syndrome: Neoliberalism and Inequality in Cape Town*. New York: Routledge, 2008.
McGrath, Susan. 'Child Poverty Advocacy and the Politics of Influence,' in *Child and Family Policies: Struggles, Strategies and Options*, eds, Jane Pulkingham and Gordon Ternowetsky. Halifax: Fernwood Publishing, 1997.
McKenzie, Brad and Brian Wharf. *Connecting Policy to Practice in the Human Services*. Toronto: Oxford University Press, 1998.
Mendieta, Eduardo. 'The Practice of Freedom' in *Michel Foucault: Key Concepts*, ed., Dianna Taylor. Durham: Acumen, 2011, pp. 111–24
Mendieta, Eduardo. 'The City to Come: Critical Urban Theory as Utopian Mapping,' *City* 14.4 (2010): 442–7.
Mendieta, Eduardo. 'The Unfinished Constitution: The Education of the Supreme Court,' *Newsletter on Hispanic/Latino issues in Philosophy* 9.1 (2009).
Mendieta, Eduardo. *Global Fragments: Latinamericanisms, Globalizations, and Critical Theory*. Albany, NY: SUNY Press, 2007.
Mendieta, Eduardo. 'Communicative Freedom, Citizenship and Political Justice in the Age of Globalization. On Seyla Benhabib's *The Claims of Culture: Equality and Diversity in the Global Era*,' *Philosophy and Social Criticism* 31.7 (2005): 739–52.
Mignolo, Walter. *Local Histories/Global Designs: Coloniality, Subaltern Knowledges, and Border Thinking*. Princeton: Princeton University Press, 2000.
Mills, Charles W. *The Racial Contract*, Ithaca, NY: Cornell University Press, 1997.
Minow, Martha. *Between Vengeance and Forgiveness: Facing History after Genocide and Mass Violence*. Boston: Beacon, 1998.
Mkandawire, Thandika P. and Charles C. Soludo. *Our Continent, Our Future: African Perspectives on Structural Adjustment*. Trenton, NJ: Africa World Press, 1999.
Moyer, Bill. *Doing Democracy: The MAP Model for Organising Social Movements*. Gabriola Island BC: New Society Publications, 2001.
Moyn, Samuel. *The Last Utopia: Human Rights in History*. Cambridge: Belknap Press, 2010.
Moynihan, Daniel Patrick. *The Negro Family: The Case for National Action*. Washington, DC: US Department of Labor, 1965.
Mouffe, Chantal. *On the Political*. London: Routledge, 2005.

Müller, Jan-Werner. *Constitutional Patriotism*. Princeton, NJ: Princeton University Press, 2007.
Munarriz, Gerardo J. 'Rhetoric and Reality: The World Bank Development Policies, Mining Corporations and Indigenous Communities in Latin America,' *International Community Law Review* 10 (2008): 431–43.
Muthu, Sankar. *Enlightenment Against Empire*. Princeton, NJ: Princeton University Press, 2003.
Nakhimovsky, Isaac. 'Vattel's Theory of the International Order: Commerce and the Balance of Power in the Law of Nations,' *History of European Ideas* 33 (2007): 157–73.
Native Women's Association of Canada. *What Their Stories Tell Us: Research Findings from the Sisters in Spirit Initiative* (2010) online: http://www.nwac-hq.org/.
Negash, Girma. *Apologia Politica: States and their Apologies by Proxy*. New York: Lexington Books, 2007.
Negt, Oskar and Alexander Kluge. *Public Sphere and Experience: Toward an Analysis of the Bourgeois and Proletarian Public Sphere*, trans. Peter Labanyi, Jamie Owen Daniel, and Assenka Oksiloff. Minneapolis: University of Minnesota Press, 1993.
Nhat Hanh, Thich. *Peace is Every Step*. New York: Bantam, 1992.
Nietzsche, Friedrich. *The Gay Science*. Cambridge: Cambridge University Press, 2001.
Nietzsche, Friedrich. 'Homer's Contest,' in *Agonistics: Arenas of Creative Contest*, eds. J. Lungstrum and E. Sauer. Albandy: State University of New York Press, 1997, pp. 35–45.
Nietzsche, Friedrich. 'The Means to Real Peace,' in *Human All Too Human*, tr. R.J. Hollingdale. Cambridge: Cambridge University Press, 1986.
Nkrumah, Kwane. *Neo-colonialism, the Last Stage of Capitalism*. London: Nelson, 1965.
Nobles, Melissa. *The Politics of Official Apologies*. New York: Cambridge University Press, 2008.
Norval, Aletta J. *Aversive Democracy: Inheritance and Originality in the Democratic Tradition*. Cambridge: Cambridge University Press, 2007.
Norval, Aletta J. *Deconstructing Apartheid Discourse*. London: Verso, 1996.
Nozick, Robert. *Anarchy, State, and Utopia*. New York: Basic Books, 1974.
O'Grady, Helen. *Woman's Relationship to Herself: Gender, Foucault and Therapy*. London: Routledge, 2005.
Oviedo Obarrio, Fernando. 'Evo Morales and the Altiplano Notes for an Electoral Geography of the Movimiento al Socialismo, 2002–2008,' *Latin American Perspectives*, Issue 172, 37.3 (May 2010): 91–106.
Owen, David. 'Transpolitical Citizenship,' in *Prospects of Citizenship*, eds. Gerry Stoker et al. London: Bloomsbury, 2011.
Owen, David. 'Democracy, Perfectionism and "Undetermined Messianic Hope",' in *The Legacy of Wittgenstein: Pragmatism and Deconstruction*, eds. C. Mouffe and L. Nagel. London: Cornell University Press, 2003, pp. 82–96.
Owen, David. 'Equality, Democracy, and Self-respect: Reflections on Nietzsche's Agonal Perfectionism,' *Journal of Nietzsche Studies* 24 (2002): 113–31.
Pagden, Anthony. 'Imperialism, Liberalism, and the Quest for Perpetual Peace,' *Daedalus* 134.2 (Spring 2005): 46–57.
Pagden, Anthony. *Lords of All the World: Ideologies of Empire in Spain, Britain and France, c.1500–c.1800*. New Haven, Conn.: Yale University Press, 1995.
Patterson, Orlando. *Rituals of Blood: Consequences of Slavery in Two American Centuries*. Washington DC: Civitas/Counterpoint, 1998.
Patterson, Orlando. *Slavery and Social Death: A Comparative Study*. Cambridge: Harvard University Press, 1982.

Pickles, John. *A History of Spaces: Cartographic Reason, Mapping, and the Geo-coded World*. London and New York: Routledge, 2004.

Pierenkemper, Toni and Richard Tilly. *The German Economy during the Nineteenth Century*. New York: Berghahn, 2004.

Pillow, Kirk. 'Imagination,' in *Oxford Handbook of Philosophy and Literature*, ed. Richard Eldridge. Oxford: Oxford University Press, 2009.

Pilon, Dennis M. *Wrestling with Democracy: Voting Systems as Politics in the Twentieth-Century West*. Toronto: University of Toronto Press, 2013.

Pitts, Jennifer. 'Political Theory of Empire and Imperialism,' *Annual Review of Political Science*, 13 (2010): 211–35.

Pocock, J.G.A. 'Deconstructing Europe,' *London Review of Books* (19 December 1991), pp. 6–10.

Pogge, Thomas. *World Poverty and Human Rights: Cosmopolitan Responsibilities and Reforms*. 2nd edn. Cambridge: Polity, 2008.

Polanyi, Karl. *The Great Transformation: The Political and Economic Origins of Our Time*. Boston: Beacon Press, 2001.

Postero, Nancy Grey. *Now We Are Citizens: Indigenous Politics in Postmulticultural Bolivia*. Stanford: Stanford University Press, 2007.

Porras, Ileana. 'Constructing International Law in the East Indian Seas: Property, Sovereignty, Commerce and War in Hogu Grotius' de Iure Praedae – The Law of Prize and Booty, or on How to Distinguish Merchants from Pirates,' *Brooklyn Journal of International Law* 31.3 (2006): 741–804.

Praeg, Leonard. 'An Answer to the Question: What is [ubuntu]?' *South African Journal of Philosophy* 27.4 (2008): 367–85.

Prashad, Vijay. *The Darker Nations*. New York: The New Press, 2009.

Preuß, Ulrich K. 'Europa als politische Gemeinschaft,' in *Europawissenschaft*, eds. Gunnar Folke Schuppert, Ingolf Pernice and Ulrich Haltern. Baden-Baden: Nomos, 2005, pp. 489–539.

Prokhovnik, Raia. 'An Interview with Quentin Skinner,' *Contemporary Political Theory* 10.2 (2011): 273–85.

Prusak, Bernard G. 'Politics, Religion, and the Public Good: An Interview with Philosopher John Rawls,' *Commonweal* 25 (September 1998): 12–17.

Rajagopal, Balakrishnan. 'The Role of Law in Counterhegemonic Globalization and Global Pluralism: The Case of the Narmada Valley Struggle in India,' *Leiden Journal of International Law* 18 (2005): 345–87.

Rajagopal, Balakrishnan. *International Law from Below: Development, Social Movements and Third World Resistance*. Cambridge: Cambridge University Press, 2003.

Ramoneda, Josep. *Después de la pasión política*. Madrid: Taurus, 1999.

Randle, Michael. *Civil Resistance*. London: Fontana, 1993.

Rawls, John. *Political Liberalism*. New York: Columbia Unversity Press, 1993.

Rawls, John. 'Justice as Fairness: Political not Metaphysical,' *Philosophy and Public Affairs* 14 (1985): 223–52.

Regan, Paulette. *Unsettling the Settler Within*. Vancouver; UBC Press, 2009.

Restakis, John. *Humanizing the Economy: Co-operatives in the Age of Capital*. Gabriola: New Society Publishers, 2010.

Rist, Gilbert. *The History of Development: From Western Origins to Global Faith*, tr. Patrick Camiller. London: Zed Books, 1997.

Robins, Steven L. *From Revolution to Rights in South Africa: Social Movements, NGOs and Popular Politics After Apartheid.* Rochester, NY: James Currey, 2008.

Robins, Steven and Bettina von Lieres. 'Remaking Citizenship, Unmaking Marginalization: The Treatment Action Campaign in Post-Apartheid South Africa,' *Canadian Association of African Studies* (2004): 575–86.

Robinson, Randall. *Quitting America: The Departure of a Black Man from His Native Land.* New York: Dutton, 2004.

Robinson, Randall. *The Debt: What America Owes to Blacks.* New York: Plume, 2000.

Rorty, Richard. *Philosophy as Cultural Politics: Philosophical Papers, Vol. 4.* Cambridge: Cambridge University Press, 2007.

Rorty, Richard. *Take Care of Freedom and Truth Will Take Care of Itself: Interview with Richard Rorty*, ed. and intro. Eduardo Mendieta. Stanford, CA: Stanford University Press, 2006.

Rorty, Richard. *Achieving our Country: Leftist Thought in the Twentieth Century.* Cambridge, MA: Harvard University Press, 1998.

Rorty, Richard. *Objectivity, Relativism, and Truth: Philosophical Papers, Vol. 1.* Cambridge: Cambridge University Press, 1991.

Rorty, Richard. *Contingency, Irony, Solidarity.* Cambridge: Cambridge University Press, 1989.

Rorty, Richard. *Philosophy and the Mirror of Nature.* Princeton, NJ: Princeton University Press, 1979.

Ruddy, F.S. *International Law in the Enlightenment: The Background of Emmerich de Vattel's Le Droit des Gens.* New York: Oceana Publications, 1975.

Sahle, Eunice N. 'Intellectuals, Oppression and Anti-Racist Movements in South Africa,' in *Theorizing Anti-Racism: Linkages in Marxism and Critical Race Theories*, eds. Abigail B. Bakan and Enakshi Dua, Toronto: University of Toronto Press, 2013.

Sahle, Eunice. *World Orders, Development and Transformation.* Houndmills and New York: Palgrave Macmillan, 2010.

Sahle, Eunice N. 'Gender, States, and Markets in Africa', in *Neoliberalism and Globalization in Africa: Contestations from the Embattled Continent* ed. Joseph Mensah. New York: Palgrave Macmillan, 2008.

Sahlins, Marshall. *Stone Age Economics.* London: Tavistock Publications, 1972.

Sandel, Michael. *Public Philosophy: Essays on Morality in Politics.* Cambridge, MA: Harvard University Press, 2006.

Sandel, Michael. *Liberalism and the Limits of Justice.* Cambridge, MA: Cambridge University Press, 1982.

Sandel, Michael. *Democracy's Discontent: America in Search of a Public Philosophy.* Cambridge: Belknap Press, 1998.

Sassen, Saskia. *Globalization and its Discontents: Essays on the New Mobility of People and Money.* New York: New Press, 1998.

Sassen, Saskia. *Losing Control? Sovereignty in an Age of Globalization.* New York: Columbia University Press, 1996.

Schell, Jonathan. *The Unconquerable World: Power, Nonviolence and the Will of the People.* New York: Henry Holt and Co, 2003.

Schell, Jonathan. *The Fate of the Earth.* New York: Knopf, 1982.

Schönberger, Christoph. *Unionsbürger: Europas Bürgerrecht in vergleichender Sicht.* Tübingen: Mohr Siebeck, 2005.

Schmitt, Carl. *Political Theology: Four Chapters on the Concept of Sovereignty*, 2nd edn. Chicago: University of Chicago Press, 2005.

Schneider, H. and D. Fassin, 'Denial and Defiance: A Socio-political Analysis of AIDS in South Africa, *AIDS* 16 (suppl): S1–S7.

Schuchter, Arnold. *Reparations: The Black Manifesto and its Challenge to White America*. Philadelphia: Lippincott, 1970.

Schumpeter, Joseph Alois. *Capitalism, Socialism and Democracy*, 6th edn. London and Boston: Unwin Paperbacks, 1987.

de Schutter, Olivier. 'The Green Rush: The Global Race for Farm Lands and the Rights of Land Users,' *HILJ* 52 (2011).

Scott, Daryl Michael. *Contempt and Pity: Social Policy and the Image of the Damaged Black Psyche, 1880–1996*. Chapel Hill: University of North Carolina Press, 1997.

Scott, David. 'Norms of Self-Determination: Thinking Sovereignty Through,' *Middle East Law and Governance*, Special Issue (Fall 2012): 2–30.

Scott, David. 'Two Traditions of Historical Others,' *Symposia on Gender, Race and Philosophy* 8.1 (Winter 2012): http://web.mit.edu/sgrp.

Scott, David. 'Stuart Hall's Ethics,' *Small Axe* 17 (2007): 1–16.

Scott, David. *Conscripts of Modernity: The Tragedy of Colonial Enlightenment*. Durham: Duke University Press, 2004.

Scott, David. *Refashioning Futures: Criticism after Postcoloniality*. Princeton, NJ: Princeton University Press, 1999.

Seekings, Jeremy and Nicoli Nattrass. *Class, Race, and Inequality in South Africa*. Scottsville, University of KwaZulu-Natal, 2006 [originally published by Yale University, 2005].

Sharp, Gene. *From Dictatorship to Democracy*, 4th edn. Boston: Albert Einstein Institute, 2010.

Sharp, Gene. *Waging Nonviolent Struggle*. Boston: Porter Sargent, 2005.

Sharp, Gene. *The Politics of Nonviolent Action*. Boston: Porter Sargent, 1973.

Shatz, Adam. 'Is Palestine Next?,' *London Review of Books*, 14 July 2011, pp. 8–14.

Shaw, Jo. *The Transformation of Citizenship in the European Union: Electoral Rights and the Restructuring of Political Space*. Cambridge: Cambridge University Press, 2007.

Shultz, Jim and Melissa Draper, *Dignity and Defiance: Stories from Bolivia's Challenge to Globalization*. Berkeley: University of California Press, 2008.

Simpson, Mike and James Tully. 'The Unfreedom of the Moderns in the post-9/11 Age of Constitutionalism and Imperialism,' in *Federalism, Plurinationality and Democratic Constitutionalism*, eds. Ferran Requejo and Miquel Caminal. London: Routledge, 2012, pp. 51–84.

Singh, Jakeet. *Beyond Free and Equal: Subalternity and the Limits of Liberal-Democracy*. PhD Dissertation, Department of Political Science, University of Toronto, 2012.

Singh, Nikhil Pal. *Black is a Country*. Cambridge, MA: Harvard University Press, 2005.

Skinner, Quentin. *Hobbes and Republican Liberty*. Cambridge: Cambridge University Press, 2008.

Skinner, Quentin. 'What does it Mean to be a Free Person,' *London Review of Books* (22 May 2008), pp. 16–18.

Skinner, Quentin. 'A Third Concept of Liberty,' *London Review of Books* 24.7 (2002).

Skinner, Quentin. *Liberty before Liberalism*. Cambridge: Cambridge University Press, 1998.

Skinner, Quentin. 'The Republican Ideal of Liberty,' in *Machiavelli and Republicanism*, eds. Gisela Brock, Quentin Skinner and Maurizio Viroli. Cambridge: Cambridge University Press, 1990.

Soja, Edward W. *Seeking Spatial Justice.* Minneapolis: University of Minnesota Press, 2010.
de Sousa Santos, Boaventura. 'Southern Europe Crises and Resistances', *The Birkbeck Institute for the Humanities*, University of London, 22 November 2012.
de Sousa Santos, Boaventura. *The Rise of the Global Left: The World Social Forum and Beyond.* London: Zed Books, 2006.
de Sousa Santos, Boaventura and César A Rodiquez-Garavito, eds, *Law and Globalization from Below.* Cambridge: Cambridge University Press, 2006.
Staggenborg, Suzanne. *Social Movements*, rev. edn. New York: Oxford University Press, 2011.
Stears, Marc. *Demanding Democracy*, Princeton, NJ: Princeton University Press, 2010.
Steinberg, Jonny. 'South Africa's Xenophobic Eruption,' Institute for Security Studies, *ISS Occasional Paper* 169, November 2008, http://www.iss.co.za/pgcontent.php?UID=3070
Stephan, Maria J. ed. *Civilian Jihad: Nonviolent Struggle, Democratization and Governance in the Middle East.* New York: Palgrave Macmillan, 2009.
Stoker, Gerry. *Why Politics Matters: Making Democracy Work.* New York: Palgrave Macmillan, 2006.
Stone, Deborah. 'For Love Nor Money: The Commodification of Care,' in *Rethinking Commodification*, Martha M. Ertman and Joan C. Williams, eds. New York: New York University Press, 2005.
Stout, Jeffrey. *Democracy and Tradition.* Princeton, NJ: Princeton University Press, 2004.
Strange, Susan. *Mad Money: When Markets Outgrow Governments.* Ann Arbor: University of Michigan Press, 1998.
Strange, Susan. *The Retreat of the State: The Diffusion of Power in the World Economy.* Cambridge: Cambridge University Press, 1996.
Surin, Kenneth. *Freedom Not Yet.* Durham: Duke University Press, 2009.
Tapia, Luis. 'Constitution and Constitutional Reform in Bolivia,' in *Unresolved Tensions: Bolivia Past and Present*, eds. J. Crabtree and L.Whitehead. Pittsburgh: University of Pittsburgh Press, 2008.
Tavuchis, Nicholas. *Mea Culpa: A Sociology of Apology and Reconciliation.* Stanford: Stanford University Press, 1991.
Taylor, Charles. *A Secular Age.* Cambridge, Mass.: Harvard University Press, 2007.
Teitel, Ruti. *Transitional Justice.* New York: Oxford University Press, 2000.
Thompson, Janna. *Intergenerational Justice.* New York: Routledge, 2009.
Thompson, Janna. *Taking Responsibility for the Past: Reparation and Historical Injustice.* Cambridge: Polity, 2002.
Thompson, Janna. *Discourse and Knowledge: Defense of a Collectivist Ethics.* New York: Routledge, 1998.
Torpey, John. *Making Whole What Has Been Smashed: On Reparations Politics.* Cambridge: Harvard University Press, 2006.
Tuck, Richard. *The Rights of War and Peace: Political Thought and the International Order from Grotius to Kant.* Oxford: Oxford University Press, 1999.
Tully, James. 'Afterword,' in *On Global Citizenship*, ed. David Owen. London: Bloomsbury 2013.
Tully, James. 'Two Ways of Realizing Justice and Democracy: Linking Amartya Sen and Elinor Ostrom,' *Critical Review of International Social and Political Philosophy* (Autumn 2013).
Tully, James. 'On the Global Multiplicity of Public Spheres: The Democratic

Transformation of the Public Sphere?', in *Beyond Habermas: Democracy, Knowledge, and the Public Sphere*, eds. Christian J. Emden and David Midgley. New York: Berghahn Books, 2012.

Tully, James. 'Legal and Governmental Pluralism: A View from the Demos,' *Middle East Law and Governance*, Special Edition (Fall 2012): 31–60.

Tully, James. 'Rethinking Human Rights and the Enlightenment: A View from the Twenty–first Century', in *Self-Evident Truths? Human Rights and the Enlightenment*, ed. Kate E. Tunstall. London: Bloomsbury, 2012, pp. 3–34.

Tully, James. 'Deparochializing Political Theory: The Dialogue and Interbeing Approach', *The Conference on Deparochializing Political Theory*, University of Victoria, Victoria, B.C., 2–4 August 2012.

Tully, James. 'Dialogue,' *Political Theory* 39 (2011): 145–60.

Tully, James. 'Citizenship for the Love of the World', *The Conference on Challenging Citizenship*, CES, University of Coimbra, Coimbra, Portugal, 3–5 June 2011.

Tully, James. 'The Crisis of Global Citizenship', *Radical Politics Today* (July 2009).

Tully, James. 'Lineages of Contemporary Imperialism,' in *Lineages of Empire: The Historical Roots of British Imperial Thought*, ed. Duncan Kelly. Oxford: Oxford University Press, 2009, pp. 3–30.

Tully, James. *Public Philosophy in a New Key, 2 vols*. Cambridge: Cambridge University Press, 2008.

Tully, James. 'The Kantian Idea of Europe: Critical and Cosmopolitan Perspectives,' in *The Idea of Europe: From Antiquity to the European Union*, ed. Anthony Pagden. Cambridge: Cambridge University Press, 2002, pp. 331–58.

Tully, James. *Strange Multiplicity: Constitutionalism in an Age of Diversity*. Cambridge: Cambridge University Press, 1995.

Tully, James. *An Approach to Political Philosophy: Locke in Contexts*. Cambridge: Cambridge University Press, 1993.

Tully, James. 'The Pen is a Mighty Sword: Quentin Skinner's Analysis of Politics,' in *Meaning and Context: Quentin Skinner and His Critics*, ed. J. Tully. Princeton, NJ: Princeton University Press, 1989, pp. 7–25.

Turok, Ivan. 'Restructuring or Reconciliation? South Africa's Reconstruction and Development,' *International Journal of Urban and Regional Research* 19 (1995).

Unger, Roberto Mangabeira. *Democracy Realized*. London and New York: Verso, 1998.

United Nations Declaration on the Rights of Indigenous Peoples. GA Resolution 61/295, 13 September 2007.

Vandormael, Alan Marc. *Civil Society and Democracy in Post-Apartheid South Africa: The Treatment Action Campaign, Government, and the Politics of HIV/AIDS*. Saarbrücken: VDM Verlag Dr. Müller, 2007.

de Vattel, Emer. *The Law of Nations or 'Principles of the Law of Nature Applied to the Conduct of Nations and Sovereigns'*, trans. Joseph Chitty, 6th American edn. Oxford: Oxford University Press, 1844 [1758].

Vázquez-Arroyo, Antonio Y. 'Universal History Disavowed,' *Postcolonial Studies* 11.4 (2008): 451–73.

Vázquez-Arroyo, Antonio Y. 'Responsibility, Violence, and Catastrophe,' *Constellations* 15 (2008): 98–125.

Vázquez-Arroyo, Antonio Y. 'Agonized Liberalism: The Liberal Theory of William E. Connolly,' *Radical Philosophy* 127 (Sept./Oct. 2004): 8–19.

de Vitoria, Francisco. *De Indis et de Ivre Belli Relectiones*, ed. Ernest Nys, trans. John Pawley Bate. Washington DC: Carnegie Institute of International Law, 1916.
Waldron, Jeremy. 'Superseding Historical Injustice,' *Ethics* 103.1, 1992, pp. 4–28.
Wallerstein, Immanuel Maurice. *The End of the World as We Know it: Social Science for the Twenty-First Century*. Minneapolis: University of Minnesota Press, 2001.
Wallerstein, Immanuel Maurice. *Open the Social Sciences: Report of the Gulbenkian Commission on the Restructuring of the Social Sciences*. Stanford: Stanford University Press, 1996.
Warner, Michael. *Publics and Counterpublics*. New York: Zone Books, 2005.
Webber, Jeffery. *From Rebellion to Reform in Bolivia: Class Struggle, Indigenous Liberation, and the Politics of Evo Morales*. Chicago: Haymarket Books, 2011.
Weber, Max. *Essays on Vocation*. Indianapolis: Hackett, 2004.
Weber, Max. *Political Writings*, ed. Peter Lassman and Ronald Speirs. Cambridge: Cambridge University Press, 1994.
Weil, Simone. 'Human Personality,' in *The Simone Weil Reader*, ed. George A. Panichase. Mt. Kisco, NY: Moyer Bell, 1977, pp. 315–17.
Weiler, J.H.H. *The Constitution of Europe*. Cambridge: Cambridge University Press, 1999.
Wellmer, Albrecht. *Endgames: The Irreconcilable Nature of Modernity: Essays and Lectures*, trans. David Midgley. Cambridge, MA: The MIT Press, 1998.
Welsh, Christine. *Finding Dawn*. National Film Board of Canada (2006)
White, James Boyd. *Living Speech: Resisting the Empire of Force*. Princeton, NJ: Princeton University Press, 2006.
White, Stephen K. *The Ethos of the Late Modern Citizen*. Cambridge: Harvard University Press, 2009.
Widdowson, Francis and Albert Howard. *Disrobing the Aboriginal Industry*. Montreal: McGill-Queen's University Press, 2008.
Wiener, Antje. *The Invisible Constitution of Politics: Contested Norms and International Encounters*. Cambridge: Cambridge University Press, 2008.
Williams, Raymond. *Keywords: A Vocabulary of Culture and Society*, rev. edn. New York: Oxford University Press, 1985.
Wingert, Lutz and Klaus Günther, eds. *Die Öffenlichkeit der Vernunft und die Vernunft der Öffenlichkeit*. Frankfurt am Main: Suhrkamp Verlag, 2001.
Wittgenstein, Ludwig. *Philosophical Investigations*, trans. G.E.M. Anscombe. Oxford: Blackwell, 2001.
Wittgenstein, Ludwig. *Remarks on Frazer's Golden Bough*, trans. Rush Rhees. Norfolk: Brynmill Press, 1987.
Wolin, Sheldon. *Democracy Incorporated: Managed Democracy and the Specter of Inverted Totalitarianism*. Princeton, NJ: Princeton University Press, 2008.
Wolin, Sheldon. 'Democracy, Difference, and Re-cognition,' *Political Theory* 21 (1993): 464–83.
Wolin, Sheldon. *The Presence of the Past*. Baltimore: The Johns Hopkins University Press, 1989.
Wood, Ellen Meiksins. 'Why it Matters,' *London Review of Books*, 25 September 2008.
Xenos, Nicholas. 'Momentary Democracy,' *Democracy and Vision*, ed. Aryeh Botwinick and William E. Connolly. Princeton, NJ: Princeton University Press, 2001.
Young, Iris Marion. 'The Logic of Masculinist Protection: Reflections on the Current Security State,' *Signs: Journal of Women in Culture and Society* 29.1 (2003): 1–25.
Young, Robert. *Postcolonialism: An Historical Introduction*. Oxford: Basil Blackwell, 2001.
Zerilli, Linda. *Feminism and the Abyss of Freedom*. Chicago: University of Chicago Press, 2005.

Index

Achmat, Zackie 155
acting otherwise 208–10, 212, 215; 'Becoming Black' *see separate entry*
Africa/African countries 82, 83, 92, 93, 94, 95, 150, 260; South Africa *see separate entry*
agency and institutions 59–62, 237–8
AIDS/HIV 155–8
Alexandrowicz, C.H. 90
Alfred, Taiaiake 74
Allen, A. 265
Ambrose, Rona 211
Anderson, P. 234
anti-war research 244
Antigone 71–6
Archibugi, D. 124, 126
Arendt, H. 35, 39, 40, 51, 53, 54, 72, 75, 225, 226, 233, 238, 240
Argentina 152
Armitage, D. 63
Asia/Asian countries 82, 83, 90, 92, 93, 94
Austin, J.L. 51
Australia 82, 94, 110
Austria 103
Awas Tingi case 94

Baartman, Reggie 178, 180
backlash 73, 74
Balibar, E. 49, 65–6, 137, 234
Barkan, E. 103
Bechtel 163, 257
Beck, U. 124, 125, 126
'Becoming Black' 174–6; acting otherwise 194–7; African gift 182–3; autobiography, examples, conversation 176–8; exemplarity: Moshoeshoe, knowledge and imagination 190–3; exemplars, democracy, citizenship 193–4; imagining blackness, imagining otherwise 188–9; interlude: Begging to the Black 183–4; legal entanglements 178–81; response 258–64; return to 'African interconnectedness' 185–8
Belenky, M.F. 207
Benhabib, S. 40
Benjamin, W. 66
Berlin, I. 39
Biko, Steve 188, 262
Bittker, B. 105–6, 108–9, 114
Blair, Tony 103
Bolivia 151, 152, 158–66, 167, 257; electoral law 160; indigenous peoples 159–60, 162–3, 164, 165, 257; labour force 161–2; post-2005 state 164–6; privatization 161, 163–4
Bondurant, Joan 241
Bourdieu, P. 62
Boxill, B. 105, 107, 112
Brecht, B. 62
Britain 103, 123, 133, 152
Brown, W. 1, 58–9, 65, 234

Calhoun, C. 125, 131, 132
Camdessus, Michel 153
Canada 48, 49, 56–7, 82; indigenous peoples 49, 73–4, 81, 94, 95, 204, 205–6, 210–11, 264; job creation policies 150; restitution settlements 103
capitalism 50, 57, 58–9, 61, 63, 65, 209, 234, 239, 241; climate change and 257; informal imperialism, the state and 235–7
Cárdenas, Víctor Hugo 160
care-workers 212–15
Carens, J. 49
Casalis, E. 190, 191, 193

Cavell, S. 15, 189, 196, 258
Central America 82
Chenoweth, E. 241
China 89–90, 92, 95, 262
citizenship: acting otherwise *see separate entry*; cosmopolitanism and multiple 126; crisis of global 227–8; Gaia 231, 257; glocal 75, 149, 202, 206, 215; market 253; political citizenship and the modern state *see separate entry*; and public sphere: making publics, becoming citizens 32, 33–5, 226–9; spaces of freedom *see separate entry*; transpolitical 126
civic engagement *see* engagement, proposals and the key of reasoning
civil and civic citizenship 43–5, 132, 151–2, 223–5, 226, 228–9, 231–2, 256–8; everyday *see* everyday and everyone, political philosophy for; political citizenship and governance 132–6, 252–6; practices of civic citizenship 53, 57, 58, 59–62, 63, 234–5, 238–9; principles of constitutionalism and democracy and 251–5
civil/civic disobedience 48, 155, 156, 227, 243
climate change 231, 239, 244, 254; capitalism and 257
Clinton, Bill 103
collective bargaining associations 60
colonialism, economic sovereignty and Vattel 87–91
colonization, internal 81–2; self-determination, indigenous peoples and 82–3, 95, 249; Vattel, colonialism and economic sovereignty 87–91; Vattel and historical characterization of non-European societies 91–6; Vattel and the Law of Nations 84–7, 248
Comack, E. 210, 211
compassion 239, 240, 241, 261, 265
Connelly, W.E. 54
constitutionalism 123, 148; civil and civic citizenship and principles of democracy and 251–5
conversation: autobiography, examples 176–8; and engagement 16–17, 26
Conyers, John 106
cooperation 202, 216, 247, 261; connecting locations and cooperating between practices of freedom 210–15

cooperatives 239, 242, 254
corporations 95, 124, 137, 148, 149, 155, 249, 262; Bolivia 161–2, 163, 166; pharmaceutical 157, 158
cosmopolitanism 122–6, 127, 250
counterpublics 34
criminal law 211
critical theory 58, 234, 235–6, 237

Dalai Lama 241
Daza, Victor Hugo 163
De Bois, W.E.B. 113, 114
decentralization 57, 160, 165, 234
decolonization 63, 148, 227–8, 232, 235–6, 237
deep ecology movement 257
Deleuze, G. 186, 187
deliberation 33, 34, 35, 36, 40, 151, 212, 229; engagement, proposals and the key of reasoning *see separate entry*
Deming, Barbara 247
Derrida, J. 258
Deutscher, I. 66
development 93–5, 248–9
Dewey, J. 35, 38
dialogical approach 101, 115–16, 249–50, 260, 262, 263–4; receptive, reciprocal and critical 242
dialogical-genealogical approach 250
Dunn, J. 51
Dussel, E. 38, 232

East India Company 92
ecological crisis 231, 239
economic sovereignty, colonialism and Vattel 87–91
education in nonviolent civic citizenship 241–4
Einstein, A. 244, 247
electoral systems 254; Bolivia 160; turnout 133
Elias, N. 123
Emerson, R.W. 196
empathy 241, 259, 260, 261
emplotment 75
engagement, proposals and the key of reasoning 13; activity of reasoning: alternative picture 14–16; conversation and engagement 16–17, 26; deliberation vs negotiation 21–2; logic of deliberation 24–8, 25, 226; logic of negotiation 22–4, 225–6; norms of reasonableness

17, 19–21, 25; philosophy and field of civic engagement 28–9; response 225–6; varieties of engagement 17–19
enmity 255; violence, power, enmity: at edges of civic freedom *see separate entry*
Escobar, A. 232, 257
Euripides 60
Europe, integration in the new 72
European Convention on Human Rights 137
European Union 122, 126, 129, 131–2, 136–8, 251–3; Charter of Rights 128; democratic deficit 252
everyday and everyone, political philosophy for 202–3, 215–16; first site: imagining/recognizing oneself as a citizen 206–10; four stories 203–6; response 264–6; second site: connecting locations and cooperating between practices of freedom 210–15
expertise 135

Farthing, L. 160, 166
feminism 35, 214
financial crisis 254
food security 95
foreign policy 135, 137
forests of Pacific Northwest 55, 76
Forman, James 105
Forst, R. 57
Foster, J.B. 257–8
Foucault and Habermas: genealogies and reconstructions 38–43, 229–30; two methods: critical theory and critical comparison 230–2
Foucault, M. 4–5, 32–3, 38–9, 40–1, 42, 51, 53, 54, 58, 74, 75, 76, 101, 102, 104, 149, 206, 209, 229–30, 231, 232, 233, 238, 241–2, 265
France 123, 135
Fraser, N. 34, 64
Frazier, E. Franklin 114
Freud, S. 72

Gadamer, H.-G. 44
Gaia citizenship 231, 257
Galtung, Johann 247
Gandhi, M. 5, 63, 64, 65, 76, 133, 226, 232, 235, 239, 240, 241, 243, 247, 254, 258
gender 162, 164, 257
Genovese, E. 114

Germany 103, 123, 127–8, 131; Weimar Republic 134
Geuss, R. 71, 121, 129
global citizenship, crisis of 227–8
global governance 127, 129, 148, 149, 153, 236, 240
globalization 74, 75, 136, 147–52, 166–7; spaces of freedom and citizenization in South Africa 152–8, 167; spaces of state reconfiguration in Bolivia 158–66, 167
glocal citizenship 75, 149, 202, 206, 215
Gotkowitz, L. 159
Gould, S.J. 207
Gramsci, A. 66
Greece 152
Gregg, Richard 241
Grotius, Hugo 84, 86, 87, 89, 90, 91, 94, 124, 125
Gutmann, H. 114

Habermas and Foucault: genealogies and reconstructions 38–43, 229–30; two methods: critical theory and critical comparison 230–2
Habermas, J. 32–4, 35, 38–40, 41–3, 49, 58, 73, 74, 101, 104, 121, 122, 124, 127–30, 131, 132, 135, 226–7, 228, 229–30, 231, 251, 252, 255
habitus 62, 75
Hardt, M. 122
Harris, F. 250
Hegel, G.W.F. 33, 36, 39, 42, 55, 121, 135
Heidegger, M. 36, 38
Held, D. 124, 126
Heraclitus of Ephesus 45
Heywood, M. 156
historical injustice *see* reparation for New World slavery
HIV/AIDS 155–8
Hobbes, T. 38, 121, 130, 234
Holocaust survivors 103
Honig, B. 137
Honneth, A. 64
Horsburgh, H.J.N. 241
Howes, Dustin 241
Huizinga, J. 54
human rights 42–3, 44–5, 49, 125, 228; European Union 128, 136, 137; German Basic Law 128; reparatory justice 102–3; South Africa 128, 155, 156–7

human service organizations/practitioners 212–15
humanism 75–6, 247–8
Humboldt, W. von 135, 255
Hunt, L. 44–5
Huxley, A. 244
Hylton, F. 161

identity politics 73, 142n73
India 82, 83, 95; Narmada dam 94
indigenous peoples 56, 238, 239, 265; Bolivia 159–60, 162–3, 164, 165, 257; Canada 49, 73–4, 81, 94, 95, 204, 205–6, 210–11, 264; ILO convention 159; reason and violence 72–4, 75, 245–6; resistance is not political freedom 62; self-determination 82–3, 95, 249, 264; treaty-making 73–4, 75, 245–6; Vattel, imperialism and rights of 81–96, 248–9
informal imperialism 124, 148, 149, 151, 152, 159, 162, 228, 256; capitalism, the state and 235–7
institutions and agency 59–62, 237–8
integration in the new Europe 72
intellectual property 157
Inter-American Court of Human Rights 94
interconnectedness 265, 266; 'Becoming Black' *see separate entry*
intergenerational communities 107, 112
internal colonization 81–2; self-determination, indigenous peoples and 82–3, 95, 249; Vattel, colonialism and economic sovereignty 87–91; Vattel and historical characterization of non-European societies 91–6; Vattel and the Law of Nations 84–7, 248
International Labour Organization 159
international law 43, 44, 57, 122, 123, 124; nation-state 136; secession 83, 94; Vattel, imperialism and rights of indigenous peoples 81–96, 248–9
International Monetary Fund (IMF) 148, 153, 163
international relations theory 122, 124, 240
intifadas, Palestinian 64–5
Iran 75, 76
Ireland 103
Ishay, M.R. 44–5
isonomia 5

Israel 64–5
Italy 254

James, W. 36, 240, 247
Japan 133
Japanese-Americans 103, 106
Japanese-Canadians 103

Kant, I. 36, 43, 49, 87, 88, 121, 123–4, 125, 132–3, 135, 230
Kelly, Petra 247
Kelsen, H. 125
Khan, Abdul Gaffar 247
King, Martin Luther, Jr 65, 240, 241, 247
Kluge, A. 34
Kohl, B. 160, 166
Korsgaard, C. 130
Krog, Antjie 175–97, 258–64
Kroker, A. 75
Kropotkin, P. 235, 239, 247
Kymlicka, W. 49

labour force 154, 161–2
Latin America 82
law: complexity 135; criminal 211; indigenous peoples 204, 264; legal entanglements: *Begging to be Black* 178–81; international *see separate entry*
League of Nations 93
liberalism 65, 100, 127, 135
literature 36; *see also* 'Becoming Black'
Locke, J. 81, 91, 135
Lozada, Gonzalo Sánchez de 160, 163

McGrath, S. 212
Machiavelli, N. 66
MacIntyre, A. 104, 109, 113, 114
McKenzie, B. 213
Malcolm X 240
Mandela, Nelson 133, 152, 153, 187, 188, 192, 254, 260, 262
Mann, M. 59, 234
Mantena, K. 244
market citizenship 253
Martin, B. 241
Marx, K. 4, 39, 63, 235, 238–9, 258
Marxist regimes 239
Mbeki, Thabo 155, 182, 184
meditation 265
Merton, Thomas 241, 247
Mesa, Carlos 163
Middle East 241

Mignolo, W. 150
migration 125–6
Mills, C.W. 38, 232
mindfulness 265
Montagu, Ashley 247
Moraka, Christopher 157–8
moral justification of reparation for New World slavery *see* reparation for New World slavery
Morales, Evo 161, 164, 166, 257, 258
morality 103, 129
Morgenthau, H. 122
Morris, W. 239, 258
Moshoeshoe, King 175, 177, 182, 188, 190–3, 260, 262
Moyn, S. 44–5
Mugabe, Robert 182
Müller, J.-W. 131
multinational corporations *see* corporations
Muthu, S. 91
Myanmar 241

Nakhimovsky, I. 88
nation-states 148, 150–1, 152, 161; political citizenship and the modern state *see separate entry*
nationalization 166
natural law 84–7, 89, 92, 93
nature 55, 76, 257–8
negotiation 151, 212, 216, 238, 241, 242–4; engagement, proposals and the key of reasoning *see separate entry*
Negri, A. 122
Negt, O. 34
neoliberal globalization (NG) 102, 147–52, 166–7, 253, 254; spaces of freedom and citizenization in South Africa 152–8, 167; spaces of state reconfiguration in Bolivia 158–66, 167
New International Economic Order 236
New Zealand 94; Maori 112
Ngewu, Cynthia 181
Nhat Hahn, Thich 241, 247
Nietzsche, F. 74, 76, 193, 196, 258
Nkrumah, K. 236
Non-aligned movement 228, 235–6
non-cooperation 243–4
non-governmental organizations 72, 149, 254
non-violence 52, 62, 63, 66, 247, 265; transformative power of 239–45
Nozick, R. 106

Obama, Barack 260
occupy movements 254
Owen, D. 54, 126, 193–4, 258
Owen, R. 239

Palestinian intifadas 64–5
parrhesia 4–5
Patterson, O. 114–15
Patton, P. 263, 264
Petrus, Jantjie 178
Pettit, P. 49
pharmaceutical firms 157, 158
philosophy, political 3–6, 232–3; post-philosophical culture 35–8, 232–3; public philosophy in the shadow of historic injustice 100–4, 115–16
Plato 4, 36
Pocock, J.G.A. 51, 52
Pogge, T. 157
Polanyi, K. 239
political citizenship and the modern state 121–2; challenge of a European polity 136–8; decline in political participation 133–4, 253–4; governance and political citizenship 132–6, 252–6; limits of cosmopolitanism 122–6, 250; political citizenship and the European polity 127–32, 251; response 250–6
Portugal 254
positivism 90
post-philosophical culture 35–8, 232–3
Postero, N.G. 160, 162–3
postnational constellations *see* political citizenship and the modern state
power 206, 209–10, 212, 213–15, 237; violence, power, enmity: at edges of civic freedom *see separate entry*
practical reasoning and acting together *see* engagement, proposals and the key of reasoning
privatization 148, 150, 154, 155, 161, 163–4, 257
public goods 148, 154, 255, 257
public philosophy 3–6, 232–3; post-philosophical culture 35–8, 232–3; in the shadow of historic injustice 100–4, 115–16
public sphere and citizenship: making publics, becoming citizens 32, 33–5, 226–9
Pufendorff, S. de 87

racialization 113, 115, 165
Rawls, J. 3–4, 28, 36, 38, 42, 48, 101, 121, 127, 130, 135, 251, 255
re-imagining civic freedom: 'Becoming black' *see separate entry*; everyday and everyone, political philosophy for *see separate entry*; spaces of freedom *see separate entry*
reason and violence 71–6, 246–8; indigenous peoples 72–4, 75, 245–6
reasonableness: engagement and norms of 17, 19–21, 25
reasoning *see* engagement, proposals and the key of reasoning
recognition 33, 57, 64, 65; emplotment: mutuality and 75; grammar of 62, 70n42; participation in deliberation 27–8; politics of 48, 134–5, 254–5
rehistoricizing the present 102
reparation for New World slavery: family lines 109–11, 113–14; harms, collective memories, reparation 111–16; public philosophy in shadow of historical injustice 100–4, 115–16; response 249–50; responsibility for injustice of slavery 105–11
reparatory justice 102–3
research, anti-war 244
Ricardo, D. 88
Robinson, R. 106, 108, 111, 114, 115
Rorty, R. 32, 35–7, 55
Russell, B. 244, 247
Russia 125

Said, E. 236
Sassen, S. 137
Schell, Jonathan 241
Schmitt, C. 3, 130, 134
Schumacher, F. 239
Schumpeter, J.A. 152
Scott, D. 232, 262
securitization 214
self 196, 265; ethics of the 216, 241–2
self-determination 236; indigenous peoples and 82–3, 95, 249, 264; internal 95
self-narrative 265
self-organizing and self-governing practices 63, 242, 266
Sharp, G. 240–1, 244, 247
Shiva, V. 63
Skinner, Q. 39, 49, 51, 52–3, 54, 102, 104, 121, 132, 233, 238

slavery *see* reparation for New World slavery
Smith, A. 88
social contract 38, 131
social movements 149, 154–5, 158, 159, 160, 161, 163, 164
social welfare state 127–8
Socrates 4–5
Soja, E. 149
Sophocles 71
de Sousa Santos, B. 239, 263
South Africa 128, 152–8, 167; 'Becoming Black' *see separate entry*; state and neoliberalism in 153–4; TAC and neoliberalizing state 154–8, 257
sovereign wealth funds 95
sovereignty 82–3, 92, 103, 112, 134, 137; European Union 136; Vattel, colonialism and economic 87–91; Vattel and the Law of Nations 84–7
spaces of freedom 147, 166–7; and citizenization in South Africa 152–8, 167; privileging of history over spatial processes 149; response 256–8; state reconfiguration in Bolivia 158–66, 167; Tully on contemporary globalization 147–52
Spain 254
Spengler, O. 55
states *see* nation-states
Stears, M. 245
Stephan, M. 241
storytelling 75, 260
Suu Kyi, Aung San 241
Switzerland 103

Tapia, L. 164
Taylor, C. 48
Thompson, Janna 103–16, 249–50
Thompson, S. 161
Thompson, W. 235
Thucydides 66
Torpey, J. 103
totalitarian societies 35
trade unions 60, 156, 160, 162, 243, 254
transitional justice 103
transnational groups/institutions/associations 124, 136
TRIPS framework 157
Trudeau, Pierre 56, 57
Tuck, R. 91
Tutu, Desmond 187, 188, 260, 262

ubuntu 181, 184, 194, 258, 259, 260–4
Unger, R. 57, 65
unions 60, 156, 160, 162, 243, 254
United Nations 92, 124, 228, 239, 244; Declaration on the Rights of Indigenous Peoples 83, 94, 95, 248; 'developed' and 'developing' states 93; self-determination 83, 95, 236
United States 56, 72, 82, 94, 102, 103; African Americans *see* reparation for New World slavery; constitutional law 128; Japanese-Americans 103, 106

Vattel, Emer de 81–2, 124; colonialism and economic sovereignty 87–91; historical characterization of non-European societies 91–6; internal colonization, self-determination and indigenous peoples 82–3, 85; Law of Nations and 84–7; response 248–9
violence 227–8, 255; indigenous peoples 56, 72–4, 75, 238, 239, 245–6; reason and 71–6, 245–8
violence, power, enmity: at edges of civic freedom 48–66; capitalism 50, 57, 58–9, 61, 63, 65, 234, 235–7; critical theory 58, 234, 235–6, 237; institutions and agency 59–62, 237–8; non-violence 52, 62, 63, 66, 239–45; practices of civic citizenship 53, 57, 58, 59–62, 63, 234–5, 238–9; primitive accumulation 63, 238–9; response 233–45

Vitoria, Francisco de 84, 88, 89, 92
voting systems 254; Bolivia 160; turnout 133

Waldron, J. 109, 113
Wallerstein, I. 37
Warner, M. 34
Washington, B.T. 113
Webber, J. 162
Weber, M. 66, 135–6, 148
Weil, S. 66, 207, 208
West, C. 37
Westlake, J. 90
Wharf, B. 213
White, H. 75
White, J.B. 208
Wiener, A. 252
Wilson, Woodrow 124
Wittgenstein, L. 15, 38, 40, 44, 45, 51, 53, 54, 55, 72, 74, 102, 104, 188, 233, 238, 258, 264
Wolin, S.S. 57, 58, 65, 234
World Bank 93, 95, 148, 153, 162, 262
World Trade Organization 148, 153, 155, 157

Young, I.M. 214
Yunus, M. 63

zero-sumness of politics 73